WELFARE ECONOI

Welfare Economics

Introduction and Development of Basic Concepts

YEW-KWANG NG
Reader in Economics
Monash University, Australia

Revised edition

MACMILLAN

First published 1979 by
THE MACMILLAN PRESS LTD
Houndmills, Basingstoke, Hampshire RG21 2XS
and London
Companies and representatives
throughout the world

ISBN 0–333–34576–2 hardcover
ISBN 0–333–34577–0 paperback

First edition reprinted once
Revised edition 1983
14   13   12   11   10   9   8   7   6
03   02   01   00   99   98   97   96   95

Printed in Malaysia

DEDICATED TO

Siang, Aline, Eve and the
welfare of all sentients

Contents

x Contents

Preface to the First Edition

The persons who are responsible for encouraging me to write this book are Ross Parish of Monash University and John Dillon of the University of New England. After labouring with my poor English on the drafts of the first few chapters, I was not only ungrateful to them but cursed them bitterly for getting me into such a dreadful endeavour. It was only because of my irrational inability to accept the economist's dictum that 'bygones are bygones' (sunk costs should not affect decisions) that I had not thrown away the first few shabby chapters but have persisted in writing to the end. However, as with learning Chinese, more or less straight sailing comes after the initial painstaking endurance. (Any reader who may toy with the idea of learning Chinese is advised either not to attempt it, or, having spent some time learning it, not to give up.) Now, looking at the finished product, I feel reasonably satisfied and am grateful for their encouragement. It seems that both irrationality and imperfect foresight (discussed in Chapter 1) were productively involved in securing the outcome. (After writing the final draft, I feel obliged to say that the final stages of standardising notations, proof-reading, etc., are rather dull, tedious, and time-consuming.)

The intended audience of this book includes advanced undergraduates, graduates, and specialists. A conflict arises from the diversity of the intended audience and is resolved by putting more technical and advanced sections into appendixes and by using asterisks (*) to denote more advanced sections which the beginner may omit without much loss of continuity. The expert may, however, be particularly interested in them. The same applies to footnotes, which usually contain bibliographical references or comment on some technical or advanced complications. Sections with double asterisks contain new arguments. An asterisk after a reference indicates that it is more advanced, mathematical, or touches on a technical point. A 'U' after a reference, e.g. Groves (1970U), indicates that it is unpublished.

It may be thought that the diversity of the intended audience will make the book an inefficient tool either as a basic textbook or as a treatise. It is hoped that the following explanations will largely dispel such apprehensions. First, a textbook is not only read by students but also by the lecturer. The former will benefit more from the basic discussion and the latter from the more advanced parts. By getting the lecturer actively interested in reading the book, more effective teaching may be achieved by using it as a text. (When using a purely basic textbook, a lecturer may not even have the patience to just read through the book.) Moreover, for the elementary student (learning welfare economics for the first time), though he may have a very slight inconvenience of having to skip some sections with asterisks in the first reading, he will find that they are useful and provide the interest for a second reading. This second reading may then bring him to a much deeper understanding of welfare economics. Furthermore, he may use this book (including Appendix 10A) as a guide to his further study. By that stage, he may find the book worth more than a basic text plus an advanced treatise (since the two usually do not completely cohere with and complement each other).

Second, as a treatise, it is also useful for the author to explain clearly the basic concepts and theories and his own opinions towards them before he embarks on his own argumentation. Experts may therefore also find the basic discussion useful. It is true that many may find it too elementary to read. But they will have little difficulty in deciding which parts to skip over. Similarly, for those (e.g. graduate students, economists not specialising in welfare economics) who have some elementary training in or understanding of welfare economics and who wish to advance their understanding, it may be desirable to review the basic concepts before going further. An explanation of the organisation of the book is provided in Section 1.5 and a summary in Section 10.1. A separate summary is also provided at the end of each chapter, before the corresponding appendix.

Partly because of the semi-treatise nature of the book and partly because it is more efficient to deal with those topics I am familiar with, the selection of the non-basic topics is admittedly idiosyncratic. But I believe that a largely unbiased coverage has been achieved for the basic topics. Nevertheless, due to space limitation, I have not been able to include detailed discussions of as many topics as I would have wished. Appendix 10A is provided as a remedy. On the other hand, due to time limitation and my other commitments, I have not been able to improve the quality of the book within its given length as much as I would have liked. Partly because of space limitation, the discussion may be a little terse in places. At the cost of some possible ambiguities, this has the advantage of provoking independent reasoning. In any case, if the reader has the patience to reread unclear parts, comprehension should not be difficult to achieve. Beginners would find lecturers' instruction and seminar discussion helpful in this respect. For average beginners, the book could thus most profitably be used under instruction.

To make the book accessible to as large an audience as possible given the content, the discussion is mainly non-mathematical and relies heavily on simple two-dimensional illustrations. Mathematics is used only when essential and appears mainly in appendixes. The conceptual discussion starts from the very basic and proceeds to the fairly complicated, including some new arguments. The main features of the book include: a methodological argument for a positive welfare economics (Chapter 1 and Appendix 1A), a proposed rehabilitation of Little's welfare criterion (Sections 3.2.2* and 3.3*), resolution of Arrow's paradox of social choice by revealing the intensities of preferences (Section 5.4*), the 'conscience effect' in externalities (Section 7.4**) and above all, a theory of third-best (Sections 9.4 and 9.5) with an extension to the equity–efficiency consideration (Appendix 9A**) and a plea for a complete study of welfare (Chapter 10). It is hoped that both the novice and the expert will find the book useful.

I am grateful to the following persons for reading and commenting on the first draft: Michael Burns, Yew-Giam Chen, John Dillon, Avinash Dixit, Theodore Groves, John Head, Murray Kemp, David Mayston, Warren Musgrave, Luat Nguyen, Amartya Sen, Manimay Sengupta, Ian Wearing, and Patrick Xavier. My special thanks must go to Mendel Weisser for very patient reading and detailed comments. I am also grateful to the publishers of *Economica, Economic Journal, Economic Record, Journal of Economic Theory, Kyklos, Public Finance,* and *Review of Economic Studies* for permission for the use here of material from my articles published in these journals. I also wish to thank the Technical Service in the Department of Geography, Monash University, for expert drawing of figures. Lastly but not least, I wish to thank Jan Ottrey for her efficiency and tolerance in typing both the first and the final drafts. (By coincidence, she and her husband Kevin make up the pair of heroine and hero, J and K, of this book.)

Monash University 1979   YEW-KWANG NG

Preface to the Revised Edition

I am glad that the book has been fairly widely used and am taking the opportunity to revise the first edition. The revision consists mainly in: (1) corrections and some misprints; (2) addition, with appropriate references and remarks in the text, of new books and articles, making the present edition up to date; (3) the incorporation of the original Addendum into Appendix 9A. I have not found it necessary to change any of the original arguments. The original Section 9A.2 has been deleted, not on the ground of incorrect argument, but because its mathematical complication may distract some readers from the central theme; it has thus been deleted to make room for additional useful references and discussions.

As far as I know, the first edition has received two favourable reviews (Walker, 1980, Winch, 1980) and one with a mixture of favourable and critical comments (Boadway, 1981). Thus Boadway twice describes the book as 'entertaining' and also as 'encyclopedic, if idiosyncratic'. He also finds the exposition of the theory of social choice 'as well done as I have seen anywhere'. But he criticises my 'distinction' between preference and welfare as falling outside 'the main stream of liberal economic thought' and can 'be used to justify all sorts of (illiberal) policy judgements'. Also, I am said to make 'some slippage... between normative and positive choice' and my theory of third best is 'belabouring the obvious'. These I regard as incorrect criticisms, and respond as follows.

First, I do not think I made a slippage between normative and positive choice in my discussion of social choice. While I am personally in favour of the Bentham SWF, I do adopt terminologies like, '*if* the following *value* premise is accepted' (p. 129, italics added), '*If* we accept the Benthamite *ethic*' (p. 158, italics added), etc.

Second, my distinction (as also made by Sen, 1973c) between welfare and preference is a matter about objective facts. It is also a fact that this distinction has been used (together with the value premise of welfare instead of preference maximisation) to justify some illiberal policies. But the distinction does not preclude one from arguing against illiberal policies on their unfavourable side- and long-run effects or on the ground that one should maximise preference, not welfare, or that the actual divergence between preference and welfare is insignificant in most cases (as I assume on p. 12). One need not have to close one's right eye to be a liberal. (Personally, I am an instrumental liberal.)

Thirdly, I find the criticism of the third-best theory as 'obvious' most unconvincing. The theory of second best was formally stated as early as 1956, with its widely recognised devastating implications for the practicability of welfare economics. Economists have attempted for decades to find a way out without much success. If my third-best theory is obvious, why has it not been advanced before to counter the negative implications of the second-best theory? And why do respectable economists like Brennan and McGuire (1975) draw the opposite conclusion to the third-best theory? Many important principles, once enunciated, appear obvious. Young budding researchers may be more impressed by complicated mathematical analyses without much policy significance than by 'simple' insights with far-reaching implications.

I should thank Jan Ottrey again for her efficiency not only in typing but also in discovering my mistakes.

Monash University 1982   YEW-KWANG NG

Common Abbreviations

AC : Average cost
CIC : Community indifference contour
CS : Compensating surplus
CV : Compensating variation
ES : Equivalent surplus
EV : Equivalent variation
GUFF : Grand utility feasibility frontier
IIA : Independence of irrelevant alternatives
MC : Marginal cost
MDE : Marginal-dollar equivalent
MRS : Marginal rate of substitution
MRT : Marginal rate of transformation
MU : Marginal utility
MV : Marginal valuation
SWF : Social welfare function
UPC : Utility possibility curve
WMP : Weak majority preference

Common Symbols

Note: Superscripts indicate different individuals, different situations, or different bundles of goods; subscripts indicate different goods of the same bundle or different indifference levels of a given preference pattern (except Chapter 7, where individuals J and K appear in subscripts).

G	:	Number of goods
I	:	Number of individuals
$xI^J y$	:	Individual J is indifferent between alternatives x and y
J, K	:	Our two individuals, Jan and Kevin
p	:	Price
$xP^i y$	:	Individual i prefers x to y
q	:	A given distribution of a collection (bundle) of goods
Q	:	A given collection of goods
$xR^i y$	:	$xP^i y$ or $xI^i y$
U	:	Utility
W	:	Welfare
x_g^i	:	Amount of good g consumed by individual i
X, Y	:	Two representative goods

1 Introduction

Welfare economics is a very important branch of economic theory. It serves as a foundation to many applied (relatively speaking) branches of economics such as public finance, cost-benefit analysis, and the economics of government policy in many areas including international trade, industry and welfare (social security, etc.). Recently, even macroeconomics is beginning to assume a microeconomic foundation and become subject to a welfare-theoretic analysis (e.g. Phelps, 1970, 1972). The increasing importance of welfare economics admits of scarcely any doubt.

Most people would agree with Pigou (1922; his work of 1912 was the first to take welfare economics as an independent study) that 'practical usefulness, not necessarily, of course, immediate and direct, but still practical usefulness of some sort' is what we mainly look for in economic investigation. In other words, bearing fruits is more important than just shedding light. To apply economics beneficially in government policies and in solving social issues we need some guidelines or criteria. Most practical policy problems are not simple enough to admit of easy answers. For example, if a change will increase the national income but make it more unequally distributed, is it desirable? If a policy will make certain groups of people better off and others worse off, should it be adopted? Should government revenue be raised more by direct or by indirect taxes? Shall we go for freer trade even if that will lead to the collapse of some industries? Should we tax or regulate pollution? To what extent should we conserve our scarce resources? Is economic growth a good thing? Can the study of welfare economics help us to answer these problems? But what is welfare economics?

(Beginners may find the methodological discussion of this chapter rather abstract. They are advised to read it, including Appendix 1A, with perhaps not much appreciation. After they have read a few more chapters, they will appreciate the methodological discussion better. However, if they cannot bear reading it, they may first read Section 1.5 and go on to Chapter 2 without much loss of continuity. More advanced readers are advised to read the methodological discussion of this chapter carefully.)

1.1 What is Welfare Economics?

Welfare economics is the branch of study which endeavours to formulate propositions by which we can say that the social welfare in one economic situation is higher or lower than in another.

The above definition of welfare economics is not much different from the following definition by Mishan. 'Theoretical welfare economics is . . . that branch of study which endeavours to formulate propositions by which we may rank, on the scale of better or worse, alternative economic situations open to society' (Mishan, 1960, reprinted in 1969b, p. 13). In fact, if we define social welfare as whatever is good, or whatever ought to be maximised, then the two definitions are identical. However, the terms 'better' and 'worse' are explicitly normative, while 'social welfare' may be given a normative or a positive interpretation. It is true that most people tend to regard 'social welfare' as a normative term. But there is no logical reason why we cannot adopt a positive definition of the term 'social welfare'. Two such definitions are presented below.

First, we may define social welfare as a vector of individual welfares

$$W = (W^1, W^2, \ldots, W^I), \tag{1.1a}$$

where W^i is the welfare of the ith individual and I is the relevant number of individuals. Here, individual welfare may be taken as an individual's well being, or more explicitly, his happiness, taking happiness to subsume both sensual pleasure and pain and spiritual delights and sufferings. How do we measure individual (net) happiness? One way to escape this difficulty is to assume that an individual is the best judge of his welfare and that he maximises his own welfare. Then, whenever he prefers x to y, he is assumed to be happier at x than at y. We may then use his utility function (which represents his preference) as an ordinal indicator of his welfare. (On ordinal versus cardinal measurability, See section 1.4.) Alternatively, we may directly define social welfare as a vector of individual (ordinal) utilities. One way or another, we have

$$W = (U^1, U^2, \ldots, U^I), \tag{1.1b}$$

where U^i is a utility function representing the ordinal preference of individual i. (For the moment, we are not concerned with the technical questions of the conditions that are necessary or sufficient for such a representation; on this, see Appendix 1B.)

A vector is said to be larger than another if and only if some of its elements are larger than, and none of its elements is smaller than the corresponding element of the other vector. Thus *if* we define social welfare as a vector of individual welfares (or utilities), we say that social welfare increases if and only if W^i (or U^i) increases for some i and decrease for no i. If welfare increases for some individual and decreases for some other individual, the change in social welfare (according to the vector definition) is undefined in sign and magnitude.

The vector concept of social welfare must be carefully distinguished from the concept of a Paretian social welfare function (SWF). The Pareto criterion says that social welfare increases if some individuals are made better off without any individual being made worse off, where 'better off' may mean 'happier' or 'in a more preferred situation'. A Paretian SWF accepts the Pareto criterion. Hence, 'increase in some W^i (or U^i) and decrease in no W^i (or U^i)' is a sufficient but not a necessary condition for an increase in social welfare. For example, for a person to live in America, it is sufficient that he lives in New York. But it is not necessary for him to live in New York; he may live in Washington, which is also in America. Similarly, if a change satisfies the Pareto criterion, it must be regarded as a good change according to a Paretian SWF. But a change need not necessarily satisfy the Pareto criterion to be regarded as a good change according to a Paretian SWF. For example, a change may make a few individuals marginally worse off but many individuals significantly better off. It may be regarded as a good change by a Paretian SWF. A Paretian SWF may be written as

$$W = f(W^1, W^2, \ldots, W^I) \tag{1.2a}$$

$$\partial f/\partial W^i > 0 \quad \text{for all } i \tag{1.2b}$$

Equation (1.2a) is an individualistic Bergson SWF (Bergson, 1938) and (1.2b) makes it Paretian. By the definition of a function, there exists one and only one value of W for each set of values of $W^i, i = 1, \ldots, I$. Thus, if we have a (specific and fully defined) Paretian SWF, we know that social welfare in an alternative situation is higher or lower even if some W^i vary in opposite directions compared with the original situation. But for the vector concept of social welfare, such a comparison is not available.

The vector concept of social welfare is of course of limited interest due to its avoidance of interpersonal comparison of welfare or utility. Most people accept the Pareto criterion as a sufficient but not a necessary condition for an increase in social welfare. But it is difficult to get people to agree on a specific Paretian SWF or to provide the necessary and sufficient condition for an increase in social welfare. Hence, what is generally accepted is a vague, unspecified Paretian SWF in the form of (1.2) but with the precise form of f unknown. Hence, the vector concept of social welfare in a sense captures the 'minimum content' of this agreement. For example, analysis dealing only with the *necessary* conditions for Pareto optimality may be based on the vector concept of social welfare only. We can then say that the vector social welfare is not maximised unless such and such hold. Then the analysis does not have to be based even on the existence of a general unspecified form of SWF, Paretian or not. One need not then be concerned with the conditions for the existence of a mathematical function. Moreover, even people who do not accept the Pareto value judgement can agree that the analysis has some objective meaning, especially if the vector (1.1b) is used. This makes it possible to interpret welfare economics as a postive study.

Another positive definition of social welfare is the utilitarian concept of the sum total of individual happiness

$$W = W^1 + W^2 + \ldots, + W^I = \Sigma_{i=1}^I W^i \qquad (1.3a)$$

If a more objective indicator is desired, one may prefer

$$W = U^1 + U^2 + \ldots, + U^I = \Sigma_{i=1}^I U^i \qquad (1.3b)$$

The advantage of adopting (1.3) instead of (1.1) is that with (1.3), social welfare is not incomparable if some W^i increase and some decrease. A difficulty with (1.3) is the problem of interpersonal comparison of welfare or utility (Section 1.4). Since these individual welfare or utility indices are to be summed, we must be able to find a common unit. In other words, the utility functions have to be unit comparable (Sen, 1970). We shall return to this problem later. At the moment, it suffices to note that, while the problem of interpersonal comparability of utility is a tricky one, it is not insoluble in principle (Section 5.4.1). It is conceivable that, perhaps several thousand (or million) years from now, neurology may have advanced to a stage where the level of happiness can be accurately correlated to some cerebral reaction which can be measured by a 'eudaimonometer'. Hence, the definition of social welfare in (1.3) is an objective definition, although the objects are the subjective feelings of individuals. Whether a particular dish is delicious is subjective. But the fact that a particular individual enjoys that dish is objective. However, before we have a perfect 'eudaimonometer', we may disagree widely in the measurement of W^i or even U^i. But if we adopt an objective definition of individual welfare or happiness or utility, such disagreement is a difference in subjective judgement of fact, not a difference in basic value judgement. (See Appendix 1A on the difference between basic value judgement and subjective judgements of fact.) The question whether we ought to pursue or maximise social welfare as objectively defined in (1.3) is however a value question. But analysis of objectively defined concepts can proceed with or without an agreement on such a value question.

It is true that, unless the objectively defined concepts are of some interest, analysis of them, while possible, is not of much relevance. For example, one may define 'X' as 'the sum of the square roots of the numbers of hairs of individuals divided by the sum of their bank-account numbers', and analyse the factors that affect X. However, such exercises are not of much interest. Hence, one would not build a welfare economics based on a definition of social welfare that appeals to no one. I shall argue later (Section 5.4.1) that the concept of social welfare defined in (1.3) is consistent with a widely acceptable set of value judgements. It is, however, unlikely that any specific concept of social welfare will find universal acceptance as the right objective we should maximise. For example, even the Pareto value judgement which seems to me so mild and reasonable has its vehement opponents. (It is, however, likely that the objection is based on a misunderstanding of the Pareto value judgement; see Section 2.1.) And such a crazy (to me anyway) objective as that of maximising the welfare of the worst off (implying zero trade-off between the welfare of the second worst off and that of the worst off) attracts overwhelming attention and a size-able group of adherents. Thus, what a welfare economist can do is to use either a concept of social welfare which he himself believes to be the right objective or one that most people or the government believes to be so, or some compromise. This is not very different from other branches of study. For example, one may investigate ways to pre-serve 'mo-shu-yu'. This line of research may prove highly useful if mo-shu-yu becomes very scarce relative to demand. If mo-shu-yu re-mains a free good, its study is not of much use but still constitutes a part of our scientific knowledge.

The advantage of adopting an objective definition of social welfare is that it enables us to regard welfare economics as a positive study. Whether welfare economics is positive or normative is by no means widely agreed upon in the profession. Let us next examine this issue.

1.2 Is Welfare Economics a Positive or Normative Study?

A positive study asks the question: what is? A normative study asks the question: what ought to be? 'These two ideas differ from one another as the understanding differs from the will, or as the indica-tive mood in grammar differs from the imperative. The one deals in facts, the other in precepts. Science is a collection of truths; art, a body of rules, or directions for conduct' (Mill, 1844, pp. 123-4). Positive propositions can be verified or falsified, or at least are verifi-able or falsifiable in principle. Normative propositions, on the other hand, cannot be true or false; they can only be persuasive or otherwise.

Now, what about welfare economics? While there is no consensus, a majority of economists seem to regard welfare economics as norma-tive. This seems to be a little curious, as a majority also regard econ-omics as a science. If economics is a science (which is positive), then welfare economics, as a part of economics, should also be a positive study. But is welfare economics perhaps not a part of economics? There is an apparent inconsistency.

The answer to our question depends on our attitude in the study of welfare economics. If we define social welfare in some positive sense, and confine ourselves to the study of the economic factors affecting social welfare, then it is a positive study. On the other hand, if we want to go a step further, and do not confine ourselves to saying that a certain measure will increase social welfare (defined in some positive sense), but try to say that a certain measure should be adopted, then we are adopting normative language. We can, however, avoid making value judgements by saying instead, '*If* the objective is such and such, then the measure should be undertaken', without committing ourselves to the value judgements behind the objective function.

A possible objection to our attempt to define the concept of social welfare in a positive sense should be considered. The term 'social welfare' has been so widely used in the normative sense that any attempt to define it positively may more likely cause confusion than clarify the issue. To forestall such objections, we may refer to the vector concept of social welfare as the welfare vector and to the Benthamite concept of social welfare as the welfare aggregate.

Little objection can be raised against the concept of welfare vector, apart perhaps from its limited usefulness. The concept of welfare aggregate raises more difficulties. Before we can aggregate individual welfares, we must be able to measure them and compare them. This leads us to consider the distinction between welfare and utility before considering the problem of utility measurability and interpersonal comparability.

1.3* Welfare versus Utility

We remarked above that one way to reduce the difficulty of measuring an individual's welfare is to take his preference as an indicator of his welfare such that whenever he prefers x to y, we infer that his welfare is higher in x than in y. There are, however, three reasons why this may not always be a good indicator.

First, the preference of an individual may not only be affected by his own welfare but may also be affected by his consideration for the welfare of other individuals. Thus it is possible for a person to prefer x to y and yet be himself less happy in x than in y because he believes, e.g., that other people are happier in x than in y. It is true that the belief that other people are happy may make him happy. But this may not be strong enough to outweigh the loss he has to suffer from changing from y to x. For example a person may vote for party x, knowing that he himself will be better off with party y in government. The reason he votes for x is that he believes that the majority of the people will be much better off with x. This itself may make him feel better and is a form of external effect. However, this external benefit may not be important enough to overbalance, in terms of his subjective happiness, his personal loss, say in income, under x. He may yet vote for x due to his moral concern for the majority. To give an even more dramatic example, consider an individual who expects to lead a very happy life. When his country is being invaded, he may volunteer for a mission which will bring him the certainty of death. The prospect of being a citizen of a conquered nation especially with the guilty conscience of failing to volunteer for the mission may not be too bright. But overall he may still expect to be fairly happy leading such a life. Yet he chooses death for the sake of his fellow countrymen. He is not maximising his own welfare. (This source of divergence between welfare and preference due to a consideration for others is discussed in Ng, 1969U, p. 43 and Sen, 1973c. On the related issue of altruism and efficiency, see Phelps, 1975.)

Some economists have difficulty in seeing the above distinction between preference and welfare, saying that whenever an individual prefers x to y, he must be, or at least believe himself to be happier in x than in y. This difficulty completely baffles me. Clearly, a father (or mother) may sacrifice his (her) happiness for the welfare of his (her) children. I cannot see why similar sacrifices cannot be made for a friend or a relative, and further for a countryman, any human being, and finally any sentient creature.

Assuming that the preference of an individual may be represented by a utility function (on which see Appendix 1B), the difference between welfare and preference discussed above may be illustrated thus. The preference of a rational individual with perfect knowledge (irrationality and ignorance will be discussed below) is in general, a function of the welfares of all individuals

$$U^i = U^i(W^1, W^2, \ldots, W^I) \tag{1.4}$$

In general, it is not true that individual i prefers x to y if and only if $W^i(x) > W^i(y)$. This is so for the special (though it may be a very important) case of a 'self-concerning' individual where $U^i = U^i(W^i)$. Even for a self-concerning individual, his welfare may still assume the following general form

$$W^i = W^i(x_1^1, \ldots, x_G^1, x_1^2, \ldots, x_G^2, \ldots, x_G^I, W^1, \ldots, W^{i-1}, W^{i+1}, \ldots, W^I)$$

$$\equiv W^i(x_{g=1,\ldots,G}^{j=1,\ldots,I}; W^{j\neq i}), \tag{1.5}$$

where x_g^j is the value of the gth variable (good, service, or activity) by the jth individual, and $x_{g=1,\ldots,G}^{j=1,\ldots,I}$ is just a shorthand way of writing the $I \times G$ variables.

A self-concerning person must be distinguished from a 'self-minding' one with $W^i = W^i(x_{g=1,\ldots,G}^{j=1,\ldots,I})$ and $W^{j\neq i}$ do not affect W^i (but may affect U^i) and a 'self-attending' one with $W^i = W^i(x_{g=1,\ldots,G}^i, W^{j\neq i})$ and $x_{g=1,\ldots,G}^{j\neq i}$ do not affect W^i except through their effects on W^j. A self-concerning person has no concern for the welfare of others except insofar as his own welfare is affected. The welfare (but not necessarily also the preference) of a self-minding person is not affected by the welfare of others. The welfare of a self-attending person is not affected by the activities of others. If a person is both self-minding and self-attending, we call him 'self-regarding', with $W^i = W^i(x_{g=1,\ldots,G}^i)$.

In our world of pervasive interdependence, the existence of a truly self-attending person is doubtful, though for certain problems it may be assumed for analytical simplicity without much loss. A self-concerning individual is more likely to exist. (If my judgement is right, over 90 per cent are self-concerning except with respect to their immediate family.) A generous person who helps others a lot need not necessarily be non-self-concerning since he may do so only because he himself feels happy doing so. Hence, operationally, it is very difficult to distinguish non-self-concerning from non-self-minding.

We may proceed to define a 'self-centring' individual as one who is both self-concerning and self-minding. He then has

$$U^i = U^i\{W^i(x_{g=1,\ldots,G}^{j=1,\ldots,I})\} = f^i(x_{g=1,\ldots,G}^{j=1,\ldots,I}).$$

If he is also self-regarding, we call him an extremely self-centring person with

$$U^i = U^i\{W^i(x_{g=1,\ldots,G}^i)\} = f^i(x_{g=1,\ldots,G}^i).$$

Shall we call a self-concerning *and* self-attending person 'self-contending'? (Some readers may find our classification of self-concerning, etc., rather artificial and useless. However, for certain problems, such distinction provides insights with policy implications; see Section 7.4**.)

Second, preference may differ from welfare due to ignorance and imperfect foresight. While an individual may prefer x to y believing he will be better off in x than in y, it may turn out to be the other way round. This is the question of *ex-ante* estimate versus *ex-post* welfare. While the *ex-ante* concept is relevant for explaining behaviour, it is the *ex-post* one which is his actual welfare.

Third, an individual may have irrational preferences. The preference of an individual is here defined irrational if he prefers x over y despite the fact that his welfare is higher in y than in x, and his preference is unaffected by considerations of the welfare of other individuals (any sentient creature can be an individual here), or by ignorance or imperfect foresight. The definition of irrationality here is such as to make the three factors discussed here exhaustive causes of divergence between preference and welfare. (The concept of irrationality differs among authors. For example, contrast ours with those of Dahl and Lindblom, 1963, pp. 38 f., and Brandt, 1966, pp. 244 ff.)

There are at least two sources of irrational preference. First, an individual may stick rigidly to some habit, custom, 'principles', or the like even if he knows that this is detrimental to his welfare and the welfare of others even in the long run, taking account of all effects and repercussions. Customs, rules, moral principles, etc. have a rational basis as they may provide simple guides to behaviour which may be, at least on the whole, conducive to social welfare. It would be too cumbersome and time-consuming if an individual were to weigh the gain and loss in terms of social welfare or his own welfare each time he has to make a decision. Thus he may stick to his routine, rules, principles, etc., without thinking about the gain and loss. If this results occasionally in decisions inconsistent with promoting his welfare and the welfare of others, it may be regarded as a cost in pursuing generally good rules. If, say, there is a change in circumstances, the adherence to some rules may result in persistent net losses in welfare, taking everything into account. An individual may stick to these rules without knowing that they no longer are conducive to welfare. Then the divergence between preference and welfare can be traced to ignorance. If he knows this and yet sticks to the rules, he is irrational.

Many readers may disagree with the definition of irrationality adopted here. For example, suppose a man sticks rigidly to the principle of honesty and would not tell a lie even if that would save his life and contribute to the welfare of others, taking everything into account. According to our definition here, he is acting irrationally. To those who are willing to accept honesty as an ultimate good in itself, he may not be irrational. But let us consider such questions as: *Why* shouldn't a person tell a lie? Shouldn't one lie to an invading army which is cruel and dishonest? If we press hard enough with such questions, I believe that most people would ultimately rely on social welfare as the justification for any moral principles such as honesty. Personally, I take the (weighted or unweighted) aggregate welfare of all sentient creatures or a part thereof as the only rational ultimate end (my basic value judgement, on which see Appendix 1A), and hence define irrationality accordingly. I know the controversial nature of this definition. But fortunately, one does not have to agree on the definition of irrationality given here to agree with the arguments of this book. If preferred, the word 'irrational' as used here could be taken to read 'irrational according to the objective of welfare maximisation'.

The second source of irrational preference is the excessive fear of danger or pain and the excessive temptation of pleasure. For example, consider a person with an aching tooth which, if not treated, will cause nagging pain for a long time but whose treatment by a dentist will cause an acute but short pain. Out of fear of the agony, the person may refuse to go to the dentist, thus subjecting himself to a greater amount of pain (assuming that the length of the nagging pain overbalances the intensity of the short pain). His refusal to go to the dentist may be due to the ignorance of the greater amount of pain or to the ignorance of the fact that the agony of dental treatment is not really so bad. Then the cause of his preference that does not contribute to his welfare is classified under ignorance. But if he knows that very well but just cannot have the determination to undergo a once-and-for-all but present agony, he is being irrational. For another example, a drunkard may vote in favour of prohibiting Sunday drinking not for the sake of the public, road safety or the like, but for forcing himself not to drink too much. But before the new law is effective, he may yet go out drinking on Sundays.

It may be objected that an individual himself is the sole judge of his own welfare and irrationality cannot therefore arise. But I think that some individuals will admit that some of their preferences are irrational. The first individual above may, after a few days, decide to face up to the dentist and agree that he should have done so days earlier. The drunkard may also agree that it is in his own interest to resist temptation.

However, the above source of irrational preference touches on the tricky philosophical question of the existence of free will. If an individual will be better off with x than with y but chooses y as x is not attainable, then obviously we would not call this an irrational preference. Thus a relevant question is whether x is within his attainable set. For example, one may argue that the individual in the first example above may have a psychological make-up that makes him *incapable* of deciding to go to the dentist before a few more days of pain help him to free himself of this incapability. Pursued to its logical conclusion, this line of argument will end up with the result that everything is predetermined and the feasible set open to any decision-maker consists only of one single point (or action). Little scope would be left for any theory of choice. To avoid this unpalatable prospect, we will not introduce too many constraints so as to leave an individual with some scope for exercising his preference. (This does not imply that the determinist view of the world is wrong. This is a matter of different types of problems; but I do not want to go into the depth of this philosophical problem.)

While we recognise the three sources of divergence between welfare and utility discussed above, it is convenient to ignore the divergence except when we come to discuss problems (such as merit goods) where the divergence is important.† In other words, in the absence of specific evidence to the contrary, we assume that, as a rule, each individual is the best judge of his own welfare and chooses to maximise his welfare. Then the question of welfare measurability coincides with that of utility measurability, to the consideration of which we now turn.

---

†Those against the use of the divergence between preference and welfare as a justification for illiberal policies may argue: (i) that the undesirable side-effects (including long-run effects) of such policies overbalance their benefits; (ii) that we should maximise preferences instead of welfare; (iii) that the divergence is insignificant in practice. But to *deny* the distinction between preference and welfare to save liberalism is to adopt the policy of an ostrich.

1.4 Utility Measurability and Interpersonal Comparability

I believe that many students of economics, like myself, have at some stage been baffled by the controversies regarding whether utility is measurable or not measurable, cardinally measurable or just ordinally measurable. Ordinal measurability involves ability to rank. With just ordinal measurability, one can say that utility at x is higher than that at y, but cannot say how many times higher, nor compare differences in utility. Thus one cannot say whether utility at x is higher than that at y by more or less than the utility at y is higher than that at z. If utility is just ordinally measurable, the utility function is said to be unique up to a positive monotonic transformation, since any positive monotonic transformation of a function $(f = g(U), g' > 0)$ leaves the ranking unchanged. On the other hand, measurability of utility *differences* would make the utility function unique up to a positive afine transformation or sometimes loosely called a linear transformation $(f = a + bU; a, b$ are constants and b is positive). This transformation leaves the proportions of utility differences unchanged. With full cardinal measurability, the only permissible transformation is a positive proportionate one (i.e $f = bU; b$ is a positive constant). One can then say how many times utility at x is equal to that at y and also know what corresponds to zero utility.

The confusion with respect to utility measurability is partly due to the use of the same term 'utility' both as a measure of subjective satisfaction and as an indicator of objective choice or preference. Another source of confusion is the insufficient distinction between measurability in principle and measurability in practice. For utility as a measure of the subjective satisfaction of an individual, it seems clear that it is cardinally measurable in principle, though the practical difficulties of such measurements may be very real. These difficulties include inaccuracies and possible insincerity in preference revelation. Moreover, even the individual himself may have difficulties in giving a precise measure. For example, I prefer a grapefruit to an orange and prefer an orange to an apple. If you ask me, 'Do you prefer a grapefruit to an orange more strongly than an orange to an apple? (Question A), then I will say, 'It depends on what kind of fruits I had in the immediate past, what sort of meal I am having'. If all these are known, then I will be able to give a definite answer. Thus, subject to practical difficulties my subjective utility is cardinally measurable. If it was just ordinally measurable, I would not just have some difficulties in answering Question A, I would dismiss it as meaningless. It seems clear that any individual will be able to compare the difference in subjective utility between having an apple and an orange and that between an orange and a house, and able to compare the difference in subjective disutility between a bite of an ant and a sting of a bee and that between a sting of a bee and having his right arm cut off.

It also seems meaningful to say that I was at least twice as happy in 1977 as in 1966. If I have a perfect memory, I may even be able to pin down the ratio of happiness, at say, 2.8. It also seems sensible for someone to say, 'Had I known the sufferings I had to undergo, I would have committed suicide long ago', or 'If I had to lead such a miserable life, I would wish not to have been born at all!' Hence, it makes sense to speak of negative or positive utility. Thus, somewhere in the middle, there is something corresponding to zero utility. 'There can be little doubt that an individual, apart from his attitude of preference or indifference to a pair of alternatives, may also desire an alternative not in the sense of preferring it to some other alternative, or may have an aversion towards it not in the sense of contra-preferring it to some other alternative. There seem to be pleasant situations that are intrinsically desirable and painful situations that are intrinsically repugnant. It does not seem unreasonable to postulate that welfare is +ve in the former case and −ve in the latter' (Armstrong, 1951, p. 269). Hence it seems clear that utility as a subjective feeling is in principle measurable in a full cardinal sense.

On the other hand, we may use a utility function *purely* as an objective indicator of an individual preference ordering such that $U(x) > U(y)$ if and only if he prefers x to y and $U(x) = U(y)$ if and only if he is indifferent; and we may not be interested in anything in addition to the above ordinal aspect of the utility function. Then any monotonically increasing transformation of a valid utility function is also an acceptable indicator and a utility function possesses only ordinal significance. For some problems (such as the theory of consumer choice), knowledge of the preference *orderings* is all that is required and hence an analyst can justifiably abstract away the cardinal aspect of the utility function. This, however, does not mean that, for problems (such as social choice) where the intensities of preference are relevant, one cannot proceed to adopt cardinal utility functions, provided due attention is paid to the problem of practical difficulties. To deny the use of cardinal utility is then to commit what may be called the 'fallacy of misplaced abstraction'. (There has been a recent trend back to cardinal utility, e.g. Mueller, 1979, Ng, 1975a, Mirrlees, 1971* and followers.)

The technical problems of the existence of a utility function that represents an individual's preference is discussed in Appendix 1B. In the text, we shall for the most part take the existence of a utility function for granted. We now turn to the problem of interpersonal comparison of utility.

Different types and degrees of comparability may be distinguished. Level comparability refers to comparison of total utilities; it answers questions such as: Is person J (Jan) happier than person K (Kevin)? Unit comparability refers to differences in utilities between situations. It answers questions such as: Is J made better off by more than K is made worse off in moving from x to y? Full comparability subsumes complete possibility of both level comparability and unit comparability. Non-comparability excludes both. In between lies partial comparability (Sen, 1970a, p. 99; 1970b) where rough but not precise comparisons of units or levels of utilities may be made. Different social welfare functions and different problems need different types of comparability (Sen, 1974, 1977b). For example, if we are interested in maximising the sum of individual utilities given the number of individuals, then what we need is unit comparability. On the other hand, if we adopt the Rawlsian criterion of maximising the welfare of the worst-off individual, what we need is level comparability. (Contrary to common belief, the general possibility of level comparability implies unit comparability under fairly general conditions; see Ng, 1982bU.)

There is a long tradition among economists in regarding statements involving interpersonal comparison of utility as value judgements (Robbins, 1932, 1938). I have argued elsewhere (Ng, 1972b; see also Appendix 1A and Klappholz, 1964, p. 105) that such statements are just subjective judgements of facts. The judgement that J is happier than K and J's gain in happiness will exceed K's loss of happiness if there is a change from x to y does not imply what ought to be done until an objective function (which necessarily involves value judgements) is specified. Thus, if our objective is to maximise the sum of utilities, we choose y; if we want to maximise the utility of the worst-off individual, we choose x (assuming that K is and will remain the worst-off individual). Judgements involving interpersonal comparison of utility are subjective judgements of fact even though the facts are the subjective feelings of individuals. However, due to this subjective nature, it is very difficult to measure individual utilities and to compare them interpersonally with any degree of precision. While such difficulties should not be underestimated, they do not make interpersonal comparison value judgements.

1.5 The Rest of this Book

The arrangement of chapters in this book is based on the following logic. After this introductory chapter, the basic topic on Pareto optimality is first covered. This emphasises the *necessary* conditions for an optimum; the next chapter on welfare criteria is concerned with *sufficient* conditions for a social improvement (qualitative). The more quantitative topic of consumer surplus is then discussed. These chapters have not adequately dealt with problems of distribution and resolution of conflict of interests. The next two chapters then address the issue of social choice and income distribution. Analysis so far has not considered market imperfections formally. Perhaps the most important of these is externality (pollution and all that: students who smoke in my class stopped doing so after this topic had been covered). A special form of externality, that of public goods, is treated in an independent chapter. With the introduction of imperfections there arises the question of second best when some of the first best optimality conditions cannot be met. This theory of second best, as well as the theory of third best recently advanced by the present writer, are discussed in Chapter 9. The last chapter touches on wider issues of welfare and speculates on the need for a complete study of happiness.

Sections and appendices in the various chapters may carry asterisks. Mostly, the ones without any asterisk are the more basic discussions essential for beginners. The ones with a single asterisk are a little more advanced topics likely to appeal to those who already have some basic knowledge in welfare economics. Those carrying double asterisks usually contain new arguments interesting to the expert. Beginners may attempt to read all sections and appendices if they find them not too demanding. In addition to all those with double asterisks, the attention of the expert is also drawn to the following: methodological issues discussed in this chapter and Appendix 1A, the assessment of Little's and Mishan's argument with respect to welfare criteria in Sections 3.2.2* and 3.3*, the recent Clarke–Groves incentive-compatible mechanism for preference revelation in Section 8.3*, the theory of third best in Section 9.4, and the concluding chapter.

Summary

Welfare economics is the branch of study which endeavours to formulate propositions by which we can say that the social welfare in one economic situation is higher or lower than in another. It can be regarded as a positive study by adopting a positive definition of social welfare or by taking the social welfare function as given. Usually, social welfare is taken as some function of individual welfares or utilities. Welfare may diverge from utility (or preference) due to a concern for the welfare of others, ignorance, and irrationality. In the absence of specific evidence of this divergence, the two are assumed to be the same. Subject to practical difficulties, individual utility can be cardinally measured; interpersonal comparisons of utility are not value judgements. Distinguishing basic value judgements from subjective judgements of fact enhances the role of economists in policy recommendation (Appendix 1A).

On Basic Value Judgements and Subjective Judgements of Fact

When there is a disagreement on policy matters, about what ought to be done, it is usually said that this is a matter of different value judgements on which no objective discussion is possible. We shall see that this is usually not true when we have made a distinction between basic value judgements and subjective judgements of fact. I shall first provide a revised (or sister) definition of Sen's concept of a basic value judgement.

1A.1 Positive Statements v. Values Judgements

Positive statements are concerned with what is, was, or will be in the objective sense; normative statements (or value judgements) are concerned with what ought to be, what is morally right or wrong, good or bad. This is a sufficiently clear distinction for our purposes. It is true that the philosophical problems of metanormative theory are by no means completely settled; there is much scope for controversy as to whether the statement 'this picture is beautiful' is positive or normative. (Personally, I regard the statement as positive if it means, 'this picture appears beautiful to me', as evaluative if it means, 'I think this is a beautiful picture', as normative if it means, 'this picture *is* beautiful!' implying that others should accept it as beautiful.) But for the present purpose, the finer distinction between the evaluative, the ethical, and the normative is not of much direct importance. I shall thus disregard this finer distinction. What I shall emphasise is the distinction between basic and nonbasic (or derived) value judgements.

1A.2* Basic v. Non-basic Value Judgements

Sen (1967, 1970a) defines basicness thus: 'A value judgement can be called "basic" to a person, if the judgement is supposed to apply under all conceivable circumstances, and it is "non-basic" otherwise' (Sen, 1970a, p. 59). For example, a person may express the judgement, 'A rise in national income indicates a better situation', (judgement A). This is not his basic value judgement if he agrees that a rise in the national income does not indicate a better situation if, for example, the poor are made much poorer. Let him revise his judgement as follows, 'For a poor country in which everyone has the same income, it will be a better situation, *ceteris paribus*, if everyone's income is to increase by the same amount' (judgement B). Now, if he will stick to this under all conceivable circumstances, shall we regard it as his basic value judgement? Let us ask him, '*Why* do you regard that as a better situation?' Suppose he replies that it is because everyone will become happier. It is then reasonable to regard judgement B as non-basic (to that individual).

In the above example, the individual may believe in the judgement, 'It is desirable to make every individual happier' (judgement C). He also sticks to judgement B under all circumstances because the conditions of 'a poor country', 'equal income', 'equal increments', '*ceteris paribus*', etc., are sufficient (or are believed to be sufficient) to make every individual happier. Thus judgement B is derived from the value judgement C and certain factual, positive statements or judgements. We shall thus call a value judgement basic to a person if it is not derived from some other value judgement and he believes in it for its own ethical appeal. Whether this definition differs from Sen's depends on the interpretation of 'all conceivable circumstances' in Sen's definition. In the above example, the individual's belief in judgement B is based on judgement C. If we ask him, 'Will you stick to judgement B even if a policy based on it does not make anyone happier?' Then presumably he has to say 'No'. (I owe this observation to Sen.) Thus, if 'circumstances in which acting in accordance to judgement B does not make anyone happier' are regarded as *conceivable* circumstances despite the fact that the individual believes that they are *sufficient* to make every individual happier, then Sen's definition may not be different from ours. In fact, with this broad interpretation of 'conceivable circumstances', the two definitions are equivalent.

I shall first show that if a value judgement is non-basic in our sense, it is also non-basic in Sen's sense (with the broad interpretation) and then show the reverse. If judgement X is based on judgement Y and some factual knowledge or judgements, this means that, given Y, X applies in the factual domain α. X may or may not apply outside α. Let us expand α to α' within which X applies and beyond which it does not apply. This is just a conceptual expansion and no actual specification of α' is necessary. Denote Ω as the universal domain, i.e. the domain of all possible (non-zero probabilities) circumstances. If $\Omega-\alpha'$ is not empty, then obviously X is a nonbasic judgement in Sen's sense. If α' is itself the universal domain, then $\Omega-\alpha'$ is empty. If we confine 'all conceivable circumstances' to the universal domain, X applies under all conceivable circumstances and is a basic value judgement in Sen's sense. But if we do not confine 'all conceivable circumstances' to the universal domain, then X does not apply beyond α' and is therefore a non-basic judgement in Sen's sense.

If a judgement Z is not basic in Sen's sense, then it applies in some domain β but does not apply outside the domain β. Suppose judgement T applies outside the domain β. It does not matter whether the individual concerned can make up his mind in a definite way. Thus, T may just stand for 'no opinion' or 'If . . ., then . . .; If . . ., then . . .'. We can then combine Z and T into a single judgement V. This combination is always possible (on which more below) since V may just stand for 'If β, Z; if non-β, T'. Then clearly judgement Z is based on judgement V and some factual statements or judgements delineating β. It is therefore also non-basic in our sense.

From the above, it may be said that, if a value judgement is non-basic in Sen's sense, it is necessarily non-basic in our sense; if it is non-basic in our sense, whether it is also necessarily non-basic in Sen's sense depends on the interpretation of 'all conceivable circumstances'. Even if we adopt the broad interpretation such that the two definitions coincide, it may still be useful to look at it in our way. Thus, in the example above, we may not be able to specify a conceivable circumstance for which the individual will relinquish judgement B until we discover his more basic value judgement C by asking him *why* B. Similarly, even if we want to stick to our definition of basicness, it may be useful to test for basicness using Sen's method. It is sometimes difficult to discover that a certain value judgement is based on another just by asking 'why?'

For example, an individual may mistakenly but sincerely believe that his belief in the judgement, 'No one shall kill a human being' (judgement D) is not based on another and is due purely to its own ethical appeal. He may not be able to answer the question, 'Why do you believe in judgement D?' He may reply, 'I believe in it because I believe in it!' It may thus seem that judgement D is his basic value judgement. But if we introduce him to the factual circumstances of euthanasia and fighting against an invading army, he may admit that he no longer accepts judgement D. His initial belief that judgement D is basic is thus mistaken. If it is truly basic, it cannot be shown to be inapplicable under any circumstances.

1A.3 Can a Person Have More than One Basic Value Judgement?

Suppose an individual has more than one, say two value judgements which he regards as basic. Then either they are not in conflict with each other under any circumstances or they are under some (or all) circumstances. If the latter is the case, then it is clear that the two judgements cannot both be basic. If the two can never give conflicting results, then we can combine them into a single one. For example, the judgements 'No female should kill a human being' and 'No male should kill a human being' are never in conflict but they can be combined into one, 'No person should kill a human being.' An individual may have many diverse basic value judgements which cannot be combined into a single statement and the only way to combine them as 'one' basic value judgement is to list them exhaustively, e.g. 'One should not murder; one should not . . .' It may then just be a semantic point whether we regard these mutually non-conflicting judgements as his numerous value judgements or as parts that form his single value judgement or value system. It is even possible that the individual himself may think that it is not possible to list all his basic value judgements exhaustively as a new one may crop up especially with the specification of a new set of circumstances. However I think that, for such cases, the numerous value judgements are likely to be non-basic. If a rational person presses himself hard enough with the question, 'Why do I think this is a good thing?', I believe that all his supposedly basic value judgements can be reduced to a few or just one single principle (his basic value judgement) that gives rise to various expressions under various circumstances. I believe that most, if not all, reasonable persons will agree that, for society, our *ultimate* end should be a maximisation of an increasing function of and only of individual welfare (see Sen, 1979b, for objection and Ng, 1981b, for defence), that is

$$W = W(W^1, W^2, \ldots, W^I), \frac{\partial W}{\partial W^i} > 0,$$

where W indicates social welfare, W^i the welfare of the ith member, and I the number of members concerned. (If we are not using a static analysis, then we have to maximise a welfare function through time, discounted to account for the uncertainty of continuing existence. If we are, as I think we should be, also concerned with sentient creatures other than human beings, we have to include their welfares.)

However, even if we can agree on a specific form of the function, this could hardly serve as our only guide under all circumstances. This is so because of the complexity of the real world and it is difficult to know whether a particular action will increase or reduce welfare. From experience, however, we learn that actions in accordance with certain principles (e.g. honesty, respecting other people's freedom, etc.) usually contribute to welfare. Eventually these principles tend to be valued for their own sake. This may explain the diversity and numerousness of 'basic' value judgements.

1A.4 Subjective Judgements of Fact

The distinction between basic and non-basic value judgements is of some importance, as remarked on by Sen (1970a, ch. 5). If two persons disagree over a basic value judgement, the only possible scientific (factual, logical) argument is for one to show to the other that the judgement in question is not really his basic value judgement. If it really is basic, no ground is left for scientific argument. One of them may of course try to persuade the other to change his basic value judgement. But this is an exercise in ethical persuasion, not scientific discussion. This does not mean that a scientist should not engage in such persuasion. A scientist is a human being as much as any other person and is entitled to engage in ethical persuasion provided he does not confuse scientific discussion with ethical persuasion, or attempt to confuse the readers.

On the other hand, if the disagreement is on factual judgements or non-basic value judgements, scientific discussion alone may be sufficient to settle the dispute. However, since our scientific knowledge is never complete, a final agreement may not be reached even for two logical persons with the same basic value judgements. This is due to possible differences in what I call subjective judgements of fact (Ng, 1972b). These are estimates made in the absence of definite scientific knowledge and hence may be influenced by the personal interests, values, experience, etc. of the person making them. For example, it has been observed that, gazing at the same statistics, left-wing economists tend to infer that progressive taxation does not have a disincentive effect, while right-wing economists tend to infer that it does (Klappholz, 1964, p. 103). However, disagreement over subjective judgements of fact can, at least in principle, be subject to further discussion and scientific testing. With the advancement of science, such differences may eventually disappear, though they are likely to be replaced by others. (On consensus among economists, see Kearl *et al.* 1979.)

As a scientist, one has no business to make any basic value judgement, and as a citizen, a scientist is no more qualified than any other citizen in making basic value judgements. But this is not so for non-basic value judgements and subjective judgements of fact. If we have any faith in the usefulness of a branch of study, we must admit that a scientist of that branch is more qualified than a layman in making subjective judgements of fact closely related to his field of study. For example, while an economist may be hard put to judge the effects on economic growth of two alternative balance-of-payments policies, a layman is likely to know nothing about the effects at all. Thus the distinction of subjective judgements of fact and non-basic value judgements from basic value judgements enhances the role of scientists in policy recommendation. If we were to lump all three under 'value judgements' and refrain as scientists from making these 'value judgements', we would have to leave everything, except the undisputable scientific facts, to the politicians.

Another source of disagreement over policy matters is due to a difference of interests, rather than a difference of values or judgements of facts. For example, leaders of a strong trade union may press on with a big wage claim, knowing full well that it will lead to further inflation and/or unemployment. On the ethical level, they may admit (though not in public) that their action is not good for society as a whole. But on the practical level, they may be guided mainly by their self-interest.

1A.5 A Summing Up

To sum up, a disagreement (especially on policy matters) may occur due to one or more of the following

(1) conflicts between personal or sectional interests;
(2) differences in basic value judgements;
(3) differences in subjective judgement of facts;
(4) differences over alleged facts or in logical analysis.

Disagreements of the fourth type can readily be resolved by objective demonstration or logical discussion. Any remaining disagreement on this score can only be ascribed to ignorance or inability to reason. Disagreements of the first type can be resolved by political compromise of some sort or by exercise of force or the threat of it. Or, especially in the long run, it may be resolved, to some extent, by educating people to be more social-minded or by making their interests more compatible. Disagreement of the second type can only be resolved by ethical persuasion. It is the disagreements due to differences in subjective judgements of fact that I think offer the most scope for further discussion, analysis, and arguments. Apart from the first type, it is also, I believe, the most important source of disagreement.

Since a non-basic value judgement is based on some basic value judgement and some factual information or subjective judgement of fact, differences in value judgements are either due to differences in basic values or to differences in subjective judgements of fact, ignoring factual and logical mistakes. It is this latter type of difference (in subjective judgements of fact) that I believe to be more prevalent. This type of difference is usually regarded as a direct disagreement over value judgements on which no further argument is possible, as a distinction between basic value judgements and subjective judgements of fact is not made. The discussion above sounds a warning against this confusion.

On the Existence of Utility Functions

Consider a set X. A set is just a collection of elements, e.g. all the students in the classroom, the rational numbers between 0 and 1, etc. Let xRy represent a binary relation between x and y, e.g. 'x is a friend of y', 'x is at least as preferable as y', 'x is no smaller than y', etc. A binary relation R over a set X may or may not satisfy certain properties. Among the properties that have been discussed, the following are most relevant of our purposes. Notations used below: $\forall$ = for any; $\in$ = belongs to; ':' = such that; $\underline{V}$ = or (does not preclude the possibility that both are true); $\Rightarrow$ = implies; $\Leftrightarrow$ = implies and is implied by (i.e. if and only if or 'iff' for short); $\sim$ = not.

(1) Reflexivity: $(\forall x \in X)\,(xRx)$

A binary relation over a set is said to be reflexive if and only if for each element of the set, the relation holds with respect to the element itself. For example, for any set of real numbers, the relation 'no smaller than' is reflexive as any number can be no smaller than itself.

(2) Completeness: $(\forall x, y \in X: x \neq y)\,(xRy\ \underline{V}\ yRx)$

For any pair of distinct elements x and y, either xRy holds or yRx holds (or both). Obviously, 'no smaller than' is a complete relation over any set of real numbers. But 'is a square of' is not a complete relation over the set of all real numbers.

Completeness is sometimes called 'connexity' or 'connectedness'; if a relation R is complete over X, then all elements of X are connected by R in some way. However, since 'connectedness' is also used to describe the property of a set itself, it is preferable to use 'completeness' to describe a binary relation over a set.

Some authors do not require x ≠ y in their specifications of completeness. In that case, completeness subsumes reflexivity; if $y = x$, $(xRy \underline{\vee} yRx) \Rightarrow xRx$.

(3) Transitivity: $(\forall x, y, z \in X: x \neq z)\,(xRyRz \Rightarrow xRz)$

The relation 'is a friend of' is not necessarily transitive for a set of persons. We do not necessarily have 'x is a friend of z' even if x is a friend of y and y is a friend of z. However, for some specific set of persons, it may be transitive. For example, take X to be the set of all students in the class. If they are all friends of each other, than the relation 'is a friend of' is clearly transitive. Suppose the class is partitioned into a left-wing and a right-wing group. All students in the same group are friends of each other and no student is a friend of someone in a different group. Then the relation 'is a friend of' is still transitive for the whole class. But it is not complete.

If a binary relation over a set satisfies all the above properties, i.e. reflexivity, completeness, and transitivity, we call it an order. If it satisfies reflexivity and transitivity, we call it a partial order. (The terminology of binary relations varies between authors; see, e.g., the table given by Sen, 1970, p. 9.)

A specific binary relation that we will be most interested in is the relation 'at least as preferable as'. This is so basic a relation that we will just use the symbol R to represent it. Thus, from now on, xRy means that x is at least as preferable as y. Now, between any ordered pair of alternatives, the relation R either holds or it does not, i.e. either xRy or $\sim(xRy)$. Hence, there are four logical possibilities, one of which is excluded by the requirement of completeness. The other three possibilities are respectively defined as xIy, xPy, and yPx as shown in Table 1B.1. Since we cannot have xRy and $\sim(xRy)$ at the same time, it can be seen that one and only one of xIy, xPy, and yPx holds if R is complete. Obviously, I stands for indifference and P for preference.

If the preference relation R over X is an order, can it be represented by a real-valued order-preserving function U such that $U(x) \geqslant U(y) \Leftrightarrow$

TABLE 1B.1

xRy	yRx	
Holds	Holds	Defined as xIy
Holds	Does not hold	Defined as xPy
Does not hold	Holds	Defined as yPx
Does not hold	Does not hold	Violates completeness

xRy? It can be seen that, if this holds, then $U(x) > U(y) \Leftrightarrow xPy$ and $U(x) = U(y) \Leftrightarrow xIy$. (Students may try to verify this as an exercise.)

Somewhat surprisingly, the answer to the question above is 'not necessarily'. If X is a finite (or infinite but countable) set, then the required U function always exists. But if X is an uncountably infinite set, then some additional condition is required before representation is assured. The standard example where representation by a real-valued function is not possible is the so-called lexicographic order. To illustrate, let X be the two-dimensional Euclidean space E^2, and R be defined by $xPy \Leftrightarrow x_1 > y_1$ or $(x_1 = y_1 \,\&\, x_2 > y_2)$ where a subscript indicates the relevant dimension, e.g. x_1 is the value of x in dimension 1. This is a lexicographic order as the conditions for an order are satisfied and dimension 1 has priority over dimension 2. As long as $x_1 > y_1$, xPy irrespective of the values of x_2 and y_2. This is similar to the order in which words are arranged in the compilation of a dictionary (lexicography).

Suppose that there is a real-valued function U representing the above lexicographic order such that $U(x) > U(y) \Leftrightarrow xPy$. For each value of x_1, let $H(x_1) = [U(x_1, 0), U(x_1, 1)]$, i.e. the closed interval bounded by the values of the function U at $x_2 = 0$ and $x_2 = 1$, given x_1. From the definition of P, $(x_1, 1) P(x_1, 0)$. Hence $U(x_1, 1) > U(x_1, 0)$. So each $H(x_1)$ is non-degenerate, i.e. it is not just a single point. Moreover if $x_1 \neq y_1$, $H(x_1)$ does not intersect $H(y_1)$. So each $H(x_1)$ contains a distinct rational number. But since there is an uncountable number of x_1, we conclude that the set of rational numbers is uncountable, which is false. So the assumed function U does not exist (Debreu, 1959*, pp. 72-3; Fishburn, 1972*, p. 58).

However, the effect of lexicographic order on the possibility of preference representation by a utility function has been over-emphasised. Some writers missed the point that, if the set is countable, representation is possible whether the order is lexicographic or not. To make representation impossible, the set must be uncountable. We will have uncountability if there is perfect divisibility. But with perfect divisibility it is doubtful that preference will still be lexicographic. The argument of lexicographic preferences is mainly based on such a question as, 'Is there some number of trinkets that will induce a starving coolie to part with one bowl of rice?' (Chipman, 1960*, p. 221). The answer to such a question may well be negative, but this does not make his preference lexicographic. With divisibility, his preference can only be lexicographic if, given that he prefers more trinkets to less, there is no number of trinkets that will induce him to part with 0.0000000 . . . 1 grain of rice. This is clearly unlikely. On the other hand, if we do not have perfect divisibility such that one grain of rice is the smallest unit, then preference representation is still possible. Nevertheless, while the practical importance of non-representation due to lexicographic preference is minimal, it remains true on a logical level that a lexicographic order over E^2 (or higher dimension – the case of one dimension is no problem) is not representable by an order-preserving real-valued function. (It may, however, be representable by vectors of real numbers; see Chipman, 1960*.)

The additional condition required to ensure representation refers to the concept of order-denseness. With R as an order on X, we say that a subset of X (denoted Y) is P-order dense in X iff: $(xPz$ and $x, z \in X-Y)$ $\Rightarrow (xRyRz$ for some $y \in Y)$.

If R partitions X into a set of indifference classes (curves or hypersurfaces) such that it is possible to draw a curve (or countable number of curves) C cutting across all these surfaces (see Figure 1B.1), then the curve C is P-order dense in X. But C contains an uncountable number of points. However, if we take a subset of C containing only points whose distances from the origin (any point of C may serve as the origin) are rational numbers, then this subset, denoted C', is countable. Moreover, since the set of rational numer is $>$-order dense in the set of real numbers, C' is also P-order dense in X.

The reason we are interested in a subset of X that is countable is evident from the following theorem. (First proved by Cantor, 1895*; and

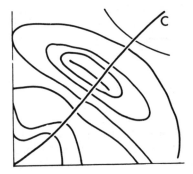

Figure 1B.1

more recently by Birkhoff, 1948*; Debreu, 1954a, 1964*; Luce & Suppes, 1965*; and Fishburn, 1970c.)

Cantor's Theorem: There is a real-valued function U on X such that for all $x, y \in X$, $U(x) \geqslant U(y) \Leftrightarrow xRy$, iff R on X is an order and there exists a countable subset of X that is P-order dense in X.

In the case of lexicographic order discussed above, there does not exist a countable subset of X that is P-order dense in X. It is also clear that if X is itself countable, then the condition of order denseness is necessarily satisfied, since we can just take $Y = X$. Hence, a corollary of Cantor's Theorem is that every order of a countable set is representable by a real-valued function.

Cantor's Theorem gives necessary and sufficient conditons for representation. Other sets of sufficient conditions are known to ensure representation. For example, if X is a connected set, a relation R on X is representable by a continuous real-valued function if R is an order and also satisfies the following continuity condition (Debreu, 1959*, p. 56; necessary and sufficient conditions for continuous utility functions are given in Fishburn, 1970c, p.36).

$(\forall x \in X)$, the sets $\{ y : yRx \}$ and $\{ y : xRy \}$ are closed.

This condition is equivalent to the requirement that a (strict) preference between any two elements is not altered if either is altered by sufficiently small amounts (Arrow and Hahn, 1971*, p. 78).

2 Pareto Optimality

The concept of Pareto optimality has occupied a major part in the discussion of welfare economics. Many theorems and optimality conditions are formulated with reference to Pareto optimality. This is so because the Pareto principle as a value judgement is widely acceptable, while other judgements involving interpersonal comparison of utility are more controversial. However, this does not mean that welfare economics has to be based on and only on the Pareto principle. Theorems and analysis which are not based on the Pareto principle or which are based on 'extra-Paretian' principles are possible and have been developed. Nevertheless, Pareto optimality has been and will continue to be one of the most important concepts in welfare economics and hence warrants careful study.

2.1 The Pareto Principle

Whenever we say that one situation is better than another, or that a situation is optimal, we must be basing our assessment, explicitly or implicitly, on a certain set of value judgements. A situation regarded as optimal according to one set of values may rank very low according to another set of values. For example, an increase in GNP, even if it includes only the production of 'goods' and does not involve any 'bads' such as air pollution, may still be regarded as a bad thing by a person who believes that man must not pursue material comforts. Thus Pareto optimality is optimal with reference to those value judgements that are consistent with the Pareto principle.

The Pareto principle says that a change is desirable if it makes some individual(s) better off without making any others worse off. This is a value judgement, but it is a very weak one both in the sense that most people will accept it and in the sense that many other value judgements subsume the Pareto principle and yet also contain something more. (An assumption, factual or value, is said to be weak if it does not assume very much and hence is likely to be realistic and/or acceptable.) For example, consider the value judgement that a change is desirable if it makes N persons significantly better off and less than N persons insignificantly worse off. No matter how it is proposed to determine what constitutes 'significantly better off', it is clear that this judgement subsumes the Pareto principle, as every change approved by the Pareto principle will also be approved by it. On the other hand, not all changes approved by it will pass the test of the Pareto principle, since in some of these changes, some persons may be made worse off. Hence, the judgement is stronger than the Pareto principle.

If one reflects on the Pareto principle, one will probably agree that it takes a rather peculiar ethic to reject it. Since some individuals are made better off and no one is made worse off, why reject the change? However, some economists come out strongly against the Pareto principle. It seems that their objections to the Paretian value judgement are based on somewhat misleading interpretations of it. For example, consider the following quotation:

> If we adopt a series of economic policies which make the richer group richer but have the poorer group at the same absolute level, then according to a Pareto-type social welfare function . . . we would be necessarily raising the level of social welfare (Nath, 1969, p. 228).

This assertion of Nath follows only from his rather peculiar interpretation of the Paretian value judgement as: 'If any change in the allocation of resources increases the income and leisure of everyone or at least of one person (or more strictly one household) without reducing those of any other, then the change should be considered to have increased social welfare'. However, the actual Paretian value judgement is that 'a change is desirable if it makes someone better off without making others worse off.'† This will yield Nath's interpretation only if an additional factual assumption is made, viz. that there is no externality in consumption. (If there are external effects in consumption, an

---

†Pareto spoke of 'benefit' and 'detriment', not 'richer'. For example, 'The points of the type *P* [i.e. Pareto optimal] are such that we cannot deviate from them to the benefit or detriment of all the members of the community.' (Pareto, 1935 – Livingstone edn, p. 1466n.)

individual may be made worse off even if his own income stays un-changed, as he may have envy for the increased consumption of others, or find it difficult to keep up with the consumption standard of his neighbours, or he may simply be made worse off by the extra empty bottles disposed of by his neighbours.) In other words, Nath confuses the value and the factual parts of the usual assumptions made by econo-mists. Alexander's argument that the generation of wants by the social process 'threatens the entire ethical basis of economics, striking in particular at Pareto-optimality' (1967, p. 110), is open to the same criticism.

Even if the Pareto principle is universally accepted, we may still have difficulties in cases where some persons are made better off and some worse off. In these cases, we cannot use the Pareto principle alone to guide our decisions. However, the Pareto principle is a sufficient value basis for many propositions with respect to the allocation of resources and even to the distribution of income. Hence, for these propositions, we naturally wish to use Ockham's razor to shave off the unnecessary assumptions, value or factual.

2.2 The Conditions for Pareto Optimality

The conditions for Pareto optimality may be divided into the first-order necessary conditions and the second-order 'sufficient' conditions. The first-order conditions have been widely discussed; see, e.g., Reder (1947, ch. II), Little (1957, chs. VIII and IX), Bator (1957), and Winch (1971, Ch. 4). The mathematical derivation of the first-order conditions is provided in Appendix 2A where all the necessary conditions are derived in one maximisation problem in contrast to the usual procedure of maximising productive efficiency and consumer satisfaction separately. The 'production of commodities by means of commodities' is also taken into account.

2.2.1 The first-order conditions

The first-order or marginal conditions may in turn be divided into the condition for exchange, the condition for production, and the top-level condition.

To begin with the optimum condition for exchange, we assume for the moment that the various amounts of the final goods have already been produced, and hence the problem is how to allocate them among the individuals in the economy. At this stage, we also assume divisibility (i.e. goods and factors of production are divisible to any desired amount), continuity ('nature does not jump'), and absence of external effects of consumption and production. Under these assumptions, the Pareto condition for exchange says that the marginal rate of substitution (MRS) between any pair of goods must be the same for all individuals consuming the two goods. This proposition may be justified by the following simple argument.

If the MRS between any pair of goods (let us call them X and Y) are different for any pair of individuals J and K, it can be shown that one individual can be made better off without making any other worse off. For example, suppose that the marginal rate of substitution of X for Y (MRS_{XY}) equals one for J and equals two for K. In other words, one X is worth (in terms of utility) one Y at the margin to J, and worth two Y to K. Thus, if we take one X from J and give it to K, and take one Y from K and give it to J, K is made better off while J stays indifferent. We could have made both of them better off if we had transferred 1.5 Y instead of one Y from K to J. The possibility of making one person better off without making any other worse off means that Pareto optimality has not been attained. This possibility can be shown to exist as long as the MRS of some pair of goods is different between any pair of individuals. Hence, for a Pareto optimum, the MRS of any pair of goods must be the same for all individuals consuming that pair of goods.

The above argument may also be illustrated in Figure 2.1 which is known as the Edgeworth-Bowley Box, or simply the Edgeworth Box. The box is formed by superimposing the inverted indifference map of K on the indifference map of J, such that the origin of K (O^K) is north-east of O^J and the axes are parallel as shown. Moreover, the width of the rectangle ($O^J M = O^K N$) measure the total available amount of X, and the height of the rectangle ($O^J N = O^K M$) measures that of Y. The symbol X^J stands for the amount of X consumed by J, etc. Any point (e.g. E) on the box represents a specific distribution of X and Y between J and K. For example, for the point E, J consumes $O^J A$ amount of X and $O^J D$ of Y and K consumes $O^K C (= AM)$ of X and $O^K B (= DN)$ of Y.

The curve $O^J E O^K$ traces the points of tangency between the two sets of indifference curves. It can be shown that, for any point which is not on the curve $O^J E O^K$, we can make one individual better off without making the other worse off, by moving to some point on the curve. For example, if the initial point is H, both individuals will be made better off if we move to any point on the curve between E and G. If we move exactly to E, J stays at the same indifference curve J_2 and K moves from a lower indifference curve K_1, to a higher one K_2. On the other

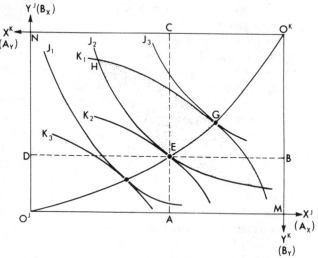

Figure 2.1

hand, if we move from H to G, J is made better off, and K stays indifferent. Hence every point between and inclusive of E and G is Pareto-superior to H. In fact, this is true for all points bounded by the two indifference curves J_2 and K_1, i.e. the shaded area. But for any point within the shaded area, a further Pareto improvement is still possible until we arrive at a point on the curve.

The curve $O^J E O^K$ is called a contract curve, since free contracting will ensure that a point on it will be reached unless our individuals engage in strategic behaviour, each attempting to gain more than the other will concede. If the number of individuals in the free exchange is large, each possessing a small fraction of the total supply of goods, no individual will have any strategic or monopolistic power and a point on the contract curve will be reached by free exchange.†

A point on the contract curve is a point of tangency between an indifference curve of J and another of K. The absolute slope of an indifference curve measures the MRS between the two goods for the individual. Hence the MRS is equalised for the two individuals for any point on the contract curve. This links our geometrical illustration with the Pareto condition for exchange.

The second Pareto optimality condition refers to production and says that the MRS between any two factors must be the same for all products and for all production units using the factors. This condition ensures that, with a constant amount of factor-endowment, the production of each good has been maximised given the amounts of other goods produced. If this condition is not satisfied, it is possible to increase the production of some product(s) without reducing that of any other product. The demonstration of this proposition is similar to that of the exchange optimum.

If the MRS between any two factors A and B are different for any two products X and Y, it can be shown that the production of one can be increased without reducing that of another. For example, suppose that the marginal rate of substitution of A for B (MRS_{AB}) equals one in the production of X and equals two in the production of Y. In other words, the marginal product of A equals that of B in the production of X but equals twice the marginal product of B in the production of Y. Thus, if we transfer one A from the production of X to that of Y, and transfer one B from the production of Y to that of X, the production of Y is increased while that of X stays the same. Moreover, outputs of all other products are unaffected since their inputs are unchanged. With the increased production of Y, we can give (divide) this extra amount

† An allocation is blocked if there exist a coalition of traders which can achieve a better outcome for each of its members with their own resources. The core of the economy is the set of all feasible and unblocked allocations. As the number of traders increases, the core shrinks. With a continuum (uncountable infinity) of traders, the core becomes a single point, the competitive equilibrium. This is called the limit theorem (proved by Shubik, 1959*; Debreu & Scarf, 1963*; Aumann, 1964*; recent results surveyed by Hildenbrand, 1977*; first discussed by Edgeworth, 1881).

of Y to (among) some (all) individual(s) in the economy and hence make him (them) better off, while no one is made worse off. Therefore, Pareto optimality has not been attained as long as the MRS between any pair of factors are different in the production of different products (and in fact also in the production of the same product in different processes). The geometrical demonstration of this proposition can be done by using Figure 2.1, reinterpreting the indifference curves of J and K to be the iso-product curves (or isoquants) of X and Y, and substituting A_X, B_X, A_Y, B_Y (A_X is the amount of factor A used to produce X, etc.) respectively for X^J, Y^J, X^K, Y^K. It can then be shown that production efficiency requires the allocation of factors at a point of mutual tangency of the isoquants, which implies the equalisation of the MRS between factors.

The third necessary condition for Pareto optimality is called the top-level optimum which relates production to preferences. It requires that, for any pair of goods, the MRS (which is equalised over all individuals, as required by the exchange optimum) be equal to the marginal rate of transformation (MRT). The MRT between any two goods is the marginal rate at which the economy can 'transform' one into another by allocating more resources to produce one and less to produce another. If the MRT is not equal to the MRS for any pair of goods, we can produce more of one good and less of another to make everyone better off. For example, if $\mathrm{MRS}_{XY} = 1$, and $\mathrm{MRT}_{XY} = 2$, then the economy can transform one X into two Y, and the individuals are indifferent between one X and one Y. Thus, by producing two units more of Y and one unit less of X, some or all individuals can be made better off.

It is convenient to summarise our three necessary conditions for Pareto optimality:

(1). *Exchange optimum*: The marginal rate of substitution (MRS) between any pair of goods must be the same for all individuals consuming the goods. (For those individuals not consuming a particular good, it is required that their MRS of this good for any good they consume be smaller, or at least not larger, than the MRS between these two goods for those individuals consuming both. Similar inequality requirements hold with respect to the following two conditions.)

(2). *Production optimum*: The MRS between any pair of factors must be the same for all production units using the factors.

(3). *Top-level optimum*: For any pair of reproducible goods, the common MRS must be equal to the marginal rate of transformation (MRT).

The exchange optimum is required to ensure that, with a given collection of goods, the allocation of these goods among individuals fulfils Pareto optimality, i.e. the utility of each person is maximised given the utilities of all others. In other words, a point *on* rather than a point inside the utility possibility (hyper-) surface (or curve, for the special case of two individuals) is reached. This utility possibility curve (UPC) is depicted in Figure 2.2. It indicates the maximum level of utility one individual can attain, given the level of the other. For example, if the level of utility for J is to stay at OG, the maximum level possible for K is OH, given the fixed collection of goods.

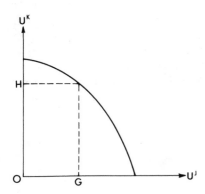

Figure 2.2

Similarly, the production optimum is required to ensure that, with a given endowment of factors, the production of each good is maximised given the amounts produced of all other goods, so that the economy is at a point on the production possibility surface (curve), or the transformation surface (curve). This production possibility curve TSP is

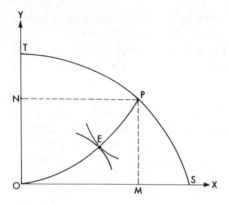

Figure 2.3

depicted in Figure 2.3. The absolute shape of this curve measures the MRT between the two goods X and Y. Each point on the curve (e.g. P) represents a given collection (OM of X and ON of Y) of the two goods. If we form a rectangular box ($OMPN$ in Figure 2.3), and draw in the two sets of indifference curves, it becomes an Edgeworth box similar to Figure 2.1. By efficient allocation of this collection of goods, we arrive at a UPC similar to that in Figure 2.2. It is derived by taking the different combination of utility levels along the contact curve OP in Figure 2.3.

The point P represents only one production possibility among a large number of such possibilities along the curve TPS. For each different production point, or each different collection of goods, we have a different UPC. If we draw all such curves in Figure 2.4, the outer envelope of all these curves, FF', is called the utility possibility *frontier*. This frontier is sometimes called a *situation* UPC referring to a given situation with fixed endowment of resources, and a UPC associated with a given collection of goods is called a *point* UPC.

As suggested by Bator (1957, p. 26), there is a short-cut to the derivation of this frontier. The short-cut is based on the top-level optimum which requires the equality of the MRS and MRT. Considering the point P in Figure 2.3, the condition for top-level optimum implies that the choice of the point P is only consistent with the optimality require-

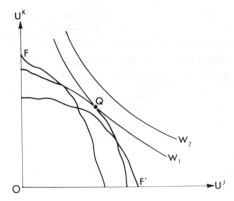

Figure 2.4

ments if the choice of a point along the contract curve *OP* happens to give the slope of the indifference curve (= MRS in absolute value) equal to the slope of *TPS* at *P* (= MRT in absolute value). As a rule, there is only one point (e.g. *E*) on *OP* that satisfies such a requirement. Hence, for each point on the production possibility curve *TPS*, we have only to plot one point in Figure 2.4. By connecting all such points we have again the utility possibility frontier *FF'* in Figure 2.4. (Some points on the production possibility curve may not have a corresponding point *on* the frontier but *inside* the frontier; see Yeh, 1972.)

All points on the utility possibility frontier (ignoring possibly positively sloped sections) satisfy the Pareto optimality conditions. Once we are at a point on the frontier, it is not possible to make anyone better off without making someone else worse off, with the existing technology of production and the existing factor endowment. Any point on the frontier thus represents *a* Pareto optimum. However, the choice between these infinite Pareto-optimal points may be made on an ethical level. (Friedman, 1980, argues that the Pareto-optimal range is small.) This choice is not a problem of Pareto optimality; it is usually relegated to a social welfare function (SWF). (A SWF is an expression specifying the level of social welfare at each combination of factors affecting welfare.) If the relevant SWF is represented by the welfare contours W_1, W_2, etc., as drawn in Figure 2.4, then a point on *FF'* which touches the highest welfare contour is chosen. In any case, once a point, e.g. Q on FF' is chosen, we can trace our steps backward to see what pattern of allocation is necessary to achieve it. Each point on the frontier corresponds to a point on the production possibility curve TPS on Figure 2.3. Hence, a point, e.g. P, may be traced from the point Q. The point P again fixes a point E on the contract curve, and hence the amounts of both goods going to both individuals are known. The point P in Figure 2.3 also specifies that OM of X and ON of Y are to be produced. Hence, looking at Figure 2.1 (interpreting the indifference curves as isoquants), we know which two isoquants are to be selected. The tangency of these two isoquants then determines the amounts of both factors to be allocated to the production of the two goods.

2.2.2* *Comparing optimal and non-optimal situations*

The above discussion and Figures 2.1 to 2.4 depict the first-order conditions for Pareto optimality. But it is a little difficult to compare an optimal with a non-optimal situation in the same diagram. To facilitate such comparisons, Browning & Browning (1976) devised the following geometrical technique.

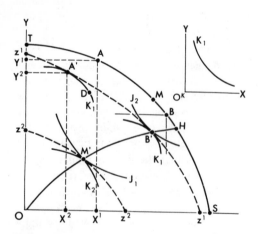

Figure 2.5

Starting from the transformation curve TS in Figure 2.5, the first step is to derive an 'availability locus', a curve which shows all combinations of the two goods available to the first individual J for which the remaining productive capacity of the economy is just sufficient to keep the second individual K on a given indifference curve, say K_1 in the small figure attached to the upper right-hand corner of Figure 2.5. This indifference map of K is inverted and its origin placed at point A on the transformation curve TS. Thus an Edgeworth box OX^1AY^1 is formed similar to Figure 2.3 and Figure 2.1. Select the point A' on K_1 where the slope of K_1 is equal to that of the transformation curve at A. This equates the MRS of K with the MRT.

Other points on the availability locus can be derived by sliding the origin of K's indifference map along the transformation curve. For example, when point B is reached, the related point on the availability locus is B' where the slope of K_1 equals that of the transformation curve at B. The whole availability locus z^1z^1 can thus be traced out. By the way it is constructed, the slope of the availability locus at any point equals both the MRS of K and the MRT at the associated allocation and production points. For example, the slope of z^1z^1 at A' equals the slope of K_1 at A' (K's MRS) and also equals the slope of the transformation curve at A (the MRT). As we move to the right along an availability locus, the output of X increases and the output of Y decreases. A point on an availability locus (such as A'), together with an associated production point (A), fixes six variables: the amounts of the two goods produced (OX^1, OY^1), J's consumption of the two goods (OX^2, OY^2), and K's consumption (X^2X^1, Y^2Y^1).

We have derived just one availability locus. But there is a whole family of availability loci, one for each indifference curve of K. For example, the availability locus associated with keeping K on a higher indifference curve, say K_2, is given by z^2z^2. This locus lies below z^1z^1 as the amounts of the two goods available to J are smaller since K is to stay on a higher indifference curve. By varying K's level of indifference, we can derive the whole family of availability loci, given the transformation curve. As the transformation curve changes, the whole family of availability loci changes. Nevertheless, we are not concerned with a change in the transformation curve.

Since there is a whole family of availability loci covering the entire production possibility set, it may be mistakenly believed that any allocation must lie on the corresponding availability locus. This is not so. For example, suppose the economy is producing at the point A but the allocation is at the point D on K_1. It can then be seen that D does not lie on the availability locus $z^1 z^1$. It is true that there is another availability locus (not shown) passing through D. However, that locus corresponds to a different indifference curve of K. Moreover, the allocation D on that different locus corresponds to a different production point on the transformation curve. Nevertheless, any Pareto-optimal allocation must lie on the corresponding availability locus. For example, if we keep K on K_1 and let J choose her most preferred consumption bundle along the availability locus $z^1 z^1$, she will consume at the point B' where the locus $z^1 z^1$ touches her highest indifference curve J_2. This will involve the economy producing at the point B and allocate at the point B'. The MRS of the two individuals will then be equal and also equal the MRT. It is then impossible to make one person better off without making the other worse off. To make K better off, the availability locus to J will then contract towards the origin (e.g. $z^2 z^2$). To stay with Pareto optimality we again allocate at the point where the new availability locus touches a highest indifference curve of J (e.g. J_1). By varying the level of indifference for K, we can then trace out the whole Pareto-optimal locus OH. In general, different points on the Pareto-optimal locus are associated with different production points on the transformation curve. For example, the allocation M' is associated with the production point M and the allocation B' is associated with the production point B. Thus, this construction allows different allocation *and* production situations to be compared in one diagram.

As an example to illustrate the use of the above construction, consider 'a competitive economy in which the government uses an excise subsidy equal to one-half of the market price of X for both consumers. The revenue to finance the subsidy is assumed to be raised with distortionless taxes, such as lump-sum taxes, so that we can ignore any possible inefficiencies introduced by the taxes and instead focus on the distortions produced by the subsidy' (Browning & Browning, 1976, p. 345, with a change in notation). When the economy has adjusted to the subsidy, the net (of subsidy) price paid by consumers for X will be one half of the price received by producers. The equilibrium production point is at E in Figure 2.6 and the allocation or consumption point is at E'. The slope of the transformation curve at E is equal to twice

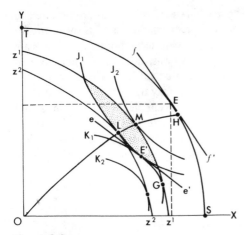

Figure 2.6

that of the indifference curves (J_1 and K_1) at E'. Thus the allocation E' is not on the availability locus (z^1z^1) corresponding to K_1. The allocation that is on this availability locus, given the production point E, is the point G where the slope of K_1 is equal to the slope of the transformation curve at E. The availability locus z^1z^1 touches J_2 at the point M and J_1 touches a lower availability locus z^2z^2 (associated with K_2) at L. The inefficiency caused by the subsidy can now be seen in Figure 2.6. At the point E', the two individuals are at J_1 and K_1 respectively. If we stay on a point on the Pareto-optimal locus between L and M, both individuals are better off in comparison to the situation at E'. The shaded area shows those allocations that are Pareto-superior to E'. However, for any point in the shaded area but not on the Pareto-optimal locus LM, there is a Pareto-superior point on LM. The choice of a different point on LM will, in general, imply a different production point on the transformation curve. As we move from the subsidy-equilibrium E' to a point on LM, production has also to be adjusted accordingly.

2.2.3 The second-order conditions

The first-order conditions are necessary but not sufficient for an optimum, since the same first-order conditions may define a minimum rather than a maximum. The second-order conditions are required to ensure that, together with the first-order conditions, it is sufficient for the attainment of Pareto optimality. These second-order conditions are usually also called the sufficient conditions. In fact, it is only in conjunction with the first-order conditions that sufficiency is assured.

To see that the first-order conditions may define a minimum instead of a maximum, let us consider a simple example of one individual and two goods, as depicted in Figure 2.7, where TS is the transformation curve, and the J's are the indifference curves. In part (a), the point P satisfies the requirement MRS = MRT and defines a maximum, since

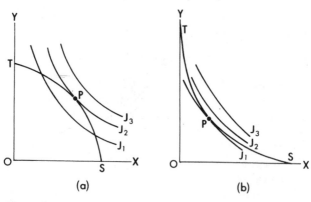

(a) (b)

Figure 2.7

J_2 is the highest indifference curve attainable. On the other hand, in part (b), the point P also satisfies the requirement MRS = MRT, but it is a point of minimum utility level along the transformation curve. To ensure that our first-order conditions do not lead us to a minimum, we require the second-order conditions as discussed below.

If all our indifference curves and isoquants are convex (to the origin), and all transformation curves are concave, it is easy to see that the possibility depicted in Figure 2.7b cannot occur. These requirements of convexity and concavity are equivalent to the assumptions of the diminishing MRS (both for goods and factors) and the diminishing

MRT.† These conditions, while sufficient (in conjunction with the first-order conditions) for a Pareto optimum, are not necessary. For example, consider Figure 2.8a, where the transformation curve TPS does not satisfy the concavity requirements. Yet the tangency point P is a maximum rather than a minimum. Hence it is seen that, for this case, what is necessary is simply that the indifference curve be more convex than the transformation curve.

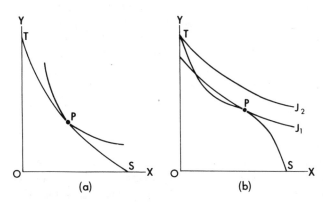

Figure 2.8

If the second-order conditions are only satisfied in the vicinity of the point where the first-order conditions are fulfilled, this point may be maximal only in this vicinity (a local maximum) and the global maximum may lie elsewhere. This is illustrated in Figure 2.8b where the

†The presence of increasing returns to scale *may* make the transformation curve convex to the origin (i.e. non-convex production feasibility set) but we may have both increasing returns and concave transformation curve at the same time. If we have constant returns to scale throughout, the transformation curve will be linear *if* we also have the same factor intensity (or input proportion) for all industries. If the factor intensities are different, the transformation curve will be concave. This diminishing MRT is caused by the fact that, if more of one product is to be produced, increased reliance has to be placed upon those factors which are more efficient (in the technical sense) in producing the other product. The degree of increasing returns to scale has to be strong enough to overbalance the effect of different factor intensities before the transformation curve is made convex.

point P represents a local maximum and T the global maximum. If the relevant functions are wholly concave and convex, a local maximum is also a global maximum (Lancaster, 1968, p. 17). In this connection, the so-called 'total conditions' (Hicks, 1939, p. 707) may be mentioned. These total conditions require that it must be impossible to increase welfare by the complete abandonment/introduction of some existing/new commodities or factors of production. If the first-order conditions are satisfied not only with respect to existing but also to potential commodities and factors as well, then the total conditions are satisfied provided that the second-order conditions are also satisfied globally. However, this proviso is rather restrictive. In practice there are such things as economies of scale, etc., which may cause the violation of the second-order conditions. Hence, an all-or-nothing comparison may have to be made. One may also extend Hicks' total conditions to include the introduction of new techniques or processes of production. This relates to the argument that the relevant MRT must refer to that achieved by the most efficient method of production (Graaff, 1957, p. 21). However, formally, one may argue that any new technique or process of production must be embodied by some factor of production. A technician or a manager who knows how to use a better method of production is then regarded as a different and superior factor than one who does not know.

2.2.4 Mathematical derivation of the first-order conditions

To assist the mathematically uninitiated, let us just derive here the exchange condition in the simple case of two individuals and two goods in given quantities. The mathematically sophisticated may read Appendix 2A* where all the optimality conditions (first-order) are derived in one maximisation problem, in contrast to the usual procedure of separating into two problems, one maximising productive efficiency and another maximising consumers' satisfaction.

The utilities of the two individuals are functions of the amounts of the two goods they consume

$$U^1 = U^1(x_1^1, x_2^1)$$
$$U^2 = U^2(x_1^2, x_2^2),$$

where x_g^i stands for the amount of the gth good consumed by the ith individual. To derive the optimality conditions, we maximise the utility level of one individual (U^1) given that of the other individual ($U^2 = \bar{U}^2$) and subject to the constraint that the aggregate amounts consumed must equal the quantities available, that is

$$x_1^1 + x_1^2 = x_1$$

$$x_2^1 + x_2^2 = x_2,$$

where x_1 and x_2 are the amounts of the goods available.

To maximise a function subject to constraints, we form a Lagrangean function by writing the constraints in the form $f(\ldots) = 0$ and add them to the objective function after multiplying them with Lagrangean multipliers (λ, α, β below)

$$L = U^1(x_1^1, x_2^1) + \lambda[U^2(x_1^2, x_2^2) - \bar{U}^2] + \alpha(x_1 - x_1^1 - x_1^2)$$

$$+ \beta(x_2 - x_2^1 - x_2^2).$$

Setting the partial derivatives of L with respect to $x_1^1, x_2^1, x_1^2, x_2^2$ to zero, we have

$$\partial U^1/\partial x_1^1 = \alpha \qquad \partial U^1/\partial x_2^1 = \beta$$

$$\lambda \partial U^2/\partial x_1^2 = \alpha \qquad \lambda \partial U^2/\partial x_2^2 = \beta.$$

After simple division, we have,

$$\frac{\partial U^1/\partial x_1^1}{\partial U^1/\partial x_2^1} = \frac{\alpha}{\beta} = \frac{\partial U^2/\partial x_1^2}{\partial U^2/\partial x_2^2},$$

which specifies the equality of the MRS between the two goods for the two individuals.

2.3 The Attainment of Pareto Optimality

After discussing the conditions for Pareto optimality, we turn now to discussing the possibility of achieving it.

It is well established that, under certain classical assumptions such as non-increasing returns, the absence of externalities, etc., a perfectly competitive economy will attain *a* Pareto optimum. (For mathematical proofs, see Appendix 2B below.) The close association of perfect competition and Pareto optimality must not be mistaken to mean that the concept of Pareto optimality is only meaningful in a perfectly competitive economy. The concept can be meaningfully applied to any economy. Moreover, an economic system other than perfect competition may also achieve Pareto optimality, at least in theory. As noted by Wiles (1964, p. 189), efficient resource allocation may be achieved in principle along three ways, viz. perfect competition, perfect central adjustment, and perfect computation, each associated respectively with the names of Lerner, Lange, and Leontief. It may be added that a system with perfect discriminatory monopolists (unlikely to exist in practice) may also achieve Pareto optimality (Pigou, 1932, ch. XVII and sec. VIII of app. III). Moreover, some rather contrived processes have also been suggested which have the required Pareto optimality property. For example, the 'greed process' as suggested by Hurwicz (1960)* can achieve an optimum even in the presence of indivisibilities and increasing returns, but it calls for more information than the competitive mechanism and is impractical as it conflicts with the behaviour of self-interest. In fact, the informational requirement of the competitive market mechanism is minimal in comparison with other processes. This has been stressed by Hayek (1945) and, together with related problems, formally analysed by Hurwicz (1972U)*, Osana (1978)*, and others; see surveys by Reiter (1977), Marschak (forthcoming)*, Hurwicz (forthcoming)*.

The crucial factor that makes perfect competition under Classical conditions capable of achieving a Pareto optimum is that no single buyer or seller of any good or factor is in a position to influence the price appreciably. The profit maximising and utility maximising behaviour of firms and consumers together with the working of supply and demand will then ensure that the equilibrium position achieved is a Pareto optimum.

To see how the conditions for Pareto optimality are fulfilled in a competitive equilibrium, first consider the equilibrium position of any consumer. Since he is unable to affect prices, his budgetary constraint is linear, a straight line in the case of two goods. Assuming non-satiation of wants, he will maximise his utility by consuming at a point P where the budget constraint touches the highest indifference curve. Since the (absolute) slope of the budget constraint measures the ratio of prices (i.e. p_X/p_Y) and the slope of the indifference curve measures the MRS, we have the equality $MRS_{XY} = p_X/p_Y$. This is true for any and every consumer, hence

$$MRS^i_{XY} = p_X/p_Y \ (i = 1, \ldots, I) \tag{2.1}$$

where X and Y stand for any two goods. (This may not seem to follow from a two-dimension figure. But we can always take one of the axes to stand for one particular good, and take the other axis to stand for all other goods. Since the equality $MRS_{XY} = p_X/p_Y$ always holds no matter which good we take to be the particular good, the equality must also hold between any two particular goods as well.) Equation 2.1 shows that the exchange optimum is attained, since the same price ratio is faced by all consumers.

Similarly, we can show that the production optimum is attained by noting the fact that a producer cannot affect factor prices. His iso-cost curves are thus linear and he produces at a point where an isoquant touches an iso-cost curve. We thus have

$$MRS^h_{AB} = p_A/p_B \ (h = 1, \ldots, H) \tag{2.2}$$

where H is the number of producers in all lines of production, and A and B stand for any two factors.

It is also not difficult to see that the price ratio between any two goods p_X/p_Y must also be equal to the MRT for all producers producing the goods. Otherwise, it would be profitable to increase the production of one and reduce the production of another. Moreover, profit maximisation also ensures that the methods of production used are efficient. The equality of MRT with the price ratio may also be seen in another way. Under perfect competition, the price of a product is equal to its marginal cost. Hence the price ratio is equal to the ratio of marginal cost which is MRT. We have thus seen that all the necessary conditions are satisfied under competitive equilibrium.† The second-order conditions are also satisfied with the assumption of diminishing

---

†We rely heavily on a large number of price-taking producers and consumers to ensure optimality. In the absence of large numbers, optimality may yet be achieved if entry/exit is free and costless such that markets become perfectly 'contestable', with potential entrants replacing the role of numerous competitors; see Baumol, Panzar & Willig (1982) for a formal analysis and Baumol (1982) for a survey.

MRS (both between goods and between factors) and the absence of increasing returns (hence ruling out convexity in the transformation curve).

We turn now to examining some of the assumptions that are made to ensure that a competitive equilibrium is necessarily a Pareto optimum. The first assumption that seems most unrealistic is that of the absence of any external effects of consumption and production, as the environment is polluted by producers and many consumers do try to keep up with the Joneses. However, the problem of externalities is so important as to warrant a separate chapter and hence we shall disregard this problem for the moment.

The assumption of diminishing MRS or convexity of indifference curves is quite weak and generally used by economists. The assumption of diminishing MRT or concavity of the transformation curve (or convexity of the production feasibility set), however, rules out, in general, increasing returns to scale. ('In general' does not mean 'always'; see the footnote on p. 45.) With the presence of increasing returns to scale, there is a natural tendency towards monopoly and hence the very existence of perfect competition is in doubt.

The assumption of perfect divisibility seems unrealistic but the inefficiency caused by indivisibility is likely to be small unless the indivisibility involved is very large, and the presence of rental services significantly reduces indivisibility, as a large indivisible unit may be rented for short periods.

The assumption of profit maximisation can be replaced by the more general assumption of utility maximisation by the entrepreneurs, since utility maximisation is equivalent to profit maximisation for the owner-managed firms (see Koplin, 1963, Ng, 1969). If there is separation of ownership from control, then utility maximisation by the managers may not result in profit maximisation for the firm. (This will happen only if transaction costs are not negligible. Otherwise it will be beneficial to both owners and managers to maximise profit and negotiate a mutually advantageous share of the spoils.) Formally, this may be regarded as a form of externality, the external diseconomy produced by managers and borne by owners.

The assumption of utility maximisation is usually employed in economics. If Pareto optimality is defined in terms of the revealed preference of the consumers, then the assumption of utility maximisation does not impose any further restriction. On the other hand, if Pareto optimality is defined in terms of the 'actual' or 'ex-post' well-being of the individuals, then utility maximisation subsumes perfect foresight, rational choice, etc. Though this is not generally true, it may still be accepted as a working hypothesis unless there is specific reason to believe otherwise, e.g. the case of addictive drugs. These problems have been touched on in Chapter 1 and will be further discussed in Section 10A.3.

Since many of the assumptions discussed above are likely to be violated in the real economy which is not perfectly competitive to begin with, the actual attainment of Pareto optimality in the level of abstraction discussed in this chapter is quite impossible. Does this mean that the concept of Pareto optimality is useless? Knowledge about the conditions for Pareto optimality, the relation between Pareto optimality and competitive equilibrium, etc. does not only give us insights into the economy but may also assist us in making improvements over the existing state of the economy These improvements need not necessarily satisfy the Pareto principle. Society may adopt changes that make more people significantly well off even at the cost of making some a little worse off. Even for such changes, knowledge about the conditions for Parteo optimality, etc. may still enable us to select those changes that are more desirable than others, e.g. making a smaller number of people worse off. But if some individuals are made better off and some worse off, with what criterion do we decide that a change is desirable? This leads us to the discussion of welfare criteria in the next chapter.

Summary

The Pareto principle says that a change is desirable if it makes some individual(s) better off without making any other worse off. Objections to this principle are usually based on some misunderstanding. The first-order conditions for Pareto optimality in a simple economy involves: exchange optimum requiring equality of MRS for any pair of goods over all consuming individuals, production optimum requiring equality of MRS for any pair of factors, and top-level optimum requiring MRS = MRT. The inability of each individual consumer and producer to affect prices renders a perfectly competitive economy Pareto-optimal under certain conditions.

APPENDIX 2A*
The First-Order Conditions for Pareto Optimality

The optimality conditions for production and those for exchange are usually derived separately (e.g. Samuelson, 1947, ch. 8; Nath, 1969, ch. 2) in two maximisation problems, one maximising productive efficiency, another maximising consumers' satisfaction. We shall derive all the first-order conditions in one maximisation problem. We shall also take account of the 'production of commodities by means of commodities'. (But we ignore the issue of time-lags.) However, to simplify notation, we shall disregard the cases of satiation and of corner maxima. A corner maximum (or corner solution) is one in which some variables take on the value of zero. For example, some goods may not be consumed by some individuals. Corner maxima can easily be allowed for by changing the equality requirements below into inequality requirements. Divisibility in the variables is assumed throughout and external effects are assumed absent. (On externalities and public goods, see Chapter 7 and 8.) Given the noneconomic factors, the utility functions of individuals may be written as

$$U^i = U^i(x_1^i, x_2^i, \ldots, x_G^i)\, (i = 1, \ldots, I) \tag{2A.1}$$

where I is the number of individuals in the economy and x_g^i is the amount of the gth good consumed (or the negative quanity of the particular labour service performed) by the ith individual. The G types of x's could either be goods or services *consumed* or productive services (such as labour) *performed*. In the latter case, we have negative amounts entering the utility function. Hence an increase in the relevant amount means a reduction in that service performed, or an increase in leisure time.

The production functions of the various x's may be written as

$$x_g = x_g(x_{1g}, x_{2g}, \ldots, x_{Gg}; z_{1g}, \ldots, z_{Rg}) \; (g = 1, \ldots, G) \qquad (2A.2)$$

where x_{hg} is the amount of the hth good or service (hereafter, we shall refer to this only as 'good') and z_{rg} is the amount of the rth natural resource used in the production of the gth good, and R is the number of different types of natural resources. We also have the following accounting identities

$$x_g = \Sigma_{i=1}^I x_g^i + \Sigma_{j=1}^G x_{gj} \; (g = 1, \ldots, G) \qquad (2A.3)$$

$$z_r = \Sigma_{g=1}^G z_{rg} \qquad (r = 1, \ldots, R) \qquad (2A.4)$$

The amounts of the R types of resources are given. If x_g is a productive service such as labour, it is not produced and hence $x_g = 0$. Then, we have, from (2A.3), $-\Sigma_{i=1}^I x_g^i = \Sigma_{j=1}^G x_{gj}$ or the equality of the aggregate labour performed by individuals and that used in the various industries.

To derive the conditions for Pareto optimality, we maximise the utility of one individual given the utility levels of all others. Without loss of generality, take this individual to be the first person (since any individual can be put in any place). Maximising U^1 subject to $U^i = \overline{U}^i$, $i = 2, \ldots, I$, and to (2A.2)–(2A.4), we form the following Lagrangean function

$$L = U^1 + \Sigma_{i=2}^I \lambda^i(U^i - \overline{U}^i) + \Sigma_{g=1}^G p_g(x_g - \Sigma_{i=1}^I x_g^i - \Sigma_{j=1}^G x_{gj})$$
$$+ \Sigma_{r=1}^R q_r(z_r - \Sigma_{g=1}^G z_{rg}), \qquad (2A.5)$$

where the λ's, p's and q's are the multipliers associated with the respective constraints. The p's and the q's may be interpreted as the (shadow) prices of goods and resources respectively, and the λ's are the weights attached to other individuals' utility levels relative to U^1. From (2A.5), we obtain the following three sets of first-order conditions by setting equal to zero the partial derivative of L with respect to x_g^i, x_{hg}, and z_{rg} respectively.

$$\lambda^i \partial U^i / \partial x_g^i = p_g \; (i = 1, \ldots, I; g = 1, \ldots, G) \qquad (2A.6)$$

$$p_g \partial x_g / \partial x_{hg} = p_h \; (g, h = 1, \ldots, G) \qquad (2A.7)$$

$$p_g \partial x_g / \partial z_{rg} = q_r \; (g = 1, \ldots, G; r = 1, \ldots, R) \qquad (2A.8)$$

where $\lambda^1 \equiv 1$.

By division, we may write (2A.6) in a proportional form to eliminate λ^i:

$$\frac{\partial U^i / \partial x_g^i}{\partial U^i / \partial x_G^i} = \frac{P_g}{P_G} \quad (i = 1, \ldots, I; g = 1, \ldots, G-1) \tag{2A.9}$$

which is the optimality condition for exchange requiring the equality of the marginal rate of substitution (MRS, ratio of marginal utilities) between any two pair of goods for all individuals consuming both goods. ('Goods' here include the negative of services performed.)

Similarly, (2A.7) may be written as

$$\frac{\partial x_g / \partial x_{hg}}{\partial x_g / \partial x_{Gg}} = \frac{P_h}{P_G} \quad (g = 1, \ldots, G; h = 1, \ldots, G-1) \tag{2A.10}$$

which is a condition for productive efficiency requiring the equality of the technical MRS (ratio of marginal productivities) between any pair of goods in all lines of production. Combining (2A.9) and (2A.10), we have

$$\frac{\partial U^i / \partial x_g^i}{\partial U^i / \partial x_G^i} = \frac{\partial x_h / \partial x_{gh}}{\partial x_h / \partial x_{Gh}} \quad (i = 1, \ldots, I; g, h = 1, \ldots, G-1) \tag{2A.11}$$

which is a top-level condition requiring the equality between the subjective MRS and technical MRS for any pair of goods consumed and used as inputs.

In addition, (2A.7) may also be written as

$$\frac{\partial x_G / \partial x_{hG}}{\partial x_g / \partial x_{hg}} = \frac{P_g}{P_G} \quad (g, h = 1, \ldots, G) \tag{2A.12}$$

which can be combined with (2A.9) to yield

$$\frac{\partial U^i / \partial x_g^i}{\partial U^i / \partial x_G^i} = \frac{\partial x_G / \partial x_{hG}}{\partial x_g / \partial x_{hg}} \quad (i = 1, \ldots, I; g, h = 1, \ldots, G) \tag{2A.13}$$

which is a top-level condition requiring the equality between the subjective MRS and the indirect (i.e. through input reallocation) technical marginal rate of transformation (MRT) between any pair of goods. Furthermore, combination of (2A.7) and (2A.9) gives

$$\frac{\partial U^i / \partial x_h^i}{\partial U^i / \partial x_g^i} = \partial x_g / \partial x_{hg} \; (i = 1, \ldots, I; g, h = 1, \ldots, G), \qquad (2A.14)$$

which is a top-level condition requiring the equality between the subjective MRS and the direct technical MRT between any pair of goods.

We have yet to extend the optimality requirement to the use of resources. In a way similar to the derivation of (2A.9) and (2A.10) from (2A.7), we may derive the following from (2A.8)

$$\frac{\partial x_g / \partial z_{rg}}{\partial x_g / \partial z_{Rg}} = \frac{q_r}{q_R} \; (g = 1, \ldots, G; r = 1, \ldots, R - 1) \qquad (2A.15)$$

$$\frac{\partial x_G / \partial z_{rG}}{\partial x_g / \partial z_{rg}} = \frac{P_g}{P_G} \; (g = 1, \ldots, G - 1; r = 1, \ldots, R) \qquad (2A.16)$$

While (2A.16) can be combined with (2A.9) to get a top-level condition similar to (2A.13), we cannot combine (2A.15) with (2A.9). This is because we assume that non-reproducible natural resources do not enter into utility functions directly. Should any natural resources enter directly into utility functions, we may just define the production function of that 'good' as $x_g = z_r$. One will then have a top-level condition for it.

In addition to the above, we may also combine (2A.7) and (2A.8) to extend the requirement for efficiency with respect to the use of goods versus resources. We have thus shown that all the necessary conditions for Pareto optimality can be derived in a single maximisation procedure. Moreover, with this approach, the MRT is also stated in the explicit form of the technical MRS, the ratio of marginal productivities (indirect MRT), or just a figure of marginal productivity (direct MRT), instead of the usual one stated in the implicit form in terms of the derivatives of the production constraint function.

APPENDIX 2B*
Pareto Optimality of Competitive Equilibrium

The proofs regarding Pareto optimality and (perfectly) competitive equilibrium, apart from those on uniqueness and stability, apply to the following four points:

(1) The existence of a Pareto-optimal state.
(2) The existence of a competitive equilibrium.
(3) Every competitive equilibrium is also a Pareto-optimal state.
(4) Every Pareto-optimal state can be sustained as a competitive equilibrium by an appropriate distribution of resource endowments.

Since proposition (3) is most relevant to our purpose and is easiest to prove, we provide the proof below which is a revision of Arrow (1951a*, Theorem 5). Basically, we have made certain assumptions implicit in Arrow's proof (such as divisibility and local non-satiation) explicit, and we have relaxed certain unnecessary assumptions such as convexity of preferences and the existence of utility functions. However, the proof concerns only the Pareto-optimal nature of a competitive equilibrium and not its existence. Additional assumptions are needed for proving the existence of a competitive equilibrium.

We shall use x_g^i to denote the amount of good (or service) g consumed by individual i. The vector x^i denotes the amounts of the G goods consumed by i. Symbolically, $x^i \equiv (x_1^i, x_2^i, \ldots, x_G^i)$. If $\bar{x}^i$ has more of some good and no less of any other good than $\overset{*}{x}{}^i$, we write $\bar{x}^i > \overset{*}{x}{}^i$. The matrix x denotes the amounts of the G goods consumed by the I individuals separately. $\Sigma_{i=1}^{I} x^i$ denotes the aggregate (over individuals) amounts of goods consumed. Symbolically, $\Sigma_{i=1}^{I} x^i \equiv (\Sigma_{i=1}^{I} x_1^i, \ldots, \Sigma_{i=1}^{I} x_G^i)$. If individual i prefers the bundle $\bar{x}^i$ to the bundle $\overset{*}{x}{}^i$, we write $\bar{x}^i p^i \overset{*}{x}{}^i$. Similarly, I^i indicates 'indifference', and R^i denotes 'p^i or

$I^{i'}$. The production feasibility (or transformation) set is denoted by T. Thus $\Sigma_{i=1}^{I} x^i \epsilon T$ indicates that the vector of aggregate amounts of goods consumed is an element of T and thus that allocation or economic state x is feasible. The set of prices is denoted by the price vector $p \equiv (p_1, \ldots, p_G)$. We are now ready to state the assumptions used.

Assumption 1   *Divisibility*: All goods are divisible.

Assumption 2   *Self-Centring*: (No externality on individuals.) The preference of each individual i is affected only by his own consumption bundle x^i (given the non-economic factors).

Assumption 3   *Rational Choice*: If an individual i chooses $\overset{*}{x}{}^i$ from a feasible set S, then there does not exist $\bar{x}^i$ in S such that $\bar{x}^i P^i \overset{*}{x}{}^i$.

Assumption 4   *Local Non-satiation*: If an individual i chooses $\overset{*}{x}{}^i$ from his feasible set S, then there does not exist $\bar{x}^i$ in S such that $\bar{x}^i > \overset{*}{x}{}^i$.

Assumption 5   *No Externality on Production*: The output of each firm is affected only by its own input usage (given the non-economic factors).

Under perfect competition, an individual i faces a given price vector p. Assumptions 1 and 4 then ensure that he always chooses a point $(\overset{*}{x}{}^i)$ on his budget hyperplane. Thus, from assumption 3, $\bar{x}^i P^i \overset{*}{x}{}^i$ implies $\Sigma_{g=1}^{G} p_g \bar{x}_g^i > \Sigma_{g=1}^{G} p_g \overset{*}{x}_g^i$, and $\bar{x}^i R^i \overset{*}{x}{}^i$ implies $\Sigma_{g=1}^{G} p_g \bar{x}_g^i \geqslant \Sigma_{g=1}^{G} p_g \overset{*}{x}_g^i$. We proceed now to define a Pareto-optimal state and a competitive equilibrium.

Definition 1: An economic state $\overset{*}{x}$ is said to be Pareto optimal in T if (a) $\Sigma_{i=1}^{I} \overset{*}{x}{}^i \epsilon T$, and (b) there is no other economic state $\bar{x}$ such that $\Sigma_{i=1}^{I} \bar{x} \epsilon T$ and $\bar{x}^i R^i \overset{*}{x}{}^i$ for all i, and $\bar{x}^j P^j \overset{*}{x}{}^j$ for some j.

Definition 2: The price vector p and the economic state $\overset{*}{x}$ is said to constitute a competitive equilibrium if (a) for each i, there does not exist $\bar{x}^i$ such that $\bar{x}^i P^j \overset{*}{x}{}^j$ and $\Sigma_{g=1}^{G} p_g \bar{x}_g^i \leqslant \Sigma_{g=1}^{G} p_g \overset{*}{x}_g^i$,, and (b) for all x such that $\Sigma_{i=1}^{I} x^i \epsilon T$, $\Sigma_{g=1}^{G} p_g (\Sigma_{i=1}^{I} x_g^i) \leqslant \Sigma_{g=1}^{G} p_g (\Sigma_{i=1}^{I} \overset{*}{x}_g^i)$.

Condition (a) in definition 2 is necessary for the equilibrium of consumers satisfying Rational Choice. Condition (b) is necessary for the equilibrium of profit maximising firms under assumption 5.

Theorem: If an economic state $\overset{*}{x}$ with the price vector p is a competitive equilibrium, it is also Pareto optimal.

58 Welfare Economics

Proof: Suppose that the reverse is true. Then there exists an economic state $\bar{x}$ such that

$$\bar{x}^j P^j \overset{*}{x}{}^j \text{ for some } j \tag{2B.1}$$

$$\bar{x}^i R^i \overset{*}{x}{}^i \text{ for all } i \neq j \tag{2B.2}$$

$$\Sigma_{i=1}^I \bar{x}^i \epsilon T \tag{2B.3}$$

From (2B.1), assumption 2, and condition (a) of definition 2, we have

$$\Sigma_{g=1}^G p_g \bar{x}_g^j > \Sigma_{g=1}^G p_g \overset{*}{x}{}_g^j \tag{2B.4}$$

Otherwise the bundle $\bar{x}^j$ would have been within the reach of individual j and the choice of the bundle $\overset{*}{x}{}^j$ would be inconsistent with rationality (assumption 3). Similarly, from (2B.2) we have

$$\Sigma_{g=1}^G p_g \bar{x}_g^i \geqslant \Sigma_{g=1}^G p_g \overset{*}{x}{}_g^i \text{ for all } i \neq j \tag{2B.5}$$

From (2B.4) and (2B.5), we have

$$\Sigma_{g=1}^G p_g (\Sigma_{i=1}^I \bar{x}_g^i) > \Sigma_{g=1}^G p_g (\Sigma_{i=1}^I \overset{*}{x}{}_g^i) \tag{2B.6}$$

But (2B.3) and condition (b) of definition 2 implies that (2B.6) is false. QED.

For the proofs of other propositions listed above, see Arrow (1951a)*, Arrow & Debreu (1954)*, Arrow & Hahn (1971)*, Debreu (1959)*. Debreu introduces producers explicitly and uses a fairly general set of assumptions. More recent literature has extended the field to cover such complications as uncertainty (Stigum, 1969*), money (surveyed by Okuno, 1976*), externalities (e.g. Osana, 1977*, Shafer & Sonnenschein, 1976*), monopolistic elements, etc. The proof of monopolistic equilibrium was pioneered by Negishi (1960–61)*, and extended by Arrow (1971a)*, Fitzroy (1974)*, Benassy (1976)*. Some recent results on the existence of competitive equilibrium are surveyed by Sonnenschein (1977)*. Temporary General Equilibrium Theory is surveyed by Grandmont (1977)*. Students who wish to be able to follow these highly mathematical analyses may start with the elementary introduction by Walsh (1970) and a more advanced treatment by Shone (1975) on modern micro-economics and Allingham (1975), Hildenbrand & Kirman (1976), or Quirk and Saposnik (1968), on general equilibrium analysis.

3 The Direction of Welfare Change: Welfare Criteria

In the last chapter, we noted that the Pareto principle (someone better off, no one worse off) is a reasonable sufficient-criterion for a social improvement. However, most policy changes make some individuals better off and some worse off. Can we still have a sufficient criterion for a social improvement? This is the issue of a welfare criterion which has caused a considerable amount of debate in the literature of welfare economics.

3.1 The Debate about Compensation Tests

The controversy on welfare criteria is associated with the distinction between the 'old' and the 'new' welfare economics. The 'new' welfare economics, marked by (i) the popularisation of the Pareto principle and the associated marginal conditions, (ii) Bergson's (1938) paper on social welfare function, and (iii) the controversy on compensation test around 1940, is not so new by today's standard. Pareto's original writings (see Tarascio, 1968) were actually published (in French) before the first edition of Pigou's *Economics of Welfare* (1912, under the title *Wealth and Welfare*), which may be regarded as a *summa* of the old welfare economics. The old welfare economists assumed measurable and interpersonally comparable utility. For example, Pigou regarded it as 'evident' that 'any transference of income from a relatively rich man to a relatively poor man of similar temperament, since it enables more intense wants to be satisfied at the expense of less intense wants, must increase the aggregate sum of satisfaction' (Pigou, 1932, p. 89). Robbins (1932, 1938) argued strongly against interpersonal comparisons of utility in scientific analysis. (I have argued in Section 1.4 and Appendix 1A that interpersonal comparisons of utility are not scientifically meaningless. But I readily admit the practical difficulties of such comparisons.) But it is also evident that most policies involve making some person better off and some worse off and hence usually a policy prescription is only possible if some interpersonal comparison is made. Kaldor (1939) attempted to get round this difficulty by resorting to the possibility of compensation.†

> In all cases, therefore, where a certain policy leads to an increase in physical productivity, and thus of aggregate real income, the economists's case for the policy is quite unaffected by the question of the comparability of individual satisfactions; since in all such cases it is *possible* to make everybody better off without making anybody worse off. There is no need for the economist to prove–as indeed he never could prove–that as a result of the adoption of a certain measure nobody in the community is going to suffer. In order to establish his case, it is quite sufficient for him to show that even if all those who suffer as a result are fully compensated for their loss, the rest of the community will still be better off than before (Kaldor, 1939, p. 550).

In effect, Kaldor proposed the criterion that there is a social improvement if the gainers can fully compensate the losers and still be better off. (Kaldor referred to an improvement from the viewpoint of production, not necessarily an all-round social improvement; see Kaldor, 1947. But the 'Kaldor criterion' is usually used with reference to a social improvement.) Hicks (1939, 1941) supported the criterion (Kaldor or Kaldor-Hicks criterion) and in fact also proposed a sister criterion (the Hicks criterion) which states that there is a social improvement if the losers cannot profitably bribe the gainers to oppose the change (Hicks, 1940). An important feature of these welfare criteria or compensation tests is that only hypothetical compensation is involved, not actual compensation. If the required compensation is actually paid, there will be no need for these criteria; the Pareto principle alone is sufficient as everyone is made better off or no worse off. Hence, these compensation tests owe both their strength and weakness to their hypothetical nature. This weakness was quickly observed by Scitovsky (1941). Using a set of Edgeworth boxes, Scitovsky showed that the Kaldor (and also

---

†On the contribution of Barone (1908) and Pareto to the compensation principle, see Chipman (1976) and Chipman & Moore (1978, p. 548n).

the Hicks) criterion may lead to a contradiction. According to the Kaldor criterion, a certain change may be proposed. But the reverse change (i.e. from the situation after the first change back to the original situation) may also be proposed by the same Kaldor criterion. A logical inconsistency is therefore involved. This inconsistency may be shown in Figure 3.1. Due to the limitation to two dimensions, we have either to assume a two-person community or to assume that the change only affects two persons, J and K, whose utility levels are represented by the two axes. But the essence of the analysis is not affected by this limitation. Moreover, the utilities assumed may also be either cardinal or ordinal without affecting the analysis. This is so because the relative position of the two curves is not altered by stretching or contracting an axis or part(s) thereof.

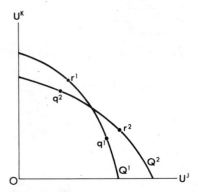

Figure 3.1

Let the original situation be at q^1 on the utility possibility curve (UPC) Q^1. It does not matter whether a UPC is assumed to represent a given collection of goods (Mishan, 1962a, p. 238, 1969a, pp. 40 ff.), a given endowment of factors of production (Robertson, 1962, p. 227), or a given set of price and output policies (Little, 1957, p. 102). What matters is that movement along the same curve is caused only by cost-less lump-sum transfers. Actually, even if we assume that cost-less lump-sum transfers are impossible we still can operate with utility feasibility curves instead of possibility curves. Which curve is relevant depends on the context in question (Graaff, 1957, p. 83). Incidentally, a utility feasibility curve shows the different combinations of utility levels (of the two individuals) attainable, taking into account the cost of transferring income. Hence, the shape of a feasibility curve depends not only on the given collection of goods (or factor endowment, etc.) but also on the initial distribution of income. Typically, the relation of a feasibility to its corresponding possibility curve is as shown in Figure 3.2, with A as the initial point. Distribution away from this point will result in a combination of utility levels (such as R) lower than that indicated by the UPC (such as S) due to the cost of redistribution.

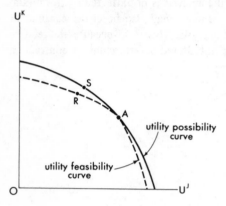

Figure 3.2

Returning to Figure 3.1, consider a change which will carry us from q^1 to q^2. This change passes the Kaldor criterion as it is possible, after the change, to redistribute income to reach a point r^2 where everyone is better off than q^1. Starting from q^2, transferring income from K to J (or making K compensate J) would enable us to travel along the curve Q^2 to the point r^2. Since r^2 is north-east of q^1, both J and K would be better off at r^2 than at q^1. According to the Kaldor criterion, therefore, the change from q^1 to q^2 is a social improvement. However, by exactly similar reasoning the change from q^2 back to q^1 also fulfils the same Kaldor criterion. This is so because we can also redistribute income from q^1 to r^1 which is north-east of q^2. Since the same criterion dictates that q^2 is socially preferable to q^1 and also that q^1 is socially preferable to q^2, a logical inconsistency is involved.

If one is sceptical about the possibility of contradiction and thinks that this may just be the result of unrestricted manipulation of UPCs one should be reminded that Scitovsky was using an Edgeworth Box consisting of commodity space with well-behaved indifference maps. In any case, the following simple example by Quirk and Saposnik (1968, p. 121) should be sufficiently convincing. Assume a community of two individuals, J (Jan) and K (Kevin), and two goods, X and Y. In situation q^1, J has two X and K has one Y; in situation q^2, J has one X and K has two Y. Suppose J prefers one X plus one Y to two X and prefers two X to one X; K prefers one X plus one Y to two Y and prefers two Y to one Y. These preference patterns are quite reasonable and satisfy the conventional diminishing marginal rates of substitution. Now, it can easily be seen that the movement from q^1 to q^2 and the reverse movement from q^2 to q^1 both satisfy the Kaldor criterion. Thus, after moving from q^1 to q^2, if the gainer (K) gives one unit of Y to the loser (J), J is made better off than at q^1 and K no worse off. Similarly, if we move back from q^2 to q^1, and the gainer (now J) gives one unit of X to K, K is made better off than at q^2 and J no worse off.

The contradiction in the Hicks criterion can also be seen by referring to Figure 3.3. Here, the change from q^1 to q^2 satisfies the Hicks criterion as it is not possible to redistribute income from q^1 to reach a point north-east of q^2. By similar reasoning, the reverse change from q^2 to q^1 also satisfies the Hicks criterion.

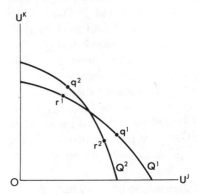

Figure 3.3

The case depicted in Figure 3.3 is more relevant than the case depicted in Figure 3.1. In the real world of many individuals and commodities, compensation is usually measured in monetary terms. Let us assume diminishing marginal utility of income so that an individual attaches higher utility to the same $1,000 if he has to pay than if he is to receive that sum. Then, for a certain utility change, he is probably willing to pay less to keep the gain (or to avoid the loss) than he has to be paid to forgo the gain (or to suffer the loss). (We say 'probably' as this statement does not necessarily follow from diminishing marginal utility. This is so because the change may move the whole marginal utility curve itself. However, we do not have to go into such details here.) For example, you may be prepared to pay a maximum amount of x to avoid the certainty of a permanent injury to your right eye, but x is likely to be far from adequate to compensate you fully for the same injury. If we take the asymmetry due to the diminishing marginal utility of income (or the concavity of the utility function, as the mathematical economists call it), then it is clear that, for a certain change, it is quite possible that the gainers may be unable to compensate the losers fully and the losers are also unable to bribe the gainers to oppose the change.

The contradiction in the Kaldor criterion may also be illustrated by using the Scitovsky CICs, i.e. community indifference curves.† (Readers not familiar with the concept of CIC may first read the appendix to this chapter or skip this paragraph.) Figure 3.4 depicts the commodity (not utility) space for a simple case of two goods X and Y. Consider the change from the q^1 distribution of the Q^1 collection of goods to q^2 of Q^2. The Scitovsky CIC C_1 corresponding to q^1 passes below Q^2. This means that, with the collection of good Q^2, we have more goods than necessary to attain the pair of individual indifference levels at q^1. Properly distributed, both individuals can be made better off. Hence, the change from q^1 of Q^1 to q^2 of Q^2 satisfies the Kaldor criterion. But the same is true for the reverse change since C_2 also passes below Q^1. The contradiction may be explained by the fact that, at q^1, the common slope of the indifference curves is much steeper than that

---

†See Mishan (1952, 1969b, p. 45). Gorman (1953)* shows that UPCs cut each other if and only if (Scitovsky's) CICs cut each other. In fact, the two maps have a common equation.

at q^2. Thus, one unit of X may be worth two units of Y at q^1, and $1Y = 2X$ at q^2. Having more of X and less of Y than Q^1, Q^2 is valued higher with the q^1 distribution and the reverse is true with the q^2 distribution. It can thus be seen that the contradiction in compensation test (and indeed the measurement of consumer surplus discussed in the next chapter) is closely related to the problem of index numbers (Samuelson, 1950).† Readers may wish to show the contradiction in the Hicks criterion using a figure similar to Figure 3.4. (Hint: draw C_1 and C_2 passing above Q^2 and Q^1 respectively.)

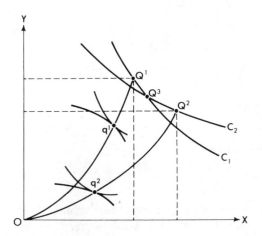

Figure 3.4

---

†For a consistent individual with non-intersecting strictly convex indifference curves, it can be shown that $\Sigma_{g=1}^{G} p_g^1 x_g^1$ (abbreviated into $\Sigma p^1 x^1$) $\geqslant \Sigma p^1 x^0$ implies $\Sigma p^0 x^0 < \Sigma p^0 x^1$ where the superscripts 0, 1 denote old and new price (p) and quantity (x) vectors. From $\Sigma p^1 x^1 \geqslant \Sigma p^1 x^0$, we infer that x^1 is preferred to x^0 (assuming no change in taste and that more is preferred to less). This is so since, with p^1 ruling, he could consume at x^0 but he chose x^1. If $\Sigma p^0 x^0 \geqslant \Sigma p^0 x^1$, we similarly infer that x^0 is preferred to x^1, ending in a contradiction. So $\Sigma p^1 x^1 \geqslant \Sigma p^1 x^0$ implies $\Sigma p^0 x^0 < \Sigma p^0 x^1$. However, for the case of more than one individual, we can have $\Sigma p^1 x^1 > \Sigma p^1 x^0$ *and* $\Sigma p^0 x^0 > \Sigma p^0 x^1$, leading to difficulties in interpreting national income data and the like.

To avoid contradiction, Scitovsky (1941) proposes that a change should be regarded as unambiguously favourable only if it satisfies both the Kaldor criterion and the Hicks criterion (or, equivalently, the Scitovsky reversal test). In terms of UPCs, this means that, for the change from q^1 to q^2 to be unabmiguously desirable, not only must the UPC through q^2 pass 'over' (north-east of) q^1, but the UPC through q^1 must pass 'under' (south-west of) q^2. This is satisfied for the movement from q^1 to q^2 in Figure 3.5. If the change from q^1 to q^2 satisfies

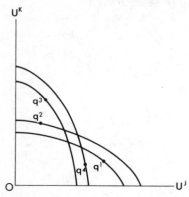

Figure 3.5

the Scitovsky criterion, the reverse change from q^2 to q^1 cannot satisfy the same criterion. The Scitovsky criterion is therefore free from contradiction in this sense. However, successive application of the criterion can still lead to cyclicity. Thus, the movements q^1 to q^2, q^2 to q^3, q^3 to q^4, and q^4 to q^1 all satisfy the Scitovsky criterion but these movements end up with the original position q^1.

3.2 Taking Distribution into Account: Little's Criterion

3.2.1 Little's Criterion and the Alleged Contradiction and/or Redundancy

Pointing out that the criteria of Kaldor, Hicks, and Scitovsky all inidicate only *potential* improvement, Little (1949, 1957, ch. v i) maintains that distributional effects have to be taken into account for a welfare criterion purporting to indicate actual improvement.† Little's criterion asks three questions: (1) Are the gainers able to compensate the losers fully and still be better off? (the Kaldor criterion); (2) Are the losers unable profitably to bribe the gainers to oppose the change? (the Scitovsky reversal test); (3) Is any redistribution good? If the answer to (3) is positive (negative) and at least one of the answers to (1) and (2) is also positive (negative), the change is proposed (rejected), assuming that direct redistribution is not feasible.

The rationale of Little's criterion is based on the following two premises: (a) the Pareto criterion: there is a social improvement if someone is made better off without anyone being made worse off, and (b) *ceteris paribus*, there is a social improvement if income distribution is made better. Consider Figure 3.3. To examine the desirability of a movement from q^1 to q^2 the point r^1 is constructed that is on the same UPC as q^1 but is just south-west of (i.e. Pareto inferior to) q^2 and hence 'represents (approximately) the same distribution as' (Little, p. 100) q^2. Now if r^1 is regarded as distributionally better than q^1, then the change from q^1 to q^2 must be a social improvement, as q^2 is superior to r^1 according to (a) and r^1 superior to q^1 according to (b).

Little's criterion has been criticised as being conducive to contradiction. In Figure 3.3, if r^2 is also distributionally preferred to q^2, then it can be shown that q^1 is superior to q^2 *via* r^2 and contradicts the demonstration in the preceding paragraph that q^2 is superior to q^1.

How can this arise? If a change from q^1 to q^2 involves a good redistribution, how can a reverse change also involve a good redistribution? When Little says that the change from q^1 to q^2 involves a good redistribution he means that a merely distributional change which will produce a point (r^1) which is distributionally (approximately) indifferent to q^2 will be a good thing (Little, 1957, p. 101). This means, as Sen (1963, p. 772) explains, that the social welfare contour passing through

---

† It may also be noted that the Samuelson (1950) criterion which requires the new UPC to lie entirely above the old one is too restrictive for a potential improvement but still insufficient for an actual improvement unless it is assumed that optimal redistribution will take place after the change. Readers may wish to confirm this assertion by drawing UPCs and welfare contours as an exercise.

r^1 is higher than that passing through q^1 which in turn must be higher than that passing through r^2 as long as the social welfare function (SWF) is Paretian, since q^1 is Pareto superior to r^2. As q^2 is again Pareto superior to r^1, r^2 cannot be on a welfare contour that is higher than q^2 unless the welfare contours intersect each other which is ruled out by consistency. In other words, the possibility that r^2 is better than q^2 is ruled out by the very SWF that says that r^1 is preferred to q^1. The alleged contradiction in the application of Little's criterion cannot, therefore, arise. However, if we have a well-defined, consistent SWF, why do we have to use a welfare criterion? Does not the existence of such a function render welfare criteria redundant? If the society or an ethical observer is able to compare the social welfare between q^1 and r^1, whey can't he compare the social welfare between q^1 and q^2 directly? (Kennedy, 1953, 1963a, 1963b, Chipman & Moore, 1978.) I wish to argue that Little's criterion is neither redundant nor inconsistent.

3.2.2* A Defence of Little's Criterion

Little's criterion is based on both Paretian improvements and distributional improvements. Does this combined use of two separate value judgements lead to inconsistency as argued by Kennedy? If our value system is such that a Pareto improvement is not a sufficient condition for a good change (e.g. that it must also have a better, or at least not worse, distribution), then the Pareto criterion cannot be used independently of other considerations (e.g. distributional). But Little assumes (reasonably) the acceptance of the Pareto criterion such that a Pareto improvement is to be regarded as a good change irrespective of what happens to any other factor (distribution included). Hence, there is certainly no problem with respect to the Pareto part in Little's criterion. With respect to the distributional part, Little does not assume (nor is it widely accepted) that we have a good change as long as the new situation has a better distribution. It may thus seem that the separate use of the distributional part is the source of the contradiction. But Little confines distributional comparison to *points on the same utility possibility curve*. Points on the same UPC by definition differ from each other *only with respect to distribution*, everything else being held constant. If r^1 is regarded as distributionally better than q^1 and r^1 and q^1 differ only with respect to distribution, then r^1 must be better than q^1 even if everything else is taken into account. Hence, the separate use of the distribution part in Little's criterion is also logically valid. If the change from q^1 to r^1 satisfies a *sufficient* condition for a good change (that it involves a better distribution on the same UPC) and the change from r^1 to q^2 satisfies another *sufficient* condition (Pareto improvement), then the change from q^1 to q^2 must necessarily be a good change. The combined use of two separate conditions is quite all right as long as each is a sufficient condition.† Even if Little's criterion is not logically inconsistent in itself, is it redundant?

Usually, a society does not have a well-defined and logically consistent SWF. The reason why a well-defined SWF is not available is partly due to the characteristic of a democratic system in which social decisions are influenced by forces generated by different pressure groups. The whole set of welfare contours in the utility space may be twisted in a certain direction when a pressure group has succeeded in its strategic threat. Choices made after this change may thus be inconsistent with those made before. This, however, is analogous to a change in taste of a consumer in the theory of demand. Frequent changes in consumers' tastes do not, however, deter us from assuming a set of non-intersecting indifference curves or the weak axiom of revealed preference. It does not seem unreasonable, therefore, to assume that we do have a well-defined SWF in terms of individual utilities, i.e. $W = W(U^1, \ldots, U^I)$. This, of course, is based on an individualistic premise that what matters are the individuals, not any mythical interest of the state above and apart from the interest of the individuals. It is also reasonable to assume that $\partial W / \partial U^i > 0$ for all i, i.e. the Pareto criterion that social welfare is an increasing function of individual utilities.

Now, does the existence of a SWF in the above form necessarily preclude the usefulness of any welfare criterion? My answer is 'No!' This is so because of possible lack of knowledge of the correspondence of a social state and a point in the utility space. If we know the exact location of every social state in utility space, the existence of a specific SWF in the above form means that we can rank all the social states

---

†Kennedy's argument that Mishan's two sufficient criteria can be replaced by a single common criterion does not apply here, as we have not placed a distributional proviso on the Pareto criterion. Even if a common criterion could be found, it would be very complicated and difficult to apply.

according to this SWF. But this exact and complete knowledge is usually if not always, unavailable. It is due to this incomplete knowledge that, I think a welfare criterion becomes useful despite the existence of a SWF in terms of individual utilities. Consider a proposal to build a new airport at a certain locality. For simplicity, assume that the relevant choice is between building that specific airport (q^2) and not building (q^1). It is known that residents in the vicinity of the proposed site (J) will be made worse off and the rest of the community (K) will be made better off. This is the knowledge available to the society, or an ethical observer. Is that knowledge sufficient for the ethical observer to make a rational choice? Not necessarily. Even if it is further known that J is relatively richer than K and that the ethical observer favours a more equal distribution of income, it does not necessarily follow that the change (from q^1 to q^2, i.e. building the airport) is socially desirable as J may suffer so much and K gain only very little by the change that even an egalitarian SWF may reject the change. If the ethical observer knows the exact position of q^1 and q^2 in cardinal utility space, he also knows the extent to which K is made better off and J worse off. But usually he does not have such precise knowledge. How then is he going to make a rational decision? It is here that the compensation test (and on a more practical and quantitative level, cost-benefit analysis) enters the scene. The use of compensation tests may reveal that K is not made better off enough by the change so as to be prepared to compensate J fully, but J is also not made worse off enough to be prepared to pay the required amount to bribe K to oppose the change. Then we know that the two utility possibility curves intersect even though we do not know the precise location of the respective points.

The next step is to ask whether our ethical observer prefers the existing situation $(q^1$ in Figure 3.3) to the situation after the payment of the bribe (r^1); the two situations differ from each other only by a lump-sum transfer of goods or purchasing power. If r^1 is preferred to q^1, we infer that q^2 is preferred to q^1, since q^2 is Pareto superior to r^1. If q^1 is preferred to r^1, then ranking of q^1 and q^2 may still be made through r^2. All this is of course the application of Little's criterion. The objection is that it may lead to contradiction. If we know the exact location of each social state (or situation) in utility space, then no contradiction can arise if the SWF in terms of utilities is well-defined. But in this case, compensation tests and welfare criteria are redundant. The usefulness of compensation tests arises from our lack of knowledge of the exact position of each social state in the utility space. While compensation tests do not establish the exact location, they give us the relative position of social states, e.g. that one is south-west or north-west of the other.

What about the possibility of contradiction? It may be thought that since the ethical observer only has a rough idea of the location of each social state in the utility space, he may prefer r^1 to q^1 and also prefer r^2 to q^2 even if he has a well-defined SWF in terms of individual utilities. This inconsistent choice will not occur if our ethical observer has taken account of the information provided by the compensation test. Before the test, since he does not have a precise idea of the location of the respective points, it is quite possible that he ranks r^1 above q^1 and r^2 above q^2 even if he has a well-defined SWF in terms of individual utilities. However, the compensation test shows that r^2 is south-west of q^1, and r^1 is south-west of q^2. Hence, no matter whether his picture of the position of the four points exactly corresponds to the 'true' picture or not, as long as they conform to the 'doubt south-west' relationship, he will not rank r^1 above q^1 and r^2 above q^2 since he is assumed to have a well-defined Paretian SWF.

What will happen if we relax the assumption of a well-defined SWF in terms of individual utilities? Inconsistency may then arise in the application of Little's criterion. (Without ruling out inconsistent distributional judgements, successive applications of Little's criterion may also lead to a situation where everyone is made worse off; see Ng, 1971c, pp. 580–1.) This inconsistency is due, however, not to any logical fault of the criterion but to the inconsistent SWF or the contradictory distributional judgements of the ethical observer. Given the inconsistent SWF, inconsistent decision will arise even if Little's criterion is not being used. The use of the criterion does not create any additional inconsistency. But does it possess any positive usefulness? My answer is 'Yes!' Without the compensation test, the ethical observer may be unable to rank q^1 and q^2 altogether. Or, if forced to rank, he is even more likely to make incorrect and/or inconsistent choice. For example, after choosing to move from q^1 to q^2, he may find that actually he prefers q^1 to q^2. Or, given a third alternative, cyclicity may also arise. Inconsistent choice is more likely to occur since, robbed of the compensation test, he has even less knowledge of the position of the respective situations. Hence, inconsistent and/or incorrect choice is more likely as the inconsistent SWF is reinforced by the lack of knowledge.

Our discussion so far may be briefly summarised. If we have a well-defined SWF in terms of individual utilities (but not in terms of social states, as in that case, the compensation test is redundant) Little's criterion may assist in making rational social choice without any inconsistent result. If the relevant SWF is not consistent, then Little's criterion may still assist social decisions but inconsistent decisions are not completely ruled out. This may be further clarified by the following analogy.

Suppose our problem is to compare the size of two solid blocks of different sides. If we can measure the lengths of all three dimensions of both blocks, the obvious criterion to use is the product of the three measures. Now suppose we are allowed only to measure one of the three dimensions and to have a look at the rectangular area formed by the other two dimensions. The analogy to Little's criterion is the following: Block A is larger than Block B if A is longer than B in the measured dimension and also looks larger in the rectangle formed by the other two dimensions. Obviously, this is a sufficient condition for A to be larger than B unless we are wrong in judging the relative size of the rectangles. However, if we are not accurate in judging the size of rectangles, we are even more likely to make mistakes by judging the size of blocks directly without measuring one of the dimensions.

3.3* Inadequacy of Purely Distributional Rankings

Little's criterion combines compensation tests with distributional judgements, in recognition of the fact that purely allocational and purely distributional rankings are inadequate. Purely allocational improvements need not necessarily improve social welfare unless we assume one of the following (or something similar): (i) Optimal redistribution of income; (ii) random distributional effects which cancel out in the long run.† Similarly, purely distributional improvements need

---

†See Polinsky (1972) for the argument that,'by 'Broadening the notion of compensation to include bundles of changes that have some effective randomness in distribution, it thereby becomes possible to leave particular individuals uncompensated and worse off for single changes, yet assure them that they can

not increase welfare as a sufficienty small cake will not help even if optimally distributed. However, in his proposed resolution of the unsettled problems in welfare criteria, Mishan (1973, 1980) downgrades the role of allocational comparison and relies on purely distributional rankings. If this is accepted, the role of economists will be significantly reduced, since economists are predominantly concerned with allocational efficiency. Nevertheless, Mishan himself has a sound intuition in not trying to reject altogther dual welfare criteria, i.e. criteria based on both allocational and distributional rankings. 'There is always hope that a little more thought may enable us to discover some redeeming features of such criteria' (Mishan, 1973, p. 776). This is in fact what the following argument will demonstrate.

With reference to Figure 3.6 (similar to Mishan's figure 2), Mishan argues that if there is another collection of goods Q^3 whose locus in utility space passes through q^1 and q^2, we shall then be able to compare q^1 and q^2 directly on distributional grounds, since q^1 and q^2 differ from each other only due to a different distribution of a single collection of goods. Moreover, by using an ingenious construction involving community-indifference curves, Mishan shows that the required collection of goods (Q^3) can, in principle, always be found,

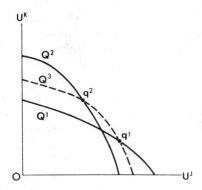

Figure 3.6

(mathematically) *expect* to be better off as a result of the entire bundle (with the probability of *actually* being worse off set a value approaching zero)' (Polinsky, 1972, p. 409.) This proposed quasi-Paretian criterion can then disregard, within certain limits, the unfavourable distributional effect of each single change.

given divisibility of goods and continuity in preferences. This can be seen in Figure 3.4. The Scitovsky CIC (Appendix 3A) C_1 corresponds to the q^1 distribution of Q^1, and C_2 corresponds to q^2. The two curves intersect at Q^3. Hence, by appropriate distribution of this Q^3 collection of goods, both the q^1 and the q^2 combinations of indifference levels for the two individuals can be attained. The UPC of Q^3 must therefore pass through q^1 and q^2 in the utility space of Figure 3.6. It is, therefore, concluded that, 'If society is assumed able to rank distributions of a single collection of goods (which has been the traditional assumption), then 'contradictory' collections [i.e. those with intersecting UPCs] can be ranked unambiguously albeit only on a distributional scale . . . If society is assumed unable to rank the distributions of a single collection of goods, then "contradictory" collections cannot be ranked at all' (Mishan, 1973, p. 762).

Mishan's conclusion does not, however, invalidate Little's criterion. Mishan concludes that 'contradictory' collections can always be reduced to a distributional ordering. But how do we know that the two collections are 'contradictory' or that the two UPCs intersect each other? This is found out by compensation tests. If the answers to questions (1) and (2) in Little's criterion have opposite signs, then the two collections are 'contradictory'. In this case, Little's criterion ranks the two situations according to the answer to question (3), which is precisely the distributional part. Nevertheless, there is an important difference between Little and Mishan with respect to distributional ranking. Little uses the intermediate points r^1 and r^2 as a reference point for comparing the distributional desirability of q^1 and q^2, but Mishan uses the direct distributional ranking of q^1 and q^2. Mishan not only uses direct comparison between q^1 and q^2 as points on Q^3, but also uses direct comparison between q^1 on Q^1 and q^2 on Q^2. In fact, in Mishan's scheme, the Q^3 collection need not actually be identified. His 'findings do not, incidentally, depend on actual identification of the required hypothetical collection of goods [Q^3] . . . Indeed nothing of significance results from knowing the composition of the hypothetical collection. For the analysis reveals that wherever there are 'contradictable' collections there will also be, necessarily, the appropriate hypothetical collection. And the purpose of confirming its existence is only to establish the fact that a comparison of 'contradictable' collections can always be reduced to a distributional ranking' (Mishan, 1973, pp. 762–3).

Given the assumption that the precise location of the relevant social states in the utility space is known, Mishan's argument seems unassailable. The points q^1 and q^2 as points on Q^3 are exactly the same points in utility-space as q^1 on Q^1 and q^2 on Q^2. Since rankings is to be made according to the utility levels of individuals, q^1 on Q^1 and q^2 on Q^2 must be ranked exactly as q^1 and q^2 on Q^3, but the latter two points differ from each other only with respect to distribution. Hence, if they can be given a direct distributional ranking, so can q^1 on Q^1 and q^2 on Q^2. However, a caution is in order, as discussed below.

Consider Figure 3.7 in which W's are the contours of a consistent and Paretian SWF and the three UPCs depict the actual utility possibilities of the three collection of goods. If these utility possibilities are known, then q^1 will be judged the best distribution of the Q^1 collection since it touches the highest welfare contour. Similarly, $q^{2'}$ is judged the best distribution of Q^2, and q^2 a 'not so good' distribution. However, when q^1 and q^2 are ranked as different distributions of the Q^3 collection, q^2 is ranked a better distribution than q^1. Is this a contradiction? One may say that this is not a contradiction since different

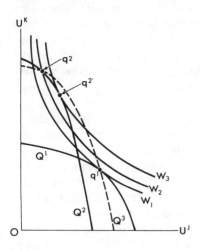

Figure 3.7

collections of goods are involved, it *is* possible that the 'not so good' q^2 distribution of Q^2 may be better than the best q^1 distribution of Q^1, and hence, as distribution of Q^3, q^2 is a better distribution than q^1. Even if this is not regarded as a contradiction, it certainly reminds us that we have to be very careful in making distributional comparison between points on different UPCs. In particular, distributional comparison for points on the same UPC is quite a different matter from distributional comparison for points on different UPCs. The point q^2 is ranked higher than q^1, but are we prepared to say that, on a purely distributional ranking, q^2 on Q^2 is better than q^1 on Q^1? It seems that most people are not prepared to say so, as q^1 is the best distribution of Q^1 and q^2 is a 'not so good' distribution of Q^2. It is true that, as points on Q^3, q^1 and q^2 differ only with respect to distribution. But as points on Q^1 and Q^2 respectively, q^1 and q^2 do not differ only with respect to distribution. If the collection Q^3 is not actually constructed, and the ethical observer, with the welfare contours as depicted, is asked to rank q^1 on Q^1 and q^2 on Q^2 on a purely distributional scale, it is quite likely that he may say that q^1 on Q^1 is superior to q^2 on Q^2 as far as distribution is concerned, though he ranks q^2 above q^1 if he is not restricted to a purely distributional comparison. Hence, while Mishan is correct in arguing that if society can rank points on the same collection it can also rank points on two 'contradictory' collections, it seems wise not to limit the latter ranking to a purely distributional ranking. Rather, the society is allowed to rank q^1 on Q^1 and q^2 on Q^2 directly, taking everything into account. (Readers are reminded that we have been assuming precise knowledge of individual utilities in this paragraph.)

If the Q^3 collection can be found not only in principle but also in practice, and it can be shown what precise distributions of that collection would result in points q^1 and q^2 in utility space, then q^1 and q^2 can be ranked on a purely distributional ranking, as points on the Q^3 UPC. However, in the real world of thousands of commodities and millions of individuals, the identification of the Q^3 collection is practically impossible, even though it exists in principle. Moreover, in practice, it is also most likely that we do not know the precise location of social states in utility space. In this case, we have to be even more careful with direct distributional comparisons of points on different UPCs.

With imprecise knowledge of individual utilities, distributional ranking is usually made with reference to money income rather than real income. In fact, in the real economy of millions of individuals and commodities, some statistical measure of equality of money income is the only practical measure of distributional desirability we can get (Mishan, 1963, pp. 345-6).† Hence, if q^1 on Q^1 and q^2 on Q^2 are to be ranked with respect only to distribution, it is quite possible that q^1 is ranked superior to q^2. This is, of course, not a necessary result since there need not be an exact correspondence between distributions of money and real income (utility). But the (purely distributional) ranking 'q^1 preferred to q^2' is quite likely. If we turn to comparing q^1 and q^2 as points on Q^3, it may happen that q^2 has a better distribution than q^1. This shows that, even if society can rank points (q^1 and q^2) on the same collection (Q^3), it does not necessarily follow that q^1 on Q^1 and q^2 on Q^2 can also be ranked *purely* on distributional merits.

From the above discussion, it may be concluded that, as purely distributional rankings are inadequate, Little's criterion which combines compensation tests with distributional judgements is superior. However, Little's criterion, like all it predecessors, is cast in static terms. Thus, in actual application of the criterion, one has to be careful not to ignore the more dynamic, less immediate effects. For example, a change may 'seem' to satisfy Little's criterion, but when account is taken of its disincentive effects, it may actually be undesirable. This issue of incentives is treated in more detail in Chapter 6 and Appendix 9A**.

Summary

Different welfare criteria in terms of compensation tests have been proposed to deal with cases where some individuals are made better off and some worse off. Kaldor's, Hicks', Scitovsky's are all logically inconsistent. Little's criterion specifies distributional improvements in addition to compensation tests. It has also been regarded as inconsistent and/or redundant. I argue that Little's criterion is not inconsistent since the

---

†If equality in the distribution of money income is representative of equality in the distribution of real income, the application of Little's criterion can never lead to a contradiction (Ng, 1971c).

alleged inconsistency arises from the inconsistent distribution judgements, not from the criterion. Moreover it is not redundant even if we have a well-defined SWF in terms of individual utilities since the SWF may not be well-defined in terms of social states and the use of Little's criterion may provide useful information. The reliance on purely distributional rankings recently proposed by Mishan is shown to be inadequate. Distributional comparisons of points on different utility possibility curves may be more difficult than comparisons of points on the same curve.

Community Indifference Contours (CICs)

When Paul Samuelson first met Tibor Scitovsky just before World War II, Scitovsky mentioned that he was writing a paper on community indifference curves. Samuelson risked a new friendship by replying: 'That's strange. Long ago I proved that community indifference curves are impossible–they don't exist' (Samuelson, 1956, p. 1). It is ironical that, not only did Scitovsky pay no attention to this negative remark and proceeded to publish his celebrated paper on CICs (Scitovsky, 1942); Samuelson (1956) himself also came up with his own version of CICs. (A contour can be a curve, a surface or a hyper-surface. The short form CICs is taken to stand for either community indifference curves or contours.) However, Samuelson's remark about the non-existence (without adopting some assumption or restriction) of CICs is not mistaken. In general, CICs are not defined on a space representing different collections of *aggregate* amounts of goods since they may depend on how the aggregate quantities of the different goods are distributed among the individuals comprising the community. For example, it is possible that all members of the community may be made worse off by a redistribution of the same collection of goods.

Scitovsky avoids the above difficulty by adopting the following approach. Instead of asking what level of community indifference is represented by a given collection of goods, let us find out what are the different collection of goods that are just sufficient, when properly distributed, to maintain each individual at a given indifference level. Given the indifference contours of all the individuals, Scitovsky's CICs can then be derived. To illustrate this diagrammatically, we take the case of two goods and start from two individuals.

The upper part of Figure 3A.1 depicts the indifference maps of the two individuals J and K. To derive a Scitovsky CIC, we keep each individual at a given indifference level, say, J at J_1 and K at K_2. In the lower part of the figure, we invert the indifference map of K onto that of J, similar to the construction of the Edgeworth box described in Chapter 2. However, the location of O^K is not determined by a *given* collection of goods. Rather, we keep K_2 tangent to J_1 at a point A. The point O^K thus determined represents a collection of goods (X^1, Y^1) that is just sufficient to attain the pair of indifference curves J_1, K_2. To attain this pair with the O^K collection of goods, we have to distribute the two goods between the two individuals at the point A where $\text{MRS}^J_{XY} = \text{MRS}^K_{XY}$. It is thus a point on the contract curve $O^J A A'' O^K$ of the Edgeworth box $O^J X^1 O^K Y^1$.

So far we have only determined one point on the Scitovsky CIC corresponding to J_1, K_2. To derive other points on the curve, we slide K_2 along J_1, keeping them tangential to each other. As we do so point O^K will trace out the Scitovsky CIC C_1. For example, we slide K_2 to K'_2, touching J_1 at A', O^K moves to $O^{K'}$. The curve C_1 thus shows the different collections of the two goods (as aggregate quantities X, Y instead of X^K, etc.) that are just sufficient to place J on the indifference curve J_1 and K on K_2. If there is a third individual, we can just invert his indifference map onto Figure 3A.1, keeping his given indifference curve tangent to C_1. We can then derive a CIC for the three persons by sliding the map as before. It can be seen that the same technique can be used for any number of individuals by successive repetition. Adding more goods prevents the use of two-demensional figures but does not change the principle involved.

Let us come back to the two-person case. We have derived the CIC C_1 corresponding to the pair of individual indifference curves J_1, K_2. Selecting a different pair, we may derive a different CIC. For example, if we keep K at K_2, and increase J's indifference level to J_2, we may then derive the CIC C_2 which lies above C_1. This is so since the pair J_2, K_2 is Pareto superior to J_1, K_2 and we need larger collections of goods to attain the Pareto-superior pair. The two CICs C_1 and C_2 are Pareto comparable. But if we select the pair J_2, K_1 and derive the CIC C'_1, it is not Pareto comparable with C_1. Moreover, we cannot be sure whether C_1 lies above C'_1 or vice versa. They may intersect, e.g. at the point O^K. This means that, with the collection of goods represented by the points O^K (i.e. X^1, Y^1), we can attain the indifference pair J_1, K_2 by distributing at the point A, or the pair J_2, K_1 by distributing at some other point (A'') along the contract curve.

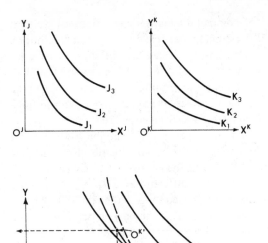

Figure 3A.1

By the method of construction, the slope of the CIC C_1 at O^K is equal to the common slope of J_1 and K_2 at A, and the slope of C_1' at O^K is equal to that of J_2 or K_1 at A''. Since, in general, the common slope of the individual indifference curves at A differs from that at A'', the slope of C_1 at A differs from that of C_1'. In other words, C_1 in general intersects C_1'. Hence, by selecting different points along a given contract curve, we can derive a family of Scitovsky CICs intersecting at the same point (O^K).

In contrast, the Samuelson CICs of the same family (i.e. derived from the same SWF) do not intersect. This is due to the nature of the way the Samuelson CICs are constructed. To construct a Samuelson CIC, we ask what are the different collections of goods just sufficient to attain a given level of community indifference (or social welfare) according to a given SWF, assuming that costless lump-sum distribution can be made to maintain optimality. It can then be shown that, with some conventional assumptions on individual preferences and the SWF, the CICs are not only 'consistent' (do not intersect) but also satisfy the 'regular' convexity requirement and can be used to derive demand functions with the conventional properties (Samuelson, 1956, p. 16).

For a specific collection of goods, say O^K in the lower part of Figure 3A.1, suppose A represents the optimal distribution according to a given individualistic SWF. Derive the Scitovsky CIC C_1 corresponding to the point A, i.e. the pair of indifferent levels J_1, K_2. Also derive the Samuelson CIC C_S through O^K according to the said SWF. What is the relationship between the two CICs? It can be seen that the Samuelson CIC (i.e. C_S) cannot lie above the corresponding Scitovsky CIC (i.e. C_1). Typically, C_S touches C_1 at O^K and lies below C_1 at other points as in the figure. Given that the SWF is individualistic (i.e. depends only on individual utilities), we do not need more goods than those represented by C_1 to attain the given level of social welfare. This is so since any collection of goods along C_1 can be distributed to attain the pair J_1, K_2 which gives the given level of social welfare. However, with a different collection of goods than O^K, the SWF may find that a different distribution is optimal. Hence, the other points on C_1 generally permit higher levels of social welfare to be attained, thus lying on higher Samuelson CICs than the one C_S.

Since the Samuelson CICs do not intersect each other, they can be more consistently used, without having to be limited to Pareto-comparable situations. However, the weakness of the Samuelson CICs is the unrealistic assumption of continuous costless lump-sum optimal distribution. Hence, the Samuelson CIC is more useful when distributional problems are not important. Apart from the assumption of costless optimal distribution, each of the following is sufficient (together with conventional individual preferences) to ensure the existence of a unique set of (hence non-intersecting) CICs: (i) the case of Robinson Crusoe economy (i.e. single individual), (ii) individuals with identical tastes and identical endowments of goods.

For the thoughtful reader, the following may be taken as an exercise. Is the assumption that all individuals have homothetic but not all identical indifference maps sufficient to ensure non-intersecting (Scitovsky's) CICs? An indifference (or any other contour) map is said to be homothetic if the slopes of the contours are all the same along any ray (straight line from the origin). The answer is given in the next paragraph.

The answer is 'No!' If the two sets of homothetic indifference curves have different shapes (say one steeper than the other on the same ray), the contract curve is not a straight line but a curve as in Figure 3A.1. Then as we move along the contract curve, the slope of the individual indifference curve may change as we are not travelling along a ray from the origin. Thus the Scitovsky CICs corresponding to these different points may intersect each other. However, if the two sets of indifference curves are not only homothetic but of identical shape, then the contract curve is the straight line $O^J O^K$ with all indifference curves having the same slope along the whole contract curve. The Scitovsky CICs then do not intersect each other irrespective of the distribution (as long as Pareto optimal). We do not then need the assumption of identical endowments. In other words, we may add another sufficient condition to ensure consistent CIC as identical and homothetic indifference maps. These conditions are however very restrictive. A marginally less restrictive condition is given by Gorman (1953)*. With some additional assumptions, it is shown that a necessary and sufficient condition to ensure a unique set of CIC is that the individual Engel curves are parallel straight lines for different individuals at the same prices. Due to some other assumptions used (e.g. individual indifference curves do not cut the axes, which, however, can be replaced by some other rather contrived condition; see Gorman 1953*, p. 68, pp. 76 ff.), this virtually implies identical and homothetic indifference maps for most interesting cases.

(For an excellent survey of problems and proposed solutions, including the 'named goods' approach by Sen, in using real income as a measure of welfare, see Sen, 1979a.)

4 The Magnitude of Welfare Change: Consumer Surplus

Our discussion of the magnitude of welfare change in this chapter is centred around the concept of consumer surplus associated with a price change. But some of the measures of consumer surplus such as compensating variation, equivalent variation, and our proposed measure marginal-dollar equivalent (see the appendix to this chapter), can also be used to measure the welfare change associated with other changes.

The concept of consumer surplus has caused a great deal of debate and confusion. While it has been regarded as superfluous, or at least the theoretical foundation of using consumer surplus as a measure of welfare change is usually regarded as suspect, its use in cost-benefit analyses and policy discussion has been widespread. In this chapter, we shall review the various measures of consumer surplus, discuss some complications, before justifying its use as an approximate measure.

4.1 The Origin of the Concept: Dupuit and Marshall

The concept of consumer surplus was first formulated around 1850 by the French engineer J. Dupuit, who was concerned with the question as to the amount of worthwhile subsidy towards the costs of constructing a bridge. He was clearly aware of the fact that a consumer will be usually willing to pay more for a good than he is actually paying. Hence, the consumer obtains an 'excess satisfaction', or a surplus.

The concept of consumer surplus gained prominence after Marshall's *Principles of Economics*. Marshall was first in introducing the concept to the English-speaking world, but was said to be less than generous in admitting Dupuit's priority (see Pfouts, 1953, p. 316).

Marshall defined consumer surplus as 'the excess of the price which he would be willing to pay rather than go without the thing, over that which he actually does pay' (Marshall, 1920, p. 124). According to this definition, the surplus is the difference of an all-or-none comparison, i.e. between (i) not being allowed to buy any quantity of the good, and (ii) buying the chosen quantity of the good at the prevailing price. As a measure of this, Marshall used the triangular area under the demand curve and above the rectangle representing the actual money expenditure of the consumer. As shown in Figure 4.1 (for the moment, disregard the dotted curves), this is measured by the curvilinear ΔAPB where OP is the price of the good.†

4.2 Hicks' Four Measures and the Average Cost Difference

Associated with the attempt to rid economic analysis of the cardinal measures of utility, Hicks (1941) introduced the concept of compensat-

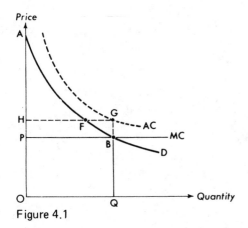

Figure 4.1

---

†As pointed out by Hicks (1941, p. 109), this Marshallian measure is not a definition but a theorem, true under certain assumptions. In his mathematical appendix, Marshall did remark on the assumption of a constant marginal utility of money. He justified this assumption on the ground that the expenditure on one particular commodity is usually small relative to total income. Any change in the marginal utility of money is neglected as of the second order of smallness. Marshall spoke in terms of marginal utility since he was interested in consumer surplus as a utility changes. Later day economists have been more concerned with consumer surplus as a more objective measure of the willingness to pay.

ing variation (discussed below). With further clarification by Henderson (1941), four measures of surplus were distinguished (Hicks, 1943). First, we see how Marshall's definition of consumer's surplus is measured in terms of an indifference map of Figure 4.2. The Y-axis represents the amount of money and the X-axis the quantity of the commodity in question. If the price of the commodity is represented by the (absolute) slope of the line AP^1 (i.e. FP/AF), the consumer will buy ON at a cost of FP, since J_1 is the highest indifference curve attainable with AP^1 as the budget line. However, the consumer is ready to pay as much as FR (amount of money) for ON (quantity of the commodity) for an all-or-none offer. This is so because after paying FR and getting ON, he is at the point R which is on the same indifference curve J_o as the point A, his initial position without consuming the commodity. Hence, Marshall's definition of consumer's surplus, being the difference between the maximum amount the consumer is willing to pay and the amount actually paid, is equal to $FR - FP = PR$.

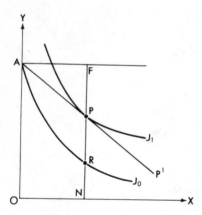

Figure 4.2

The above measure refers to the surplus of a consumer when he is able to buy a good at a given price in comparison to the case where the good is not available. Consumer surplus need not be confined to this all-or-none comparison and may refer to a change in prices. We shall illustrate below the four measures of consumer surplus for a price fall; the case of a price rise can be similarly illustrated.

First, let us look at the definitions of the four measures of consumer surplus:

(1) Compensating variation (CV) of a change in prices (or other variables, if we are not confined to changes in prices) is the amount of compensation (usually in monetary terms) that can be taken from an individual while leaving him just as well off as *before* the change;

(2) Compensating surplus (CS) is the amount of compensation that can be taken from the individual while leaving him just as well off as *before* the change if he were constrained to buy at the new price the quantity of the commodity he would buy in absence of compensation;

(3) Equivalent variation (EV) is the amount of compensation that has to be given to the individual, in the absence of the change, to make him as well off as he would be with the change;

(4) Equivalent surplus (ES) is the amount of compensation that has to be given to the individual, in the absence of the change, to make him as well off as he would be with the change if he were constrained to buy at the old price the quantity of the commodity he would buy in absence of compensation.

If the change in price is a rise instead of a fall, then we cannot take any positive amount of money from the consumer but have to pay him (i.e. take a negative amount) to make him as well off as before the price rise. The measures are then negative in sign. (Note: CV of a price fall, $p^0 \rightarrow p^1 = -$EV of the reversed price rise, $p^1 \rightarrow p^0$, and EV of a price fall $= -$CV of the reversed price movement. The same is true for CS and ES. As an exercise, readers may verify this having understood Figure 4.3.) It may also be noted that the difference between the variation measures (i.e. CV and EV) and the surplus measures (CS and ES) is that, for the former, no constraint is imposed on the consumer and he is free to choose any quantity he likes. This will become clearer in the following diagrammatic illustration.

Consider Figure 4.3a. As the price of the good in question falls from p^0 to p^1, the consumer moves from the point A on the indifference curve J_0 to the point B on J_1. It can be seen that, for this price fall, the four measures (all positive) are: CV $= Y^0 Y^1$, CS $=$ BC, EV $= Y^0 Y^2$, ES $=$ AD. (For an explanation as to why CV and EV may be unequal, see the appendix to this chapter.)

In Figure 4.3b, an ordinary demand curve dd' is derived from the in-

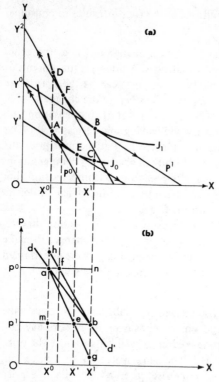

Figure 4.3

difference map in Figure 4.3a. When the price falls from p^0 to p^1, the consumer increases his purchase from X^0 (or p^0a) to X^1 (or p^1b). If the consumer has to pay the CV of Y^0Y^1, he will end up at E instead of at B. Hence, the curve aeg is the compensated (or Hicksian) demand curve from the point a (and refers to the indifference curve J_0). (If the good were inferior, aeg would lie to the right of dd'.) Similarly bfh is the compensated demand curve as the consumer is kept at the indifference curve J_1. It can then be seen that, while in Figure 4.3a consumer surplus is measured as distances, in Figure 4.3b it is measured as areas, as follows:

$$CV = p^0p^1ea$$

$$CS = p^0 p^1 ea - egb$$

$$EV = p^0 p^1 bf$$

$$ES = p^0 p^1 bf + afh$$

When the price is p^0 a marginal decrease in price benefits the consumer by $p^0 a$. As price falls continuously from p^0 to p^1, the total amount of money that can be taken from him while leaving him just as well off without the fall (i.e. on indifference curve J_0) is thus the area $p^0 p^1 ea$, remembering that, as compensation is extracted from the consumer, he is travelling along the compensated demand curve aeg, not the ordinary one dd'. For CS, since the consumer is constrained to purchase the quantity X^1 while he in fact prefers to purchase X', he will be made worse off if we extract $p^0 p^1 ea$ from him. Hence, CS is measured by $p^0 p^1 ea - egb$; this little triangle being the loss he suffers by having to stick to the constrained quantity. This is so since he has to pay the unit price p^1 while his marginal valuation for the units between X' and X^1 is indicated by the height of the compensated demand curve eg. For ES, he is also made worse off by the constraint. But here, it is the amount we have to pay him and so ES exceeds EV by the little triangle afh.

The Marshallian measure is the area $p^0 p^1 ba$ which falls somewhere in between the four measures. If the income effect is negligible, the consumer demand is not affected by the payment of compensation. Then the compensated demand curve coincides with the ordinary demand curve and all the five measures are equal. If readers have not been puzzled by this multiplicity of measures, two further measures (Machlup, 1940, 1957) may be added:

(1) The Laspeyre cost difference of a price change is the amount of compensation that could be taken from the consumer while leaving him just able (not necessarily willing) to buy the original bundle of goods he bought before the change.

(2) The Paasche cost difference is the amount the consumer would have to be paid to have just enough money to buy the new bundle of goods at the original prices.

For the case of a price fall illustrated in Figure 4.3b, the Laspeyre cost difference is measured by the rectangle $p^0 p^1 ma$ and the Paasche cost difference by $p^0 p^1 bn$. A useful exercise for readers to do at this point is to indicate the two cost differences (as vertical distances) in Figure 4.3a. While the two cost differences do not seem to measure the consumer surplus very accurately, they have the advantage of being easily calculated from actual market data. For most practical purposes, the average of the two cost differences may be a good enough approximation. Let us call this the average cost difference (ACD). When the demand curve is linear, ACD equals the Marshallian measure.

4.3 Which Measure?

Which of the many measures is appropriate depends partly on the availability of information and partly on the problem in hand.† For example, since the CS measures involves a quantity constraint but need not directly involve relative prices, it is more useful for measuring the welfare cost (loss in surplus) due to quotas, price controls and rationing. On the other hand, the CV measure is useful in measuring the costs of distortions in relative prices due to taxes, subsidies, tariffs, etc. (Hause, 1975, p. 1148). For another example, if we want to actually compensate for the loss (or extract payment for the gain), CV is the appropriate measure. In the absence of the required information, we may use the Laspèyres cost difference if we do not want to over-compensate (over-extract) or the Paasche cost difference if we do not want to under-compensate. If compensation (payment) is not actually intended, CV may not be appropriate. (See Appendix 6A.) If what we want is a measure of the gain or loss involved but not to effect actual compensation, then the Marshallian measure has the following advantage over the variation measures as discussed by Winch (1965).††

Consider Figure 4.4, where dd' is the ordinary demand curve and ae is a compensated one. For a price fall from p^0 to p^1, the Marshall/Winch measure of consumer surplus/gain is the area $p^0 p^1 ba$, and the

---

†Information is usually more difficult to obtain for the Hicksian measures than for the Marshallian one. Seade (1978) shows that the Hicksian values of surplus can be computated from not too complicated formulae provided that Engel curves are linear. This proviso is fairly restrictive. However, see Hauseman (1981)*, who argues that the Hicksian values can be derived from the market demand functions (of prices and income), first using Roy's identity to integrate and derive the indirect utility function.

††Winch's argument in favour of the Marshallian measure involves some technical ambiguities but the basic point is, in my opinion, valid and interesting, provided the measure is taken as an approximate one; see the text below.

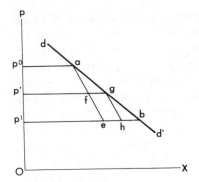

Figure 4.4

CV is the area $p^0 p^1 ea$. However, let us divide the price fall into two steps: from p^0 to p' and from p' to p^1. For the step p^0 to p', the Marshall measure is $p^0 p' ga$ and the CV is $p^0 p' fa$. For the step p' to p^1, the Marshall measure is $p' p^1 bg$. The CV depends on whether the consumer has actually to pay the amount $p^0 p' fa$ for the first step of price fall. If he has paid, then the relevant compensated demand curve is the section fe and the CV for the second step of price fall is the area $p' p^1 ef$. The CVs for the two steps of price fall will then sum to $p^0 p^1 ea$, the CV of the total price fall. However, if he does not have to pay the amount $p^0 p' fa$, he will be consuming at the point g if the price is p'; fg being the income effect of the amount $p^0 p' fa$. Thus the relevant compensated demand curve for the second step of the price fall is the section gh. The CV of this second step of price fall will then be $p' p^1 hg$. The CVs for the two steps of price fall will then sum to $p^0 p^1 hgfa$ which is larger than the CV of the total price fall (taken as one single step from p^0 to p^1) by the area $fehg$. If we regard the price fall from p^0 to p^1 as consisting of a large number of small steps, and if the consumer does not actually have to pay the compensation, the CVs will sum to an amount close to the Marshall measure. In the limit, when the number of steps approach infinity, the two measures approach each other. Thus, if we are not interested in the actual amount we can extract from the consumer (without making him worse off) but in a measure of his gain, Marshall's measure seems to be preferable.

Marshall's measure must, nevertheless, be taken as no more than an approximate measure of the consumer gain except for some very restrictive cases (on which see Chipman & Moore, 1976). For each marginal price change, Marshall's measure converges towards the CV (and also EV) and may be taken as an accurate measure of the consumer's gain. However, for a non-infinitesimal price change, though Marshall's measure is just a sum (or integral) of the marginal measures, it is, in general, just an approximate measure due to the following reason. As the price changes, the marginal utility of money (MUM) changes, in general. Thus, the sum of the marginal measures may no longer be a perfectly accurate measure of the consumer gain (or loss) in utility. The condition of constancy in MUM for the Marshall measure to be accurate must be carefully explained. It is not the constancy in MUM as money income increases but the constancy in MUM as prices change (see Samuelson, 1942, Patinkin, 1963, Currie, Murphy, Schmitz, 1971, p. 751 n1). The MUM may stay approximately constant for a particular price change. But to ensure that Marshall's measure is accurate for any price change, we need to have constancy in MUM with respect to all prices. This is a rather restrictive condition. Thus, in attempting to use the area under the demand curve as a perfect measure, Winch (1965) has been a little over-zealous. For one thing, if it were a perfectly accurate measure, we would not have the problem of path-dependency of the measure for changes in prices of more than one commodity discussed below.

4.4* Aggregation over Commodities: The Issue of Path-Dependency

The discussion above refers to changes in the price of one single commodity. What if the prices of more than one commodity are to change? How do we measure the change in consumer surplus? To illustrate this problem of aggregation over commodities, let us consider first a simple case involving two commodities, say tea and coffee.

In Figure 4.5, the original demand curve for tea D_T^0 is drawn given that the price of coffee is P_C^0 as well as given the prices of all other commodities and the consumer's income. Similarly, the price of tea is at p_T^0 for the demand curve for coffee D_C^0. Can we say that the consumer's surplus from being able to consume both tea and coffee at p_T^0 and P_C^0 respectively, relative to the case where tea and coffee are totally unavailable (which is equivalent to prices being infinite), is measured by $\Delta p_T^0 ab + \Delta p_C^0 cd \equiv (1) + (2)$?

To answer this question, let us conceptually raise the price of tea

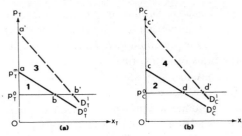

Figure 4.5

from p_T^0 to infinity (or make tea unavailable), keeping the price of coffee at p_C^0. The loss of consumer surplus is measured by the area denoted (1). Let us next raise the price of coffee to infinity. *If the demand curve for coffee stays at D_C^0 after tea is made unavailable, the loss of consumer surplus is measured by the area (2).* Thus, in comparison to the original situation, the total loss in consumer surplus is measured by (1) + (2). However, the demand curve for coffee will be unaffected by a change in the price of tea only if the consumption of coffee is independent of tea. If coffee is either a complement or a substitute for tea, then the demand curve for coffee will move as the price of tea changes. For this specific case, it is likely that tea and coffee are substitutes.† Hence, as tea is not available, the demand curve for coffee may move rightward to D_C^1. The loss of consumer surplus as coffee is also made unavailable is thus $\Delta p_C^0 c' d' \equiv (2) + (4)$. The total consumer surplus involved for tea and coffee at p_T^0 and P_C^0 is thus measured by (1) + (2) + (4) which exceeds (1) + (2) by (4). If coffee were a complement of tea, the demand curve D_C^1 would lie to the left of D_C^0 and the measure would be smaller. Thus, we cannot measure the consumer surplus of two or more goods by the sum of the areas under the existing demand curves except for the special case of independent goods. We have to take the measure step by step. (For an alternative measure using 'total' demand curves, see Berry, 1969, Gwilliam & Nash, 1972.) This however is not what is known as path-dependency, which is discussed below.

†Note, however, that X may be a (gross) substitute for Y and yet Y is not a substitute for X. The same is true for (gross) complementarity. For net substitutes/ complements, we cannot have this asymmetry with standard assumptions concerning the utility function. The difference between gross and net substitutes/ complements is that one includes the income effect and the other does not. It is the possible difference in income effects that gives rise to the asymmetry of gross substitutes/complements. See Green (1976, pp. 69-70).

When measuring the total consumer surplus of tea and coffee, we first raised the price of tea (to infinity) and let the demand curve for coffee move in response to this. But we could have taken the logically equivalent way of raising the price of coffee first. We would then have arrived at a measure of total consumer surplus of (2) + (1) + (3) where D_T^1 is the demand curve for tea when coffee is unavailable. The two alternative measures of total consumer surplus will be equal if and only if (3) = (4). If (3) ≠ (4) our measure of total consumer surplus will depend on which procedure or path we take. This is what is meant by path dependency (Hotelling, 1938, Silberberg, 1972, Burns, 1977). There are in fact many other possible paths of measurement even for the case of just two goods. For example, we can raise the price of tea by a little bit, then raise the price of coffee, then raise the price of tea further, etc.

Under what conditions will (3) = (4)? It can be seen that if $\partial x_C / \partial p_T = \partial x_T / \partial p_C$ at all sets of prices, then the two areas must be equal. Let us now use the more general notations g, h (instead of C, T) so that we may interpret our results more generally, referring to any two goods. The notation $\partial x_g / \partial p_h$ is the effect of a partial change (i.e. other prices and M, the income of the consumer, are being held constant) in the price of good h on the quantity demanded for good g. By the Slutsky equation, it can be split into a substitution effect and an income effect.

$$\frac{\partial x_g}{\partial p_h} = \frac{\partial x_g}{\partial p_h} |U| - x_h \frac{\partial x_g}{\partial M} \qquad (4.1a)$$

$$\frac{\partial x_h}{\partial p_g} = \frac{\partial x_h}{\partial p_g} |U| - x_g \frac{\partial x_h}{\partial M} \qquad (4.1b)$$

where $|U|$ means that the utility level is being held constant so that the movement is along an indifferent contour. If the consumer's utility function satisfies certain mild conditions (such as strict quasi-concavity,† continuous first- and second-order derivatives), it can be shown

---

†Strict quasi-concavity, together with some other conditions, ensures the existence of demand functions; see Malinvaud (1972, pp. 24–9). A (strictly) quasi-concave utility function yields indifference curves or surfaces (strictly) convex to the origin. A real-valued function $f(x)$ defined on a convex set X is quasi-concave if and only if: $f\{\lambda x + (1 - \lambda)y\} \geqslant min\{f(x), f(y)\}$ for all $\lambda: 0 < \lambda$

that $\partial x_g / \partial p_{h|U|} = \partial x_h / \partial p_{g|U|}$. (See, e.g., Green, 1976, p. 312; Malinvaud, 1972, p. 36.) Then the condition for $\partial x_g / \partial p_h = \partial x_h / \partial p_g$ boils down to the equality of the income elasticities for the two goods.

$$\frac{\partial x_g}{\partial M} \cdot \frac{M}{x_g} = \frac{\partial x_h}{\partial M} \cdot \frac{M}{x_h} \qquad (4.2)$$

If (4.2) holds, the two income effects in (4.1) will be equal.

In terms of integrals, the area (1) in Figure 4.5 may be written as

$$\int_{p_T^0}^{p_T^m} x_T dp_T$$

where the integration is taken at $p_C = p_C^0$. Thus, for a change in the prices of a number of goods, the change in consumer surplus may be measured by†

$$-\int_{p^0}^{p^1} \sum_{g=1}^{G} x_g dp_g \qquad (4.3)$$

where the initial price vector is $p^0 \equiv (p_1^0, p_2^0, \ldots, p_G^0)$ and p^1 is the new price vector. Some of the prices may be unchanged. The measure in (4.3) depends, in general, on the path of integration. However, with some 'regular' conditions, if (4.2) holds for all g, h whose prices have changed, then (4.3) will give a path-independent measure of the change in consumer surplus. While (4.2) may hold for some goods, it is unlikely to hold for all goods since this implies that all goods have an income elasticity equal to unity as the increase in income must be spent. Nevertheless, for relatively small changes in prices, the income effects, even if unequal, will not be significant. Secondly, even for large changes in prices of many goods, and even if the income effects involved are not negligible or equal, they are still likely to be largely offsetting to each

---

<. 1 and for any two distinct points x and y in X. If strict inequality holds, we have strict quasi-concavity. The notation 'min' means the minimum of what follows. For quasi-convexity, reverse the inequality sign and change 'min' into 'max'.

†Hotelling (1938) first generalised the measure of consumer surplus to multi-price changes. For an intuitive argument and application to transportation, see Glaister (1974).

other in the ways they affect the measures of surplus along different paths such that, while the measure (4.3) may be path dependent, the differences involved are likely to be small for most changes and are likely to be negligible compared to inaccuracies due to statistical and informational problems.†

If the shape of the demand curves is not known, an approximation may be used. Harberger (1971, p. 788) derives the following approximate measure of welfare change in terms of changes in consumption

$$\Sigma_{g=1}^{G} p_g^0 \Delta x_g + \tfrac{1}{2}\Sigma_{g=1}^{G} \Delta p_g \Delta x_g \tag{4.4}$$

For cases where the income level is unchanged, we have

$$\Sigma(p_g + \Delta p_g)(x_g + \Delta x_g) = \Sigma p_g x_g. \text{ Hence } \Sigma p_g \Delta x_g = -\Sigma x_g \Delta p_g - \Delta p_g \Delta x_g.$$

Substituting this into (4.4) yields

$$- \Sigma x_g \Delta p_g - \tfrac{1}{2}\Sigma \Delta p_g \Delta x_g \tag{4.5}$$

which is the generalisation of the average cost difference to multiprice changes. In terms of Figure 4.3b, if only the price of X falls, we can express the approximate measure either as the area $p^0 p^1 ba$ (which is equation 4.5) or as the area $X^0 X^1 ba$ plus the area $(p^0 p^1 ma - X^0 X^1 bm)$, since this is the amount of the change in expenditure on the consumption on other goods.

4.5* Aggregation Over Individuals: The Boadway Paradox

The discussion above refers to one individual. If more than one person is involved, can we use the area under the market demand curve or the sum of compensating variations (ΣCV) as a measure of the gain or loss of the group as a whole? The problem of distribution arises if the gain or loss is not uniform across all individuals. This is especially so if some individuals gain and some lose. Can we say that, if $\Sigma CV > 0$, gainers can more than compensate losers and the change (in prices or other factors) will at least lead to a *potential* Pareto improvement? It is very tempting for one to give an affirmative answer but Boadway (1974) discovered the following paradox.

---

† Ignoring 'contrived' paths of integration, e.g. ones that repeatedly go through a path and back from another many times to magnify the small difference involved.

To elucidate the paradox, let us consider a simple case where the change involves a pure redistribution. For more complicated cases involving changes in the collection of goods, readers are referred to Boadway (1974, pp. 932–4). Consider a simple exchange economy with two goods, X and Y, and two individuals, J and K, as illustrated in the Edgeworth Box (see Chapter 2) of Figure 4.6. Assuming optimal alloca-tion, we are confined to the contract curve $O^J O^K$. A purely distribu-tional change takes us from q^1 to q^2. Since this is a purely distribu-tional change, it is clear that the gainer J cannot compensate the loser K fully and still be better off herself. With full compensation, we can, at best, move back to the original point q^1, with no one being any better off. After the movement to q^2 the price ratio of the two goods is indicated by the line cd. Hence, in terms of compensating variation, the movement involves a positive CV of ac (using Y as the numeraire) for individual J, and a negative CV of bc for K. Thus, $\Sigma CV = ab$ and is positive, despite the fact that J cannot really fully compensate K and be better off herself. What has gone wrong with the ΣCV measure? What is the explanation of the paradox?

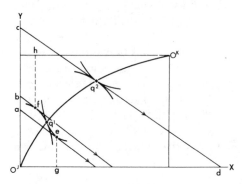

Figure 4.6

After paying ac amount of compensation, J would be no worse off (in comparison with the original point q^1) only if she could be allowed to consume freely at the unchanged price ratio. She would then con-sume at e. Similarly, K would be not worse off receiving bc only if he could consume at f. However, the two points e and f are inconsistent with each other, since the sum of the amounts of X consumed by J and

K ($O^J g$ + $O^K h$) would add up to more than the total available amount of X in the economy. Thus J and K cannot simultaneously consume at e and f respectively. The CV measure assumes that the price ratio (slope of cd) can be unchanged and each individual may choose whatever point of consumption he prefers at this price ratio and his budget (after compensation). But this may not be feasible (as shown above) if the compensation involved is large enough to change the equilibrium price ratio. If the common slope of the indifference curves at the point q^1 is equal to that at q^2, it can be seen that compensation will not change the price ratio. Then ΣCV will be equal to zero, accurately reflecting the fact that full compensation is *just* possible with no one made better off. In general, the payment of compensation does tend to change the equilibrium set of prices. Hence, the Boadway paradox is logically very real. Nevertheless, in the real economy where a certain change is small relative to GNP, the payment of compensation is unlikely to change prices significantly. Even if prices are changed, the effects of the changes are likely to be mutually offsetting. The remaining net divergence, if any, is likely to be negligible compared with inaccuracies in data collection. Thus, if ΣCV is big enough to overbalance data inaccuracies, we can be quite safe in concluding that full compensation is possible. Hence, for most cost-benefit analyses, the use of ΣCV is quite acceptable. It seems, therefore, that Boadway is too pessimistic in his conclusion: 'If some persons gain and others lose, we cannot interpret a positive surplus as an indication that the gainers could compensate the losers and a negative surplus that they could not. The magnitude and sign of the surplus are not related to the ability to compensate losers . . . ' (Boadway, 1974, p. 938). While the relation is not a perfect one, it is certainly an overstatement to say that the two are unrelated.

4.6** The Approximate Nature of Surplus Measurement

The welfare of an individual is a subjective state of mind. Hence, any non-approximate measurement has to reflect this subjective character, e.g. the concept of just noticeable difference (see Section 5.4.1). However, it is convenient (in economic calculation, almost essential) to have some objective measures such as a monetary measure. Nevertheless, since the relation between units of any external yardstick of welfare such as money and internal unit of welfare (however defined) is in general not a constant, such objective measures can be, by their very nature, no more than an approximate measure of welfare, even abstracting from the problem of inaccuracies in practical data collection. If we recognise that the surplus measurement and in fact any other objective measurement of welfare must be regarded as approximate only, then all the problems of path dependency, inconsistencies, etc., shrink into insignificance unless the discrepancies involved are substantial. (For a case where this is so, and our corresponding proposed measure to overcome the substantial divergence, see Appendix 4A on the concept of marginal dollar equivalent.)

To illustrate the approximate nature of any surplus measurement, consider the argument by Hause (1975, pp. 1150-1) that the EV and ES measures have the following advantage over the CV and CS measures. Starting from a given initial point x^0 (say a bundle of goods consumed), the consumer moves to a new point x^1 due to a certain change (in prices, quotas, etc.). Starting from the same initial point x^0, he moves to x^2 with another change. An ideal measure of welfare change ΔW should possess the following property: $\Delta W(x^0 \rightarrow x^1) > \Delta W(x^0 \rightarrow x^2)$ if and only if x^1 is preferred to x^2. It can be seen that the EV and ES measures possess this property while the CV and CS measures do not, in general. (Readers may attempt to show this as an exercise before consulting Figure 4.7a where this point is shown for the surplus measures. The point can also be similarly shown with respect to the variation measures, using price lines.) The reason is that the equivalent

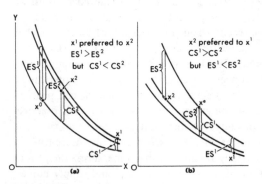

Figure 4.7

measures use the initial point as the welfare reference point while the compensating measures use the end point as the reference point. In the above comparison, the initial point is fixed but the end points are not. This explains why EV and ES satisfy the required property while CV and CS do not. But this argument by Hause seems to me to look at only one side of the coin. For any given end point x^e, the ideal measure of welfare change for different points x^1, x^2 taken as the original point should possess the following property: $\Delta W(x^1 \to x^e) > \Delta W(x^2 \to x^e)$ if and only if x^2 is preferred to x^1. It can then be seen that CV and CS possess this property but EV and ES do not. (See Figure 4.7b.) Hence neither pair can be regarded as superior to the other. Both measures may be acceptable as approximate measures for changes whose effects are thinly spread (cf. Appendix 4A).

4.7* Some Uses of Surplus Measurement

Apart from the problems discussed above, there are also other complications associated with the measurement of consumer surplus (Foster & Neuburger, 1974, Mohring, 1971, Schmalensee, 1976). The same is true for the corresponding measure of producer surplus, i.e. the area above the supply curve and below the price line. (See Berry, 1972 and Currie, Murphy & Schmitz, 1971 for surveys.) However, most of the issues may be dismissed, on the level of policy relevance, as being of little practical significance since any inaccuracies involved are likely to be much less than those due to lack of information. Moreover, until we derive something better, an imperfect measure is better than no measure at all. (For some recent arguments in favour of using consumer surplus as a measurement of welfare change, see Burns, 1973, Harberger, 1971, Hause, 1975, Willig, 1976.) It is true that some prominent economists once regarded the concept of consumer surplus as 'superfluous' (e.g. Samuelson, 1947, p. 198) since theoretical analysis can proceed without it. This is because they were not concerned with practical policy matters where not only the direction of change but also the magnitudes of gains or losses involved are important. Moreover, in many cases, the only practically feasible means of measuring the gain or loss may be an estimation of the relevant demand and supply curves. Some simple examples of how surplus measurement can be used to aid policy decisions are outlined below. (For a survey of the uses of consumer and producer surpluses, see Currie, Murphy & Schmitz, 1971.)

Consider an industry (practical examples are electricity, telecommunication services to a remote small town) with falling average cost (AC) over the relevant range. As illustrated in Figure 4.1, the marginal cost (MC) curve is shown as horizontal but this is not essential for the problem here. If the demand curve lies wholly below the AC curve as shown in Figure 4.1, any uniform (non-discriminating) price charged would fail to yield sufficient revenue to cover total cost. With marginal cost pricing, the loss equals PBGH. Does this mean that the supply of the good in question is undesirable? The answer is 'not necessarily', even abstracting from questions of externalities (see Chapter 7) and merit goods (see Section 10A.3). With OQ amount of consumption at the price OP, the amount of consumer surplus is measured by (curvilinear) $\triangle APB$. This is larger than the loss $PBGH$ if $\triangle AHF > \triangle FBG$. Thus, the supply of the good may be desirable despite the loss. A government subsidy or the public provision of the good may be called for. However, the subsidy or the loss has to be financed somehow. Since the raising of more taxes may involve allocation and administrative costs, the gain in supplying the good has to be weighed against the costs involved. (There are also other problems such as the check to empire-building type public investment, rent-seeking, second best, etc., some of which will be discussed in later chapters.)

Now consider the cost (loss in surplus) of a sales tax to a competitive industry. Figure 4.8 depicts the pre-tax demand curve dd' and supply curve ss' and the corresponding equilibrium point e. The imposition of a per-unit tax of fg increases the post-tax consumer price to Oa and lowers the producer price (net of tax) to Ob, and reduces the quantity from On to Om. The loss in consumer surplus is measured by the area $cega$ and the loss in producer surplus by the area $bfec$. The tax revenue equals $bfga$. Hence, the net loss (total loss in consumer surplus and in producer surplus less the tax revenue, sometimes called the excess burden of taxation) equals the curvilinear $\triangle feg$. Alternatively, we may concentrate on the reduction in the quantity produced and consumed. The reduction by mn amount of production saves resources valued at $mnef$. But this same mn amount of the good is valued by consumers at $mneg$. The net loss is again $\triangle feg$. This measure is based on the partial equilibrium setting in which the effects of the tax on the prices of the other goods are taken as negligible. This is not always a permissible assumption especially if the good in question has close substitutes or complements. Then a correct measure of welfare change has to sum the change in surpluses over many goods (see Section 4.4 above). Unless the supply curves for other goods involved are horizontal and there is no distortion (taxes/subsidies not justified on efficiency grounds, monopolistic power, etc.) in these goods, the measure for welfare loss thus obtained will in general differ from the partial equilibrium measure of Δfeg.

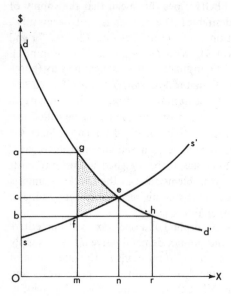

Figure 4.8

Now consider a legal maximum price of Ob (assumed effective) that reduces the quantity supplied to Om. Will this result in the same welfare cost of Δfeg? The answer is 'no' even disregarding the general equilibrium problem just mentioned. In the previous case where the price is increased to Oa due to the tax, consumers who continue to consume the good place a marginal valuation on it no lower than Oa. Thus the loss in the mn amount of consumption is measured by $mneg$. But in the case of a legal maximum price of Ob, consumers who place a marginal valuation as low as *rh* (=*Ob*) may also consume the good while those who place a much higher value may have to go without the good. Thus the total value of the *Om* amount of consumption will be approximately equal to *Om/Or* times the area *Orhd*, assuming that all consumers have an equal chance of obtaining the good. By comparison with the original equilibrium consumption of *On*, the loss is equal to *Oned* − *Om/or* · *Orhd* which can be shown to be larger than *mneg*, given that the demand curve is downward-sloping. Hence, the net loss will be much larger than Δ*feg*. In fact, it can be shown that the net loss is larger than the area *ced* times *mr/Or*. If the demand curve has a very high vertical intercept, this could be an amount many times larger than Δ*feg*.

It is true that consumers who value the good highly may go earlier for the queue. Hence it is more likely than random that they will get the goods. The value of the *Om* amount of consumption is then likely to be larger than *Om/Or* times *Orhd*. But on the other hand, the additional costs of queuing, etc. have to be added. Thus it remains true that the total net loss is likely to be much larger than Δ*feg*.

A similar analysis to the above may also be applied to the case of a quota of *Om*, raising the price to *Oa*. In this case, the loss in *mn* amount of consumption is valued at mneg. But the saving in resources is no longer measured by *mnef*. With a higher price (*Oa*), less efficient producers may also supply part of the market. It is again true that, since more efficient producers will enjoy a larger producer surplus or rent, they are more likely to obtain the limited quotas. But the resources invested in securing the quotas must be included in the calculation of costs.

From the above analysis, it may be concluded that, for the same amount of quantity adjustment (*mn* in Figure 4.8), the loss is usually much lower if it is achieved *through* the working of the market mechanism (by taxes/subsidies, etc.), than if it is achieved by administrative regulations (such as legal price, quotas, etc.).

Summary

Different measures of consumer surplus (Dupuit-Marshall, CV, EV, CS, ES, Laspèyres, Paasche, and average cost differences) are illustrated. Which measure is appropriate depends on the problem. If compensation is not actually intended, Marshall's measure has an advantage over CV, as argued by Winch. But Marshall's measure is path-dependent. Where price changes of more than one good are involved, the measure may give different results depending on which good is measured first, etc. Since the payment of compensation may affect prices and since the CV measure is based on a fixed set of prices, a positive ΣCV does not ensure that gainers can more than compensate losers (Boadway's paradox). However, these complications shrink into insignificance if we recognise that any objective measure of subjective welfare must necessarily be approximate in nature, since the differences due to such complications are small in most practical cases. Where the differences are large, a different measure (marginal dollar equivalent; see Appendix 4A) is proposed. This is the number of times a change is worth a (marginal) dollar in utility terms. It is also shown that the loss in consumer surplus due to price control, rationing, etc., may be many times larger than the traditional triangular measures (Section 4.7).

CV, EV or Marginal Dollar Equivalent?

For most practical applications, it is likely that the difference in the sum of compensating variations (ΣCV) and the sum of equivalent variation (ΣEV) is likely to be overwhelmed by the inaccuracies in data collection. For changes whose effects are thinly spread, no significant differences are likely to arise. However, it cannot be ruled out that, if the effects are concentrated, the two measures may differ by a substantial amount and even differ in sign. As a dramatic example (for another example, see Mishan, 1971, p. 19), consider a somewhat eccentric farmer content with living simply on his farm. The society is considering building a highway and the most suitable path is across his farm. The farmer is not prepared to move for any sum of compensation (i.e. $CV = - \$\infty$) but is willing to pay only $1,000 for the benefit of not having to move (EV = $-$\$1,000$). (In terms of Figure 4A.1, his marginal utility curve may look like the dotted curve.) The only loss he will suffer from moving to another farm is the trouble of moving, which he is willing to pay $1,000 to avoid. But since additional wealth is not of much use to him, he would stick to his farm rather than become a billionaire.

For each individual, the CV measure of a change equals the negative of the EV measure of the reverse change and vice versa. Hence, the difference in ΣCV and ΣEV means that, whichever measure we decide to use, we may end up in a contradiction. In the example of the eccentric farmer above, suppose that ΣCV and ΣEV for the *rest* of society lie between $1,000 and $\$\infty$. Thus, for society as a whole, ΣEV > 0 and ΣCV < 0. But consider the reverse change. The decision to build the road has been taken and the proposed change is that the decision be reversed. Then again we have ΣEV > 0 and ΣCV < 0 for this reversed change. Thus, if we use ΣEV as the criterion, we will recommend the building of the road as well as recommend that the decision be reversed. Similarly, using ΣCV, we will recommend not to undertake the building but if the undertaking has somehow been made, we shall recommend not to reverse it even if it does not cost anything to do so.

For an approximate measure, the logical possibility of a contradiction is not an important objection unless the divergence involved is large. For cases where CV and EV differ greatly such as the road-building example, I suggest the use of the sum of marginal-dollar equivalent (ΣMDE) to remove one source of the contradiction, namely the diminishing marginal utility of income.

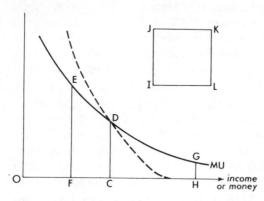

Figure 4A.1

The difference between CV and EV can most clearly be appreciated by using a cardinal-utility approach (by no means necessary). In Figure 4A.1, the curve MU measures the marginal utility of income. Suppose the individual's income is OC and consider a change that will increase his total utility by the area IJKL but leave his income and MU unchanged over the relevant region. (The case where these are changed is considered in Figure 4A.2.) By construction, the area CDEF = IJKL = CDGH. Hence, his CV for the change is measured by FC and his EV is measured by CH. Due to the diminishing marginal utility of income, CH > FC. This (that EV > CV) is usually true but not necessarily so even if we assume diminishing MU unless we also assume that the MU curve is not substantially lowered with the change. The size of (positive) CV is limited by the amount of the individual's income OC, but the size of (positive) EV can be arbitrarily large. For example, the EV of giving a blind person his sight may be infinite.

If the change that benefits the individual by *IJKL* also cost the society an amount *IL* either measured by CV or EV (if the costs are dispersed, $\Sigma CV = \Sigma EV$), should the change be made? By construction, $CH > IL > FC$. In terms of aggregate net benefit, the answer is 'yes' or 'no', depending on whether ΣEV or ΣCV is used as a criterion. Should we just use an average of the two measures? While this may be the most simple way out for most practical cases of cost-benefit analysis, it is not difficult to think of cases where this will not do. For one thing half an infinity is still an infinity and scarcely anyone would suggest that society should spend its entire (or even half of its) GNP to give sight to one blind person, assuming that it can be done at, and only at, such a cost.

Before coming to our solution to the problem of conflicting ΣCV and ΣEV measures, we shall first examine the more general case where both the *MU* curve and the income level of an individual may be affected by the change (project, etc.). In Figure 4A.2, the *MU* curve is shifted upward (the case of a downward shift can be analysed similarly) from MU^0 to MU^1 and the income level of the individual is also increased from Y^0 to Y^1. If the total gain in utility to the individual is equal to *IJKL*, then $C'F'$ measures his CV and CH his EV, where $C'D'E'F' = IJKL = CDGH$ in area.

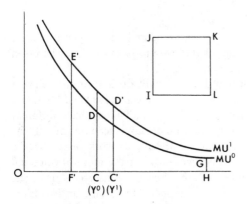

Figure 4A.2

If income is actually to be taken from (or given to) the individual, then CV (or EV) is the appropriate measure. But if the compensation test is only hypothetical, CV (EV) usually under-estimates (over-estimates) the gain to the individual due to the diminishing marginal utility of income. Now we wish to derive a monetary measure that is free from such inaccuracy. Since the purpose of the exercise is to see, before the change is carried out, whether it is worth undertaking, it seems reasonable that we should use the marginal utility (*CD*) at the existing income level Y^0 (*OC*) as a yardstick. (Moreover, this marginal utility has a significance across different individuals if we accept the incentive argument discussed in Appendix 9A.)

By using *CD* as a yardstick, we mean that, if the utility gain to the individual is measured by the rectangle *IJKL*, and if by construction *IJ* = *CD*, then *IL* is the amount of monetary measure we are after. We shall call this measure the 'marginal-dollar equivalent' (MDE) of the gain. It is the number of times the gain is worth the gain of a marginal dollar. The MDE can be measured in two ways: one via the CV and the other via the EV.

$$\text{MDE} = \int_{Y^1 - CV}^{Y^1} MU^1 \, dY / MU^0 (Y^0) = C'D'E'F'/CD \qquad (4\text{A}.1)$$

$$\text{MDE} = \int_{Y^0}^{Y^0 + EV} MU^0 \, dY / \dot{M}U^0 (Y^0) = CDGH/CD \qquad (4\text{A}.2)$$

Barring inaccuracies, the two measures should give equal results. If the results diverge, the average of the two measurements may be taken to minimise the effect of inaccuracy.

If we know the marginal utilities of individuals over the relevant range both before and after the change, we can calculate ΣMDE and make a decision accordingly. But different individuals have different utility functions. In practice, we cannot take account of all the differences in individual preferences and have to work in terms of a typical individual and make allowances only for the more obvious and serious cases of abnormalities. Both common sense and analytical simplicity suggest that it may be reasonable to assume an iso-elastic form of marginal utility function (i.e. the marginal utility curve has the same elasticity throughout),

$$MU = Y^{-\rho}; U = Y^{1-\rho}/(1 - \rho), \tag{4A.3}$$

where Y represents the amount of income and ρ is a positive constant. In the special case of $\rho = 1$, $U = \log Y$. This has some support from some psychological studies which show that, apart from extreme values, Sensation $= k \log$ Stimulus, where k is a positive constant (Weber-Fechner law).† One of the weaknesses of this function is that utility approaches infinity as income approaches infinity. I do not believe that an individual can have infinite happiness no matter how great is his income. It seems likely that ρ will increase as income gets very high. But for the relevant range ρ may be taken to be approximately constant.

The introduction of a policy change (a project, etc.) may affect MU. However, in the absence of specific knowledge of how MU is affected, we shall take (4A.3) to represent the utility functions of individuals both before and after the change. Hence the approximate measures for MDE are:

$$MDE \simeq (Y^0)^\rho \int_{Y^1-CV}^{Y^1} Y^{-\rho} dY \tag{4A.4}$$

$$MDE \simeq (Y^0)^\rho \int_{Y^0}^{Y^0+EV} Y^{-\rho} dY \tag{4A.5}$$

Where both measures are available and differ, we take

$$MDE \simeq \tfrac{1}{2}(Y^0)^\rho \int_{Y^1-CV}^{Y^1} Y^{-\rho} dY + \tfrac{1}{2}(Y^0)^\rho \int_{Y^0}^{Y^0+EV} Y^{-\rho} dY \tag{4A.6}$$

A policy measure is then recommended for acceptance or for rejection according to whether the sum of MDE over all individuals, i.e. ΣMDE^i is positive or negative.

† Luce & Edwards' (1958) criticism of Fechner does not apply to this particular function. Some studies show that the sensation scale is better described as a power function, with the value of the exponent varying from case to case. See Sternbach & Tversky (1964).

The ΣMDE measure removes a source of contradiction in the ΣCV or ΣEV measure (due to diminishing marginal utility). But it is still no more than an approximate measure (see Section 4.6 above). In particular, if MU changes due to a *shift* in the whole curve (i.e. $C'D' \neq CD$ in Figure 4A.2), contradiction may still arise. (This source of possible contradiction is already present in the ΣCV and ΣEV measure.) In principle, if we know all the *MU* curves before and after the change and can attach social significance to them, we can devise a measure free of contradiction. But this would be little short of providing a fully defined social welfare function. At any rate, it is unlikely that the shift in *MU* will be an important source of contradiction. (Our argument in Appendix 9A will reinforce this belief.)

5 Social Choice

The concept of Pareto optimality leads us to situations where it is impossible to make someone better off without making others worse off. But it does not offer any guidance to the choice involving making some better off and some worse off. In Chapter 3, we discussed welfare criteria that provide sufficient conditions for a social improvement. But what we obtained there is still incomplete in two aspects. First, in cases where the compensation test is met but the distributional one is not, or vice versa, we have no answer. Second, the criterion (Little's) we find acceptable is based on some judgements about distributional desirability. How do we obtain such judgements? In Chapter 4, the discussion of the magnitude of welfare changes reduces (not completely) the inadequency of Chapter 3 in the first aspect. But the incompleteness with respect to the second aspect has not been overcome. Thus we still need something more. If we have a specific social welfare function (SWF), the vacuum can then be filled. But how do we get a specific SWF? If there is a super-Stalin, he may say that, 'The SWF should just be my preference function. Whatever I prefer or whatever I think is good for society should prevail.' But the solution by resorting to a super-dictator is not a palatable one to most people. The problem of social choice is to see whether we can derive our social preference *based on* the preferences of individuals, satisfying certain reasonable conditions. This seems simple enough and nothing more than the basic requirement of (minimal) democracy. But a formidable difficulty is encountered in this problem of social choice – the impossibility theorem of Arrow.

5.1 Arrow's Impossibility Theorem

Arrow (1951b) calls his theorem the *General* Possibility Theorem, since he first proves another theorem, the Possibility Theorem, for the special case of two alternatives. However, as the answer of the General Possibility Theorem is negative, it is also called the Impossibility Theorem or the General Impossibility Theorem. In simple terms, the theorem states that a rule (or a constitution) for deriving, from *individual orderings* of social states, a *social* ordering consistent with some reasonable conditions cannot be found in general.

A first glimpse of the content of the theorem may be provided by the well-known 'paradox of voting'. Assume a three-person group faced with a choice of three alternatives. A simple and obvious way of arriving at a collective ordering is to say that one alternative is preferred to another if a majority holds such preference. Now suppose that the preferences of the three individuals are as shown below,

$$xP^1 yP^1 z; zP^2 xP^2 y; yP^3 zP^3 x,$$

where x, y, z are the three alternatives and P^i stands for 'is preferred to' for the ith individual. It can be seen that a majority prefers x to y and a majority prefers y to z. According to the rule of majority voting, we may say that the group prefers x to y, and y to z. By transitivity, which is usually accepted as a condition of logical consistency, x should be preferred to z. But actually a majority of the group prefers z to x. This shows that the rule of majority voting for making social or collective choice may result in cyclicity ($xPyPzPx$) and *a fortiori* may fail to satisfy the requirement of transitivity. What Arrow proves in his theorem is that the difficulty illustrated by the paradox of voting is *general*, i.e. we cannot find *any* method or rule for passing from individual to collective ordering, satisfying some reasonable conditions. For example, even if we make our rule to be one of unanimity, intransitivity may still arise, as shown below. Suppose

$$xP^1 yP^1 z; zP^2 xP^2 y.$$

It may be seen that, according to the unanimity rule, xPy and yIz (since we do not have a unanimous preference between y and z, to make the social preference complete, we have to declare indifference). From transitivity, xPz. But there is actually no unanimous preference of x over z.

We come now to discuss Arrow's path-breaking contribution. He defines a social state to be 'a complete description of the amount of each type of commodity in the hands of each individual, the amount of labour to be applied by each individual, the amount of each productive resource invested in each type of productive activity, and the amounts of various types of collective activity such as municipal services, diplomacy and its continuation by other means, and the erection of statues to famous men' (Arrow, 1951b, 1963, p. 17). Each individual in the community has a definite ordering of all conceivable social states in terms of their desirability to him. But 'desirability' need not be determined by the commodity bundle which accrues to him. 'The individual may order all social states by whatever standards he sees relevant' (Arrow, 1950, pp. 333–47).

Both individual and social orderings are required to satisfy two rather weak axioms:

Axiom A: Completeness: *For all x and y, either xRy or yRx, where R stands for 'preferred or indifferent to'.*

Axiom B: Transitivity: *For all x, y, and z, xRy and yRz imply xRz. In other words, if x is preferred or indifferent to y and y is preferred or indifferent to z, then x must be preferred or indifferent to z.*

It may be noted that, although Arrow discusses his theorem in terms of social states, his argument is generally applicable to the choice of any set of alternatives, whether it is the set of social states confronting a society, a number of candidates to be elected, or a number of alternative actions to be decided by a committee. The two crucial requirements are that more than one individual is involved and that the collective ordering is to be based on the individual orderings of the alternatives.

Arrow next defines a constitution as 'a process or rule which, for each set of individual orderings $R^1, \ldots, R^I$ for alternative social states (one ordering for each individual), states a corresponding social ordering of alternative social states R' (Arrow, 1951b, 1963, p. 23).† And Arrow requires the constitution to satisfy the following five 'natural conditions'.

† Arrow first used the term 'Social Welfare Function'. This is not exactly the same as Bergson's SWF, which is numerical. In the last chapter of the second edition of his celebrated book, Arrow (1963, p. 105) agrees to use the term 'constitution' instead. Recently the concept of a social welfare functional (D'Aspremont & Gevers, 1977, Sen, 1970a, 1977b) has become popular. This specifies a social ordering from a set of individual utility or welfare *functions*. I do not find this concept necessary as Independence (p. 142) is compelling. On the close connection between the two approaches, see Theorem 1 of Roberts (1980b)*.

(1) **Free Triple**: *There are at least three among all the alternatives under consideration for which all logically possible individual orderings of these three alternatives are admissible.*

This condition is to ensure that the problem will not be made trivial by being confined to highly restricted sets of individual orderings. For example, if the orderings of all individuals over all the alternatives have to be exactly the same and no other pattern of ordering is admissible, it is quite trivial that we can have a constitution saying that the social ordering be the same as the common individual ordering. However, if we allow our individuals to order the alternatives freely, even if such freedom is allowed over only three alternatives, we are faced with the difficulty of social choice.

(2) **Positive Association of Social and Individual Values**: *'the social ordering responds positively to alterations in individual values, or at least not negatively. Hence, if one alternative social state rises or remains unchanged in the ordering of every individual without any other change in these orderings, we expect that it rises, or at least does not fall, in the social ordering'* (Arrow, 1951b, 1963, p. 25).

(3) **The Independence of Irrelevant Alternatives** (IIA): *'the choice made by society from a given environment depends only on the orderings of individuals among the alternatives in that environment. Alternatively stated, if we consider two sets of individual orderings such that, for each individual, his ordering of these particular alternatives in a given environment is the same each time, then we require that the choice made by society from that environment be the same when individual values are given by the first set of orderings as they are when given by the second'* (Arrow, 1951b, 1963, pp. 26-7).

This condition has caused much controversy partly due to an inadequate understanding of it. Sen (1970a, pp. 89ff.) provides a penetrating observation that there are two different aspects involved in IIA. The first is the 'irrelevance' (or 'independence') aspect referring to the fact that the social ordering of any two alternatives (or any other subset of alternatives) must depend only on individual preferences of these alternatives, not on individual preferences for other irrelevant alternatives. Many people find this requirement unacceptable. This is probably due to their neglect that each social alternative is a complete specification of *all* the relevant aspects of a social state. Recognising this, the independence aspect is a very reasonable requirement. (See p. 144 below.) The second is the 'ordering' aspect requiring that social ordering of any two alternatives be based only on the individual *orderings* of these alternatives and not on anything else, e.g. preference intensities or cardinal utilities.† Both aspects of IIA are quite reasonable if our knowledge is confined to the *orderings* or ordinal preferences of individuals (Plott, 1972). If relative intensity of preferences or interpersonally comparable cardinal utilities are somehow available, then the ordering aspect of IIA need not be accepted. With the introduction of cardinal preferences, however, we have gone outside the scope of the original problem posed by Arrow, since he requires the constitution to derive a social ordering based on individual *orderings*. Nevertheless, the possibility of aggregating cardinal utilities is a meaningful one and is within the confines of social choice (Section 5.4).

(4) **Citizens' Sovereignty**: *The social ordering must not be imposed. The social ordering is imposed if there is some pair of alternatives x and y such that the society can never express a preference for y over x no matter what the preferences of all individuals are. Even if all individuals prefer y to x, the social ordering is still xRy.*

This condition again is quite reasonable as it only requires that the social ordering over any pair of alternatives must be based somehow on individual orderings or not be totally independent of these individual orderings.

(5) **Nondictatorship**: *The constitution must not be dictatorial. The constitution is dictatorial if there is an individual such that for every pair of alternatives, if he prefers the first over the second, the social ordering must also rank the first over the second, regardless of the orderings of all the other individuals.*

This definition of Dictatorship has not definitely included such persons as Stalin and Hitler as dictators. The requirement of Nondictatorship is therefore very mild. If we allow Dictatorship, a constitution can easily be defined which requires the social ordering to be the same as the ordering of the dictator.

† Some writers, e.g. Quirk & Saposnik (1968, p. 110), were aware of these two distinct aspects of IIA, but Sen provided a more detailed discussion. The ordering aspect is also involved in condition 2 and many conditions used by other authors. Osborne (1976)* further divides the ordering aspect into individualism and ordinalism, and calls the irrelevance aspect localism.

The original Arrow's General Possibility Theorem states that there is no constitution that simultaneously satisfies axioms A and B and conditions 1 to 5 as outlined above. Arrow's proof is sketched below:

Arrow uses the concept of a decisive set. A set of individuals is decisive for alternative x against y if their unanimous ranking of x as preferred to y is sufficient to establish that x is socially preferred to y, regardless of the orderings of all other individuals. Arrow first proves that, for a free triple, if an individual is decisive for any one alternative against any other, then he is also decisive in every pair of alternatives (Arrow, 1951b, p. 56). Hence no single individual can be decisive by the requirement of Nondictatorship. On the other hand, since unanimity must determine social ordering by conditions 2 and 4, at least one decisive set can always be found. Select that decisive set that contains the smallest number of individuals. Without loss of generality, let it be decisive for x against y. Divide this decisive set which is denoted by V_1 into V', a single individual in V_1 and V_2, the set of all other individuals in V_1. This division is possible since a decisive set cannot contain less than two individuals. Suppose the individual orderings are as follows:

V' prefers x to y and y to z;
all individuals in V_2 prefer z to x and x to y;
all individuals in V_3 prefer y to z and z to x;

where V_3 is the set of all individuals not in V_1. This pattern of preference is admissible since x, y, z constitute the free triple.

Since V_1 is decisive for x against y, the social ordering must rank x preferred to y. Individuals in V_2 prefer z to y but all other individuals prefer y to z. If the social ordering were z preferred to y, V_2 would be decisive for z against y. But this contradicts the assumption that V_2 is one individual less than the smallest decisive set. Thus the society must prefer y to z or be indifferent between y and z. By transitivity, x must be socially preferred to z. However, all individuals other than the single individual V' prefer z to x. So he is decisive for x against z. But no single individual can be decisive to satisfy Nondictatorship. This shows that, given the two axioms, the five conditions cannot be satisfied simultaneously. Before reading on, readers are invited to try for themselves to discover any inadequacy in the preceding proof.

The proof is incomplete because it refers only to the free triple. It shows that if other conditions are satisfied, Nondictatorship is violated for the free triple. If we consider the general case of more than three alternatives, then all the five conditions may be satisfied for these alternatives, though not for some three alternatives. That an individual is decisive over three alternatives does not mean that he is a dictator over all the alternatives. Hence Nondictatorship need not necessarily be violated. Arrow's original definition of a decisive set is also, strictly speaking, not appropriate, since 'regardless of the preferences of all other individuals', and 'all other individuals have the reverse preference' are not exactly the same thing. A pedantic note may also be added that, if the set of individuals is infinite (obviously not relevant), Arrow's theorem does not apply; see Fishburn (1970a)*, Kirman and Sondermann (1972)* and Hansson (1976)*.

The inadequacy of Arrow's original proof was first discovered by Blau (1957) who shows that the proof could be saved by slightly revising condition 2 and by replacing Free Triple with Free Orderings.

Free Orderings: *All logically possible orderings are admissible.*

Arrow (1963) also replaces the revised condition 2 (2') and condition 4 by a mild version of the Pareto principle.

Weak Pareto Principle: *If every individual prefers one alternative to another, then society also prefers the first to the second.*

This condition is deducible from conditions 2', 3 and 4 and is almost universally accepted. It is weaker than the usual Pareto principle since it requires strong preference for all individuals. Arrow then proves the revised impossibility theorem: Free Orderings, IIA, Weak Pareto, and Nondictatorship are inconsistent, given axioms A and B. The proof (Arrow, 1963, pp. 97-100) is very similar to the original proof. First it is shown that no single individual can be decisive for any pair of alternatives. This is so because if an individual is decisive for any alternative against any other, he is also decisive for all pairs of alternatives (with any number of alternatives) by Free Orderings, IIA, and Weak Pareto. Then a decisive set with the smallest number of individuals is selected. With the same argument as in the preceeding proof it is then shown that a contradiction must result.

Another revision of the theorem is suggested by Murakami (1961) in which Nondictatorship is replaced by:

Strong Nondictatorship: *Among the triples of alternatives satisfying Free Triple, there is at least one for which no individual is a dictator.*

Arrow accepts this extension of the notion of a dictator as very reasonable, since its violation implies that there is a dictator for every choice on which there can be real disagreement.

It may be concluded that Arrow's theorem is established under either of the following two sets of conditions (with axioms A and B):
(i) Free Orderings, IIA, Weak Pareto, and Nondictatorship
(ii) Free Triple, IIA, Weak Pareto, and Strong Nondictatorship.

(The Comment by Bailey (1979) on the Arrow-Murakami proof that no *minimum* number of alternatives is imposed misses the point that a social-choice rule should give reasonable results for any number of alternatives. His proposed rule (equal endowments with free exchange) is 'imposed', as it fails to base the choice of the distribution of endowments on individual preferences.)

5.2 The Impossibility Propositions of Kemp-Ng and Parks

Arrow's impossibility theorem has far-reaching implications. For one thing, it shows that we cannot have a reasonable rule to derive our SWF or simply a social ordering from the *ordinal* preferences of individuals. (The existence of a SWF presupposes a social ordering.) Since the concept of a SWF is crucial in welfare economics and since many economists are reluctant to use cardinal utilities, a dilemma is posed. Some economists, notably Little (1952) and Samuelson (1967), attempt to solve this dilemma by rejecting Arrow's theorem as irrelevant to welfare economics. Specifically, it is maintained that what is relevant to welfare economics is a SWF for a given set of individual orderings. It is true that individual preferences may change. But for any new set of individual orderings, we have a new SWF. The Arrow impossibility result only applies by requiring that the same rule is used to derive the new SWF (or social ordering) from the new set of individual orderings as the one used for deriving the old SWF from the original set of individual orderings. By not restricting ourselves to observe such inter-profile consistency, i.e. the same rule over different profiles or sets of individual orderings, we can free ourselves from the Arrow paradox.

The above argument to bypass Arrow's impossibility result is not really convincing. As individual preferences over social states or alternatives change, it is reasonable that society's ordering or SWF over social states should change. But why should the *rule* of deriving the social ordering change? For example, if we use majority rule for a given set of individual orderings, why should we shift to say unanimity for another set of individual orderings? It seems unreasonable to change

the rule unless it is not acceptable even with the original set of preferences.† Nevertheless, even ignoring the requirement of interprofile
consistency, one can show that there does not exist a reasonable rule
to derive a social ordering based only on individual orderings. Even if
we agree to operate with a fixed set of individual preferences, we still
have the impossibility result. This was established almost simultaneously and independently by Kemp and Ng (1976) and Parks (1976).
The two papers use different sets of assumptions. Roughly speaking,
Parks adopts a stronger assumption with respect to the diversity of
alternatives and individual preferences and Kemp and Ng adopt a
stronger assumption with respect to democratic requirement (Anonymity in contrast to Nondictatorship). Due to his set of assumptions,
Park's proof is very similar to Arrow's. Hence the elucidation below
follows that of Kemp & Ng. (For extensions, see Pollak, 1979, Roberts,
1980c*.)

Kemp & Ng (1976) first prove that we cannot construct a real valued
SWF based only on individual orderings under a fairly mild set of
assumptions. But since the proof of the first proposition is fairly complicated, we shall present their Proposition 2 which rules out a reasonable
social ordering based only on (a given set of) individual orderings. The
assumptions (or conditions) used are the following three.

(1) **Mild Diversity of Preferences**: *There exist three social alternatives
x, y and z, and two individuals J and K such that (a) these two individuals strongly order (i.e. no indifference) x, y, z , (b) they differ
strongly in their rankings of two pairs chosen from {x, y, z} and agree
on the ranking of the remaining pair, and (c) other individuals are indifferent between x, y and z.*

By strong difference in preference on a pair of alternative x and y,
we mean: xP^Jy and yP^Kx or vice versa. If the allocation of G goods to
I individuals are among the variables defining the set of social alternatives, as relevant to welfare economics, it can be shown (Kemp & Ng,
1976, pp. 60-1) that Mild Diversity is a very reasonable condition. (See
also Kramer, 1973*.)

---

†See, however, McManus (1975*, 1978*) for the argument that, e.g., society
may want to give different weights to the preference of an individual depending
on whether he is a drug addict. But how does society agree first on discounting
the preferences of addicts? McManus' proposal does not provide a satisfactory
solution to Arrow's impossibility result, not to mention the impossibility propositions of Kemp–Ng (1976) and Parks (1976).

(2) **Strong Pareto Principle**: *For any two alternatives x and y, ($xR^i y$ for all i) implies (xRy), and ($xR^i y$ for all i and $xP^j y$ for some j) implies (xPy).*

(3) **Anonymity plus Orderings Only**: *For any x, y, z, w (not necessarily distinct alternatives), if ($x\bar{R}^i$ y for all i) implies x$\bar{R}$y, then ($z\bar{R}^i w$ for all i) imples zRw, where $\bar{R}^i$ stands for one (not necessarily the same for all i) of P^i, I^i and contra P^i, similarly for $\bar{R}$, and ($\bar{\bar{R}}^1$, $\bar{\bar{R}}^2$, ..., $\bar{\bar{R}}^I$) is any permutation of ($\bar{R}^1$, $\bar{R}^2$, ..., $\bar{R}^I$).*

This last condition expresses two requirements simultaneously. First, it requires that all individuals be treated anonymously on an equal footing. This requirement is of course stronger than Nondictatorship. (Anonymity is not used in Proposition 1 of Kemp & Ng.) However, it is still a reasonable democratic requirement. If different weights are to be used, how are they to be decided? Secondly, the condition above requires that the social ranking of any two alternatives must be based only on the individual rankings of them. Apart from a reasonable independence or irrelevance aspect, this can in turn be split into two parts: (i) that only *individual* preferences count and not anything else, (ii) that only the *ordinal* aspect of individual preferences, i.e. orderings or rankings, count, and not the intensities of preferences. This last aspect (orderings only) need not be a reasonable condition to impose on the social ordering for anyone, myself included, who is willing to take preference intensities into consideration. However, since our purpose here is to show the impossibility of a reasonable social ordering based on individual *orderings*, this is a natural condition to impose. (Samuelson, 1977 completely misses this point; see Kemp & Ng, 1977 and Appendix 5A. Mueller (1979) is aware of this point but unconvincingly interprets Samuelson as believing in the necessity of cardinality.)

Impossibility Proposition: *Given Mild Diversity of Preferences, there does not exist a social ordering satisfying Strong Pareto and Anonymity plus Orderings Only.*

Proof: From (1), there exists x, v, z such that xI^iyI^iz for all individuals $i \neq J, K$ and such that either (i) xP^JyP^Jz and zP^K/xP^Ky or (ii) xP^JyP^Jz and yP^KzP^Kx. Since the proof proceeds on much the same line in each of the two cases, let us confine our attention to the first. From (2), we infer that xPy. From (3), x and z must be socially indifferent. From transitivity, zPy. (An ordering presupposes transitivity.) This violates (3) since yP^Jz and zP^Ky while other individuals are indifferent. Q.E.D.

The impossibility proposition above shows that, even if we confine ourselves to a given set of individual preferences, we cannot construct a reasonable social ordering based on individual *ordinal* preferences. Thus the Little-Samuelson attempt to escape Arrow's paradox leads us to a blind alley. This is a deadly blow to those who dislike cardinal utilities or who believe in the sufficiency of ordinal utilities (e.g. Samuelson, 1947, pp. 277–8, 1967, 1977, 1981). But it does not rule out the possibility of constructing a SWF based on cardinal utilities (Section 5.4.1). One needs of course some aggregating procedure or interpersonal comparison as well. Disallowing interpersonal comparison, one can establish impossibility results even with cardinal utilities (DeMeyer & Plott, 1971, Kalai & Schmeidler, 1977, Osborne, 1976*, Sen, 1970a, pp. 123-30). However, interpersonal comparability without cardinality is not sufficient. For example, Anonymity is a form of interpersonal comparison. With Orderings Only, we have shown above that it does not provide a reasonable result. (See Ng, 1982b, for the necessity of interpersonal cardinal utilities, and Roberts, 1980a*, for a comprehensive analysis of comparability without cardinality.)

5.3*   Can the Paradox of Social Choice be Resolved?

Arrow's theorem has implications not only for welfare economics but also for political science since it implies that all methods of voting and election (including majority rule) based on rankings are irrational in some sense. Many attempts have been made to overcome or by-pass the impossibility result. We have already seen that the attempt by Little and Samuelson leads us nowhere. What about the others? Since Arrow's theorem (after the revision) is valid, the proposed solutions of the paradox must consist in either relaxing the requirement of (especially social) rationality (i.e. axioms A and B) or by relaxing some of Arrow's conditions, especially IIA and Free Orderings. The last alternative usually takes the form of imposing restrictions on the admissible sets of individual preferences.

Just before the publication of Arrow's article (1950), Black (1948) showed that, if the preferences of all individuals are single-peaked, it can be shown that group decisions based on majority rule are transitive. This assumes that the alternatives can be arranged in one dimension (see Grandmont, 1978*, for a generalisation to multi-dimensions), and each individual selects his first preference, and the farther any alternative departed from it on one side or the other, the less he would favour it. The shape of the evaluation curve would then be either Λ-shaped or monotonically increasing or decreasing, as shown in Figure 5.1. There is no constraint on how we arrange the alternatives. In other words, we may arrange the alternatives in any one-dimensional order; as long as there is one way of arrangement which gives a single-peaked preference curve for *every* individual, the condition of single-peakedness is met.

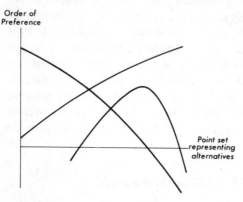

Figure 5.1

The assumption of single-peaked preference implies the violation of Free Triple (and *a fortiori* Free Orderings). However, single-peaked preference is quite likely for some alternatives, e.g. the possible sizes of a numerical quantity such as the price of a product, the height of a tax, etc. If an individual prefers $10 to $5 (say, for a per unit pollution tax), he is unlikely to prefer $5 to $8. Nevertheless, many problems of social choice may involve more than one dimension, and individual preferences may be so complicated and diverse that no arrangement of the alternatives would result in a single-peaked preference curve for every individual. Moreover, even for the simple case of the choice of a one-dimensional numerical quantity it is still possible that the requirement of single-peaked preference may not be satisfied. For example, take the case of the number of F–111 planes. One individual may have the preference pattern that the lower the number of planes bought (by Australia) the better. Another individual may prefer more planes to less, up to 10. The third individual may prefer no planes to any number of planes.

But he may yet prefer four planes to three planes because he regards four as the minimum operationally useful number of F-111 planes. Rather than wasting money on three planes, it may be more sensible to spend a little more money to keep a workable team of four F-111's. Hence the preference of this individual has two peaks, at zero and at four. If we rearrange the order of the alternatives to give a single peak for this individual, the preference of at least another individual will be made double-peaked. It may thus be concluded that the assumption of single peaked preference, though likely to be realised in some cases, cannot be taken to prevail generally. As the rule of social choice is to be applied in many alternative sets of preferences most of which are unknown at present, the requirement of Free Orderings is very compelling. The attempt to solve the paradox of social choice by imposing restrictions such as single-peakedness on individual preferences does not seem to be very promising. (On other restrictions on preferences, see Grandmont, 1978*, Inada, 1970, Pattanaik, 1971, Slutsky, 1977.)

Whilst the requirement of single-peaked preference violates Free Triple, many other solutions presently to be discussed violate IIA. This condition involves both the 'independence' and the 'ordering' aspects. If the intensities of preference can somehow be revealed, the 'ordering' aspect need not be accepted. However, many attempts to solve the problem by revealing intensities of preference (or 'cardinalisation') also violate the 'independence' aspect of IIA. This is a drawback of such schemes. If the intensities of preferences can be known, we would still expect the social ordering or SWF to be a function of the ordinal and *cardinal* preferences of individuals of the relevant alternatives. The choice between x and y should be a function only of the individual orderings and intensitives of preferences of x and y, but should be independent of an irrelevant alternative z.† The compelling reasonableness of the independence aspect of IIA is also demonstrated by Hammond (1977), who shows that, even if the constant set of individuals has constant and consistent tastes, dynamic social choice may still be inconsistent unless the social choice rule satisfies the independence aspect of IIA (which Hammond calls a generalisation of IIA).

† Hansson (1969) shows that, if we impose Anonymity (or neutrality between persons) and Neutrality (between alternatives), no group decision function can satisfy IIA unless it always declares all alternatives equal. While Hansson regards this as an argument against IIA, it is more reasonably regarded as an alternative impossibility theorem if we stay within the orderings-only framework.

To show how both aspects of IIA are violated in some attempts at cardinalisation, consider the following procedure of voting which is free of intransitivity. 'Each elector is asked to vote in the following manner. Faced with a subset of the set X of all conceivable alternatives, he assigns to that alternative which he ranks highest (i.e. from which he expects to get the greatest utility) the number 'one'. The remaining alternatives are assigned numbers according to the utility expected from them relative to that expected from the most desired alternative . . . The numbers assigned to each alternative are summed over all electors and that alternative is chosen which has the greatest total. The alternative with the second highest is ranked second, and so on' (Kemp & Asimakopulos, 1952, pp. 196-7; see also Weldon, 1952, p. 452, and Hildock, 1953, p. 81).

The procedure clearly violates the 'ordering' aspect of IIA. That it also violates the 'independence' aspect can also be shown. Suppose that my first alternative x is ranked very low by all other numerous voters who are roughly equally divided between y and z. The utility I expect from y is twice that of z, say 10 units and 5 units respectively. If the utility I expect from x is 100 units, I have to vote 1 to x, 0.1 to y and 0.05 to z. In this case, suppose the sum over all voters indicates that z has a fractionally larger total than y. However, if the utility I expect from x is 20 units instead, I have to vote 1 to x, 0.5 to y and 0.25 to z. With all other votes unchanged, y may then have a larger total than z instead. Thus, even if all individual preferences (both ordinal and cardinal) with respect to y and z remain exactly unchanged, the social ordering of y and z will be affected by my preference with respect to x, an alternative which will certainly be ranked lower than both y and z. This is certainly an undesirable outcome. Even if we hold all individual preferences fixed, the social ordering of y and z will still depend on whether x, or some other alternative, is included in the set of alternatives at all. Again an undesirable outcome. (Observant readers may have noticed that IIA is stated with reference to a change in individual preferences. But since the example used by Arrow himself to illustrate the spirit of IIA refers to a change in the set of alternatives, it has frequently been taken to assume this second meaning as well. If we eschew the ordering aspect, both meanings of IIA are just an extremely reasonable property of independence.)

Buchanan & Tullock (1962, pp. 330-2), Coleman (1966), and others also propose a method of voting (log-rolling) whereby the relative intensities of preferences may be revealed. (See Miller, 1977, for a survey.) Basically, voters are allowed to enter into vote trading agreements or actual exchange of votes. For example, if J feels strongly against alternative z, she may agree with K that she (J) will rank y (her second preference and K's first preference) first, provided K agrees to vote z (K's second preference) last. This increases K's chance of getting his first preference and also increases J's chance of preventing the adoption of her worst alternative.

It has been shown by Park (1967) that the method of vote trading cannot, in general, arrive at a stable equilibrium. Mueller (1967) also argues that vote trading agreements cannot be relied upon to reveal the true preferences of individuals and that the resulting set of policy decisions will fall short of being socially optimal. 'If the number of voters is not so large as to preclude the formation of partially stable coalitions, it is too small to remove completely the monopsony power a voter will be able to enjoy over any issue of vital importance to him' (Mueller, 1967, p. 1310). Nevertheless, it remains true that, if vote trading is possible, we will tend to move closer to a social optimum, and the social decision will tend to be transitive. Arrow rejects the log-rolling argument on the ground that 'a social state is a whole bundle of issues, and I presupposed that all possible combinations of decisions on the separate issues are considered as alternative social states. That this included log-rolling seemed to me so obvious as not to be worth spelling out' (Arrow, 1963, p. 109). This argument misses the point that, with log-rolling, the relative intensities of preference are revealed somewhat and hence we may no longer wish to be bound by the ordering aspect of IIA. However, social decision with log-rolling violates IIA not only in its ordering aspect but also its irrelevance aspect. This can be seen most clearly where the alternatives concerned are small in number. A change in individual preferences with respect to some alternatives or the removal of one alternative changes the possibility of vote-trading so much that the social ordering of the unaffected alternatives may change. (Cf. Wilson, 1969, p. 339.)

Quite distinct from log-rolling, another proposal along the lines of cardinal utility is made by Harsanyi (1953, 1955).† Each individual is to indicate 'what social situation he would choose if he did not know what his personal position would be in the new situation chosen (and in any

† See also Vickrey (1945).

of its alternatives) but rather had an equal *chance* of obtaining any of the social positions existing in this situation,† from the highest down to the lowest' (Harsanyi, 1955, p. 316). If the preferences of the individual satisfy a certain reasonable set of rationality axioms, they must define a cardinal SWF equal to the sum of the utilities of all individuals in the society. But these utilities are those judged by him rather than the actual utilities of all the individuals, unless we heroically assume that each individual has perfect information not only with respect to the objective but also the subjective circumstances (psychology, ability to enjoy, etc.) of all individuals in different alternatives. Hence the SWFs of different persons thus derived may differ from one another to the extent of the lack of factual information and differences in personal judgements regarding the utilities of other individuals, not to mention the possibility of false preferences. We are still left with the decision of choosing among or aggregating the various individual SWFs, and have to face the paradox of social choice at this level.

Sen (1969) shows that, if we are interested only in the best social alternative, rather than the social ordering of all the alternatives, then the impossibility theorem does not apply. In other words, it is possible to have a social *choice* function which denotes the best or chosen alternative while satisfying all Arrow's requirements. However, with one addditonal reasonable condition Sen is able to revive the impossibility theorem in relation to social choice function. This additional condition requires that if both x and y are in the chosen set out of a set S_1, then if x is chosen from a larger set S_2 that includes S_1, so must y be chosen (Sen, 1969b, p. 384, 1970, p. 17). The fact that the relaxation of social rationality does not provide a very promising escape route is further confirmed by a number of contributions (e.g. Mas-Colell & Sonnenschein, 1972*, Fishburn, 1974*, Ferejohn & Grether, 1977b*) establishing impossibility results with very mild requirements on social rationality such as acyclicity (of strict preferences).

Despite Arrow's theorem, the actual functioning of democractic vot-

---

†Or, rather, if he had an equal chance of being "put in the place of" any individual member of the society, with regard not only to his objective social (and economic) conditions, but also to his subjective attitudes and tastes. In other words, he ought to judge the utility of another individual's position not in terms of his own attitudes and tastes but rather in terms of the attitudes and tastes of the individual actually holding this position — Harsanyi's note.

ing systems seem to work well or at least seems to be acceptable. What is the explanation? There are a number of contributions which may provide such an explanation, and question, with partial success, the significance of Arrow's theorem. Thus Tullock (1967a) attempts to show that the theorem is not important in practice. While no decision process will meet Arrow's conditions perfectly, a very common decision process meets them to a very high degree of approximation, and this explains the practical success of democracy. The General Impossibility Theorem is therefore generally irrelevant in this sense. Arrow admits that Tullock (1967b) has 'argued convincingly that if the distributions of opinions on social issues is fairly uniform and if the dimensionality of the space of social issues is much less than the number of individuals, then majority voting on a sincere basis will be transitive' (Arrow, 1970, p. 19; see also Davis & Hinich, 1966). However, Mackenzie (1967, pp. 144-51) and Taylor (1968) argue that Arrow's theorem is still very relevant in dealing with small voting bodies such as committees which typically consist of small numbers of members. In a computer simulation it has been shown that 'the difference made by adding more dimensions is small . . . that percentage of cycles declines as the numbers of committee members increases' (Tullock & Campbell, 1970, p. 101). But 'it has not been demonstrated that cycles in small committees are trivial, nor has it been shown that they are important' (Tullock & Campbell, 1970, p. 104; see also Sen 1970a, pp. 163-6 and references therein).

While majority voting may be acceptable as a workable rule on the level of practical decision, even a minute probability of cycles is quite disturbing on the level of logic. Though majority voting will be used for a long time to come, theorists will keep searching for a better alternative, if not the ideal. We have examined some representative attempts in this search and have found them wanting in some respect or other. In the next section, we shall discuss two other attempts both involving ways of revealing the intensities of preferences.

5.4* Revealing the Intensities of Preferences

Numerous ways of revealing the intensities of individual preferences (rather than just orderings) have been proposed, some of which are discussed in the preceding section; two further approaches merit special discussion.

5.4.1 Finite Sensibility and Welfare Aggregate

The first approach is based on the concept of finite sensibility, the recognition of the fact that human beings are not infinitely discriminative. For example, suppose an individual prefers two spoons of sugar (x) to one (y) in his coffee. If we increase the amount of sugar continuously from one spoon, we will reach a point y' (say 1.8 spoons) for which he cannot tell the difference between x and y'. There may exist another point y'' (say 1.6 spoons) for which he is indifferent to y' but he prefers x to y''. Hence, with finite sensibility, a perfectly rational individual may have intransitive indifference.

The concept of finite sensibility was touched on as far back as 1781 by Borda and in 1881 by Edgeworth. (Thus, when I was giving a seminar at Nuffield College early in 1974, upon which my 1975a paper is based, a participant interjected, 'Why can't you wait a few more years until 1981?') Edgeworth took it as axiomatic, or, in his words 'a first principle incapable of proof', that the 'minimum sensibile' or the just-perceivable increments of pleasures for all persons, are equatable (Edgeworth, 1881, pp. 7ff., pp. 60 ff.). Armstrong (1951), Goodman & Markowitz (1952), and Rothenberg (1961) have also discussed the problem. It has also been explored in decision theory and the psychological literature, using the term 'just noticeable difference'. (See Fishburn, 1970b, for a survey.)

With intransitivity of indifference, the (explicit) preference of an individual can no longer be represented by a utility function U^i such that $xR^iy \Leftrightarrow U^i(x) \geqslant U^i(y)$. However, it can be shown that his 'underlying preference' (roughly speaking, his preference if he were infinitely sensitive) may still be represented by a utility function.[†] In terms of his

---

[†] Luce (1956) defines a semiorder which effectively requires that two levels of preference should overbalance one level of indifference, i.e. $xPyPzIw \Rightarrow xPw$, etc. Fishburn (1973*) provides necessary and sufficient conditions for a semiorder to be closed-interval representable. These conditions involve some very technical concepts of countability and density requirements. Ng (1975a) provides sufficiency proof of representation by adopting standard assumptions on explicit preference and showing that the underlying preference must then satisfy certain conditions well-known to ensure the existence of utility functions.

explicit preference, the utility function may be scaled to have the following property: $yP^ix \Leftrightarrow U^i(y) - U^i(x) > a$; $xR^iy \Leftrightarrow U^i(y) - U^i(x) \leqslant a$, where a is a constant, i.e. any positive number (e.g. one) used to represent a utility difference of a maximal indifference. Using this utility function for each individual and some assumptions of purely technical nature, Ng (1975a) shows that the only acceptable SWF is just the unweighted sum of individual utilities (the Bentham SWF), if the following value premise is accepted. (For other arguments in favour of utilitarianism, see Fleming, 1952, Harsanyi, 1955, Maskin, 1978, Sugden & Weale, 1979, and Ng, 1981c, for a survey.)

Weak Majority Preference Criterion (WMP): *For any two alternatives x and y, if no individual prefers y to x, and (1) if I, the number of individuals, is even, at least I/2 individuals prefer x to y; (2) if I is odd, at least (I-1)/2 individuals prefer x to y and at least another individual's utility level is not lower in x than in y, then social welfare is higher in x than in y.*

The reason why WMP leads us to the utilitarian SWF is not difficult to see. The criterion WMP requires that utility differences sufficient to give rise to preferences of half of the population must be regarded as socially more significant than utility differences not sufficient to give rise to preferences (or dispreferences) of another half. Since any group of individuals comprising 50 per cent of the population is an acceptable half, this effectively makes a just-perceivable increment of utility of any individual an interpersonally comparable unit. This is illustrated below.

Confining to the case where the number of individuals is even, as long as 50 per cent of the population are made noticeably better off and the other 50 per cent unnoticeably worse off, social welfare increases according to WMP. Conversely, as long as 50 per cent are made noticeably worse off and the other 50 per cent unnoticeably better off, social welfare decreases. Thus, taking the limit, social welfare stays unchanged as 50 per cent of the population are made just unnoticeably better off and the other 50 per cent just unnoticeably worse off (reasonably assuming that social welfare is a continuous function of individual utilities).

In Figure 5.2 (Ng & Singer, 1981) all the I individuals are arranged along the horizontal axis and individual utilities are represented by the vertical axis. Starting from an initial situation x, let the curve x repre-

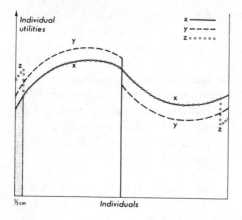

Figure 5.2

sent the utilities of the various individuals. For example, if each individual occupies a distance of one-third of a centimetre (along the horizontal axis), the utility of the first individual in situation x is the shaded area. The curve x need not be continuous. This does not affect our argument. Consider another situation y which, in comparison to x, involves making the first $I/2$ individuals just unnoticeably better off and the rest just unnoticeably worse off. From WMP and the argument of the preceding paragraph, social welfare remains unchanged. Now, starting from situation y (see the curve y), consider another situation z. In comparison to y, z involves making another 50 per cent (the first individual, and the second half of all individuals except the last one) unnoticeably better off and the other 50 per cent (the last individual and the first half of all individuals except the first) unnoticeably worse off. Hence, social welfare again remains unchanged. Since there is no change between x and y, or between y and z, social welfare must be the same at x as at z. Comparing x and z, we see that all have exactly the same levels of utilities except the first and the last individuals. The first individual's utility has increased by two units and the last decreased by two units. This demonstration does not depend on the choice of these two particular individuals, since WMP applies to any 50 per cent of individuals. Thus we may conclude that, irrespective of the initial situation, if we increase the utility of any one individual by two units and decrease that of any other by two units, holding those of all others unchanged, social welfare must remain unchanged. Effectively, this will lead us to the Bentham SWF of the unweighted sum of individual utilities. (See Ng, 1975a, for a formal proof.)

But is WMP an acceptable value premise? Roughly speaking, WMP says that, if at least half of the people say 'yes' and no one says 'no', then a change must be recommended. As a sufficiency condition, it is much more acceptable than majority rule and the Pareto principle. The latter says that, if some individual prefers x to y and no individual prefers y to x, then the society should prefer x to y. In addition to this, WMP requires that at least half of the population prefer x to y. Thus anyone who accepts *either* the Pareto principle *or* majority rule must logically accept WMP.

It may be objected that, with finite sensibility, the Pareto principle should refer to the underlying preferences and not the explicit preferences. The WMP criterion is not necessarily weaker than this interpretation of the Pareto principle. Nevertheless, I find that WMP is a very acceptable premise on its own. Ideally, as a variable in the SWF, the preference of an individual should refer to his actual feeling of well-being, not an ex-ante revelation of preference or actual choice. Though we may have to use revealed preferences except where divergences are significant and obvious, in principle we are referring to actual feeling. Now, in comparing two social states x and y, if no individual feels worse off and a majority feel better off at x, there seems to be no ground to deny that social welfare is higher at x. (Here we abstract from possible differences in the welfare of other sentients such as animals. Personally, I would put them into the SWF.) If a majority prefers x to y, it may be better to choose y provided the minority *more strongly* prefers y to x. But for the case satisfying WMP, there is no individual in the minority who *feels* any worse off, not to mention 'more strongly worse off'.

The main objection to WMP and the resulting Benthamite SWF is that it may lead to very unequal distribution of income. Apart from in-centive effects, it is doubtful that differences in sensibility will lead to a great inequality of income if we apply the Bentham SWF. Psychological studies in pain sensation show that the pain thresholds are very close for different individuals (e.g. averaging 230 ± 10 standard variation), as are the number of just noticeable differences (Hardy, 1952, pp. 88,

157). If there are more differences in the capacity to enjoy income, these are probably due to 'learning by doing' and a long-run SWF will take account of that.

If we ask ourselves why do we want to give more weight to the poor, we may have a number of answers. The most obvious one is that incomes of the poor meet more urgent needs. But this is taken care of by reckoning in terms of utilities instead of incomes. Secondly, it may be said that the consumption of the rich is self-defeating due, e.g. to the snob effect, the desire to keep up with the Joneses, etc., while the consumption of the poor (if spent on, say, education and health) may have very beneficial long-run effects. This again can be taken care of by allowing for all forms of externalities, etc. If some inequality still persists after taking all effects into account, I cannot see why this is not an optimal distribution if it maximises aggregate welfare. Consider the much-cherished principle, 'From each according to his ability; to each according to his needs' (which I personally approve of, assuming no disincentive effect). Why doesn't it read, 'An equal amount of work from each; an equal amount of income to each?' If a weak man is tired by four hours of work, it is better for a stronger man to work longer to relieve him. Similarly, if a less sensitive man does not enjoy the extra income much, it is better that a more sensitive man receives more of it. What prevents us from seeing such a simple analogy?

For choices involving risk, there is a problem as to whether we should maximise welfare as a function of expected utilities, i.e. $WE = W(E^1, \ldots, E^I) \equiv W(\Sigma_{s=1}^{S} \theta_s U_s^1, \ldots, \Sigma_{s=1}^{S} \theta_s U_s^I)$, or expected welfare as a function of *ex-post* utilities, i.e. $EW = \Sigma_{s=1}^{S} \theta_s W(U_s^1, \ldots, U_s^I)$, where θ_s is the probability of state s and S is the number of all possible states. There seem to be good grounds for adopting either method. If welfare is a sum (unweighted or weighted with constant individual weights k^i) of utilities, then the two methods are equivalent. Thus $EW = \Sigma_s \theta_s \Sigma_i k^i U_s^i = \Sigma_i k^i \Sigma_s \theta_s U_s^i = WE$. Hence the Bentham SWF we obtained frees us from the agonising choice of maximising WE or EW, and we may use either one, as convenience dictates. Looking at the matter from the opposite sequence, one may say that the fact that EW and WE are both appropriate objective functions lends support to WMP and the Bentham SWF. If welfare is not a sum of individual utilities, then the maximisation of EW or WE will not, in general, yield the same result.† Therefore, if either one is a reasonable objective function, the other cannot be so unless social welfare is a sum of individual utilities.

The acceptance of WMP (and the resulting Benthamite SWF) has far-reaching implications spelt out briefly in Ng (1975a, section 8) and in more detail in Ng (1975U). Here we shall just discuss the implication with respect to social choice. If we adopt the rule of basing our social ordering on the summation of individual utilities, it can be seen that the rule will satisfy all Arrow's axioms and conditions (except the ordering aspect of IIA) as well as some other reasonable conditions such as anonymity, neutrality, and path-independency (on which, see Plott, 1973*, and Ferejohn & Grether, 1977a*). Anonymity is satisfied since every individual is treated similarly in the summation of utilities. With the fulfilment of anonymity, nondictatorship is satisfied *a fortiori*. It is also obvious that the Pareto principle (either weak or strong version) is satisfied since $xP^iy \Rightarrow U^i(x) > U^i(y)$. The utilitarian decision rule can also be shown to be 'responsive' to individual preferences in a stricter sense (Arrow, 1977U). However, since the ordering aspect of IIA is not satisfied, our rule does not constitute a counter-example to Arrow's theorem. Nevertheless, having taken account of the intensities of preferences, this ordering aspect becomes itself irrelevant. Thus our analysis shows that the paradox of social choice can be resolved, at least in principle, on a rational basis satisfying reasonable conditions. But the practical problems of doing so remain very real, due to the difficulties of utility measurement. In this sense, Arrow's theorem is still very significant. However, these practical difficulties can be reduced by using indirect measurement, as suggested in Ng (1975a). Another way of measuring preferences is the second approach we are going to discuss, the incentive compatible mechanism for preference revelation or the demand revealing process.

---

† If WE and EW always yield the same result, we have $WE = W(\Sigma_s \theta_s U_s^1, \ldots, \Sigma_s \theta_s U_s^I) = EW = \Sigma_s \theta_s W(U_s^1, \ldots, U_s^I)$. Differentiation with respect to U_s^i gives $\partial W / \partial E^i = \partial W / \partial U_s^i$ at any given situation. Such an equality cannot hold through for every set of θ's unless W is a sum (unweighted or weighted with constant individual weights) of its arguments.

5.4.2 An Incentive Compatible Mechanism for Preference Revelation

The incentive compatible mechanism for preference revelation was independently proposed by Clarke (1971) and Groves (1970U, 1973). (Both presented conference papers in 1970. Vickrey discussed a similar mechanism in 1961 but was not aware of its full significance.) Tideman & Tullock (1976) conspicuously bring the mechanism in relation to the problem of social choice. Here we shall discuss the simple case of two alternatives: the treatment of the continuous case can be found in Section 8.3 in relation to public goods.

The essence of the preference revelation mechanism is to ask each individual to state the (maximum) amount of money he is willing to pay to have his preferred alternative; but, instead of actually paying this stated amount, he has to pay – if his 'vote' changes the society's decision – an amount (i.e. the Clarke-Groves tax) equal to the cost (of so changing the social choice) on the rest of the society. The social choice is simply decided by calculating (summing over all individuals) the total amount of money voted for each alternative and the one with the highest figure is chosen. (We shall consider a generalisation to avoid the predominant influence of the rich presently.) Consider the simple case of four voters illustrated in Table 5.1. If all voters vote sincerely, alternative x will be chosen since $20 > 19$. Voter 1's stated figure of \$8 is effective in shifting social choice from y to x. He has thus to pay \$7 (= \$10 + \$9 − \$12), the cost of so shifting social choice on the rest of the society. Similarly, voter 2 has to pay \$11 (= \$10 + \$9 − \$8).

TABLE 5.1

Voter	Differential values of alternatives	
	x	y
1	8	0
2	12	0
3	0	9
4	0	10
Total	20	19

Voters 3 and 4 do not have to pay since their votes do not affect the outcome.

Will the above mechanism provide the correct incentive to voters to reveal their true preferences. Take voter 3 who prefers y to x. If \$9 reflects his true preference, exaggerating by less than \$1 does not change the outcome. To change the social choice into y, he has to state a figure of more than \$10 (exaggerating by more than \$1). But if y is chosen due to exaggeration, he has to pay \$10 (= \$8 + \$12 − \$10) which is more than he really wishes to pay to have y. Acting on his own, each individual will find it to his own advantage to report truthfully. (We ignore here the problem of the disposal of the Clarke–Groves taxes which are discussed in Section 8.3.) However, if voters 3 and 4 come together, they may agree to state the figures of, say \$30 and \$40 respectively. If voters 1 and 2 do not engage in such collusion, voters 3 and 4 will have shifted the social choice in their favour at no cost to themselves, as each of them has to pay nothing (since \$12 + \$8 < \$30). It is true that the problem of collusion and strategic misrepresentation is present in other voting schemes as well, but the Clarke–Groves mechanism is especially vulnerable in this respect.† In fact, if no other voters engage in collusion, any two voters preferring the same alternative can always ensure its choice at no cost to them by each stating an arbitrarily large figure. (The 'optimal mechanism' of Groves & Ledyard, 1977a, is less vulnerable but is not coalition-proof.) Thus, an essential condition for the mechanism to work is to ensure non-collusion, a very difficult task to achieve in practice. (see, however, Tideman & Tullock, 1981, and Section 8.3* below.)

Even forgetting about the difficulty created by collusion, the preference revelation mechanism is still unlikely to be acceptable as a method

---

†In fact, all non-dictatorial voting (using only 'rankings' or orderings) on more than two alternatives are manipulable by misrepresentation (Gibbard, 1973*, Satterthwaite, 1975*). Most reasonable decision processes using only orderings are manipulable by even a *single* individual. The Clarke–Groves mechanism overcomes this to a large extent. On the difference in approach between the 'strategies' and the 'revelation' literatures, see Sen (1978U). On strategic voting, see also Barbera (1977)*, Dummett & Farquharson (1961), Farquharson (1969), Pattanaik (1978), Sengupta (1978)*, and a special symposium issue of *Review of Economic Studies* (scheduled for April 1979)* on incentive-compatible mechanisms and strategic voting. Blin & Satterthwaite (1978) show the logical similarity of Arrow's theorem and the impossibility of strategy-proof group decisions. For a collection of papers on these and related issues, see Laffont (1979).

of social choice since most people would regard it as giving 'unduly' high influence to the rich. This difficulty is partly solved by a generalisation of the mechanism proposed by Good (1977). Instead of calculating the *unweighted* sum of (dollar) figures by all individuals for each alternative, we calculate the sum using any weight for each individual as desired.† For example, if we want to discount the figure voted by a rich man, his $10 may count only as $5. The reverse weight is used for calculating his tax. If he has to pay $2 for the unweighted case, he now has to pay $4. This method allows us to use differential weighting without damaging the incentive for preference revelation. Good (1977, p. 66) suggests that a possible weighting system is the inverse proportionality to wealth (financial + human). Since human wealth is very difficult to estimate, it is more practical that income is used as a proxy. With this inverse proportionality weighting system, a rich man will have the same degree of influence as a poor man. Whether this is desirable, it seems to me, depends on the nature of the issue of social choice involved. For political issues such as the election of a president or a parliament, it is consistent with democratic tradition to let all voters, rich or poor, have the same voting power. For economic issues, it seems that a distinction between two different types of issues is necessary. Problems like the provision of public (final) goods concern the consumption or enjoyment of the fruit of production. For this class of issue, the adoption of the inverse proportionality weighting system seems to suggest that the distribution of the fruit of production should be absolutely egalitarian. In practice, we need some degree of inequality to maintain incentives. Given this, it is inefficient to adopt a weighting system. (A fuller development of this argument against weighting can be found in Appendix 9A.) On the other hand, problems like the regulation of the process of production and distribution (patent, tariff, etc.) fall into a different class. The fact that society agrees to let a more hard-working man have a larger share in the fruit of production does not mean that he should also have a larger say with respect to future production and distribution. Otherwise, those who become rich by luck, illegal means, and/or initial hard work may be able to perpetuate their riches without further effort.

†Or, more generally, the original figure for each individual i can be transformed into another figure using a continuous strictly increasing bounded function f^i such that $f^i(0) = 0$.

Apart from the problem of collusion, the Clarke-Groves mechanism is by no means ideal. For one thing, if income effects are not negligible, social choice generated by the scheme may be cyclic. This is so because the amount of money a person is prepared to pay to have x instead of z need not be equal to the amount he is willing to pay to have x instead of y plus the amount he is willing to pay to have y instead of z, even given xP^iyP^iz. Thus I am willing to pay $10,000 to prevent the little finger on my left hand from being cut off. After losing it, I would be willing to pay $11,000 to prevent the loss of the little finger on the right. However, I am willing to pay only $19,000 ($< $10,000 + $11,000) to prevent the loss of both fingers. This is so because the first $10,000 was not actually paid. If I had to actually pay it, I would be only willing to pay $9,000 to prevent the loss of the second finger. Thus the cyclicity involved is similar to the contradiction in the Kaldor-Hicks compensation test. In fact, the use of the Groves-Clarke mechanism is the application of compensation test plus an ingenious design to motivate preference revelation. (Cf. Groves, 1979.)

In closing this section, it may be reiterated that the practical difficulties of using the cardinal utility approach remain very real. However, since this approach seems to provide the most sensible way out of the paradox of social choice and since all practical solutions are not ideal in every respect, further work to reduce the shortcomings of this approach seems desirable.

5.5 The Possibility of a Paretian Liberal

Since readers who encountered the topic of social choice for the first time may have found this chapter a little tough going, I shall try to placate them by closing it with a light section discussing informally the 'impossibility of a Paretian liberal' discovered by Sen (1970c).

The (weak) Pareto principle says that if everyone prefers x to y, the society should prefer x to y. Liberalism says that there are certain choices which an individual should have a decisive say irrespective of the preferences of others. 'Whether you should sleep on your back or on your belly is a matter in which the society should permit you absolute freedom, even if a majority of the community is nosey enough to feel that you must sleep on your back' (Sen, 1970c, p. 152). Both principles seem extremely reasonable, but Sen says that it is inconsistent to adhere to them simultaneously. He illustrates this impossibility by the following interesting example.

There is one copy of a certain book, say *Lady Chatterley's Lover* (or should we say *Portnoy's Complaint* instead?), which is viewed differently by two individuals J and K. The three alternatives under consideration are: that J reads it (x), that K reads it (y), and that no one reads it (z). Madam J, who is a prude, prefers most that no one should read it, but given the choice between either of the two reading it, she would prefer reading it herself rather than exposing gullible Mr K to bad influences. (Prudes, as Sen was told, tend to prefer to be censors rather than being censored.) Mr K however, prefers that either of them should read the wonderful book rather than neither. Furthermore, he takes delight in the thought that prudish J may have to read the book, and his first preference is that J should read it. The set of individual orderings we have is thus

$$zP^J xP^J y; \quad xP^K yP^K z.$$

For the choice between x and z, i.e. between J reading the book or no one reading it, liberalism dictates that J's own preference should be decisive; no one should be forced to read a book he doesn't like. So the society should prefer z to x. Similarly, for the choice between y and z, K's preference should be decisive. Hence the society should prefer y to z. From the Pareto principle, the society should prefer x to y since all individuals prefer x to y. So social preference becomes cyclic, as $xPyPzPx$. Liberalism seems to be inconsistent with (even the weak) Pareto principle.

Despite Sen's impossibility result, I still profess to be a Paretian liberal, as most readers probably would. Partly because of space limitation and partly as an exercise, I leave it to readers to think of a way out of Sen's paradox themselves. The interested reader is referred to the discussion by Aldrich (1977), Farrell (1976), Gibbard (1974), Ng (1971b, 1973U), Rowley (1978), Gaertner & Krüger, 1981, etc. (For a survey, see Sen, 1976.) Readers interested in the topic of social choice are referred to recent surveys by Mueller (1976, 1979), Sen (1977a, forthcoming), Kelly (1977), and to Roberts (1980a,b,c)* for a comprehensive analysis of questions of interpersonal comparison, cardinality, inter *vs* intra-profile approaches.

Summary

Arrow's impossibility theorem shows that any rule used to derive a social ordering from individual orderings is undesirable in some respect. Majority rule does not provide a consistent social ordering since it may be cyclic. The Little–Samuelson attempt to dismiss Arrow's theorem as irrelevant to welfare economics is countered by Kemp, Ng, and Parks, who have established impossibility results even operating within a given set of individual orderings. Other attempts to bypass Arrow's paradox by restricting individual preferences, relaxing social rationality, etc., are shown to be restrictive and/or undesirable in some respects. A more promising escape is to attempt to reveal the intensities of individual preferences and hence to operate beyond just individual *orderings*. Using the concept of finite sensibility, a marginal indifference can be used as an interpersonally comparable unit of utility. The Weak Majority Preference Criterion says that x should be preferred to y if no one prefers y to x and at least half of the population prefer x to y. With this criterion it is shown that the rule of social choice must be the utilitarian SWF of the unweighted sum of individual utilities. The relevance of the 'incentive-compatible mechanism' for social choice is also discussed.

APPENDIX 5A**

The Incompatibility of Individualism and Ordinalism

In the proof of their impossibility propositions that there does not exist a reasonable SWF or social ordering based only on individual ordinal preferences, Kemp & Ng (1976) use a condition (Orderings Only, i.e. the second requirement of condition 3 in Section 5.2) which is very objectionable in itself (Samuelson, 1977). However, it reflects the requirement that social ordering is to be based on and only on individual *orderings*. The fact that, in combination with other reasonable conditions, we get an impossibility result means that if we want to have a reasonable social ordering, it cannot be based only on individual orderings. Either cardinal preference information or something other than individual preference is needed. In other words, either ordinalism or individualism has to give way. Let us first discuss this informally before proving a formal proposition and commenting on a related paper by Mayston (1980). First we have to state the condition of orderings only formally.

(A3) Orderings Only: *The social ordering of any two social alternatives depends only on the I individual orderings of the alternatives. Formally, for any (not necessarily distinct) x, y, z, w, if $(x\bar{R}^i y \Leftrightarrow z\bar{R}^i w$ for all i) then $(x\bar{R}y \Leftrightarrow z\bar{R}w)$, where $\bar{R}^i$ stands for one (not necessarily the same for all i) of P^i, I^i, and contra P^i, and the $\bar{R}$ stands for one of P, I, and contra P.* (Kemp & Ng 1976, with minor notational changes; note also the unconventional notation $\bar{R}$ which may stand for *contra* preference.)

To see the implication of this condition (A3), consider Samuelson's example of a society with 100 units of chocolates to be distributed to two self-centring individuals who prefer more chocolates to less. (A3) implies that if it is socially preferable to take something (say 1 or 50 chocolates) from J who had all the chocolates in order to give to K who had none, then it must be socially desirable to give all the chocolates to K. This is clearly a very unreasonable implication. I myself will stay with Samuelson to be the last group of persons on earth to accept it. (Nay! I will never accept it.) But I shall argue that the only acceptable alternative is to reject either individualism or ordinalism.

Most people find it reasonable to take some chocolates from J (who had all 100 units) and give them to K because otherwise K would be starving. Those units of chocolates given to K meet more urgent needs than if consumed by J. But this is speaking in terms of cardinal utilities. In purely ordinal utility terms, we cannot distinguish whether an individual prefers 50 units to 0 unit more strongly than he prefers 100 units to 50 units. However, for those (myself included) who find it sensible to speak in terms of intensities of preference, it is quite sensible to use the cardinal utility approach. It is the pure ordinalists who cannot accept this.

Is there an alternative way out of the Kemp-Ng impossibility? Yes, by rejecting individualism. Social preference then need not be based only on individual preferences (cardinal or ordinal). In particular, social preference may depend on the objective specification of social states such as the amounts of commodities consumed by individuals. For example, the particular social state (50, 50) (i.e. 50 units of chocolates to each individual) may be selected as the best alternative based on the objective amounts of chocolates consumed and not on the cardinal utility approach of urgent versus not urgent needs of the last paragraph. But it is clearly unreasonable to base social choice on objective specification of social states irrespective of individual preferences. What if the 100 units of chocolates are very essential to J who uses them to cure a curious disease while K only slightly prefers more chocolates to less and uses them for the fun of throwing them into the sea and could have used a slightly inferior substitute of stones in abundant supply? Should not (100, 0) be socially preferable to (50, 50). What if K is not self-centring and both individuals prefer (100, 0) to (50, 50)? Clearly, social preference based on objective specification of social states may violate the Pareto principle. To avoid this violation, the so-called social preference over the objective specifiction of social states has to be carefully designed to be consistent with individual preferences, especially in a multi-commodity society with diverse individual preferences. To be consistent with the Pareto principle, social choice has to be confined to the Pareto optimal frontier determined by individual preferences. If social ranking of a pair of alternatives in this frontier is based only on individual orderings, we have (A3). (More on this below.) If it is based on intensities of preferences as well, we have to reject ordinalism. It cannot be said to be based on the objective specification of social states since what social states are in this Pareto-optimal frontier depends on individual preferences. If we want to stick to individualism, the only relevant differences between different social states are individual ordinal and cardinal preferences. Hence, objective specification cannot be used or can only be used as indirect indicator of cardinal preferences if we want to stick to individualism.

Let us now establish the incompatibility of individualism and ordinalism more formally. Let the set of individuals be denoted by $N = \{1, \ldots, i, \ldots, I\}$ and the set of social alternatives be denoted by S. Let μ be the set of all numerically bounded functions which may be defined on $S \times N$. Any *set* of individual preferences (cardinal or ordinal) is then represented by some $u \in \mu$. In other words, $u(x, i)$ is the utility of individual i in state x. The problem of social choice is to rank each pair of alternatives such that the overall ranking R over S is logically consistent.

Weak Individualism: *Social choice is a function of and only of individual preferences, $R = f(u)$. Non-preference variables do not affect the form of f.*

Independence: *Given non-preference variables, the social ranking between any pair of alternatives (x, y) is a function of and only of individual utilities at these two alternatives. $R(x, y) = g\{u(x), u(y)\}$, where $u(x)$ is the vector $u(x, i)$, $i = 1, \ldots, I$. The form of g may be affected by non-preference variables.*

Independence captures the irrelevance aspect of Arrow's Independence of Irrelevant Alternatives, but does not demand its ordering aspect (Sen, 1970a, pp. 89ff.). It is therefore extremely reasonable (Plott, 1972). Since social alternatives are mutually *exclusive* and each alternative is a complete specification of all the relevant aspects of a social state, one naturally does not want the choice between x and y to be affected by preferences with respect to z.

Combining Weak Individualism and Weak Independence, we have

Individualism: $\forall x, y \in S, R(x, y) = g \{u(x), u(y)\}$ *with the form of g fixed.*

The relative social desirability of any pair of alternatives depends only on the desirabilities (utilities) of these alternatives to the individuals. This is extremely reasonable, remembering again the mutually exclusive nature of social alternatives.

Ordinalism: *If u^1, $u^2 \in \mu$ are such that $u^2(x, i) = \phi^i\{u^1(x, i)\}$ for all x and all i, where ϕ^i is a positive monotonic transformation for each i, then u^1 and u^2 are two equivalent pieces of information (written $u^1 \approx u^2$) and are to be treated similarly.*

Proposition: *Individualism and Ordinalism imply* (A3).

> *Proof*: If the precondition of (A3) is satisfied, $x\overline{R}^i y \Leftrightarrow z\overline{R}^i w$ for all i. Suppose the social ranking is $x\overline{R}y$, we have to show that $z\overline{R}w$. Take a $u^1 \in \mu$ that represents the given set of individual preferences (reminding that each u is defined over $S \times N$). Then from Individualism, $g\{u^1(x), u^1(y)\}$ dictates $x\overline{R}y$. Since $x\overline{R}^iy \Leftrightarrow z\overline{R}^iw$ for all i, we may select a $u^2 \in \mu$ such that $u^2 \approx u^1$ and such that $u^2(z) = u^1(x), u^2(w) = u^1(y)$. From Ordinalism, u^1 and u^2 are to be treated in the same way. Then from Individualism $g\{u^2(z), u^2(w)\}$ will dictate $z\overline{R}w$. Q.E.D.

The proposition above shows that Individualism and Ordinalism imply (A3) (Orderings Only) which presumably no one accepts. If we want to reject (A3) which I think we should, we must either reject Individualism (this rejection is I believe unreasonable) or reject Ordinalism (in my view the only reasonable way out).

Some professed individualistic ordinalist may attempt to get away with the above proposition by saying that there is an element of independence in the definition of Individualism above. By accepting just

Weak Individualism and Ordinalism without accepting Independence, (A3) need not be implied. However, anyone who understands the true meaning of independence will certainly accept it provided he also understands that social states are mutually exclusive and each state is a complete specification of all relevant factors. Most people reject independence on the ground of a misunderstanding. For example, it is often said that whether one (and society) prefers Carter or Reagan to be the president may depend on whether a potential third candidate (L) is alive or dead. For example, one may believe that Reagan is a better president if L is around to do some mischief and Carter is better if L is not around. Then one's choice between two alternatives may depend on a third. This however is based on an incomplete specification of social states. If whether L is around is a relevant consideration, then a complete specification will not just involve Carter versus Reagan but rather Carter with L around; Carter without L; Reagan with L; etc. This may pose some practical difficulties in the actual election of candidates but does not pose a problem at the level of generality we are operating on.

Since social states are mutually exclusive, it is perfectly reasonable that, if social preference is to depend only on individual preferences, the social ranking of any two alternatives must be a function only of the individual rankings of and/or intensities of preferences between these two alternatives. In other words, Individualism as we defined it, though it may be said to incorporate an element of independence, is truly individualism and is quite reasonable.

It is true that, due to the lack of perfect information to reveal the intensities of individual preferences, we may wish to use the number of intermediate alternatives (or rather steps of preferences) to give us a rough guide as to the intensity of preference (Goodman & Markowitz, 1952, Mayston, 1975U*). But the use of intermediate alternatives is reasonable only if it gives us some indication of the intensity of preference. Then independence is not really violated. Rather, the availability of the intermediate alternatives just give us more information about intensities of individual preferences on the relevant alternatives. Social ranking of any two alternatives is still a function of these individual preferences of these two alternatives. In fact, with finite sensibility and enough information on the intermediate alternatives, we could go all the way to construct fully cardinal utility functions and base our social choice on these cardinal utilities (Section 5.4.1). On the other hand, if the intermediate alternatives do not provide or are not regarded as providing an indication of the intensity of preference, then it is unreasonable to use the number of intermediate alternatives or any other aspects of other alternatives to determine the social ranking of any given two alternatives. For example, suppose $xP^J yP^J z$ and $yP^K zP^K x$. Is it reasonable to say that y should be socially preferred to x since J prefers x to y in one step but K prefers y to x in two steps? When we introduce more alternatives, we may find that the one step becomes 10 steps and the two steps remain at two steps, even if the individual ordinal and cardinal preferences with respect to all the alternatives remain unchanged. Thus, unless intermediate alternatives can give us some indication of preference intensity, they should not alter social ranking. This can be seen even more clearly in the following case.

Consider the divisible case with an uncountable infinity of alternatives and infinite sensibility. Let us also confine attention to the intermediate range (in which no individual is in bliss or in hell) which is usually the only relevant range in practice. (If one believes in the general possibility of individualistic ordinalism, then presumably one has to tackle this case.) Then for any individual, and for any relevant social alternative x, there is an uncountable infinity of alternatives preferred to, indifferent to, and inferior to x. And for any two relevant alternatives x, y such that not $xI^i y$ there is an uncountable infinity of alternatives 'in between' x and y. Thus, if we eschew information about the objective amounts of commodities, etc., and consider only individual orderings, we see that, for any two pairs of alternatives x and y, z and w, if $xP^J y$, $zP^J w$, $yP^K x$, $wP^K z$ (no other individual or all others are indifferent), the standing of x against y with respect to individual orderings is exactly the same as that of z against w, even if account is taken of the number of alternatives or steps of preferences in between, above and/or below. Then if we choose $x\bar{R}y$, how can we not choose $z\bar{R}w$ *if* social choice is to be based only on individual orderings? Hence, unreasonable as it is, (A3) has to be accepted if social choice is to be based only on individual orderings.

Consider Figure 5A.1a where the arrows indicate the direction of individual preferences. Suppose that social choice is xIy. Mayston (1980) argues that, contrary to (A3) which requires zIw, we should have wPz due to 'secondary Pareto dominance'. This is very reasonable (given xIy) since the difference between z and w is less than the difference

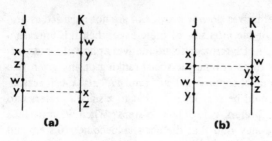

Figure 5A.1

between x and y for J but the reverse is true for K. If society regards the preference of x over y by J as just overbalanced by the dispreference of K and declares xIy, then it is reasonable to require wPz as argued convincingly by Mayston. However, Mayston fails to see that, unless we rely on information concerning the intensity of preference (violating ordinalism) and/or nonpreference information (violating individualism), we simply cannot declare xIy to begin with without also committing ourselves to zIw, and thus violating secondary Pareto dominance. To see this, consider Figure 5A.1b which is derived from Figure 5A.1a by just compressing the scale of K. Since absolute scale is arbitrary for ordinal preferences, both figures give us exactly the same ordinal information. Then, instead of declaring xIy, why not declare wIz instead which implies xPy from secondary Pareto dominance? As far as individual orderings are concerned, the standing of x against y is exactly the same as the standing of z against w. Unless we use something other than individual orderings (intensities of preferences of non-individualist procedures such as tossing a coin or relying on objective specification), there is just no way of discriminating between the two pairs. (In Mayston's language, the required social weighting function or social marginal rates of equivalence cannot be constructed at all.)

From the above discussion, it may be concluded that if we do not want to accept (A3) with its unreasonable implications, we must reject either individualism or ordinalism. A reasonable individualistic ordinalist exists only under illusion. (At the risk of being redundant, may I add that the above argument against ordinalism in no way affects the sufficiency of ordinalism for the analysis of a consumer's choice instead of social choice.)

6 The Optimal Distribution of Income

6.1 Conceptual Determination of Optimal Distribution

What is the optimal distribution of income? As any constrained optimisation problem, this depends on the form of the objective function and that of the constraint. Since we are interested in optimality from the social point of view, the relevant objective function is the SWF. The relevant constraint can be expressed as a utility possibility frontier if we agree that social welfare is a function of individual utilities. (Or individual welfares. Abstracting away the differences between preference and welfare, the two are equivalent; see Section 1.3.) Factors other than individual utilities are either regarded as not relevant to social welfare or are being held constant. In Section 2.2.1 we derived a utility possibility frontier by taking the outer envelope of the numerous utility possibility curves each corresponding to a specific collection of goods. This may be regarded as rather restrictive or purely economic, since, by varying only the collection of goods, other (social, etc.) factors must be held constant. By changing these other factors, a different utility possibility frontier may emerge. Conceptually, this generalisation can easily be taken into account by taking the outer envelope of the various utility possibility frontier, calling it the grand utility possibility frontier. Second, we may also take account of the possible costs of and constraints on redistribution which reduces the grand utility possibility frontier into the grand utility feasibility frontier (GUFF). (On the relationship between a utility *possibility* and utility *feasibility* curves or frontiers; see Figure 3.2.)

Given a GUFF, the point of optimal distribution depends on the form of the SWF. This is most vividly illustrated in Figure 6.1 for the simple case of two (or two groups of) individuals. The given GUFF is the curve UU'. It does not extend beyond the point U and U' as, e.g. a constraint defining GUFF is that each individual must not be pushed lower than his 'misery point'. The frontier has an upward-sloping section on each end (UD and $U'A$), reflecting the fact that, as one individual is made very worse off, the other suffers as well, due to sympathy or fear of a revolution perhaps. If we accept the Pareto principle, the upward-sloping sections are ruled out and the choice is confined to the section AD. The point A will be chosen by the élitist (maximax) SWF maximising the utility of the best-off individual (J). In contrast, the point D will be chosen by the Rawlsian (maximin) SWF maximising the utility of the worst off individual (K). Both these points are clearly extreme choices since they imply zero trade-off or vertical and horizontal welfare contours respectively. For example, a policy-maker acting in accordance with the maximin SWF would be prepared to sacrifice enormous amounts of utilities of other people (including the second worst off) even if that will increase the utility of the worst off only marginally. The maximax SWF goes to the other extreme. The Bentham SWF selects a point somewhere between these two extremes, specifially, point B where the GUFF touches a highest negatively-sloped 45° line (a Benthamite welfare contour).†

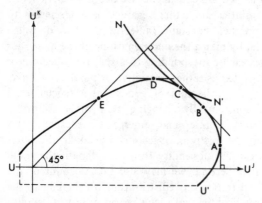

Figure 6.1

†The alleged equivalence of Rawls and classical utilitarianism by Yaari (1981) is based on a number of contrived interpretations and unreasonable assumptions including: the maximum welfare aggregate constrained by resources is a constant (W) independent of the choice of social state and population size (N) so that average welfare can be maximised first (U^*) and then population size chosen to satisfy the constrained welfare aggregate, $N = W/U^*$ (Yaari, 1981, p. 17).

While the maximin point D is an extreme choice within the confine of Paretian SWFs, people with extreme egalitarianism may go beyond it to choose the point E. This involves the blind pursuit of equality as such without regard to its contribution to individual well-being since it opts for equality even at the expense of making all individuals worse off. A more appealing solution is at the point C, the outcome of maximising the product of individual utilities, with welfare contours (e.g. NN') as rectangular hyperbolas. An operational disadvantage of this Nash solution,† in comparison the Bentham solution, is that it is based on individual utility functions with known origins, whilst the Bentham solution is invariant with respect to shifts in these origins. Conceptually, the Nash SWF is open to a stronger objection, especially in the general case of I individuals. If one individual has zero utility, it does not matter whether the other 999,999 individuals have extremely high or extremely low utilities, since the products of utilities in both cases are the same. When some individual utility becomes negative, the Nash SWF becomes ridiculous. Even if we are confined to non-negative utilities, its acceptability is still doubtful since, according to the Nash SWF, $W(U^1 = 1000, U^2 = 1, U^3 = 1, \ldots, U^{1,000,000} = 1) > W(U^1 = 1000, U^2 = 0, U^3 = 1000, U^4 = 1000, \ldots, U^{1,000,000} = 1000)$. But it seems to me clearly ethically desirable to provide decent life for 999,998 fairly miserable individuals even if this involves making an equally miserable Mr 2 a little bit worse off still. Similarly, according to the Nash SWF, $W(U^1 = 2000, U^2 = 1, U^3 = 1, \ldots, U^{1,000,000} = 1) > W(U^1 = 0, U^2 = 1000, U^3 = 1000, \ldots, U^{1,000,000} = 1000)$. But I am prepared to sacrifice 2000 utils of the well-off Mr 1 (whoever he is) if the rest of the one million miserable individuals can be made fairly happy. Even if we exclude zero utility, the above results still follow since any sufficiently small utility will do. (Kaneko & Nakamura's (1979) support of Nash's SWF is based on the objectionable Condition II; see Ng, 1981c.)

The several forms of SWF discussed above are of course only a few out of a large number of possible SWFs. The main point of this section is to show that, given a GUFF, the optimal point depends on the specific form of the SWF. Once a point in the utility space is chosen, not only is the optimal distribution of income determined, but the optimal set of

†Nash (1950). To be fair, it must be noted that Nash was dealing with the more positive problem of the outcome of bargaining, using the initial position as the origin. But the principle of maximising the product of utilities has been used by others (e.g. Fair, 1971) in a normative context.

non-economic policies are also determined, if they are included as variables affecting the feasible combination of utilities. It is possible, though not very likely, that the same point in the utility space can be achieved by two or more different combinations of income distribution and noneconomic policies. If such is the case, society will be indifferent between these combinations.

6.2 Utility Illusion

Since there are numerous forms of SWF, which one should we select? In Section 5.4.1, we note that the acceptance of a very reasonable value premise, the Weak Majority Preference Criterion, implies that we must subscribe to the Bentham SWF. When the utilitarian philosophy was first propounded, it was regarded as a radical principle used to justify such progressive measures as the progressive income taxation. Nowadays, egalitarianism has won so much mileage that many people want to go beyond Bentham and adopt a strictly quasi-concave SWF with welfare contours strictly convex to the origin of utility space such as the Nash welfare contour NN' in Figure 6.1. However, I believe that this is due more to some kind of illusion than to genuine rational ethical radicalism. It is true that problems such as the 'right' form of SWF have to be solved ultimately by resorting to some value judgements which cannot be true or false. Nevertheless, certain value judgements can be shown to imply, or to imply the rejection of, certain other value judgements. Moreover, one may also be able to convince some people that their *adherence* to certain value judgements may be based on illusion. The possibility that strictly convex welfare contours may be based on what I call 'utility illusion' (Ng, 1975a) is discussed below.

If we have to draw our welfare contours not in a utility space but in an income space with axes representing the income levels of different individuals (holding other relevant variables constant), most people will agree that the contours should be convex to the origin. This is due to the belief that, for any given individual, a marginal dollar meets more important needs when his income is low than when his income is high. Hence, the marginal income of an individual is given a diminishing weight as his income increases. We thus have strict convexity in the welfare contours (in an income space). If we use utility not only as an ordinal indicator of choice but also as reflecting the degree of subjective satisfaction, we have, for each individual, diminishing marginal utility of income. Given interpersonal comparison of utility and equal capacity for enjoyment, unequal distribution of a given amount of total income (abstracting from incentive effects, etc.) diminishes total utility by denying more urgent needs and satisfying less urgent ones. This egalitarian ethic may however, be, carelessly carried over to the distribution of utilities. Since unequal distribution of income usually implies unequal distribution of utilities, the two are sometimes regarded as equivalent. Thus unequal distribution of utilities is condemned along with unequal distribution of income.

Consider a simple example. Given a fixed total income of $100, we may prefer ($50; $50) (i.e. $50 to each of the two individuals) to ($70; $30), assuming similar capacity to enjoy income. Then, when asked to choose in terms of utils, we may say we prefer (50 utils; 50 utils) to (70 utils; 30 utils), believing that the former is just a more equal distribution of the same total income as the latter. However, given diminishing marginal utility of income and similar capacity for enjoyment, the former must involve a smaller total income. If our preference for equality in the distribution of a given total income is based on the diminishing marginal utility of income, it does not follow that a more unequal distribution of a *larger* total income is inferior.

If the objection to unequal distribution of a given total income is based only on the diminishing marginal utility of income (plus perhaps such arguments as externality or utility interdependency which can all be taken account of by reckoning in terms of utilities), then the preference for a more equally distributed but smaller aggregate *utility* over a larger aggregate utility must involve double-counting (or double-discounting). A larger but less equally distributed total income is already discounted by reckoning in terms of utilities rather than incomes, with diminishing marginal utility, interpersonal comparability, utility interdependency, etc. If unequal distribution of utilities is again to be discounted, this second level of discounting cannot be based again on the diminishing marginal utility of income or utility interdependency.

6.3 Theories of Optimal Income Distribution and Taxation: Lerner and Mirriees

Classical economists, including Pigou, seemed to be quite free of utility illusion; they justify equal distribution of income mainly on the ground of diminishing marginal utility, assuming equal capacity to enjoy income. Abstracting away such questions as incentive effects, that equal distribution maximises total utility (and hence the Bentham SWF) is an obvious implication of such assumptions. The assumption of diminishing marginal utility of income, which is implied by the Weber–Fechner law (on which, see Section 6.5), is regarded by most people as reasonable. The assumption of equal capacity to enjoy income is open to more criticisms. However, Lerner (1944) successfully relaxes this assumption. Even if different individuals may have quite different capacities to enjoy income, it can be shown that equal distribution of a given total amount of income maximises expected total utility provided that we do not have any knowledge with respect to the capacity levels of different individuals. This argument is illustrated in Figure 6.2 for the case of two individuals.†

The given total amount of income is $O^J O^K$ and the amount given to J is measured rightward from O^J and that given to K is measured leftward from O^K. It can clearly be seen that, with diminishing marginal utility and equal capacity, i.e. when both individuals have the same MU curve such as $MU^{J'}$ and MU^K, equal distribution at the point E maximises total utility. However, if J has a lower MU curve, say MU^J, total utility is maximised at the point A. Starting from the equality point E, if we transfer AE amount of income from J to K, this increases K's utility by $ACDE$ but reduces J's utility only by $ACFE$, with a net gain of CDF. However, if we do not know (even on a probabilistic level) who is more capable of enjoyment, we could equally probably have given EB (= AE) amount of income from K to J. This increases J's utility by $EFHB$ but reduces K's utility by $EDGB$, with a net loss of $FDGH$. Since $FDGH > CDF$, the expected gain of unequal distribution of income with no knowledge of the actual distribution of capacity is negative.

The above argument is based on the assumption that the total amount of income is independent of its distribution. This ignores the costs of achieving the desired distribution, including the disincentive effect. Since factors affecting the ability to earn income (e.g. inheritance, intelligence, motivation, luck, etc.) are not equally distributed, the pre-tax distribution of income is usually far from equal. Consider a

†For a critical survey of Lerner's argument, see Friedman (1947). For formal statements of Lerner's argument, see Sen (1969), McManus, Walton & Coffman (1972). For the generalisation of Lerner's argument to any SWF which is quasi-concave in individual utilities, see Sen (1973b). For variable production, see Bennett (1981).

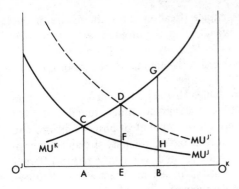

Figure 6.2

principle method of redistribution, income taxation. The more progressive the income taxation, the more equal the post-tax distribution, but the higher is the disincentive effect likely to be. Having to pay a larger proportion of their extra income in taxes, people *tend* to work less and undertake less risky but profitable ventures. It is true that empirical studies are inconclusive with respect to the extent of the disincentive effect of taxation. But empirical studies refer to what may be called the gross disincentive effect which includes the income effect. When the post-tax wage rate is reduced, an individual tends to work less due to the substitution effect but also tends to work more due to the income effect as leisure is probably a non-inferior good. The gross effect depends on the balance of these two opposing tendencies. The excess burden of taxation however depends on the net disincentive effect, i.e. the pure substitution effect. (See Appendix 6A.) This net disincentive effect is almost necessarily negative. At the post-tax income, an individual would probably choose to work more if his income/leisure trade-off has not been distorted by taxation. Taking account of this excess burden, what is the optimal schedule of income taxation? This problem is tackled by Mirrlees, a mathematician who became an economist. This problem of Mirrlees (1971)* may appear to be an ordinary simple maximisation problem. But it is really much more complicated due to the fact that the government's choice of a tax *schedule* to maximise a SWF is subject to the *freedom* of taxpayers with respect to work/leisure choice. Realising fully the nature of this complication, one does not wonder that the problem was not tackled before Mirrlees. (Sheshinski, 1971U*, analyses a similar problem from a slightly different perspective stressing the amount of educational investment as a variable.)

To make the problem tractable, Mirrlees adopts a number of simplifying assumptions, including a common utility function for all individuals which depends only on the amount of post-tax income and the amount of work. 'Differences in tastes, in family size and composition, and in voluntary transfers, are ignored. These raise rather different kinds of problems, and it is natural to assume them away' (Mirrlees, 1971*, p. 175). The SWF is Benthamite, i.e. the integral (since individuals are distributed along a continuous scale of different earning skills) of individual utilities. The maximisation of the SWF by choosing the tax schedule is subject to the requirement that a given amount of tax revenue be raised. Thus, the amount of government expenditure is regarded as a separate problem. Without assuming a specific form of utility function (which determines the work/leisure choice, given the level of skill and the tax schedule) and a specific form of the distribution of skills, one is expecting too much to expect stronger results than the following obtained by Mirrlees: (1) the marginal tax rate lies between 0 per cent and 100 per cent; (2) in a large class of cases, consumption and labour supply vary continuously with the skill of the individual; (3) there will usually be a group of people in the lower end of the scale of earning abilities (the crippled?) who ought to work only if they enjoy it. 'The optimum tax schedule depends upon the distribution of skills within the population, and the labour–consumption preferences of the population, in such a complicated way that it is not possible to say in general whether marginal tax rates should be higher for high-income, low-income, or intermediate-income groups' (p. 186). However, the two equations that Mirrlees obtains to characterise the optimum tax schedule are of a reasonably manageable form so that the schedule can be calculated without great difficulty once the forms of the utility and skill distribution functions are specified.

Taking a specific example (with a positive revenue requirement) where the utility function is a sum of the (natural) logarithm of consumption and the logarithm of leisure, and the skill distribution is lognormal, Mirrlees (1971*, p. 202, table II) calculated the optimum tax schedule which is progressive in terms of average rates (increasing from negative to 14.5 per cent for the top 1 per cent) and regressive in terms of marginal rates (decreasing from 23 per cent to 17 per cent). Mirrlees had expected that the rigorous analysis of income taxation in the utilitarian manner will provide an argument for using high tax rates to achieve equality, and expresses surprise (p. 207) that it has not done so. It is true that the specific results depend on the specific functional forms chosen and a different choice will yield different rates (see, e.g. Atkinson, 1973, table 2; the choice of a different SWF will also affect the outcome; see Helpman, 1974). But the regressivity of marginal rates is still present.

The regressivity of marginal tax-rates is not too surprising if we realise that, in Mirrlees' model, the optimal marginal tax-rate for the person with the highest earning is zero. The reason for this apparently astonishing result is not difficult to see. For any tax schedule that does not involve a zero marginal tax-rate for the top person, let us amend the schedule making the *marginal* rate zero after the income level of the top person. This will induce him to perform a little extra work since he now has to pay no tax for the extra earning. (This assumes smooth indifference curves. However, at least he will not work less. For a geometrical illustration, see Sadka, 1976, figure 4.) This makes him better off and no one worse off (due to the use of a utility function that rules out utility interdependency). The total amount of tax-revenue collected is not smaller than before since the tax schedule has been amended only at the range in which no one was operating before. Though we now impose no tax on the marginal income of the top person, that income was not earned before and hence no tax was collected on that income level despite a positive tax rate. Some readers may wonder, if this argument is true, why we don't make the marginal tax-rate zero for all persons instead of just for the top person. The explanation is that the tax schedule is to apply to all individuals simultaneously: we do not have a separate schedule for each person. If we make the marginal rate zero at an income level lower than the income of the top person, this will reduce the amount of tax collected from the top person (and those tax-payers in between). Such amendments to the tax schedule may then not be feasible. (If the number of individuals is finite, it is possible to design a complicated discontinuous tax system whereby every tax-payer is faced with a zero marginal rate at the relevant income level. Ignoring administrative and informational cost, this is indeed a necessary condition for optimality.)

Should we then advocate marginal tax-rates regressive to zero at the top end? My answer is 'no', or at least 'not necessarily', for the following reasons. First, in practice, the incomes of the very rich are mostly 'unearned', and it is doubtful that making the marginal tax-rates regressive to zero will induce the very rich to work appreciably harder. Secondly, the analysis above ignores utility interdependency or external effects. Increased earnings of the rich may make the non-rich worse off since it is likely that individual utility is not only a function of absolute income but also of relative income. The failure to account for this is a major weakness of Mirrlees' analysis. (Research to account for this has emerged: Boskin & Sheshinski, 1978*, analyse optimal linear income taxation with utility dependent on relative income. The empirical study of Kapteyn and Van Herwaarden (1980) ignores work-incentives.) In private correspondence (in 1975), Mirrlees agreed that the problem of utility interdependency is an interesting one but remarked that utility interdependency need not necessarily tend to remove regressivity since envy may make people work harder. Keeping in a high income group may make other people feel worse off but may also make them do more work to keep up with the rich. Since the whole income tax system has a predominant disincentive effect, inducing people to work harder produces a positive result. However, if my (subjective) judgement is right, the negative effect of high incomes is likely to predominate.

6.4 General Discussion

The analysis of Mirrlees concentrates on the choice of a tax schedule to strike an optimal balance between the need to provide incentives to work and the reduction of inequality due to differential earning skills. This is one of the most important issues. Thus, the reduction in income taxes (larger reductions for higher income levels) introduced in February 1978 in Australia was justified on the ground of incentives. Nevertheless, this is not the only relevant issue: the difference in skills is not the only cause of inequality, income taxation is not the only means of achieving equality, equality of income distribution is not the only problem in economic justice, etc. However, due to space limitation, these issues cannot be discussed in detail. Interested readers are referred to the following works and references listed therein: Atkinson (1975, 1976), Atkinson & Harrison (1978), Collard et al. (1980),

Danziger, Haveman & Plotnick (1981), Griliches *et al.* (1978), Hochman & Peterson (1974), Juster (1978), Krelle & Shorrocks (1978), Meade (1976), Okun (1975), Pen (1971), Phelps (1973), Rivlin (1975), Sen (1973a), Taubman (1975), Tinbergen (1975), Thurow (1981). What is given below is no more than a brief résumé-type treatment.

Since work is not the only source of income, it is obvious that skill differential is not the only source of inequality. In fact, the reverse misconception, i.e. the belief that property incomes account for more than they really do, is more likely to prevail (Pen, 1971, p. 10). Recent empirical studies show that property incomes in advanced economies account for a small and declining share in total income, and the inequality of the personal distribution of income has also been narrowing. While not doubting the basic validity of these studies, it must be noted that they do not reflect hidden illegal incomes. Inequality due to these incomes is regarded by most people as even more contrary to economic justice. But these types of income existed long ago. Hence, it is likely that inequality has narrowed even if we take them into account. However, it remains true that if inequality due to these dubious forms of income can be reduced, it will be even more conducive to the attainment of economic justice. But this is easier said than done (Pen, 1971, section VII-4). With respect to tax evasion, it seems clear that a simple system of linear income tax (with constant marginal rates but increasing average rates) will not only save a lot of administrative costs but will also reduce tax evasion substantially. Mirrlees' analysis shows that the optimal tax schedule is regressive (in marginal rates). If we take account of utility interdependence, the regressivity may be eliminated or even reversed. But when we consider administrative costs and tax evasion, it may be true that a linear income tax is not far from the optimum. Then we are left only with the choice of the fixed marginal rate and the level of exemption or minimum post-tax income. (For an analysis, see Atkinson, 1973.) After taking account of tax evasion, the progressive income tax systems in many countries are not very progressive anyway, since, with progressivity in marginal rates, there are more incentives and opportunities for evasion for higher income groups. A constant marginal rate eliminates much scope for tax evasion by income-splitting. Any residual loss of equality is likely to be overbalanced by the gains in incentives and reduced administrative costs (including the time costs of tax evasion). This is so especially if we also introduce other measures to reduce inequality in pre-tax incomes and to create equality of opportunity.

In fact, some people believe that equality of opportunity is more important than equality of income as (1) equality of opportunity will lead to equality of income, and/or (2) inequality of income is not an injustice if there is equality of opportunity. The latter is especially so if the inequality of income is a result of differences in motivation and in choices with respect to work/leisure, risk/security, pecuniary/non-pecuniary aspects, etc. (Friedman, 1953, Taubman, 1975). However, even if we use a broader concept of income (full income?) that takes account of these non-monetary factors, it is still unlikely that equality of opportunity will lead to complete equality of (full) income, since men are not born equal in physical fitness and mental ability. Should this type of inequality be tolerated or removed? Different persons may have different answers to this ethical question. If we accept the Benthamite ethic, it is likely that such inequality should be reduced but not removed. The difficulty lies in the choice of the right extent and methods used.

Even if we opt to achieve equality of opportunity alone, the problem is by no means a simple one. For one thing, the concept of equality of opportunity is not a very precise one. For example, with respect to education, does equality of opportunity mean that each student should pay the same fee or does it mean that each student should receive the same amount of education? And what do we mean by 'the same amount of education'? Do we measure education by the amount of input or by the amount of output? With differences in intelligence and motivation, equality in educational inputs implies inequality in output and equality in output (if at all possible) implies inequality in input. The application of the Benthamite principle seems to suggest that there should be output-regressivity (the able ending up better off) with input-progressivity or regressivity depending on the utility function (Arrow, 1971b). Optimising education and income redistribution policies simultaneously, Ulph (1977) shows that optimal education policies are more regressive than suggested by Arrow. It may also be noted that, while many supporters of the principle of equality of opportunity believe that equality in educational input will produce substantially equal output, or at least that substantial equality in output can be achieved by input-progressivity, recent empirical and theoretical studies emphasise the reverse. Education may not do much to change the innate difference in ability and, apart from a learning process, may serve mainly as a screening process sorting out the (inborn) intelligent from the less intelligent (Arrow, 1973, Battalio, Kagel & Reynolds, 1977, Jencks, 1972, Liu & Wong, 1982, Riley, 1979, Spence, 1973, Stiglitz, 1975, Taubman, 1976).

Ambiguity may also arise in applying the principle of horizontal equity which requires the equal treatment of people in the same circumstances. The difficulty lies in the interpretation of 'the same circumstances'. If Mrs J with one child receives $\$x$ in child-endowment, should Mrs K receive the same amount as she also has one child? Or should the income of the family be admitted as a relevant factor in defining the circumstances so that, e.g., the rich receive no endowment? If we admit all factors in the definition of 'circumstances', the content of horizontal equity becomes vacuous since there are no two persons who are exactly similar. Alternatively, if we do not include all factors, different criteria of horizontal equity may be inconsistent with each other. Moreover, each may be inconsistent with the Pareto principle (Stiglitz, 1976U). What about vertical equity, which requires the appropriate different treatment of people in different circumstances? This depends much on the criterion used to judge the appropriateness of treatment. Should we go for 'From each according to his *choice*, to each according to his *contribution*', or for 'From each according to his *ability*, to each according to his *needs*'? A fundamental liberal may insist on 'choice' instead of 'ability' since no person should be forced to work against his will. (A fundamental liberal believes in liberalism as an utlimate moral principle; an instrumental liberal believes in liberalism because it is generally consistent with some ultimate end, e.g. utilitarianism; see Ng, 1973U.) A utilitarian can only be an instrumental liberal and must at least allow for the hypothetical exception to the freedom of choice. But, taking account the harmful effects (especially in the long run) of forced labour, utilitarians may become practically identical with fundamental liberals with respect to freedom of work. With respect to remuneration, the Benthamite utilitarian principle will probably settle at something between 'contribution' and 'needs', taking account of incentive effects, etc. In other words, the Bentham SWF is willing to trade off efficiency for equality to some extent. But what are the appropriate methods to achieve a favourable trade-off? We have discussed Mirrlees' approach to the use of income taxation and have briefly touched on the provision of equality of opportunity. We turn now to discussing briefly some other forms of taxation.

If the government is omniscient, knowing the potential of all individuals, it can design a system of lump-sum taxes on different persons to achieve the objective of equality without any loss in efficiency. But this is an unobtainable ideal. However, it has been suggested that this ideal may be better approached if we tax individuals according to their measured capabilities, such as IQ instead of their incomes. (See, e.g., Tinbergen 1972.) Unfortunately, the practical difficulties, especially the problem of evasion by hiding one's real capabilities, are overwhelming. Mirrlees (1971, p. 208) believes that 'high values of skill-indexes may be sought after so much for prestige that they would not often be misrepresented'. But I suspect that, once these indexes are used for taxation purposes, most people will take pride in being able to register a low value. (Cf. the proposal of ladies being tolled on their beauty, gentlemen on their valour, with self-assessment to be the rule!)

Another form of taxes to achieve equality (especially of opportunity) is death and gift duties. To achieve the objective of equality at a low cost on efficiency, it has been proposed that the progressivity of the duties should be based not on the size of the estate but on the size of the individual bequest, the wealth of the beneficiary, and/or the total amount of bequest and gift received by the beneficiary. This may result in very little disincentive effect since one can reduce the tax rate by leaving a moderate amount to each of a number of persons who are poor and/or have not received much inheritance and gift. In particular, it will encourage people to distribute their estate to more relatives and friends instead of concentrating on a most favoured person. While there are some practical difficulties in implementing this proposal, they are not insurmountable (Meade, 1964, pp. 55-8).

Taxation is not, of course, the only means to achieve equality. Other measures to achieve equality may be divided into two groups. The first includes measures to remove man-made, institutional barriers in order to create equality of opportunity. The second includes measures that go further to impose restrictions on activities that lead to inequality even with equality of opportunity. This second type of measure not only results in substantial loss in efficiency but usually leads to infringement on freedom (Bauer, 1976). The pursuit of equality may have important side-effects.

6.5 Concluding Remarks

In the first section of this chapter, we have noted that optimal distribution can be put in terms of a SWF and a GUFF. Different people may disagree widely on the form of both SWF and GUFF. In Section 5.4.1, I argued in favour of a specific SWF—the unweighted sum of individual utilities. But the shape of GUFF is much more difficult to ascertain. The following factors are relevant here: (1) the degree of diminishing marginal utility of income, (2) the extent of incentive effects, (3) the nature and extent of utility interdependency, (4) the social rate of discount, (5) administrative and other costs (e.g time spent on evading taxes, infringement on freedom, etc.) of pursuing equality.

There is evidence in psychological studies that, apart from extremal values, the just noticeable increment to any stimulus value is a constant proportion of that value. Written as the Weber-Fechner law, Sensation = k log Stimulus.† If we take this general law as applicable to the utility of an individual as a function of his income, then we may write U = k log Income. The marginal utility of income then diminishes by the same proportion as income increases. Economists have also done some studies on the marginal utility of income, usually based on some simplifying assumptions (Fisher, 1927, Frisch, 1932, Van Praag, 1968, Clark, 1973, Van Herwaarden, Kapteyn & Van Praag, 1977). While studies have also been done on the extent of disincentive effects, no definite conclusion is available. The nature and extent of utility interdependency is even more elusive, especially if we take account of long-run effects. For intertemporal considerations, the social rate of discount becomes relevant. Some people argue that, while it is reasonable to discount future consumption if future generations will be richer, it is unreasonable to discount future utility from the social point of view. This argument ignores the fact that we are not perfectly sure of the continued existence of the human society. Thus a small uncertainty discount can be justified though it is difficult to agree on a precise value. We are on similar imprecise territory as we move to our last item on the matter of freedom and other noneconomic factors. We have a long way to go before the practical choice of distributional policies can be mainly based on more objective factors.

Summary

Given a utility possibility or feasibility frontier, the choice of an optimal point (related to income distribution) depends on the form of

---

†Luce & Edwards' (1958)* criticism of Fechner does not apply to this particular function.

SWF. The common 'egalitarian' inclination to adopt welfare contours convex to the origin may be due to 'utility illusion', the double discounting of incomes of the rich. With a given total income, diminishing marginal utility, and no knowledge of individual utility functions, equal distribution maximises the expected sum of utilities. Some degree of inequality is usually needed to maintain incentives to work. The choice of an income tax schedule to strike an optimal balance between incentive and equality as analysed by Mirrlees shows that, for a particular choice of the relevant functional forms, the average tax-rate is progressive but the marginal rate is regressive. Since Mirrlees' analysis ignores utility interdependency and administrative costs, perhaps a linear tax schedule over a significant income range is not far from optimal.

The Excess Burden of Taxation: Can it be Negative?

This appendix shows that (1) the excess burden of taxation is positive even if the gross disincentive effect is zero; (2) a measure of excess burden based on compensating variation (CV) may give a misleading negative figure.

6A.1 Gross Versus Net Disincentive Effect of Taxation

Consider Figure 6A.1 illustrating the choice between leisure and income by an individual. His pre-tax opportunity line is OP^0, the absolute slope

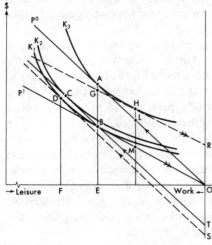

Figure 6A.1

of which is his given wage-rate. A proportional income tax shifts his opportunity line to OP^1 and he moves from A to B. For the specific case of this figure, A and B are on the same vertical line. Thus the gross disincentive effect is zero; he chooses to work the same amount despite the tax. The amount of tax collected is AB. If we impose a lump-sum tax of the same amount OT and leave him with the same income/leisure trade off as before, i.e. so that TC is parallel to OP^0, he will choose the point C. Since B is on a lower indifference curve than C, the income tax involves an excess burden despite the fact that its gross disincentive effect is zero. In monetary terms, this excess burden may be measured by TS since we could have imposed a lump-sum tax OS while leaving him at a point (D) no worse off than B. The net disincentive effect is EF.

6A.2 A Negative Excess Burden?

As illustrated in Figure 6A.1, the imposition of an income tax shifts the opportunity line from OP^0 to OP^1 and the individual moves from A to B. We showed that the excess burden can be measured by TS. However, there are alternative ways of measuring excess burden. A popular method is to take the difference between the loss in consumer surplus and the tax revenue collected. Adopting the usual CV measure, the loss in surplus is measured by OR $(= BG)$. Since the tax revenue collected is AB, this measure of excess burden gives us a negative figure–AG. How can this be so?

If a negative excess burden is possible, we may increase taxes all round to create excess surpluses! This is obviously impossible. This CV measure of the loss in surplus OR is the amount of money we have to compensate the individual to make him no worse off than before the tax. If this compensation is actually paid, he will move to H. But at this point, the amount of tax collected is only LM which is less than OR by HL. If the compensation is not actually paid, the tax revenue is AB. Our CV measure then gives a misleading impression of a negative excess burden. This again shows that if the compensation is not actually to be paid or collected, the measure is not satisfactory in some respect. In this particular case, it gives a totally misleading figure. The Marshall measure and the CS, ES (all equal AB) are also misleading since they indicate that the excess burden is zero.

Usually, CV is measured in monetary terms. In the two dimensional diagrammatical framework, it is measured in terms of the good on the Y axis. For the usual cases of a change in the price of X, the maximum amount of Y the individual can obtain remains unchanged. For the case of an income tax illustrated in Figure 6A.1, this maximum amount changes with the tax. It is the maximum amount of X (leisure) which remains unchanged. Had we measured CV in terms of leisure, the measure of excess burden of taxation would then not be negative (in the present case where no inferior good is involved). (This paragraph is written after discussion with my colleague, Mike Burns.)

7 Externality

We noted in Chapter 2 that an equilibrium situation of a perfectly competitive market economy is Pareto optimal under certain conditions. One of these conditions is the absence of (unaccounted for) external effects. But external effects are pervasive. Important forms of external effects such as pollution have recently come to the fore of public discussion. There is also a growing professional literature on the economics of the environment (surveyed by Fisher & Peterson, 1976). In this chapter, we shall see how the presence of external effects may cause non-optimality and how this can be alleviated. Before doing so, we shall first discuss the concept and classification of external effects.

7.1 The Concept and Classification of Externalities

Obviously, for an external effect to be present, there must first be an effect. Some party K (the affecting party) must produce an effect on some other party J (the affected party). The effect must not just be present but must have some (positive or negative) welfare significance. For example, if water flows from my neighbour's garden hose into my garden, a physical effect is there. But if I do not care about it one way or the other, we will not say that an externality exists. Second, the affecting party is usually a person or a group of persons or something (animals, institutions, etc.) under the control of some person(s). It is possible to speak of the external effects of, say, wild animals and use this to justify certain measures against them. But the usual methods of tax/subsidy, bargaining, etc., will not be applicable. The affected party is also usually a (or a group of) person(s) or something owned by some person(s). However, if the welfare of some nonhuman beings such as that of animals enters into our objective function, then it is quite logical to include them as possible affected parties.

The mere presence of a welfare-relevant effect by one party on another does not necessarily constitute an externality; some additional conditions are needed for the effect to be considered as 'external'. For example, as you buy a number of oranges from a shop, there is presumably a positive effect on your welfare. However, this is an exchange relationship rather than an external effect as you *pay* for the oranges. Thus, externality refers only to those benefits or damages that are not paid for; market relationships are not external effects.

Another possible additional condition is to require that externality refer only to the *incidental* effects and not the primary or intended effects (Mishan, 1971, p. 2). Thus, the factory does not emit smoke for its own sake but the smoke is incidental to the production process. On the other hand, one's welfare is obviously affected by murder, robbery, rape, companionship, etc. But these are the primary, intended effects and are not usually described as externalities. Instead, they are just referred to as outright illegal activities, or social activities. However, the distinction between primary and incidental effects is an ambiguous one. If a group of hooligans enjoy themselves by throwing stones, some of which break windows, is the breakage a primary or an incidental effect? If air pollution becomes so severe that we ban all forms of smoke, isn't the emission of smoke as much an outright illegal activity as the breaking of windows? Moreover, couldn't the effect upon the victim of such outright illegal activities as rape be regarded as the incidental effect of the drastic attempt by the rapist to achieve (perhaps psychopathic) sexual fulfilment? The factory manager is interested in his production, not in polluting the atmosphere. Similarly, the rapist may be interested in his sexual satisfaction, not in inflicting harm on the victim. It seems, therefore, quite logical to speak of the external effects of offenders on victims or society in general. In fact, according to this general interpretation of externality, most illegal activities are made illegal on the ground of their harmful external effects.

More formally, we shall say that an externality exists when the utility function of an individual (or the cost or production function of a firm) depends not only on the variables under his control but also on some variable under the control of someone else where the dependence is not effected through market transaction (cf. Heller & Starrett, 1976). Thus,

$$U^J = U^J(x_1^J, x_2^J, \ldots, x_G^J, x_1^K) \tag{7.1}$$

where U^J is the utility of individual J, x_g^J is the level of the gth activity by J. In this case, the first activity of K has an external effect on J.

Assuming differentiability, the externality at $x_1^K = \bar{x}_1^K$ (where $\bar{x}_1^K$ is a particular given level of the activity) is said to be a marginal one if $\partial U^J/\partial x_1^K \mid_{x_1^K = \bar{x}_1^K} \neq 0$, and an infra-marginal one if $\partial U^J/\partial x_1^K \mid_{x_1^K = \bar{x}_1^K} = 0$ but $\neq 0$ for some $x_1^K < \bar{x}_1^K$. Thus if $\partial U^J/\partial x_1^K$ is as depicted in Figure 7.1a, it is a marginal external economy (benefit) over the range OC, an infra-marginal one over the range CD, and a marginal external diseconomy (cost) after D. It is of course possible for some externality to be a marginal diseconomy or economy throughout its entire range.

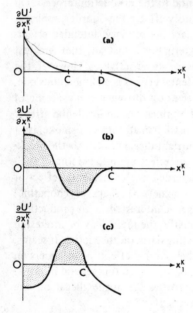

Figure 7.1

The usual definition of infra-marginal externality as $\partial U^J/\partial x_1^K \mid_{x_1^K = \bar{x}_1^K} = 0$, $\int_0^{\bar{x}_1^K} \partial U^J/\partial x_1^K \neq 0$ leaves cases illustrated in Figures 7.1b and 7.1c without a name. Here, the two shaded areas are equal in size and hence $\int \partial U^J/\partial x_1^K dx_1^K$ is equal to zero after/at the point C in Figure 7.1b/7.1c. While such cases are unlikely to occur frequently in practice, they are logically quite possible and may be termed infra-marginal mixed externalities. An example of this mixed externality is Kwang's laugh. The first few of these high-pitched laughs are usually regarded as very amusing (but sometimes offending). Further laughs are regarded as disturbing until people get used to them.

If the activity x_1^K affects not only the total utility of J but also the marginal utility of some relevant activity of J, it is said to be a non-separable externality. We have $\partial^2 U^J/\partial x_g^J \partial x_1^K \neq 0$ for some x_g^J. On the other hand, if $\partial U^J/\partial x_1^K \neq 0$ for some value of x_1^K but $\partial^2 U^J/\partial x_g^J \partial x_1^K = 0$ for all relevant x_g^J, it is a separable externality. An example of a non-separable externality is the emission of smoke that also reduces people's preference for wearing white shirts.

If K's activity affects J but J's activity does not affect K, there is a unidirectional externality. If they are mutually affected, there is a reciprocal externality. A classic example is the case of an apple-grower and a bee-keeper who both benefit from the activity of the other, as the bees help to fertilise the apple-flowers which on their part provide the bees with the material to make honey.

7.2 Divergence from Optimality and the Tax/Subsidy Solution

The analysis of externalities can most simply be undertaken by a partial equilibrium approach, assuming an existing unidirectional externality. (Ng, 1980, justifies corrective taxes/subsidies for normal cases in a general equilibrium setting.) This is done in Figure 7.2 which differs from Figure 7.1 in two aspects. First, to speak in monetary terms, we have converted the (net) marginal utility curves into the (net) marginal valuation (MV) curves. This can be done by dividing $\partial U^J/\partial x_1^K$ by the marginal utility of money. Second, while the MV of K is still measured in the vertical axis in the normal direction, that of J is measured in the opposite direction (southward from the origin). For the case depicted in Figure 7.2, we have an external diseconomy and hence J's valuation of K's activity is negative. Due to the way J's valuation is measured, her MV curve (MV_J) lies in the upper section of the figure.†

Since K undertakes the activity x_1^K himself, his MV is positive at least over some range of the activity. However, since his MV curve is measured net of the costs of undertaking the activity, it must meet the horizontal axis somewhere; otherwise K will extend his activity indefi-

†If MV_J depends on some activity under J's control, the curve MV_J should trace out the MV_J for the utility- (or profit-) maximising choice of J for each given x_1^K; see Gifford & Stone (1975).

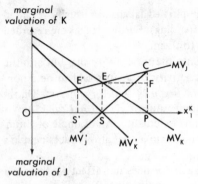

Figure 7.2

nitely. As drawn in Figure 7.2, MV_K cuts the horizontal axis at P. Assuming that K maximises his utility, he carries his activity up to P. At this point, his net MV of the activity is zero. But he is imposing a marginal damage of PC on J. This is therefore not a socially optimal solution. The latter occurs at S where the two MV curves intersect.† The traditional Pigovian solution to this divergence between private and social optima is to impose a tax (a subsidy for the case of external economy) on the activity. The marginal tax rate is equal to the negative marginal valuation of J. After the imposition of this tax, the new net MV curve of K will be MV_K'. K will then be induced to reduce his activity level to the socially optimal point S, ignoring income effects. In the presence of income effects, the marginal valuation curve of K may move slightly due to his payment of taxes. Hence the social optimal point S may also move slightly. However, the solution remains Pareto optimal. For a more detailed illustration of this point see Ng (1971a, pp. 176–7).

However, it has been argued that full optimality cannot be attained by the imposition of the above unilateral tax (Buchanan & Stubblebine,

---

†Feasibility of lump-sum transfer may be assumed to side-step the distributional issue. However, according to the argument of Appendix 9A, this assumption is not really necessary. We have also been assuming the satisfaction of second-order and total conditions (on which see Section 2.2.2). For the argument that the presence of external diseconomies tends to push the production possibility curve inward except for points of specialisation, hence making the violation of the second-order condition more likely, see Baumol and Bradford (1972). (Cf. also Starrett, 1972*, Otani & Sicilian, 1977*.) For an analysis of total conditions, see Gould (1977).

1962, p. 383). At the point S, J's (absolute) marginal valuation of the activity is not equal to K's marginal valuation (net of tax). Hence, there is an incentive for them to bargain and achieve a new level of the activity S' which, however, is not the socially optimal point. By moving from S to S', J gains the area $S'SEE'$ and K loses $S'SE'$. So there is a net gain of SEE' to be shared between J and K. But this is not a social improvement since there is a loss in tax revenue $S'SEE'$. To prevent this non-optimal outcome, Buchanan & Stubblebine propose that J should also be taxed to ensure that she will take the costs imposed on K into account. This second tax on J should be positively correlated with K's *reduction* in his activity level from the point P, or *negatively* related to x_1^K, thus shifting MV_J to MV_J', to intersect MV_K' at the social optimal point S. If this tax on J is positively correlated with K's *increase* in his activity level, it will shift MV_J upward (recalling that J's marginal valuation is measured southerly from the origin), making its intersection with MV_K' further away from the social optimal point S.

The proposed bilateral taxation may be superfluous. If bargaining between the parties concerned is possible, a Pareto optimum may be achieved without any taxation. If bargaining is impossible (owing, for example, to the high cost of coming to an agreement and enforcing it), a single tax on K may be sufficient to achieve the optimum. Nevertheless, bilateral taxation may be relevant where bargaining is possible but is deemed unjust or is more costly and the government decides to use the taxation solution. But of course, the costs of administering the bilateral taxation must also be taken into account.

Bilateral taxation may also serve two other purposes. In our example illustrated in Figure 7.2 above, if J can avoid the external diseconomy (e.g. by moving to another place) at a cost less than K's cost of reducing the nuisance (i.e. *ESP* in Figure 7.2), then it would be desirable for J to do so rather than have K reduce his activity level. But with the enforcement (or expected imminent introduction) of the unilateral tax, J, in maximising her own utility, is not motivated to do this unless she is required to pay an amount equal to the cost (or the reduction in utility) incurred by K to reduce the externality. Second, the amount of diseconomy borne by J is difficult to discover in practice. Under a unilateral tax system, she is motivated to exaggerate her damage so as to raise the rate of tax on K and hence to reduce the activity of K further. But if J is required to pay a tax equal to the cost borne by K to reduce the externality, J will not benefit from the reduction of K's activity beyond

S. J will therefore be motivated to report her damage function truthfully (Ng, 1971a, pp. 173–4). Similarly, since K also has to pay for the damage sustained by J, he will also be motivated to report his MV function truthfully. In fact, one can show that, even given an exaggerated report of one party, the other party will still find that honesty is the best policy under the bilateral tax arrangement. Dishonesty does not only harm the other party but the dishonest party itself. Unfortunately, this happy result does not generalise to the case where J and/or K consists of a number of individuals/firms with different MV functions. For example, suppose K is a polluting firm and J consists of a large number of affected individuals. First take the case where these individuals have identical MV curves. As illustrated in Figure 7.3, each individual MV curve is MV_J^i. Hence the vertical summation of these n individuals' MV_J^i gives $\Sigma_{i=1}^{n} MV_J^i = nMV_J^i$, whose intersection with MV_K gives the social optimal point S. If each individual is required to pay $1/n$ of the cost imposed on K in having to reduce the externality (curve PD in Figure 7.3), each will be motivated to reveal her MV curve truthfully, provided she believes that other individuals will on average report truthfully. Thus, for any single individual j, if she believes that all other individuals' reported MV curves sum to $\Sigma_{i \neq j} MV_J^i = \Sigma_{i=1}^{n-1} MV_J^i$, she will figure that, if she also reports truthfully, the aggregate reported MV_J will intersect MV_K at S. If she exaggerates or under-reports her MV, the actual level of x_1^K will diverge from the point S. Since she is required to pay for $1/n$ of the cost imposed on K and since her own MV is equal to $1/n$ the aggregate MV, it will be to

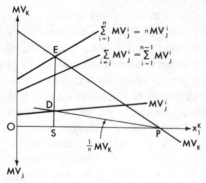

Figure 7.3

her own advantage to have x_1^K reduced to precisely the point S where $\Sigma_{i=1}^n MV_J^i$ intersects MV_K and MV_J^i intersects $1/nMV_K$.

The analysis above may seem to be based on the assumption that the true MV_K curve is somehow known. If we relax this assumption, does the result change? The answer is 'no'. For any given reported $MV_{K'}$ whether it is the true one or not, each individual will be motivated to make the level of x_1^K occur at the intersection of $\Sigma_{i=1}^n MV_J^i$ with the reported MV_K. Hence the above conclusion is not affected by false revelation by K. Moreover, since K has to pay a tax equal to $-\Sigma MV_J^i$, he will also be motivated to reveal MV_K truthfully.

Unfortunately, if we introduce differences in individual MV curves, we run into trouble. Individuals with high (absolute value) MV will be motivated to exaggerate and those with low MV to under-report their true MV. We cannot count on these two opposite tendencies precisely offsetting each other to produce a true aggregate MV. If we try to avoid this difficulty by making each individual pay according to her reported MV, we run into trouble in another direction. Each individual may then try to under-report her MV in order to reduce her own payment. This is the well-known free-rider problem in the literature of public goods. This difficulty may be overcome by using a more complicated mechanism, as shown below. (For a more detailed discussion and the relevant references on this mechanism, see Section 8.3*. Beginners may skip the following paragraph.)

Basically, the scheme consists of: (1) asking each individual to report her marginal valuation function; (2) sum the reported marginal valuation functions for all individuals in J and tax individual (or firm) K according to the negative of this sum, i.e. $-\Sigma_{i=1}^n MV_J^i$; (3) tax each individual j in J according to $MV_K - \Sigma_{i \neq j} MV_J^i$, positively correlated with the *reduction* in x_1^K from the point where $MV_K = \Sigma_{i \neq j} MV_J^i$. These three points are illustrated in Figure 7.4. Given the reported MV of all other individuals, an individual j in J has to pay taxes according to T_j as x_1^K is reduced beyond the point Q. If she reports her true MV_J^j the sum of reported MV_J^i will intersect MV_K at R where MV_J^i is equal to T_j. Thus, at this margin, she has no incentive to exaggerate or underestimate her damage. If she exaggerates (underestimates) her damage and reports her MV curve to be something higher (lower) than her true MV_J^j curve, then $\Sigma_{i=1}^n MV_J^i$ will intersect MV_K at a point to the left (right) of R. She

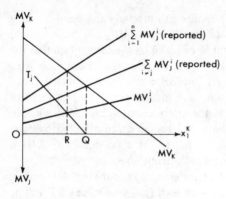

Figure 7.4

will gain from the resulting reduction in x_1^K (taxes), but the gain is more than offset by the increase in taxes (x_1^K). This is true whether other individuals report truthfully or not. Moreover, since this is true for each individual (j can be any one in J), each will in fact be reporting truthfully. Similarly, since K has to be taxed according to ΣMV_J^i, he is also motivated to report truthfully. Therefore, the resulting bilateral taxes may lead to an optimal level of x_1^K. (For some complications, see Section 8.3*.)

7.3 Other Solutions

We have already mentioned bargaining in passing. This is indeed one of the possible ways to solve the problem created by externality. In our example illustrated in Figure 7.2 above, J and K may come to a mutual agreement between themselves. K may agree to reduce his activity to the point S. By doing so, he is losing the area ESP but J is gaining the area $ESPC$. So the net gain is EPC. If J also agrees to pay K an amount of money equal to, say, the area $ESPF$, then both parties will be made better off than the initial position at P. Hence, provided that the costs of coming to the agreement and enforcing it (loosely referred to as transaction costs) are not too high, both parties will have the incentive to do that. One possible objection to this solution is that many people may think that it is unjust that J, the sufferer of K's activity, should have to pay K to reduce the activity. This equity question can be taken care of by appropriate assignment of property rights. If J has the 'amenity right', then K has to pay J in order to undertake the activity. As will be shown in Section 7.5, a Pareto optimal outcome may still emerge provided the transaction costs are not too high.

Apart from transaction costs, there is another important difficulty in reaching voluntary bargaining agreements. Referring again to Figure 7.2, J is interested in reducing the amount of payment to K towards the minimum amount ESP, and K is interested in increasing it towards the maximum amount $ESPC$. In between these maximum and minimum amounts, there are a large number of possible amounts of payment which will still make both parties better off. The actual outcome depends on their relative skill and toughness in bargaining. It is possible that they may not be able to come to any agreement at all. While it is true that some agreement is better than no agreement, both of them may be acting on the assumption that the other party will give in first. This sort of strategic behaviour by the parties involved may prevent the reaching of agreement. Such a prospect will reduce the incentive to both parties to enter into negotiations.

When we take account of game-strategic behaviour, K may carry his activity beyond his private optimal point P (Shibata, 1971). This means that he has to sustain a net loss at the margin. He may do it in the belief that J is damaged even more and hence may be willing to settle on terms more favourable to K. While such rather unethical behaviour is not very likely to be adopted by many people, the possibility that some persons may act very unscrupulously cannot be ruled out. This poses a further problem to the bargaining solution. Another shortcoming of the bargaining approach is its effect on future decision-making including the possibility of encouraging blackmail. This will be discussed in Section 7.5 below.

If the two parties involved are both business firms, then bargaining may go beyond an agreement to reduce/increase the level of activity involved. The two firms may agree to merge into one firm, effectively internalising the pre-existing external effect. With a single management, the pre-existing external effect can be taken into account and is no longer an external effect. But the informational and organisational costs may increase (Alchian & Demsetz, 1972). Logically, this merger solution may also be adopted if the two parties concerned are households.

Another way of tackling the problem of externality is for the government to undertake some form of direct control. This may be either outright prohibition, making the activity completely illegal, or some milder regulations such as the zoning of residential areas in which no factory can be built, the division of smoking and non-smoking sections in public places, compulsory installation of pollution-reducing devices, etc. In particular, a certain quota on the maximum permissible amount of externality may be specified. Economists are generally in favour of making quotas freely transferable. Thus, if we do not want a certain pollutant to exceed X units, we may issue X units of such quotas which are either distributed proportionally, or better still, sold to the polluters who may exchange (for money) these quotas as their needs for them change. Then a producer who can only reduce his pollution at a high cost is motivated to pay for the quota while those who can do so at low costs are motivated to cut down their pollution levels. Thus the same overall reduction in pollution level can be achieved at a lower overall cost to society as a whole. (See, e.g., Parish, 1972, Baumol & Oates, 1975.)

In the choice between alternative methods of tackling the externality problem, one has not only to consider their respective ability to achieve the desired result but also the costs (informational, administrative, etc.) of their implementation. It is likely that different external effects will be best solved by different methods, including that of doing nothing. (The different methods to tackle externalities discussed above are applicable only to normal external effects. There is a special type of externalities which is inherently not amenable to these usual methods of solution even assuming no informational, administrative, and transaction costs. This refers to externalities of usually noneconomic activities such as social interaction that change their characters once taxes/subsidies, etc., are introduced. For a discussion of these non-amenable externalities and the associated indirect externalities, see Ng, 1975d.)

7.4** The Conscience Effect

Our analysis of externalities above is based on the assumption of no divergence between welfare and preference. Now let us relax this assumption that individual K is self-centring with respect to the activity

x_1^K. (A self-concerning individual's utility or preference is affected only by his own welfare but his welfare may be affected by others' welfare; a self-minding individual's *welfare* is not affected by others' welfare; a self-centring individual is both self-minding and self-concerning. See Section 1.3 above.)

Consider Figure 7.5. The curve MV_K^a is the (net) marginal valuation of K if the activity x_1^K does not have any external effect. Now introduce the external effect as represented by MV_J. If K is self-centring, his MV curve remains unchanged and our analysis above applies. However, if K is not self-minding, the fact that J is adversely affected by x_1^K may reduce MV_K even if K is self-concerning. Suppose this reduces his MV curve (in terms of his own welfare) to MV_K^b. Moreover, if K is not self-concerning, his MV (in terms of his preference) may be further reduced to MV_K^c. He will then carry the activity up to the point P^c which may be to the right or left of S. But is S still the point of social

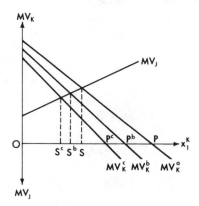

Figure 7.5

optimum? Since, in terms of welfare, the MV curve of K is MV_K^b, it seems that the social optimum point is now S^b. It is likely that S^b still lies to the left of P^c. This is so because K, even if not completely self-concerning, is unlikely to have equal concern for J's welfare as for his own. If K is self-concerning, then MV_B^c and MV_B^b coincide. It may then seem that the analysis of previous sections applies provided MV_J^b instead of MV_K^a is taken as the relevant marginal valuation curve for K.

However, as will be shown below, some interesting new results emerge even for a self-concerning individual provided that he is not also self-minding.

Consider Figure 7.6, where the marginal valuation curve of K is reduced from MV_K^a to MV_K^b due to the presence of external diseconomy as indicated by MV_J. The social optimal point is *apparently* at S^b where MV_K^b intersects MV_J. Now suppose we impose a Pigovian tax on K. Will this move MV_K^b down to $MV_K^{b'}$ to intersect the horizontal axis at S^b as in the analysis of the preceding sections? Not necessarily, even ignoring income effects. In fact, it may move up to $MV_K^{a'}$. K's MV curve is reduced from MV_K^a to MV_K^b due to the external diseconomy imposed on J. Now that he has to pay a tax (or some other form of compensation) to account for the externality, his MV curve may well revert to MV_K^a, which, after subtracting the tax, gives $MV_K^{a'}$. K will then carry the activity up to the point S which is socially optimal since his MV curve has reverted to MV_K^a. Two interesting observations may be made. First,

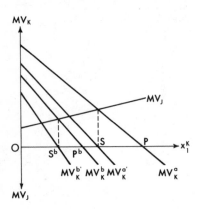

Figure 7.6

the diseconomy-producing activity may increase (from P^b to S in Figure 7.6) after the imposition of the optimal Pigovian tax. This must not be confused with the argument of Buchanan & Kafoglis (1963) and Baumol (1965) that 'the presence of external benefits may very conceivably call for reduced output and activity levels on the part of those who produce these economies' (Baumol, 1965, p. 32). This is due to the reciprocal nature of the externality–such as communicable disease. Thus a public health programme may decrease medical expenditures as compared with uncoordinated private health programmes, where many individuals–fearing that they are unprotected–are apt to take very strong measures of self-protection. 'However, the reduction of aggregate resources is not caused by the reduced output and activity levels on the part of those who produce the external economies, but rather by a reduction in resources committed by those who are benefited by the external economies' (Ng, 1971a, p. 180). In contrast, for our case discussed in Figure 7.6, it is the party (K) producing the externality who makes the 'counter-normal' adjustment. Secondly, the affecting party may be made better off or worse off by the tax, and the same applies to the affected party. In the analysis of the previous sections, the affected party is always made better off (ignoring the unlikely Giffen effect) and the affecting party always made worse off. (If the tax proceed is used for compensation, then of course both parties could be made better off.) Referring back to Figure 7.6, that the affected party may be made worse off is due to the fact that the activity level may increase after the imposition of the tax. That the affecting party may be made better off is due to the fact that he may gain more than the amount of the tax as he is now *not* engaging in an activity detrimental to someone else without paying for it. This may be called the conscience effect.

As drawn in Figure 7.6, P^b lies to the left of S. This may be regarded as impossible, but consider the following two real-life examples. After learning that a vacant block in our street is a common dumping ground, I also started dumping grass cut from my front lawn into that block. Being aware that this is the property of someone else, I refrained from dumping grass from my back lawn. However, if my next door neighbour is right in saying that grass dumped in the block quickly decomposes and does not really do any harm, the optimal Pigovian tax on dumping cannot be more than a few cents. If something like a dumping meter were installed so that one could dump legally by pressing a coin into the meter, I may be prepared to pay for the dumping of grass from my backyard as well.

Factors other than the direct feeling of guilt may contribute to the reduction in valuation placed on the activity that produces external diseconomy. The value to the owners of a polluting factory may not only be reduced by the guilt feeling of the owners themselves, but also by that of their employees since the latter will, presumably, require some wage premium to compensate them for the unpleasant feeling. If the labour market is not perfect so that such a premium does not exist, then the value to the owners may not be reduced but the producers' surplus of the employees is reduced. Moreover, the employees will be more likely to engage in industrial disputes either to obtain wage increases or in direct protest over the pollution. The decision by the unions to ban the building of the Newport power station in Victoria on the ground of its environmental impact involves many factors but may at least be partly analysed using our framework. Had the principle of Pigovian taxes been enforced, the SEC (State Electricity Commission) might have taken the environmental effects more conspicuously into account. An independent body could have estimated the external costs involved for which the SEC would be required to pay. If it were still to regard Newport as the best site, then the decision might have been accepted as socially optimal and the costly dispute between the unions and the government might not have happened. (It may be true that the real motive of the unions is power politics instead of a concern for the environment. But without a reasonable pretext, they may not be able to initiate the dispute.) A Newport power station of a size smaller than the one that does not take adequate account of environmental effects could have been built despite the Pigovian tax. In fact, the tax is not imposed and Victoria ends up with a stalemate between the unions and the government which is probably much more costly.

The case depicted in Figure 7.6 may also be doubted on the following ground. If K's valuation of the activity is reduced by more than the external cost due to the conscience effect, why does he not pay for it voluntarily? This may be explained by imperfect knowledge and transaction costs. But if transaction costs are prohibitive for voluntary payment, isn't it likely that they will be prohibitive for the taxation scheme? This may be so for many cases such as the grass-dumping example given above. For many other cases, the reverse may be true.

This is especially so if the number of individuals affected by an external effect is large. The transaction costs of paying for the damages are then likely to be very high. Yet it may not be too costly to impose a tax based on a reasonable estimate of the total damages.

We have argued that a Pigovian tax may actually increase the level of a diseconomy-producing activity due to the conscience effect. But such examples may be called extreme cases. The cases more likely to occur in practice are shown in Figure 7.7. Here, P^b lies to the right of S and the imposition of the tax reduces the activity. While this is less startling in the effect on the activity level, it is noteworthy in another aspect.

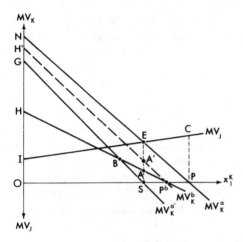

Figure 7.7

Both parties to the externality may be made better off without any compensation from the tax revenue. Party J gains from the reduction of the activity from P^b to S. K also gains if $\triangle OGS > \triangle OHP^b$, or equivalently, if $NHAE > NGSE + ASP^b$. ($\triangle OGS > \triangle OHP^b$ implies $\triangle GHB > \triangle BSP^b$ which in turn implies $NHAE > NGSE + ASP^b$.) The RHS is the amount of tax he pays plus his loss in reducing his activity from P^b to S, and the former is his gain due to the conscience effect. This may still be regarded as an extreme case since the total conscience effect is still larger than the external effect. A more likely case is for the conscience effect to move K's marginal valuation from MV_K^a to the dashed curve. Then $NH'A'E < NGSE = IOSE$. K will then be made worse off by the tax. But his loss is less than the amount indicated by the traditional analysis due to the conscience effect. The area $NH'A'E$ is ignored in the traditional analysis. For cases where the conscience (and the associated disturbance) effects are significant, corrective taxes do not just lead (after accounting for the tax revenue but ignoring transaction costs) to gains in triangular areas like $\triangle EPC$, but also to gains in areas of trapezoids like $NH'A'E$. If the conscience (including the associated disturbance) effects are not insignificant, the importance of the externality problem is greatly enhanced. Even if the conscience effect is relatively small, it should not be lightly ignored as it is of first-order magnitude in comparison to the traditional second-order cost of a marginal misallocation.

7.5* The Coase Theorem and Liability Rules

One of the most controversial topics on the problem of externality involves the so-called Coase theorem (Coase, 1960). Essentially, it is argued that the problem of externality is a two-way one. To avoid harm to J would inflict harm on K. In the absence of transaction costs, the two parties will agree to an optimal outcome irrespective of who has to pay compensation. Hence, the assignment of property rights does not affect the outcome.

Referring back to Figure 7.2, a certain activity of K affects J, say through the emission of smoke. If K has the right to emit smoke, he will carry his activity up to P. But in the absence of transaction costs, J will agree to pay K to reduce his activity to the level S. On the other hand, if K does not have the right to emit smoke, he will pay J for letting him do so. The optimal level of the activity will still be arrived at. At this optimal point S where the two MV curves intersect, no further gain is possible.

Several qualifications to the above argument have to be mentioned. First, if income effects are not negligible, the MV curve of each party will be different, depending on whether he has to pay or to receive compensation. Thus the point of intersection of the two curves may differ according to the assignment of property rights. However, while the presence of income effects affects the activity level, it does not affect the Pareto optimality nature of the outcomes. It just means that a different Pareto optimum will be reached due to a change in distribution effected through different assignments of property rights (Ng, 1971a, pp. 176–7).

Secondly, the proviso 'in the absence of transaction costs' is important. Where transaction costs are not negligible, we do not expect that a Pareto optimal outcome will necessarily be achieved by mutual agreement. Moreover, even in the absence of transaction costs, we observed above (Section 7.3) that the presence of game-strategic behaviour alone may prevent the reaching of an optimal solution. It is possible to extend the definition of transaction costs to include the cost arising from game-strategic behaviour or any other factor that impedes the attainment of Pareto optimality. Then Coase's theorem will be formally valid but will become just a tautology (Calabresi, 1968, Swan, 1975). In the real world where transaction costs, strategic behaviour, blackmailing, etc., are all present or possible, the best assignment of property rights becomes a tremendously complicated matter even if only the efficiency and not the equity aspect of the problem is being considered (Walsh, 1975, Ng, 1975b). As an example, consider the first-party-priority rule.

Barring strategic behaviour, if the transaction costs of reaching an agreement between the two parties to an existing externality are negligible, a Pareto-optimal outcome will emerge no matter how the property right is assigned. However, the assignment of property rights will affect future decisions. For example, if the party affected by factory smoke is entitled to receive compensation, this tends to encourage people to build houses close to the factory with no regard to the smoke effect since they will be compensated. This may result in socially inefficient decisions. Moreover, blackmailers who really have no intention of building houses nearby may threaten to do so in order to extort payment from the factory. In the absence of 'transaction costs' (in its all-inclusive definition), all relevant parties will come to a Pareto-optimal agreement. But while the assumption of negligible transaction costs between two parties may be reasonable for some cases, the 'transaction costs' between one party and all potentially affected parties (including blackmailers) must be enormous. Hence inefficiency will most likely emerge.

To overcome the above weakness of the bargaining solution, I have proposed that, in order to avoid inefficiency and blackmailing, it is generally the second party rather than the affecting party who should have to pay compensation (Ng, 1971a, p. 171). Ensuing discussion shows that the first-party-priority rule is not without limitation. While the affected-party-priority rule encourages people to pretend to be affected parties, the first-party-priority-rule may encourange people to pretend to be the first parties. For example, predicting an expansion of the residential areas, shrewd but unscrupulous people may set up smoke-emitting factories on the outskirts of a city, waiting to profit from the compensation paid by future residents there. However, since it is usually more difficult to ascertain the true second party (from blackmailers) than the true first party, the first-party-priority rule may still be of some merit, though many other factors have also to be taken into account. One of the basic difficulties of the bargaining solution is that, no matter how we assign property rights or what liability rule we adopt, it tends to be 'one-sided', and fails to tackle the two-sided nature of the externality problem adequately. The payment of compensation only makes the payer take into account the cost he imposes on others, failing to make the receiver and prospective receivers of compensation take account of the cost they impose on the payer. In this view, it seems that the bilateral tax/subsidy scheme is superior, provided that it is not too costly to administer.

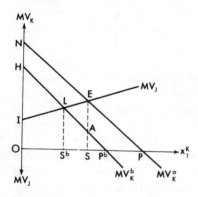

Figure 7.8

Thirdly, the Coase theorem ignores the conscience effect. Consider Figure 7.8 where K's MV curve is MV_K^a if the activity does not involve any unpaid-for external cost. The presence of this cost represented by MV_J reduces K's MV curve to MV_K^b. If J compensates K to reduce his activity from P^b to S^b, the net gain of the *activity* (not the change in the activity level) after this mutual agreement is $\Delta HIL = HOS^b L$ (K's benefit) $- IOS^b L$ (J's loss). On the other hand, if K compensates J for damages sustained, he will have a better conscience and so his MV curve is MV_K^a. The activity level will occur at S. More importantly, the net gain will now be ΔNIE which is larger than ΔHIL by $NHLE$. This extra gain is due to the conscience effect. In fact, the gain from the conscience effect may be larger than $NHLE$. This is so because the valuation K places on the payment by J may be less than its face value. It is likely that one would rather receive money from some neutral source than from someone who is externally affected by one's activity. On the other hand, such conscience effects are unlikely to operate if the affected party (say, householders) receives compensation from the affecting party (say, a smoke-emitting factory). Thus, even in the absence of transaction costs and strategic behaviour, it may be better for the affecting party instead of the affected party to pay compensation even if we ignore the question of equity. Nevertheless, this may contradict the first-party-priority rule. Again, this suggests the possible superiority of the bilateral taxation scheme. At the risk of repetition, it must be noted that the actual choice of a method of tackling an externality has to take many factors into account, including the costs of administration.

Summary

An externality is present when a utility/production function depends on a variable not under the control of the relevant consumer/producer and the dependence is not effected through the market relationship. If an activity of a person exerts an external diseconomy/economy on others, the level of the activity tends to be higher/lower than socially optimal. Different methods may be used to tackle this problem: a Pigovian tax/subsidy on the external diseconomy/economy according to the marginal external cost/benefit involved, mutual agreement with compensation between the parties involved, government regulations, etc. The Coase theorem says that, in the absence of transaction costs, a Pareto-optimal outcome will be arrived at by mutual agreement irrespective of whether the affecting or the affected party has the liability to pay compensation. However, liability rules may be important if we take account of issues such as blackmailing, equity, etc. Nevertheless, my proposed 'first-party priority rule' also has some limitations. Liability rules may also be important due to the 'conscience effect' whereby the affecting party's welfare may be reduced by the fact that he is adversely affecting the welfare of others without paying compensation. This conscience effect may make the problem of externality much more important than suggested by traditional analysis.

8 Public Goods

In the previous chapters, especially Chapter 2, we have been mainly concerned with an economy of private goods. But public goods are an (increasingly) important part of the economy. We discussed problems of externality in the last chapter and a public good is, in a certain sense, a special kind of externality in consumption. However, our discussion of externalities is mainly concerned with the 'small number' case where one party affects another. Most important external effects such as pollution affect large numbers of individuals. These external effects (public bads) may be regarded as involving an external diseconomy aspect and a publicness aspect. Hence, this chapter is not only relevant for the more traditional issue of the provision of public goods but also for the solution of the problem of public bads as well as other social issues involving a large number of individuals simultaneously.

8.1 Basic Characteristics of Public Goods

What is the basic characteristic that distinguishes public goods from private goods? Of the several criteria that have been suggested, two have been widely discussed. First, the same unit of a public good can be consumed by many individuals: its availability to one does not diminish its availability to others. This is called 'non-rivalry' in consumption. Examples of goods possessing this characteristic are national defence and (radio and television) broadcasting. My tuning in to a certain broadcast in no way reduces its availability to other receivers. On the other hand, once I have eaten an apple, it can no longer be consumed by others. Two persons may share an apple but then they will each be eating only half. Thus such goods as apples, bread, etc. are private goods. However, there are goods which fall between the polar cases of purely public and purely private goods. For example, books in libraries can be borrowed by different readers over different periods but not at the same time. In fact, even books on my own shelves have some degree of publicness since my students and colleagues quite often drop in to borrow them. However, for this case, since there is a prime beneficiary/owner, it is best regarded as a good with external effects, i.e. common consumption externality, instead of a public good. (The borrowing imposes negligible costs on me except when, occasionally, some borrowers forget to return books *and* I forget who borrowed them.)

The second characteristic related to public goods is 'nonexcludability'. Once the good is provided for some individuals, it is impossible or at least very costly to exclude others from benefiting from it. Defence is again a good example. It is also difficult to exclude people from receiving television signals. But licensing can be used as a (usually not very effective) way and cabled television as an effective but costly method of exclusion. Moreover, exclusion cost is almost never zero even for purely private goods since the production and distribution of all goods require the maintenance of law and order.

A characteristic which is both similar to and the opposite of nonexcludability is 'nonrejectability'. Defence again may be cited as an example. Once your country has been defended from foreign invasion, you are also defended, even if you prefer the chaos created by invasion. But nonrejectability is more important in the issue of 'public bads' (pollution and all that).

If a good is perfectly nonrivalrous, once provided, it *can* be made available to all individuals concerned at no additional cost. If a good is both perfectly nonexcludable and nonrejectable, it *must* be consumed at the same amount by all individuals concerned. The qualification 'concerned' here refers to a possible distinction between local, national and global public goods. For example, certain forms of broadcasting are effective only within a given geographical region while others can be picked up almost all over the world.

A characteristic that is of relevance here is that of 'decreasing (average) costs'. Quite often, a good may not be perfectly nonrivalrous, like broadcasting (given the programme, the place and strength of transmission), but once some units of it are produced, additional units can be supplied at very low costs. For example, the marginal cost (MC) of supplying your copy of this book is probably only a small fraction of the price since the bulk of the costs of publication consists in the fixed costs of writing, typing, editing, administration, typesetting, etc. However, many economists regard the question of decreasing costs as a separate issue from that of public goods since the production of both public and private goods may be subject to the condition of decreasing, increasing, or constant costs. Basically, this is due to two different dimensions of the good involved. For example, the publication of a book involves both the length (and/or quality) and the number of copies made (or more generally, the number of consumers served). For a pure public good, the MC with respect to the second dimension is zero but may be decreasing, increasing, or constant with respect to the first dimension. In the following paragraph, this first dimension is therefore being held constant.

Average costs (ACs) may be decreasing due to a substantial fixed cost component or to decreasing MCs. The latter case is however very rare and unimportant. (For this case, 'decreasing costs' as such need not have anything to do with publicness.) Let us therefore concentrate on the case of substantial fixed costs. For concreteness, consider the publication of this book. Once the book is to be published, the fixed costs are committed and can be used to serve any number of readers without diminishing its availability to others. It clearly possesses the characteristic of nonrivalry. It is true that the MC of printing and distributing additional copies is not zero. But we may treat it as a separate part. Moreover, this is true for most public goods. Take television, a very pure form of public good. The broadcasting part is a pure public good. But you need a television receiver (plus electricity consumption) to benefit from the broadcast. Clearly, a TV set is not costless and is a private good. It corresponds to a copy of this book, while the broadcasting corresponds to the writing and publication (as such) of the book. The main difference is that TV broadcasting and TV receiver sets are usually produced by quite separate groups while the same is not true for the publication of books. Nevertheless, in some cases of cabled broadcasting, both the broadcasting and the receiving sets are provided by the same organisation. On the other hand, it is also conceivable that the public good aspects of books may be recognised so that books approved by some independent selection committees may have their fixed costs paid for and supplied to competitive distributors at MCs and allow free copying. In fact, some universities and research institutions are fulfilling a small part of this function by subsidising the publication of books though, with limited funds, they usually price their books to minimise loss instead of at marginal costs (which may involve more losses).†

It may be objected that, if we regard the fixed cost component of a good as a public good, virtually all goods are public goods or possess a public good aspect. It is true that the production of most goods involves fixed costs (e.g. capital equipment) *in the short run*. But if the capital equipment is utilised close to capacity, output cannot increase without significantly increasing the MC. If the total market demand is large relative to the output of a firm, perfect competition ensures a long run equilibrium of price = MC = AC. This is then a clear case of a private good. Even if the efficient size of production is large and we have a monopolist operating at the range of decreasing AC, the industry may still be more efficiently run by private enterprise, though the fixed-cost component may be regarded as possessing a public good aspect. This is partly a problem of the relative importance of the fixed cost component and partly a problem of the relative efficiency of private versus public production.

Some economists (notably Musgrave, 1959, 1969a) emphasise the nonexcludability aspect of public goods, arguing that, with excludability, nonrivalrous goods can be effectively provided by private production. But if we do not regard public production as a necessary and sufficient condition for a public good, it seems analytically more fruitful to regard nonrivalry as the basic defining characteristic and accept other characteristics such as nonexcludability, nonrejectability as factors that make the good more difficult to be provided by private production. On this view, we can then have excludable public goods, nonexcludable public goods, etc.

8.2 Optimality Conditions and Provision of Public Goods

Due to the nature of a public good, the (top-level) optimality condition for its provision is quite different from that for private goods in the form $MRS^i = MRT$ discussed in Chapter 2. In the case of a pure

---

†After writing the first draft, I came accross Baumol (1977), who argues along similar lines but more forcefully. He maintains that public goods are just special cases of decreasing costs and/or externality and do not provide an *independent* justification for government subsidy.

private good, the sum of the amounts consumed by various individuals equals the (net) amount produced. In the case of a pure public good, the total amount produced is (or at least can be) simultaneously consumed by all individuals. Due to this difference, it can be shown (see Appendix 8A) that the Pareto-optimality condition for the supply of a public good is characterised by $\Sigma MRS^i = MRT$, i.e. the *sum* over all individuals of the marginal rate of substitution (of the public good for a numeraire private good) be equal to the marginal rate of transformation (Samuelson, 1954, 1955). The reason for this optimality condition is not difficult to see. Once a public good is provided, it can be enjoyed by all individuals. Pareto optimality requires that it be made available to all, and it is the sum of the marginal benefits over all individuals that should be compared with the MC of providing it in determining the optimal amount of the public good. The MRS and MRT are just respectively measures of the marginal benefits (or marginal valuations) and marginal costs in terms of numeraire good.

The condition for the optimal supply of a public good is illustrated in Figure 8.1. For simplicity, assume that there are only two individuals whose marginal valuations of the public good X (measured along the horizontal axis) are represented by MV^J and MV^K respectively. Abstracting from income effects, these MV curves also correspond to

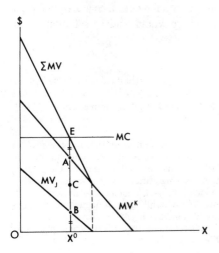

Figure 8.1

individual demand curves.† The vertical sum of the individual MV curves (denoted ΣMV) intersect the MC curve at the point E. This determines the optimal amount X^0 of the public good. At this amount of the good, $\Sigma MV (= BX^0 + AX^0 = EX^0) = MC$. ‡

However, the optimality condition discussed above is formulated within a framework devoid of institutional considerations, ignoring e.g. the method of financing the provision of public goods. Hence the condition refers to an ideal which may or may not be possible to realise. Moreover, when we take account of the relevant complications in the real world, it may or may not be desirable to stick rigidly to the optimality conditon (Stiglitz & Dasgupta, 1971, Lau, Sheshinski & Stiglitz, 1978*). This will become clearer after the discussion in the rest of this section.

Once a pure public good is produced, it does not cost anything to make it available to more individuals. Thus it seems desirable to make it available to all. But should those who have access to the public good pay for the cost of producing it? Suppose we charge each individual a price equal to $1/I$ the cost of producing the public good, where I is the number of individuals. Then those individuals who benefit only slightly from the good may choose not to consume it. This may be undesirable, since the cost of making the good available to them is zero. Let us then charge these individuals a low price and charge those who benefit more a higher price, etc. (Ideally, each individual would face a marginal price equal to his marginal valuation and we would achieve a Lindahl equi-

---

†Income effects may shift MV curves. Hence, strictly speaking, the optimal supply of a public good is not independent of the way it is financed; see Strotz (1958), Samuelson (1969), McGuire & Aaron (1969), Bergstrom & Cornes, 1981*. However, for most cases, within the relevant range of cost-shares, the degree of indeterminacy is trivial.

‡The MC curve is drawn as horizontal in Figure 8.1, which is not essential for the analysis. A horizontal $MC = AC$ curve may be due to the condition of constant costs of production. Alternatively, we may define the units of X such as to make the cost curve horizontal. If there is a significant fixed cost element, there will then be an initial section of X which is subject to an all-or-nothing choice. If the MC in producing the 'natural unit' of the public good is decreasing, this may overbalance the diminishing MV to result in increaseing MV curves in X defined to make the cost curve horizontal. On the importance of cost-efficiency in the provision of public goods, see Olson (1974).

librium.†) But then consumers may try to conceal their true MV so as to qualify to pay a low price, resulting in an under-supply of the public good. (This is the problem of preference revelation, often referred to as the 'free-rider' problem, to be discussed further below.) What about making the public good free, financing it from general taxation? But the collection of tax revenue may involve costs in addition to the revenue raised, i.e. 'excess burden' of taxation. Taking account of the budget constraint of the public sector, it may be better to charge a positive price even for pure (but excludable) public goods (Baumol & Ordover, 1977). A positive price reduces the amount that has to be financed from taxation and hence reduces the excess burden of taxation though at a cost of discouraging some consumers from consuming the full amount of the public good produced. It is a matter of striking an optimal balance between the two inefficiencies. Moreover, without charging a price how do we know the extent to which the public benefits from the public good? In the case of a private good, consumers have to pay for it and hence their preferences are revealed through their willingness to pay. If they do not have to pay directly for the consumption of public goods, how do we know that it is worth the costs of supplying them? (Again, the problem of preference revelation.) Thus making consumers pay for public goods, though involving some inefficiencies in comparison to the ideal, may be superior to the alternative of making them free. The problem of the optimal provision of public goods is more complicated than the simple condition $\Sigma MRS = MRT$ discussed above.

It has been argued that, for an excludable public good, under-supply will not be a problem since the competitive market can provide the good effectively. In fact, Thompson (1968) goes so far as to claim that over-supply will result. However, he assumes that producers have full knowledge of the demand curves of all consumers and can thus extract all their consumer surplus. If there is freedom of entry and no decreasing cost in production, competition for the surplus will then force down

---

†For an exposition of Lindahl's analysis, see Johansen (1963). See Roberts (1974) on the more technical aspects (such as existence) of the Lindahl solution. For a survey of the advanced literature of general equilibrium with public goods, see Milleron (1972)*.

the price and lead to over-supply. Demsetz (1970) does not rely so much on the rather questionable assumption of perfect knowledge but regards a public good as essentially analogous to joint supply. 'Just as the slaughtering of a steer provides goods to both leather users and meat consumers, so the production of a public good, by definition, yields benefits that can be enjoyed by more than one individual' (Demsetz, 1970, p. 293). In other words the same public good consumed by different individuals is regarded as different 'goods'. But what is overlooked is the following important distinction. For the case of joint supply, there is a large number of consumers competing for each of the jointly supplied good. This condition, among others, ensures that competitive private production of jointly supplied goods is efficient. On the other hand, for the case of a public good, each 'good' has, by definition, only one consumer. This makes the argument that the private production of excludable public goods is as efficient as the case of competitive joint supply questionable (Head, 1977).

A more convincing argument on the (theoretical possibility of) competitive private production of a public good is that of Oakland (1974). In contrast to Thompson, Oakland assumes that producers have no knowledge of the differences in the willingness to pay of different consumers. Hence, any *given* unit of the public good must be sold to all consumers at the same price. Nevertheless, *different units* may be sold at different prices. In the case of television tapes taken as perfectly substitutable (though no one wants to view the same tape twice) and produced at constant cost, the same price will be charged for each tape to all consumers, but different tapes may command different prices. Consumers with low demand will consume only the low-priced tapes while those with high demand will consume low-priced *and* high-priced tapes. This is best illustrated in Figure 8.2 for a simple case of three consumers. (Similar to figure VI in Head, 1977.)

Assuming freedom of entry, the price for any unit of the public good will be lowered to yield no profit. But since, from the definition of a public good, the same unit can be sold to different consumers, this price also depends on the number of consumers for that unit. For the case illustrated in Figure 8.2, the first X^3 units can be sold to all the three consumers at a price equal to $1/3\ AC$. At this price, individual 3 will consume no more than X^3. But the other two individuals are pre-

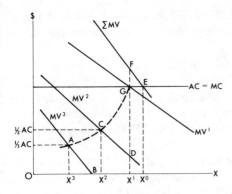

Figure 8.2

pared to pay for additional units even at a higher price. Thus $X^2 - X^3$ units can be produced and sold at $1/2\,AC$ to them. Similarly, $X^1 - X^2$ units are produced and sold to individual 1 only. It may appear impossible that we can have an equilibrium with different prices charged for different units of the same good. But all producers are making zero profits. No producer can increase his price due to free entry. While most producers (except those selling to all consumers) would be able to increase their profits if they could lower their prices only to *new* consumers, this cannot be done as the original customers would demand the same treatment and freedom of entry would ensure that these demands would be met. Moreover, there is no opportunity for arbitrage among consumers since individuals who consume the higher-priced units have already purchased the lower-priced ones.

While private production of a public good in the Oakland model is feasible, it falls short of the ideal in two respects, as Oakland himself recognises. First, total production X^1 falls short of the optimum X^0. Secondly, some individuals are excluded from consuming some of the units produced even though their consumption would not add to costs. For example, in the case of Figure 8.2, individual 2 does not consume those units from X^2 to X^1 even though his MV is still positive at X^2. Nevertheless, since the ideal is seldom attainable in practice, these two shortcomings need not be regarded as significant unless the welfare costs involved are very large. For the case illustrated in Figure 8.2, these costs (areas $AX^3B + CX^2X^1D + FGE$) are relatively small. If this is typical of the actual cases, private production is quite acceptable. But is it typical?

It is difficult to find a good practical example of a public good produced under Oakland's conditions. In particular, the differential prices charged for different units of the same public good sold to different sets of consumers do not seem to exist. Why the divergence between the theoretical feasibility and the actual world? The following explanation may be offered.

Observing Figure 8.2, one may note that if MV^1 (the highest individual MV curve, assuming non-intersecting MV curves) intersects the horizontal cost curve at a point to the left of X^2, no additional units of the public good can be produced under Oakland's conditions beyond X^2. In other words, no unit can be produced for only one individual. This is likely to be true for the case of a large number of individuals where the cost curve is high relative to individual MV curves. Consider Figure 8.3 depicting the case of just ten individuals with MV curves concentrated at the lower-middle range, as is likely'in most actual cases. As we connect the intersection of MV^{10} with $1/10 \ AC$, MV^9 with $1/9 \ AC$ and so on, we find that the curve has an almost horizontal section AB, an upward-sloping section BC and becomes vertical and turns leftward after C (corresponding to X^8), in contrast to the positively sloped curve ACG in Figure 8.2. This means that no more than

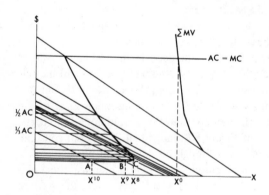

Figure 8.3

X^8 amount of the good can be produced under the Oakland model. This may fall significantly below the social optimal level X^0, and the associated welfare cost may be significant. However, it seems that three different prices (1/10 AC, 1/9 AC, 1/8 AC) are still feasible for the corresponding three different sections. This is so at the level of abstraction of the Oakland model but may no longer be so if we take into account a number of practical considerations discussed below.

In the case of thousands of individuals, the cost of production is likely to be many times higher than an average individual MV curve and higher than the highest individual MV curve. Who will view a television programme if he has to pay for the entire cost of production? In this case, the almost horizontal section AB is likely to be flatter still, consisting of hundreds of practically horizontal sections. This may make it administratively impracticable to charge different prices for this section. Moreover, who cares about a difference between $100 and $99.999? Thus all units before point B are likely to be sold under a single price. On the other hand, the upward sloping section BC is likely to shrink further into a tiny section and may even vanish altogether in the case of many individuals, especially if the individual MV curves are very concentrated towards the lower-middle section. While we have drawn the cost curve as hortizontal right from the level of zero output, in practice, there is likely to be a certain minimum size for efficiency. If BC has shrunk into something much smaller than this minimum size, this section of the market cannot exist. Then we will observe a uniform price and a sub-optimal level of output.

Even if the above considerations are not sufficient to rule out differential prices, indivisibility in the units of the public good may do the trick. Consider the following hypothetical example. The dramatic death of a once famous singer makes the reproduction of some of his records profitable. Consumers go mainly for his name and hence regard each of his records as a perfect substitute for any other. The cost of producing each record is also the same. Ignoring the small MC of making extra copies, the reproduction of each record is an indivisible unit of the public good. Suppose 1,000 copies of the first record are reproduced at a total cost of $1,000 and sold to 1,000 consumers at $1 a copy. Some of these consumers would like to purchase additional (but different) records by that singer at a higher price. But if less than

500 are willing to pay $2, less than 333 are willing to pay $3, etc., the reproduction of the second record is not a profitable proposition. If it is possible to reproduce half a unit of the second record at a cost of $500, there may be, say, 400 consumers each willing to pay a price of $1.25 for it. We may then observe the differential prices. But indivisibility in record production rules this out.

In addition to the above considerations, it may be added that the production of many public goods is subject to the condition of decreasing AC over a wide range of output, making the competitive production of these public goods even more unlikely. (A more interesting model of private production may therefore be that of a monopolist. Brennan, Head & Walsh, 1979, analyse a profit-maximising monopolist producer of a public good charging differential Oakland prices; see also Brito & Oakland, 1980, Burns & Walsh, 1981). Nevertheless, the lack of real-world examples does not make Oakland's analysis useless.

> Several considerations can be brought to bear on this issue. (*1*) While it is true that under present arrangements examples are difficult to come by, we need not take such arrangements as given. Thus one could imagine market provision of broadcasting, and outdoor recreation facilities such as parks, police, and fire protection. Before rejecting private provision of such excludable services as an alternative, we must know some of its characteristics. (*2*) There is increasing pressure on state and local governments to consider user finance for many of their activities. The present analysis sheds light on the outcome of a decentralised self-supporting finance arrangement . . . (Oakland, 1974, p. 938).

Our discussion above supplements Oakland's analysis by showing that the problem of under-production is likely to be quite serious and differential pricing may not be practical.

8.3* An Incentive-Compatible Mechanism for Preference Revelation

As we have discussed above, preference revelation is a very important issue in the provision of public goods. But the free-rider problem has long been regarded as intrinsically unsolvable in our world of imperfect knowledge and individual self-interest. Thus the discovery of an *incentive-compatible* mechanism whereby self-interested individuals are induced to reveal their true preference for public goods can be rightly hailed as a landmark in the theory of public goods. In fact, Tideman & Tullock (1976) regarded the proposed mechanism as being so important that they had to warn readers that it will not cure cancer or stop the tides!

The mechanism was discovered by Clarke (1971, 1972, 1980) and Groves (1970U, 1973, 1976); see also Groves & Loeb (1975), Groves & Ledyard (1977a)*. Hence, we shall call it the Clarke–Groves mechanism.† It may also be noted that the problem of incentive-compatible mechanisms has also been discussed by Dreze & Poussin (1971)* and by Malinvaud (1971)*. However, their approaches are quite different from that of Clarke and Groves. Basically they adopt a game-theoretic framework and assume that a consumer adopts a minimax strategy. Hence, their proposed mechanisms seem more relevant for cases where the numbers of (all 'pessimistic') individuals concerned are small and where the process is an on-going (in contrast to a once-and-over) one.

While the Clarke–Groves mechanism has been developed to take account of some complicated aspects such as general equilibrium (e.g. Groves & Ledyard, 1977a*, 1980*, Pethig, 1979) and dynamic procedures (Green & Laffont, 1978a), we shall just discuss the more essential parts of the mechanism, mainly following the exposition by Tideman & Tullock (1976). Consider Figure 8.4a where X, measured along the horizontal axis, may be taken either as the number of units of a public good defined to cost $1 each or just the total $ expenditure on the public good. The horizontal line through the $1 mark then represents the MC curve. The Clarke–Groves mechanism may be broken down into the following steps.

---

†Green & Laffont (1977a)* show that this is the only class of mechanisms with the desired properties. Vickrey (1961) described a similar mechanism in connection with optimal counter-speculation policy and price auction procedure, but was not fully aware of its significance. On various alternative versions of the mechanism, see Loeb (1977). For a fairly comprehensive bibliography on the literature on demand-revealing mechanisms, see the introduction on the special issue (Spring, 1977) of *Public Choice* on the topic. A monograph tackling specifically problems of incentive-compatible mechanisms is Green and Laffont (1978b).

Step 1: Each consumer is allocated a (percentage) share of the total cost of providing the public good, with $\Sigma s^i = 1$ where s^i is the cost-share of individual i. Thus the cost of production of the good (irrespective of the amount produced) is adequately covered by these levies. For the moment, we may take the method of determining the shares as given, either by convention, by equal shares or determined arbitrarily.

Step 2: Consumers are then asked to report their MV curves (they need not be linear) which are then summed vertically to give $\Sigma_{i=1}^I MV^i$ whose intersection with the MC curve determines the amount of the public good to be supplied as X^0. (Income effects are again ignored: see the first footnote on p. 192 and also Bradford & Hildebrandt, 1977*

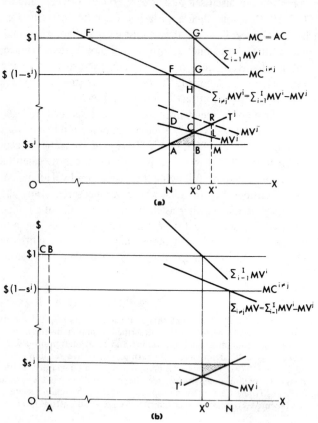

Figure 8.4

which shows how the market demand functions for private goods may be used to reveal preferences for public goods.)

Step 3: Each consumer j, *in addition to* his share in the total cost of production discussed in step 1, has to pay a Clarke-Groves tax determined in the following manner. A horizontal line is drawn through the point $\$(1-s^j)$. This line is labelled $MC^{i \neq j}$ since it is the MC to all consumers other than j. The curve $\Sigma_{i \neq j}MV^i = \Sigma_{i=1}^{I}MV^i - MV^j$ is then drawn in. This is the aggregate MV of all consumers other than j. It intersects the $MC^{i \neq j}$ curve at a point (F) to the left of X^0 since the MV^j curve lies higher than the line through $\$s^j$ at the point X^0. (The reverse case is illustrated in Figure 8.4b). The Clarke-Groves tax on consumer j is then the difference between $MC^{i \neq j}$ and $\Sigma_{i \neq j}MV^i$ from the point N to X^0 or the (curvilinear) ΔFHG. Drawing T^j as the mirror image of $\Sigma_{i \neq j}MV^i$, the tax also equals the shaded ΔABC, where $BC = HG$. For the case where MV^j lies below s^j at the point X^0 illustrated in Figure 8.4b, $\Sigma_{i \neq j}MV^i$ intersects $MC^{i \neq j}$ at a point to the right of X^0. The Clarke-Groves tax is then the difference between $\Sigma_{i \neq j}MV^i$ and $MC^{i \neq j}$ from the point N to X^0, or the shaded triangle.

The three steps described above are the basic outlines of the Clarke-Groves mechanism. We turn now to examine its rationale and the reason why it works. The point N is the amount of the public good that would be supplied if individual j were to report his MV as identical with his cost-share, i.e. the horizontal line through $\$s^j$. This is the level of supply preferred by all consumers other than j, as a group, given s^j, since it is at this point (N) that $\Sigma_{i \neq j}MV^i$ intersects $MC^{i \neq j}$. By reporting a MV^j curve either above or below $\$s^j$, consumer j causes the amount of the public good provided to differ from N. Thus, from the viewpoint of all other consumers, they suffer a loss measured by the shaded triangle. By making consumer j pay precisely this shaded triangle, he is thus motivated not to attempt to increase or reduce the supply of the public good from the point N, unless by doing so he gains more than the loss to other consumers. He will then find it in his own interest to report his MV truthfully. To see this more clearly, suppose he overstates his MV to be $MV^{j\prime}$, in Figure 8.4a. This will cause the public good to be supplied at $X^\prime$. His MV on the extra amount $X^0 X^\prime$ is the area $CX^0 X^\prime L$. But he has to pay an extra $X^0 X^\prime MB$ in cost-share *plus* an extra $CBMR$ in the Clarke-Groves tax. Thus the net loss of misreporting is ΔCLR. Similarly, if he under-reports, it can be shown that his forgone benefit exceeds his saving in his cost-share and tax. Thus, the best strategy for him is to report his MV curve truthfully. This argument for an individual j is true for any $j = 1, \ldots, I$. Hence all individuals will be motivated to reveal their true preferences.

It may be noted that the assignment of cost-shares is to ensure adequate finance for meeting the cost of providing the public good. *If* this cost can be met in a way not affecting individual motivation, then we could start with no pre-assigned cost-shares. The Clarke–Groves tax would still induce the revelation of true preferences as we have shown towards the end of Section 7.2 with respect to externality (where no cost of production need be met). The Clarke–Groves tax for a typical consumer would then be a larger amount, being $\Delta F'HG'$ in Figure 8.4a for consumer j.

Since the cost of providing the public good is already adequately met by the cost-sharing arrangement, the collection of the Clarke–Groves tax represents the surplus of the process. In the case where the number of individuals is large, this surplus can be used for the benefit of the group as a whole without any significant effect on incentives to reveal true preferences. But strictly speaking, a sophisticated individual may take into account the effect of his reported MV curve on the amount of Clarke–Groves taxes others have to pay. If he has a share in the benefits of the surplus, he may then be motivated to misrepresent his preference. This is consistent with the impossibility results by Hurwicz (1972)* and by Ledyard & Roberts (1974U)* that there exists in general no resource allocation mechanism that yields 'individually rational' Pareto optima which are also incentive-compatible for each individual. But this impossibility result is derived by ignoring the costs (time, trouble, and conscience) of behaving in a strictly 'rational' fashion. Hence, at least in the case of large numbers, the surplus of the Clarke–Groves tax can safely be used for the group as a whole without any adverse effect on preference revelation. Otherwise we would not have correct preference revelation for private goods either. However, for the case of a small number of individuals, this adverse effect may be significant, for two reasons. First, each individual will then have a higher share in the benefits from the surplus. Secondly, the surplus itself will be relatively a much larger amount as the Clarke–Groves tax on each individual decreases rapidly with the number of individuals (Green, Kohlberg & Laffont, 1976*). How do we overcome this difficulty?

Tideman & Tullock (1976) have an interesting suggestion to make on the disposal of the Clarke-Groves surplus. They suggest that the surplus should be wasted and be regarded as a cost in the process of preference revelation. They justify this partly on the ground that, for the case of a large number of individuals, the surplus is only a small amount relative to the cost of providing the public good. Nevertheless, as we argued in the preceding paragraph, it is in cases of small numbers that the problem of surplus disposal is a real problem. But cases of small numbers usually involve relatively larger amounts of surplus. This difficulty can largely be solved by slightly revising the assignment of cost-shares discussed in Step 1 above. Right from the beginning, a lower estimate is made on the total amount of Clarke-Groves taxes that will be collected. Out of the total cost of production, an amount equal to this estimate (say, $OABC$ in Figure 8.4b) is set aside. In other words, costs in excess of this estimated amount are then assigned to be shared by the various consumers. In this revised scheme, the amount of surplus is still likely to be positive since the estimate is a lower estimate (to avoid losses to a high degree of confidence), but it is likely to be a small amount. Then this small amount of surplus can either be wasted, or, better still, donated to some outside body.

Tideman & Tullock also have an interesting proposal with respect to the assignment of cost-shares whereby a Lindahl equilibrium may be approximated.† An official is appointed to assign the cost-shares, 'with the stipulation that from his pay we are going to subtract some multiple of the sum of the triangles [i.e. the Clarke-Groves taxes] for all the voters [i.e. consumers]. The person assigning the fixed [cost] share would be motivated to try to minimise the triangles. In the limit, if he were able to perfectly achieve his goal, there would be no triangles and no loss (or surplus); we would have a perfect Lindahl equilibrium, with each voter paying for public goods according to his marginal evaluation' (Tideman & Tullock, 1976, p. 1156). With advanced econometric method, Tideman & Tullock believe that the official would be able to

---

†Compare the use of unanimous auction election to achieve a Lindahl equilibrium discussed by Smith (1977). This method has the advantage of making no one worse off (each individual has a veto power) but also the disadvantage of a possible stalemate, as happened in one of the five experiments conducted by Smith (1977, p. 1132). Smith and others have also done experiments with the incentive-compatible mechanism; see Smith (1979, 1980).

do quite well (though not perfectly, otherwise there would be no need for preference revelation) despite the fact that there is one piece of information he is not allowed to use in assigning the cost share of any individual – that individual's reported MV curves in previous choices. Otherwise, the individual may be motivated to understate his MV curve so as to obtain a lower cost-share in the future.

So much for the theory of the Clarke–Groves mechanism; what about its practicability in actual decision making? One difficulty which is regarded as 'serious' by Tideman & Tullock is the fact that, for the case of a large number of consumers, each has very little incentive to go to the trouble of putting in a report at all since each report has very little effect on the amount of the public good supplied. This difficulty seems to be relatively easy to resolve as long as there is, as is likely, some section (especially if it is a representative one) of the population that does report. For those who fail to report their MV curves are just taken to be their assigned cost shares (i.e. the horizontal line through $\$s^j$). In terms of purely economic incentives, it is those whose cost shares differ more from their MV at the margin (in either direction) who have greater incentive to report, since the gain to each in reporting (such as ΔACD in Figure 8.4a) is then larger. Thus, one may expect that the reporting section may be non-representative of the population in this sense. However, it may be representative in the following sense. As long as the above divergence is equal in each direction (i.e. as high a proportion of people with low MV relative to cost shares reports as people with high MV relative to cost shares), the resulting supply of the public good will still be optimal from the view of the whole population. Even if the reporting section is non-representative of the population in this latter sense, the resulting supply of the public good is still optimal from the view of the *reporters* since nonreporters still have to pay their cost shares. A possible source of non-representativeness of the reporting section may be due to the epistemological problem discussed below. It may happen that the more educated section of the population will have a higher percentage of reporters. If they also have higher than average MV, this may exaggerate the aggregate MV. However, this bias will not be present if these better educated people are already allocated higher cost shares in accordance with, say, econometric estimates of their MV. This is so because, in the estimation of aggregate MV, we add all the reported MV curves and the cost shares of the nonreporters. This estimated aggregate *MV* will be less steep than the true one but will still intersect the *MC* curve at approximately the same place. If desired, econometric methods may again be used to correct (approximately) for the divergence in the steepness. If the better educated sections are not allocated higher cost shares, the estimated aggregate *MV* may be non-representative of the whole population. Whether we should then use statistical methods to adjust for this bias depends on whether we want to achieve optimality for the reporting section or for the whole population or whether the failure to report should be taken as giving up one's potential gain of ΔACD.

Apart from the basic difficulty of coalition (see Section 5.4.2), the more important practical difficulties of the preference revelation scheme are epistemological, political, and administrative.† A participant must not only know how to reveal his preference by drawing his *MV* curve correctly, he has also to understand the whole rationale of the scheme so that he knows that it is advantageous to him to report truthfully. Anyone who has experience in marking undergraduate examination papers will have doubts that an average citizen is able to achieve such an understanding. Perhaps what can be hoped is that he may trust the assurance of the expert and proceed to draw his *MV* curve at his very best. Second, assignment of cost-shares may not be politically acceptable. Whether the assignment is equal, arbitrary, or decided by the Tideman–Tullock official, it is likely that many individuals will claim that their shares are 'excessive'. Perhaps a politically more acceptable method of cost assignment is to tie the cost-shares to some extent with income levels since income is one of the major determinants of *MV* and since this would be more consistent with the present method of financing public goods. Third, the costs of admini-

---

†Groves & Ledyard (1977b, p. 107) also 'present five warnings intended to dampen any premature urge to adopt a constitutional amendment to institute one of these demand-revealing mechanisms'. Except with respect to the difficulty creation by coalitions, I agree basically with the argument by Tideman & Tullock (1977) that these limitations are not very significant. While all known group decision mechanisms are subject to manipulation by coalitions, the demand-revealing mechanisms seems particularly vulnerable; see the second half of Section 5.4.2 above. On some practical issues,, see also Bohm (1979). For a comparison of survey and hedonic approaches to the empirical measurement of the value of public goods, see Brookshire, Thayer, Schulze & D'Arge (1982).

stering the scheme for the large-number case must be prohibitive. Nevertheless, these costs can be significantly reduced by requiring only a sample of the population to report their MV curves (Green & Laffont, 1977b). While all individuals have to pay the assigned cost-shares, only those in the sample have to report and pay the Clarke-Groves taxes.

The sampling method has another advantage as it can be used to mitigate the difficulty due to coalition by making the sample secret. If only 2,000 out of 200 million individuals have to report, it will be rather costly for any individual in the 2,000 to find a partner, especially if attempts at coalition-forming are declared illegal. In addition, if the time of sampling and the time of reporting are made as close as possible, coalitions may be well nigh impossible. Another method to suppress coalition is to disallow vertical MV curves. In our present continuous case, the counterpart of reporting an arbitrarily high value (see the discrete case discussed in Section 5.4.2) is for the coalition members to report the same vertical MV curve. For most public goods, it can be reasonably assumed that vertical MV curves are impossible to prevail. If individuals are constrained to report reasonably downward sloping MV curves, there will be a cost (in terms of the Clarke-Groves tax) to each coalition member in sticking to the agreed false MV curve. Hence, if the reports are also classified confidential, each coalition member will have an incentive to betray the coalition and report truthfully himself. (On some other difficulties of coalition-forming, see Tullock, 1977.)

Apart from the difficulties mentioned above, we have the additional problem that many of the publicly provided goods such as education are not pure public goods. These goods may be publicly provided more on the ground of external benefits, merit wants, distributional considerations, etc. than on the ground of nonrivalness in consumption. Hence, we cannot simply rely on the Clarke-Groves mechanism discussed above to determine the optimal provision of public goods. For one thing, even if one is prepared to accept that an individual is the best judge of his own interest with respect to his consumption of private goods, one may reasonably be sceptical that an average citizen can know the extent to which he will benefit from an additional expenditure on preventive public health-care that may, among other things, reduce the probability of the outbreak of communicable diseases.

Moreover, the beneficiaries of the expenditure on health-care may include those unborn at the present who are thus unable to report their *MV* curves.

While the possibility of actually using the Clarke–Groves mechanism for most public goods is remote, its potential for application in some specific cases cannot be denied. Moreover, even if the Clarke–Groves mechanism has rather limited practical applicability, it must still be regarded as an important theoretical contribution since it shows that the problem of preference revelation is essentially one of practical difficulty instead of intrinsic intractability.

8.4* Income Distribution as a Peculiar Public Good: The Paradox of Redistribution

While the concept of public goods is an important one, few practical examples of a *pure* public good can be found. It has however been suggested that, since some people may have a preference over the distribution of income as such (excluding the effects on their own income levels), income distribution may be regarded as a pure public good. (On some empirical applications of the concept of income distribution as a public good, see Orr, 1976, and Morawetz, 1977.) In this sense, income distribution is indeed the purest of all public goods, since it meets all the tests of a pure public good. 'Exclusion is impossible, consumption is nonrival; each individual must consume the same quantity' (Thurow, 1971, pp. 328-9). It can, however, be shown that income distribution as a public good has a peculiar nature which renders the traditional analysis inappropriate in some sense. This peculiar nature may be called the paradox of redistribution (Ng, 1973a). It refers to the fact that, on counting the compensating or equivalent variations, it seems that a Pareto redistribution of income (i.e. one that makes someone better and no one worse off due to utility interdependency; see Hochman & Rodgers, 1969, and the ensuing discussion) is possible, though in fact it is impossible. The Pareto optimality condition for a public good must correspondingly be revised as it is no longer in the simple form of aggregate MRS. A verbal and geometrical discussion is provided below; the mathematics is in Appendix 8A.

A Pareto improvement requires that no one be made worse off. If some individuals are made worse off by the production of a public good, e.g. a super-highway, the Pareto criterion may yet be met if they are sufficiently compensated, and the rest of the community is still better off after paying the compensation. In other words, if the maximum amount of money the gainers are willing to pay for a public good exceeds the cost of production plus the amount necessary to compensate the losers, a Pareto improvement is still possible. While this is true for other goods, it is not so for the peculiar public good, income distribution. In order to arrive at some income distribution while making no one worse off, those made worse off must be compensated. But once this compensation is paid, income distribution itself has been changed.

A highly simplified example may be helpful at this point. In a community of one rich man and two poor men, supose that the poor men are strong egalitarians and each of them values each dollar transferred from the rich man to be shared equally by the two poor men at one dollar, i.e. 50 cents in excess of what he himself receives. Suppose also that the rich man is self-centring and cares only for his own income. The aggregate benefit of the transfer of one dollar is therefore $2 which is larger than the cost of $1 to the rich man. The poor men are willing to pay a higher sum ($2) to buy a unit of the public good 'distributional equality' than that necessary to compensate the loser (the rich man). Assuming negligible administrative and efficiency costs, a Pareto improvement should be possible in the 'production' of this public good if it is a normal public good. But as income distribution is a peculiar public good, no Pareto redistribution may be possible at all. Thus, in the example, as the rich man is self-centring, he has to receive exactly one dollar in compensation for each dollar transferred to the poor. The society may decide to supply the public good 'equality' since the amount people are willing to pay exceeds the cost of production (which is negligible here) plus the necessary amount of compensation. However, if the redistribution is to remain Pareto optimal, the rich man has to be paid back with exactly the same amount transferred. This leads back to exactly the initial situation. We have thus illustrated that, with the peculiar public good income distribution, a Pareto improvement may not be possible even though the counting of compensating or equivalent variations suggests the reverse. (This paradox of redistribution is not the same as the Boadway paradox due to a change in price discussed in Section 4.5.)

The argument above is not based on the fact that the rich man is self-centring. Even if he derives some satisfaction from a more equal distribution, a Pareto redistribution may still be impossible unless he (or they, in the case of many rich men) places a higher valuation on a more equal distribution than the amount of money he has to give up. If this is so, the Pareto redistribution will be automatically achieved in the case of one rich man just by his voluntary transfer. However, in the case of many rich men, some coordinated action may be necessary and a Pareto optimal redistribution may not be realised in the free market because of the problems of strategic behaviour, negotiating costs, information, etc.

Our argument may be put in a more general way geometrically. Consider Figure 8.5 where the horizontal axis represents some measure of income distribution X. The point E represents complete equality and O complete inequality. $\overline{X}$ is the initial point. The curves B^1, B^2, B^3 represent the total benefits (to the three individuals) of each level of income distribution X, as compared to the existing point $\overline{X}$. B^s is the vertical summation of B^1, B^2 and B^3, and hence is the benefit curve for the whole society. If redistribution can be achieved without cost, the optimal supply of 'equality' is indicated, according to the counting of compensating or equivalent variations, by the point H where the curve B^s attains its maximum. But it can clearly be seen that the point H is not Pareto superior to $\overline{X}$ as the third individual is made worse off.

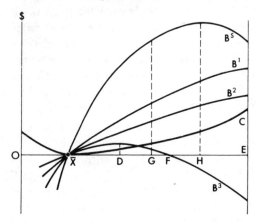

Figure 8.5

To stay within the framework of Pareto redistribution, no person must be made worse off. thus a constraint is set that redistribution must not make any benefit curve become negative. The segment FE is hence ruled out. The segment OD is also ruled out because within it everyone can be made better off. This leaves us with the segment DF. Since B^s is positively sloped within this segment, it appears that F is preferable to D. But for individual 3, D is preferable to F. Hence, if F is achieved by an indivisible jump from $\bar{X}$, it is a Pareto redistribution; no one is made worse off. But if the movement is a continuous one, that part of redistribution from D to F is no longer a Pareto improvement.

In the figure, the 'net marginal social benefit' of equality is still positive in the segment FH (i.e. B^s is positively sloped). But redistributing income from $\bar{X}$ to this segment is not Pareto improvement. The amount of money the society is willing to pay for redistribution is larger than the necessary compensation to make the losers not worse off, yet the society is not able to achieve this level of equality if the Pareto criterion is to be satisfied. This suggests that income distribution cannot be analysed in exactly the same terms as other public goods, despite the fact that it meets all the tests of a public good. To those not content with Pareto redistribution, this also seems to provide some gunpowder for their argument that the Pareto criterion is not sufficient.

To inject a dose of 'realism', introduce the costs of redistribution as measured by the curve C. Redistribution beyond the point G will then reduce total net benefit, where G is the point at which the difference between B^s and C is greatest. (In Figure 8.5, the second-order condition is satisfied.) The range in which it is Pareto optimal with respect to the initial point $\bar{X}$ (this range being DF when the cost of redistribution is ignored) depends on how the cost of redistribution is shared between the individuals. This Pareto range must lie to the left of G.

The analysis above is simplified by the assumption that X perfectly and uniquely describes every possible income distribution. In practice, the following two cases are usually regarded as equivalent distributions: (1) \$10,000 to J and \$5,000 to K; (2) \$5,000 to J and \$10,000 to K. Thus different patterns (from the individuals' viewpoint) may be associated with the same level of X. If we insist on defining each level of X as associated with only one pattern of distribution, we are still confronted with vastly discontinuous benefit curves. For example, distribution patterns (1) and (2) will be ranged close together on the X-

axis, but individual *J* or *K* will value them very differently. This complication, however, does not vitiate the principle of the analysis above. (For an extension of the analysis, see Kleiman, 1978.)†

8.5* Economic Theories of Clubs

As not many goods are *pure* public goods, generalisations to account for different types and degrees of 'impurity' may be desirable. One such generalisation is the recognition that, for any given amount (and/or quality) of a public good, each consumer's satisfaction may be a function of the number of individuals consuming it. While some individuals may prefer to swim alone, most seem to prefer a reasonable crowd. However, as the capacity of the pool is overtaxed, most swimmers may suffer a loss in enjoyment. Thus, at least after a certain point, an additional consumer imposes a cost in the form of reduced utility on existing consumers. The number of consumers then becomes a variable to be optimised in the 'economic theory of clubs' analysed by Buchanan (1965) and Ng (1973b, 1974a). The relevant Pareto optimality condition requires that any individual in the club (i.e. consuming the public good) must derive a total benefit in excess of (or at least equal to) the aggregate marginal cost imposed on all other consumers in the club, and that the reverse holds for any individual not in the club. Instead of focusing on the number of consumers directly, Oakland (1972) takes the crucial variable to be the degree of congestion which in turn depends on the capacity of the public good and its degree of utilisation. (On impure goods, see De Serpa, 1978. For a geometric review of the economics of congestion, see Porter, 1978.)

An alternative framework (Tiebout 1956, Pauly 1970, McGuire 1974) for the theory of clubs is to assume an indefinitely large number of individuals (uncountable infinity has been used) forming themselves into many clubs of the same or different sizes depending on the assumptions with respect to homogeneity or heterogeneity in tastes. Under certain conditions, the assumption of an infinite number of individuals allows each individual (club) to maximise his (its) own benefit (average benefit) without violating the requirement of Pareto optimality since

†The paradox of redistribution (of income) differs from the paradox of redistribution (of voting weights) discussed by Fischer & Schotter (1978). The latter refers to the increase in the Shapley–Shubik and Banzhaf power indices as voting weights decrease.

each individual can join a club which suits his preference best. The assumption of infinite individuals is crucial for this result. To see this, consider a simple contrasting example of a finite number of individuals, zero congestion, and positive benefit of joining additional clubs. Thus, ideally, any club should be made available to any willing consumer. It is then clear that decentralised, non-discriminating financing cannot simultaneously meet the cost of production and the requirement of optimality. The proposition (Auster, 1977, pp. 425-6) that competitive production results in the optimal provision of public goods in long-run equilibrium under the condition of imperfect information is therefore at best of limited applicability since there are usually not enough consumers to ensure the optimality of a competitive solution even if one exists.

The framework of an infinity of individuals is suitable for problems where the number of clubs for the same good is large and the population can be taken as mobile across clubs such as in the case of group segregation in housing. The previous Buchanan–Ng framework that concentrates on each particular club is preferable where these conditions are not satisfied, e.g. where the location of consumers is given and transportation is not costless, and/or where there is one or a few clubs. (On the application and generalisation of the Buchanan–Ng framework, see e.g. Dodsworth, 1975, De Serpa, 1977, Sandler, 1977.) Berglas' (1976) criticism of Ng (1973b) is based on the failure to distinguish the two different frameworks. My analysis aiming at Pareto optimality or maximising total benefits of the *whole population* has also been mistaken as maximising total benefits of *one club* which can be shown to be, in general, non-Pareto optimal (Helpman & Hillman, 1977, Brennan & Flowers, 1980). Note the last section in Ng (1973b) which attempts, apparently not very successfully, to clarify this and similar confusions in advance. My reply to critics appears in Ng (1978b, 1981a). (Buchanan has personally confirmed with me that his framework in fact agrees with my interpretation and is not the Tiebout framework as some critics maintain.)†

---

† For a recent survey of the theory of clubs, see Sandler and Tschirhart (1980). This survey gives Buchanan the best of both worlds by using an ingenious but contrived interpretation; see Ng (1982aU), which also shows why the reallocation of the private good is unnecessary for Pareto optimality as such, contrary to Sandler and Tschirhart (1980, p. 1493).

Summary

Nonrivalry in consumption of a public good means that the optimality condition is in terms of the sum of the marginal rates of substution. Even with possibility of exclusion, problems arise with the private production of public goods. The Oakland model of differential prices may not be practically feasible. The recent proposed incentive-compatible mechanism whereby individuals might be motivated to reveal their true preferences is examined in some detail and its practicability is discussed. Viewing income distribution as a public good, we may have the paradox of redistribution where, on counting the compensating variations, it seems that a Pareto redistribution is possible, though it is in fact impossible. Two contrasting frameworks of the economic theory of clubs are also outlined. (The paradox of universal externality discussed in Appendix 8A refers to the impossibility of expressing the Pareto optimality conditions in the simple terms of MRS.)

The Paradox of Redistribution and the Paradox of Universal Externality

The Pareto optimality condition for a pure public good may be derived in the following model of one public good X and G private goods. (The number of public goods can easily be increased; see Samuelson, 1954.) First the utility functions of the I individuals may be written as

$$U^i = U^i(x_1^i, \ldots, x_G^i, X) \ (i = 1, \ldots, I), \tag{8A.1}$$

where x_g^i is the amount of the gth private good consumed by individual i. The production constraint may be written as

$$F(x_1, \ldots, x_G, X) = 0, \tag{8A.2}$$

where $x_g \equiv \Sigma_{i=1}^G x_g^i$. Note the difference between public and private goods: the total amount of the public good, X, enters the utility functions of all individuals simultaneously. Note also that, for simplicity, we have written the production constraint in the implicit form, in contrast to Appendix 2ᴀ.

To derive the Pareto optimality conditons, we maximise U^1 subject to $U^i = \bar{U}^i, i = 2, \ldots, I$ and to the production constraint (8A.2). Defining $\lambda^1 \equiv 1$ and $\bar{U}^1 \equiv 0$, the relevant Lagrangean function is

$$L - \Sigma_{i=1}^I \lambda^i (U^i - \bar{U}^i) - \theta F(x_1, \ldots, x_G, X) \tag{8A.3}$$

The first-order conditions are

$$\lambda^i U_g^i = \theta F_g \ (i = 1, \ldots, I; g = 1, \ldots, G) \tag{8A.4}$$

$$\Sigma_{i=1}^I \lambda^i U_X^i = \theta F_X, \tag{8A.5}$$

where $U_g^i \equiv \partial U^i / \partial x_g^i$, $U_X^i \equiv \partial U^i / \partial X$, $F_g \equiv \partial F / \partial x_g$, $F_X \equiv \partial F / \partial X$.

As in Appendix 2A, we may write (8A.4) in the proportional form

$$U_g^i / U_G^i = F_g / F_G \quad (i = 1, \ldots, I; g = 1, \ldots, G - 1), \tag{8A.6}$$

which is the equality of the MRS across all individuals and with the MRT.

Since $\lambda^i U_G^i$ is equal to θR_G for all i, we may also rewrite (8A.5) in the proportional form by dividing it with $\lambda^i U_G^i$ and θF_G.

$$\Sigma_{i=1}^I U_X^i / U_G^i = F_X / F_G, \tag{8A.7}$$

which is the equality of aggregate MRS with the MRT, the standard optimality condition for a public good illustrated in Figure 8.1.

Instead of a normal public good, now consider X as some measure of income distribution. The utility functions (8A.1) are unchanged. But we have

$$X = X(M^1, \ldots, M^I) \tag{8A.8}$$

where $M^i = \Sigma_{g=1}^G p_g x_g^i$ is the income of individual i and p_g is the price of the gth good.

Ignoring the costs of redistribution for simplicity, we write the production constraint as

$$F(x_1, \ldots, x_G) = 0 \tag{8A.9}$$

The relevant Lagrangean function in our maximisation problem is now

$$L = \Sigma_{i=1}^I \lambda^i (U^i - \bar{U}^i) - \theta F(x_1, \ldots, x_G). \tag{8A.10}$$

The corresponding first-order conditions are

$$\lambda^i U_g^i + \Sigma_{k=1}^I \lambda^k U_X^k X_i p_g = \theta F_g \quad (i = 1, \ldots, I; g = 1, \ldots, G), \tag{8A.11}$$

where $X_i \equiv \partial X / \partial M^i$, $U_X^k \equiv \partial U^k / \partial X$.

In proportional form, (8A.11) may be written as

$$\frac{U_g^i + p_g \Sigma \lambda^k U_X^k X_i}{U_G^i + p_G \Sigma \lambda^k U_X^k X_i} = \frac{F_g}{F_G} \quad (i = 1, \ldots, I; g = 1, \ldots, G - 1) \tag{8A.12}$$

Given the utility-maximising choice of consumers, $U_g^i / U_G^i = p_g / p_G$. Thus (8A.12) may be simplified into

$$U_g^i/U_G^i = F_g/F_G \ (i = 1, \ldots, I; g = 1, \ldots, G - 1), \tag{8A.13}$$

or the equality of MRS over all individuals and with MRT.

However, (8A.13) gives us only the first-order conditions for private goods. It says nothing about the income distribution X. Since we have ignored the costs of redistribution, we should be able to derive condition $\Sigma \text{MRS} = \text{MRT} = 0$ or $\Sigma U_X^k/U_G^k = 0$ if X were a common public good. From (8A.11), we have

$$\Sigma \lambda^k U_X^k = (\theta F_g - \lambda^i U_g^i)/X_i p_g \tag{8A.14}$$

But we cannot even express the LHS in the form of ΣMRS. We cannot divide it through by $\lambda^k U_g^k$ since, from (8A.11), $\lambda^i U_g^i$ may vary over i due to the term X_i which differs, in general, over i. This impossibility of expressing the Pareto optimality conditions in the simple form of MRS or ΣMRS has been called 'the paradox of universal externality' (Ng, 1975c). For the present case, the difficulty involves only one good, X. The conditions for all other goods can still be expressed in the simple form of MRS as shown in (8A.13). But in the presence of complete universal externality where the consumption of each good by each individual enters into the utility function of at least another individual, no Pareto optimality condition can be expressed in the simple form of MRS. The Lagrangean multipliers λ^i (which 'convert' one individual's utility into equivalent units of another) can be eliminated from the Pareto conditions only by a complicated process which makes them tremendously complex. If we want to avoid this complexity, we are left with the paradox that we have to retain the λ's which signify interpersonal comparison of utility just to express the conditions for Pareto optimality which is free of interpersonal comparison. This paradox of universal externality is analysed in some detail in Ng (1975c)* and will not be repeated here.

9 First, Second or Third Best?

In Chapter 2, we discuss the necessary conditions for Pareto optimality and how these conditions can be fulfilled. A factor that makes fulfilment of the necessary conditions difficult in a market economy is monopolistic power, which is quite impossible to eliminate in the presence of increasing returns to scale characteristic of many sectors in the economy. The presence of external effects (Chapter 7) makes things even more complicated. In principle there may exist a system of tax/subsidy such that all necessary conditions can be fulfilled and a first-best Pareto optimum achieved. But this may not be politically or institutionally feasible. (In the presence of 'nonamenable' externalities, the first best is inherently impossible to achieve even abstracting from the problems of political feasibility, costs, and information. Non-amenable externalities include those external effects such as social interaction which change their character once tax/subsidy, regulation, bargaining, etc., are introduced to internalise the effects. See Ng, 1975d.) For one reason or another, if the necessary conditions cannot be satisfied for some sectors of the economy, what is the best we can do for the rest of the economy? This is the problem of second best.

For example, first-best Pareto optimality requires the equality of marginal rate of substitution (MRS) and the marginal rate of transformation (MRT) for every pair of goods produced and consumed. Under certain conditions, this would be fulfilled if perfect competition prevailed in every sector of the economy (Section 2.3 and Appendix 2B). Suppose however that the X industry is competitive and the Y industry is monopolised. The price of $X(p_X)$ is then equal to its marginal cost (MC_X) but p_Y exceeds MC_Y. The MRS_{XY}, being equal to p_X/p_Y due to the utility-maximising behaviour of atomistic consumers, is therefore not equal to MRT_{XY} ($= MC_X/MC_Y$). Assuming that we have no way of affecting the decisions in these two industries, MRS_{XY}

$\neq \text{MRT}_{XY}$ is then a constraint which prevents the achievement of a first-best Pareto optimum. We are then left to do the next best thing, i.e. to achieve a second-best Pareto optimum which is subject not only to the usual technological constraints on production possibilities but also the above additional constraint created by the presence of a monopoly. (The necessary conditions for a second best are still optimal in the Pareto sense given the additional constraint. The usual contrast between 'Pareto conditions' and 'second-best conditions' may give the misleading idea that a second-best optimum is not optimal in the Pareto sense.) To achieve a second-best optimum, should we make MRS = MRT for every other pair of goods? Given that some first-best conditions cannot be fulfilled, is it better to fulfil as many of the rest as possible? In particular, if the government cannot control the distortive private sector, should it put its own house in order by pricing public utilities at MCs? The theory of second best says that the answer is 'NO!' This has some devastating implications for the practicability of welfare economics. In particular, there seems to be very little scope for the valid application of 'piecemeal' welfare policies. We shall first discuss the theory of second best and the various attempts to salvage welfare economics from its full implications before presenting a theory of third best.

9.1 The Theory of Second Best

Though Samuelson (1947, pp. 252-3) was aware of the principle contained in the theory of second best, it was not widely discussed until the 1950's, when a number of writers working in different fields of economics (e.g. Viner, 1950, Meade, 1955a, 1955b, and Ozga, 1955, on custom unions and tariffs; Little, 1951, and Corlett & Hague, 1953, on taxation) encountered the problem of second best. Lipsey & Lancaster (1956) generalised the principle into the celebrated 'general theory of second best'.

The theory of second best usually refers to the achievement of Pareto optimality, though it is applicable to other optimisation problems. For simplicity, a simple constrained maximisation problem is used for enunciation. In maximising a differentiable objective function of n variables

$$F(x_1, x_2, \ldots, x_n) \tag{9.1}$$

subject to a differentiable constraint on the n variables

$$G(x_1, x_2, \ldots, x_n) = 0 \tag{9.2}$$

the necessary conditions can readily be obtained as

$$F_i/F_n = G_i/G_n \ (i = 1, \ldots, n - 1), \tag{9.3}$$

where a subscript after a functional notation denotes partial differentiation, i.e. $F_i \equiv \partial F/\partial x_i$, etc., and corner solutions are ignored. (9.1) may be interpreted as a social welfare function since the n variables may represent the allocation of the G goods to I individuals, i.e. $n = I \times G$. One may have $W = W(U^1, \ldots, U^I) = F(x_1^1, x_2^1, \ldots, x_I^1; x_1^2, \ldots, x_G^I)$. (9.2) may be interpreted as a production constraint and may take the form $G(\Sigma x_1^i, \ldots, \Sigma x_G^i) = 0$. (9.3) specifies the equality of MRS and MRT.

A second-best problem arises if there is some additional constraint(s) in the form such as

$$F_1/F_n = kG_1/G_n, k \neq 1. \tag{9.4}$$

Maximising (9.1) subject to (9.2) and (9.4), we form the following Lagrangean function $L = F(x_1, \ldots, x_n) - \lambda G(x_1, \ldots, x_n) - \mu(F_1/F_n - kG_1/G_n)$, where λ and μ are the Lagrangean multipliers.† The following necessary conditions are obtained by equating to zero the partial derivatives of L with respect to the x's and by writing the resulting equations in the proportional form. (Following Morrison, 1968, p. 113, we have corrected a minor algebraic error in the original equation of Lipsey & Lancaster, 1956, p. 26.)

$$\frac{F_i}{F_n} = \frac{G_i}{G_n} \cdot \left[\frac{1 + \dfrac{\mu}{\lambda G_i} \cdot (Q_i - kR_i)}{1 + \dfrac{\mu}{\lambda G_n}(Q_n - kR_n)} \right] \ (i = 2, \ldots, n - 1) \tag{9.5}$$

---

†Allingham & Archibald (1975)* argue that, with an additional constraint, it is strictly speaking not valid to assume *in advance* that the economy should still operate at the boundary of the production constraint (9.2). However, they show that this (i.e. productive efficiency) is still optimal in the second-best solution. Hence, we shall ignore this technical methodological point.

where $Q_i \equiv (F_n F_{1i} - F_1 F_{ni})/F_n^2$, $R_i \equiv (G_n G_{1i} - G_1 G_{ni})/G_n^2$ and a double subscript denotes second-order differentiation, e.g. $F_{1i} \equiv \partial^2 F/\partial x_1 \partial x_i$.

In general, the expression in square brackets in (9.5) is not equal to unity. This means that the conditions for second-best optimality differ from the conditions for first-best optimality even for those variables which are not subject to the additional constraint(s). In terms of marginal analysis, if we are unable to equate MRS and MRT for some pair of goods, it is then better to deviate from this equality for all pairs of goods except where the bracketed expressions happen to equal unity.

To show the principle of second best vividly, the following diagrammatic illustration (adapted from McManus, 1959,* and Winch, 1971) is useful. Consider a simple economy producing three goods X, Y, and Z under conditions of constant cost. By suitable choice of units for the three goods, one unit of each can be transformed into one unit of any other. The aggregate amount of the three goods produced is then a constant. Any combination of the three goods produced can then be represented by a point in the equilateral triangle XYZ in Figure 9.1, with the amount of X produced measured by the (perpendicular) distance of the point to the side facing the vertex X, etc. For an equilateral triangle, the sum of the distances of any point in the triangle to the three sides

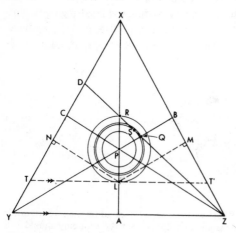

Figure 9.1

is a constant. (Students with a logical mind may wish to prove this as a revision exercise of their secondary school geometry.) Assume that the SWF may be represented by a community indifference map (Appendix 3A) on $\triangle XYZ$. This involves some restrictions but is used purely for simplification (in reducing the number of variables to facilitate geometrical treatment) and does not affect the essence of the argument.

Typically, the point P of the highest level of community indifference occurs in the interior of $\triangle XYZ$. Given continuity of preference, lower levels of indifference are represented by 'rings' (not necessarily circular) enclosing the point P, as shown in the figure.† For a given amount of X represented by the distance between TT' and the side YZ, TT' is the locus of the different combinations of Y and Z that can be produced. Recall that the amounts of Y and Z are measured as distances to the sides XZ and XY. For example, if the economy is operating at the point L, the amount of Y equals LM and that of Z equals LN. Along TT', the point L touches the highest CIC (community indifference curve). It is thus a point at which, for the given amount of X, the community's MRS_{YZ} equals MRT_{YZ} (which equals unity in this simple case). If we translate the different combinations of Y and Z along TT' into an ordinary two-dimensional figure (not shown) with Y and Z measured along the two axes, the production possibility or transformation curve for Y and Z (with the given X) is a $45°$ negatively inclined straight line. If we draw in the CICs in that figure, L will correspond to the point where the transformation line is tangent to a highest CIC. The curve XA (not necessarily perpendicular to YZ) is the locus of all points such as L where, for some given amount of X, the corresponding transformation curve (such as TT') touches the highest CIC. Hence, along XA, we have $MRS_{YZ} = MRT_{YZ}$. Similarly, along YB, we have $MRS_{XZ} = MRT_{XZ}$, and along ZC, we have $MRS_{XY} = MRT_{XY}$. The three curves intersect at a common point, P. This is so since MRS must equal MRT for the remaining pair of goods if they are equal for any two pairs. The point P is the first-best optimum where MRS = MRT for all pairs of goods.

---

†This is true despite the fact that a special method of measuring the various amounts of goods (distances to sides) is used since a small movement in the plane of Figure 9.1 corresponds to a small movement in the ordinary three-dimensional commodity space.

Now let us introduce a second-best complication. Suppose that, for one reason or another, MRS_{XY} cannot be made equal to MRT_{XY}. Instead of operating at a point along ZC, we are constrained to operate along a point along, say, ZD where $\text{MRS}_{XY} \neq \text{MRT}_{XY}$. Given this constraint, what is the best we can do? Should we try to make MRS = MRT for as many other pairs of goods as possible? Obviously we cannot achieve such an equality for both the remaining two pairs of goods (i.e. X, Z and Y, Z) since MRS = MRT for any two pairs implies the same for the remaining pair, but $\text{MRS}_{XY} \neq \text{MRT}_{XY}$ is given as a constraint. In other words, MRS ≠ MRT for any one pair of goods implies an inequality for at least another pair. But it is possible to have MRS = MRT for one pair of goods, either X, Z (i.e. at the point Q) or Y, Z (i.e. at the point R). But either Q or R is on a lower CIC than the point S where the constraint ZD touches the highest CIC. The point S is the second-best optimum which generally involves MRS ≠ MRT for all pairs of goods unless the constraint ZD happens to touch the highest CIC at the point Q or R, which is unlikely. We have thus illustrated diagrammatically the second-best principle that, once some necessary conditions cannot be fulfilled, it is in general no longer desirable to fulfil the rest even if feasible.

Given some second-best constraint, the resulting necessary conditions are different from the first-best necessary conditions even for the free sector. If the second-best conditions were simple and easy to fulfil, the problem of second best would not create much difficulty. Unfortunately, the second-best conditions (Equation 9.5 above) are generally very complicated, involving not only first-order derivatives but also second-order cross-partial derivatives. In economic terms, this means that the second-best conditions depend not only on the values of (ratio, of) marginal costs and marginal rates of substitution, but also on the degrees of complementarity or substitutability between goods in the constrained sector and those in the free sector, and the effects of increased production of a good on the marginal costs of another. This involves tremendously more complicated information than what is related to the first-best conditions. Moreover, this is so even if the second-best constraint applies only to one pair of goods. In the real economy where we have second-best constraints (due to monopolistic power, externalities, taxes/subsidies, etc.) in many sectors of the

economy in a complicated way, the resulting second-best conditions
are well-nigh impossible to define, let alone to fulfil. (Cf. Sandler,
1978.)

The principle of second best is not difficult to comprehend intui-
tively. If some goods produce important external diseconomies, their
price/(social) MC ratios will be lower than others, *ceteris paribus*. These
sectors are therefore over-expanded from a social point of view. If the
government cannot do anything directly to affect the private sector, it
may no longer be desirable to price its own products (e.g. public
utilities) at MCs. For example, for those public products which are
very complementary to the products of the over-expanded sectors, it
may be better to price above MCs so as to indirectly discourage their
over-expansion.

The difficulty due to insufficient knowledge of the relevant interrelationships (complementarities, etc.) is only part of the problem of
second best. In addition, even if we had the required information, it
would still be practically impossible to fulfil all the complicated conditions as the administrative costs may be prohibitive. (See Allingham
& Archibald, 1975*, on the difficulty of attaining a second-best optimum through decentralisation.) Though we can achieve neither the
first best nor the second best, it will not be too bad if we can at least
make some improvements over the existing state. Unfortunately, the
theory of second best says further that, by trying to satisfy as many
(short of all) conditions as possible, it is by no means certain that we
will not in fact make matters worse. This is true not only with respect
to the first-best conditions, but also to the second-best conditions.
Given some second-best constraints, the conditions for optimality
for the free sector become the complicated second-best conditions.
But unless we can satisfy all these second-best conditions, it is in
general not desirable to satisfy as many as possible. This can be shown
to be true by forming a second-stage second-best (or 2½th best) problem whereby the non-satisfaction of some second-best conditions is
taken as an additional constraint. One can then apply the theory of
second best all over again to arrive at the above negative conclusion
with stronger force, since the second-stage second-best conditions are
even more complicated.

Most, if not all, economic analyses, are based on the assumption that the first-best optimality conditions are satisfied 'in the rest of the economy' or 'for other aspects of the economy'. For example, when one is analysing the appropriate policy for a particular sector, it is analytically useful to assume that optimality prevails in other sectors. Even for general equilibrium-type analyses where all sectors are taken into account, usually only one or two problems are considered, and other problems are assumed solved. For example, when analysing externality, it is assumed that problems of monopolistic power, etc., do not arise, and vice versa. From the theory of second best, it seems that all these analyses are useless. By adjusting the economy to take account of externalities alone, we may be making matters worse if there exist other distortions in the system. Similarly, by studying a (proper) subset of the economy, even considering all problems including externality, monopoly, etc., the resulting policy recommendation may be worse than doing nothing unless the complicated interrelationships of this subset and the rest of the economy are taken into consideration. It seems that, to make any improvement at all, we must analyse the whole economy and take every problem into account. We must leap right to the summit to be sure of an improvement. But it is clear that this task is epistemologically, administratively, and politically impossible.

Before readers conclude from the above negative results that welfare economics is useless and hence decide to throw this book away, they are advised to read the rest of this chapter on the ways out of the second-best difficulty.

9.2 Softening the Blow of Second Best

First, it may be noted that not all constraints give rise to complicated second-best conditions such as Equation 9.5. (Cf. Mishan, 1962b.) For example, some constraints take the form that a certain variable (e.g. output of an industry) must not exceed or fall short of a certain value, e.g.

$$x_1 \leqslant \bar{x}_1 \tag{9.6}$$

Maximising (9.1) subject to (9.2) and (9.6), we still obtain the first-best conditions (9.3) except for $i = 1$, for which we have

$$\frac{F_1}{F_n} = \frac{G_1}{G_n} + \frac{\theta}{\lambda G_n} \tag{9.7}$$

where θ, the multiplier associated with (9.6), is equal to zero if (9.6) is ineffective and λ need not have the same value as in the previous second-best problem. Hence only the constrained sector need be adjusted; piecemeal welfare policy is sufficient here. This is true even if there are several constraints of the type (9.6). Constraints which place maximum or minimum values on certain variables such as the amount of consumption, production, import, export, input usage, etc. will reduce in general the maximum value of the objective function, but do not lead to complicated second-best conditions.

The point that constraints of the type (9.6) do not lead to complicated second-best conditions can be illustrated in Figure 9.1. Let the constraint be that the value of X must not be greater than the distance between TT' and YZ. It can then be seen that the highest indifference curve is reached at the point L where $\text{MRS}_{YZ} = \text{MRT}_{YZ}$. In fact, the constraint, if effective, confines the economy to the line TT', and simple first-best condition for the pair YZ confines it to the line XA. Hence, these two equations (together with the production constraint) already define the maximum point L and hence the corresponding values of X, Y and Z. In this simple case of three variables, we cannot add another effective constraint (such as on the value of Y) without leaving economy with no degree of freedom. But in a many-variable case, a number of constraints of the type (9.6) can be added without affecting the necessary conditions of the unconstrained variables. However, complicated necessary conditions will result if the added constraint is specified in the form of an inequality of an orginal first-best condition such as (9.4). Since the real economy does not lack constraints of this type, we still have to face the difficulty of second best.†

---

†Since this involves a *pair* of goods, McManus (1959)* regards it as really 'two constraints for the price of one'. This is a problematical interpretation. It is true that if the additional constraint takes the form of, say, $p_1 = kMC_1$, $k \neq 1$, we can still achieve a first-best optimum by making $p_i = kMC_i$ for all i, if the economy is vertically integrated, i.e. no interfirm transaction of intermediate goods. (See Kahn, 1935. With intermediate goods, some complication is present; see McKenzie, 1951.) In a constrained maximisation problem where the constraint is

There is a special case where the first-best conditions still apply in the second-best solution for all variables other than those subject to additional constraints of the form (9.4). This is the case where both the objective and constraint functions (i.e. Equations 9.1 and 9.2) are separable functions. A function $f(x_1, x_2, \ldots, x_n)$ is separable if it can be expressed as $f^1(x_1) + f^2(x_2), \ldots, + f^n(x_n)$. For example, the function $z = 2x^2 + 3y^4$ is separable but the function $z = 2x^2 y^3 + 4$ is not. The function $z = \log x^2 y^3$ is separable as it can be expressed as $z = \log x^2 + \log y^3 = 2 \log x + 3 \log y$. It is clear that every second-order cross-partial derivative of a separable function is zero. Thus if (9.1) and (9.2) are both separable functions, we have $F_{ij} = G_{ij} = 0$ for all $i \neq j$. Then Q_i and R_i in (9.5) are all zero for $i = 2, \ldots, n - 1$. The square-bracketed expression in (9.5) becomes unity for $i = 2, \ldots, n - 1$ and hence first-best conditions are retained.

The above happy result follows from the assumption of separability; the issue is the interpretation of this assumption. Davis & Whinston (1965, pp. 3, 12) emphasise that 'separability is not an unduly restrictive assumption. If there are no technological externalities, there must be separability in terms of the decision units (consumers and producers) in the general equilibrium model . . . In such situations "piecemeal policy" is all that is required'. If this conclusion is true, then the second-best theory loses a great deal of its significance. As a welfare economist, I very much hope that this is so. Unfortunately, the assumption of separability is actually much more restrictive than the mere absence of externality (Ng. 1972a), as shown below.

For (9.2), if it is interpreted as a production constraint, then the mere absence of externalities will not, in most cases, make it a separable function. Take a very simple example of three goods, X, Y, Z with the production functions

$$X = A_X, Y = B_Y, Z = A_Z B_Z; A_X + A_Z = \bar{A}, B_Y + B_Z = \bar{B}, \qquad (9.8)$$

---

effective, there are only $n - 1$ degrees of freedom. The $n - 1$ necessary conditions in (9.3), together with the constraint equation, determine the n variables. A constraint of the form $p_1 = kMC_1$ need not violate any of the conditions MRS = MRT, provided other sectors price appropriately. But if the additional constraint is due to the monopolistic power of the first industry, it will make $p_1 > kMC_1$ after we have made $p_i = kMC_i$ (Lipsey & Lancaster, 1959). In the more recent formulation of the second-best problem by Allingham & Archibald (1975)*, this problem of the number of constraints seems to be better handled.

where $\bar{A}$ and $\bar{B}$ are the fixed quantities of the two inputs. No externality is involved as the output of each commodity is only a function of its own inputs. From (9.8), we have $X = \bar{A} - A_Z = \bar{A} - Z/B_Z = \bar{A} - Z/(\bar{B} - B_Y)$. The production constraint is then

$$X - \bar{A} + Z/(\bar{B} - Y) = 0, \tag{9.9}$$

which is not a separable function in terms of X, Y and Z. We can manage to separate any one variable but not all three variables. The presence of nonseparability in this example of simple production functions indicates that the assumption of separability is very restrictive in the real economy of thousands of products and inputs.

Turning to the objective function (9.1), if it is an individual utility function, the assumption of separability is equivalent to (Edgeworth) independence in *all* goods. This of course is a very restrictive assumption since complementarity and substitutability are very common phenomena in consumption. If (9.1) is some SWF or community preference function, F_{ij} will still be non-zero in general even in the absence of externality as the complementarity and substitutability at the individual preference level will be reflected at the social preference level. It can be concluded that the absence of externality alone is far from sufficient to ensure separability in both the objective and the constraint functions. Separability is too restrictive an assumption to make the special case of Davis & Whinston interesting. (Similarly, the analysis of McFadden, 1969 is misleading. His definition of 'externality-free' is much more restrictive than the absence of technological externalities. His 'externalities' include normal forms of economic interdependency whereby the production or consumption possibility of an economic agent depends, through the market, on the production and consumption of others.) However, separability is not a necessary condition to yield the required special case. Examining (9.5), it can be seen that $F_{ij} = G_{ij} = 0$ for all $i \neq j$ is sufficient but not necessary to make the square-bracketed term equal to unity. A weaker sufficient condition is $F_n F_{1i} = F_1 F_{ni}$ and $G_n G_{1i} = G_1 G_{ni}$ for all $i = 2, \ldots, n - 1$. Dusansky & Walsh (1976) show that this is satisfied if the functions are 'partially weakly separable'. Though this is a less restrictive assumption, it is still unlikely to prevail in most cases. In economic terms, $F_n F_{1i} = F_1 F_{ni}$ means that the degree of complementarity (or substitutability) between the ith good and the first good is the same as that between the ith good and the nth good. It is quite likely that this may be so for some goods, but extremely unlikely to hold for all goods. Rapanos (1980) notes that a still weaker sufficient condition is $F_i/F_n = G_i/G_n = (Q_i - kR_i)/(Q_n - kR_n)$ for all $i = 2, \ldots n - 1$. However, calling this the equality of the marginal rate of substitution and the marginal rate of distortion may make the restriction appear misleadingly simple, which it is not (see Jewitt, 1981). Boadway & Harris (1977)* also show that a piecemeal policy that sets consumer prices proportional to MC in some subset (this includes the whole) of the controllable sector is very unlikely to be valid.

Green (1961), assuming a single primary resource and constant returns to scale, shows that, if all goods are substitutes, the second-best optimum involves price/MC ratios between the largest and smallest constrained ratios. A similar result is established by Kawamata (1977)* using more general assumptions. (For an open economy, see Lloyd, 1974.) Integrating the contributions of Green (1961), Foster & Sonnenschein (1970)*, Bruno (1972)*, and Kemp (1968), Hatta (1977)* shows that, in an economy of linear production constraints (constant costs), a policy which reduces all price distortions uniformly will improve welfare if the economy is stable in the Marshallian sense. Moreover, a policy which brings the highest distortion to the level of the next highest will improve welfare if the good with the highest distortion is substitutable for all other goods and the economy is Marshall-stable. The requirement of substitutability is not difficult to see. If the good with the highest distortion has a perfect complement, the two together may be regarded as a single good which need not then have the highest level of distortion. It may also be noted that the assumption of linear constraint is to nullify the effect of G_{ij} in (9.5) and hence allow concentration of the effect of F_{ij}, that of complementarity or substitutability. These assumptions involve fairly strong restrictions. Moreover, some of the measures, such as uniform reduction of all distortions, may not be politically feasible. Hence, though the above results provide some useful insights, they are not sufficient to overcome the difficulty of second best. In the next section, we examine quite a different approach to the solution of the second best problem. (The following two sections are based on Ng, 1977a.)

9.3 A Theory of Third Best

In maximising the objective function (9.1) subject to the constraint

(9.2), the first-order necessary conditions, ignoring corner-solutions (which can be allowed for), are the $(n - 1)$ conditions in (9.3).† If the second-order conditions are also satisfied throughout, (9.3) defines a global maximum. Thus if we satisfy (9.3) for all $i \neq j$, the value of the objective function will attain the maximum value as (9.3) is also satisfied for j, as illustrated by the curve F^1 in Figure 9.2. Hence we have the following trivial proposition.

Proposition 1:   *First-best rules for first-best worlds*

In Figure 9.2, the curve F^1 relates the value of the objective function to the direction and degree of divergence from the first-best rule for the variable under consideration and may be called the relation curve for short. For most cases, it is reasonable to expect that the relation curve is concave. As we diverge more and more from the first-best rule, the marginal damage increases. Take a specific example of the first-best rule of price = MC. The relation curve will be concave (in a first-best world) if

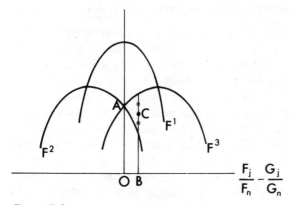

Figure 9.2

---

†Though we have only $n - 1$ first-order conditions in a system of n variables, the system is not indeterminate since there is the constraint equation (9.2). While the variables in the whole system are simultaneously determined, if one likes, one may regard each of the first $n - 1$ variables as directly determined by the corresponding first-order condition and the last variable (i.e. the numeraire or money supply) as directly determined by the resource constraint equation, i.e. the need (for feasibility + optimality) to operate at full employment.

the demand curve is downward-sloping and the *MC* curve is either up-ward-sloping, constant, or downward-sloping but everywhere less steep than the demand curve. To put it more concisely, we have concavity if the algebraic slope of the demand curve is everywhere smaller than that of the *MC* curve. It is, of course, possible to construct cases where the concavity condition is not satisfied. But the condition may be violated on either side of the curve. In the absence of more precise knowledge, it is reasonable to say that the *expected* 'average' curve is concave.

Now introduce some distortion preventing the fulfilment of the first-best rule for a set of variables. The theory of second best says that the value of the objective function is no longer, in general, maxi-mised by observing the first-best rule for variables where this is feasible. If the distortion is truly of a second-best nature, the second-best rules (first-order conditions) are typically extremely complicated. (See equation 9.5.) However, if we can have all the relevant information costlessly and apply the second-best rules without significant additional costs, then we have again, trivially,

Proposition 2: *Second-best rules for second-best worlds*

Here, a 'second-best world' is defined as a situation where some second-best distortion is present but costs of information, etc. are negligible. But first-best and second-best worlds are of course not of much practical interest. Though the second-best solution has been termed 'optimal feasible', it is really neither optimal nor feasible if we take account of administrative costs and informational inadequacy. What is really opti-mal feasible may be called the third best since the real world is better characterised by what may be called a third-best world where both distortions and informational costs exist. With the presence of signifi-cant costs of acquiring information, an integral part of the optimisa-tion problem is the choice of the amount of information we shall acquire. This problem of the economics of information is not, in general, independent of the other aspects of the optimisation problem. However, to deal with one issue at a time, let us for the time being assume that the information problem has been solved. In other words, we already know the amount of information we will acquire. This will be termed the 'available' amount of information.

The available amount of information may conceivably range more-or-less continuously from perfect information to perfect ignorance. But it is convenient to adopt the following classification:

(1) *Informational Poverty* where the available information is insufficient to provide a reasonable probabilistic judgement regarding: (a) the direction and extent of divergence of the second-best optimum from that resulting from the application of the first-best rule in the presence of the second-best distortion; (b) the shape and skewness of the relation curve apart from its general concavity;

(2) *Information Scarcity* where the available information is sufficient for such a judgement but is not perfect;

(3) *Informational Abundance*, i.e. perfect information. This last case has been dealt with (proposition 2); we shall now consider Informational Poverty and Informational Scarcity.

With Informational Poverty, what is the appropriate policy to adopt in the presence of second-best distortion? We noted before that the relation curve in a first-best world is likely to be concave, attaining its maximum at $F_j/F_n - G_j/G_n = 0$. With the introduction of second-best distortion, the relation curve may of course change its position as well as its shape. However, under Informational Poverty, we do not know in which direction it is likely to move. Moreover, we do not know whether it is skew, or the sign of its skewness. Under these conditions, it is not difficult to establish:

Proposition 3: *First-best rules for third-best worlds with Informational Poverty*

To see the reason behind this proposition, consider Figure 9.2 where F^1 is the relation curve under first-best conditions. With a second-best distortion, the relation curve will, in general, diverge from F^1. But with Informational Poverty, we do not know in which direction it is likely to move. As a representation, F^2 and F^3 are drawn as two equally likely curves. Moreover, both curves are symmetrical as we do not know the sign of skewness, if in fact they are skew. It is then easy to see that, if we stick to the first-best rule, the expected value of the objective function is OA. If we diverge from the first-best rule in any direction and in any degree, e.g. to the point B, the expected value of the objective function is BC, smaller than OA.

It is, of course, not necessary that, in the face of risk, we should maximise the expected value of the objective function. However, it is reasonable to assume that what we are maximising is a concave function of the possible values of the function F. In other words, we are either risk-neutral or risk-averse. With this additional reasonable assumption, proposition 3 then follows.†

We turn now to examine the case of Informational Scarcity. Suppose, for some reason, we expect the relation curve to be skew as shown in Figure 9.3. A right-hand or positive divergence from the first-

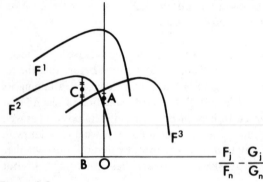

Figure 9.3

best rule causes a sharper reduction in the value of the objective function than a left-hand or negative divergence. Then the expected value of the objective function with first-best rule, OA, is smaller than BC, the expected value resulting from a negative divergence from the first-best rule. Furthermore, if we have reason to believe that the relation curve is more likely to move leftward than rightward, there is another reason to prefer a negative departure from the first-best rule.

---

†For a different argument in favour of first-best rules based on voters' distrust of bureaucracy, see Faith & Thompson (1981).

Of course, this second consideration may happen to counterbalance the first consideration (that of skewness). An optimal policy is taken by considering the effects of these factors as well as the degree of risk-aversion we possess. We shall call such policies third-best policies. We have, thus:

Proposition 4: *Third-best rules for third-best worlds with Informational Scarcity*

The third-best policies depend on the available amount of information as well as the administrative costs involved. With Informational Poverty third-best policies converge with first-best ones. With perfect information and negligible costs of administration, third-best policies converge with second-best ones. Hence both first-best and second-best policies are special, polar cases of the general third-best policies. Thus, if we relax the assumption that the available amount of information is already given, the latter becomes an important variable in the system. As a simplified illustrative model, we may write our objective function as dependent on the amount of information ι and the policy to be pursued, π, i.e. $Q = Q(\iota, \pi)$ where the functional form reflects the cost of obtaining information, administrative costs of carrying out the policies as well as the given environment in the economy. With uncertainty, we really do not know what will definitely happen for any particular choice of ι, π. But Q may be regarded as the expected utility or whatever is being maximised. Thus the subjective probability estimates and the attitude towards risk will also influence the form of the Q function. Hence the Q function may differ from the F function in 9.1 above. Assuming differentiability and a noncorner solution, Q is maximised at $Q_\iota \ (\equiv \partial Q/\partial \iota) = 0$, $Q_\pi = 0$ as illustrated in Figure 9.4a, where M is a typical third-best solution.

The shapes of the contours are determined by costs of getting information, administrative costs, and other factors mentioned above. The two ridge lines trace out the loci of the optimal value of one variable (ι or π) given the other. Both lines may be expected to be positively sloped. If the cost of information is sufficiently high, we may have a corner-solution of O in Figure 9.4b. However, it is not possible to have a corner solution at any other point of the vertical axis. Given Informational Poverty, the best policy is to stick to first best. If the costs of

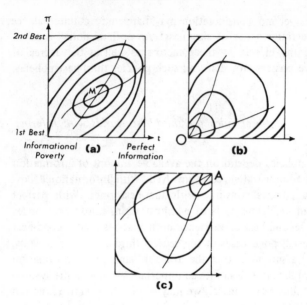

Figure 9.4

getting information are very low (unlikely to prevail), we may have a corner solution diagonally opposite to the origin at A in Figure 9.4c. It is, however, logically possible to have a solution along the vertical line below A: due to administrative costs, perfect information does not necessarily mean that a second-best policy is optimal.

In practice, neither ι nor π are likely to be unidimensional and the functional relationships are known only very imperfectly. But since the theory of third-best deals precisely with situations where precision is lacking, the above simple model may at least be accepted as a first approximation. To illustrate further the difference between Informational Poverty and Informational Scarcity, let us consider a specific example.

Suppose that a good X has an important external diseconomy which justifies, assuming a first-best world, a Pigovian tax of $\$M$ per unit. Now we know that the actual economy is not first-best. Thus the $\$M$ tax may actually worsen the situation if, for example, X is highly complementary to Y and Y produces important external economies which for some reason cannot be dealt with directly. A situation where we have knowledge about the characteristics of the goods closely related to X corresponds to our case of Informational Scarcity. The first-best rule will have to be appropriately revised in view of this knowledge. On the other hand, if X does not have any clearly identifiable close substitute or complement, or if those goods closely related to X do not exhibit any marked characteristics (such as strong non-amenable external effects, high degree of monopoly), then the appropriate policy is to adopt the first-best rule of $\$M$ tax on X, unless there is some other reason to justify a specific divergence. It is possible that, if we have all the detailed interrelationships and characteristics of the whole economy, the second-best tax on X may be $\$(M + N)$. But it is also possible that it is $\$(M - N)$. We do not know which way to diverge from $\$M$ unless we have such detailed knowledge. A marginal increase in our knowledge of the rest of the economy is likely to be of no help at all. For example, the additional knowledge that good Z is closely related to V is of no use at all unless we also know other interrelationships which lead us back to X.

It may be argued that, in the presence of Informational Poverty, we really do not know whether the adoption of first-best rules will improve matters even only in a probabilistic sense. Since we have no information, we know nothing; we may as well stay with the status quo instead of imposing the $\$M$ Pigovian tax. (This is the line taken by Brennan & McGuire, 1975. I am grateful to Brennan for clarifying his position in private discussion and correspondence.) This argument ignores the fact that, while we do not have adequate information on the rest of the economy to form any reasonable judgement, we do have specific knowledge that the good X imposes an external *diseconomy* (instead of just an externality with no knowledge of its sign, i.e. whether a benefit or a cost) valued at about $\$M$ per unit. To refuse to impose the tax on the ground of second-best would be a failure to make use of this specific piece of information. This would not be an optimal policy according to our theory of third-best. This theory shows that piecemeal policies can be justified and analyses based on first-best assumptions on the rest of the economy can be useful. Thus, despite the theory of second-best, welfare economics can still be a worthwhile study.

We turn now to discussing, in a very loose way, some of the factors that may affect the nature of third-best policies, taking account of the efficiency aspect of the problem. The distributional aspect is considered in Appendix 9A which attempts to justify the separate consideration of efficiency and equity on third-best grounds, hence tremendously simplifying economic policy making.

9.4 Towards a Third-best Policy

What a third-best policy is depends, of course, on the specific case under consideration. What can be given here is no more than a general discussion of a few factors that are likely to be important for most cases. We shall first consider the shape of the relation curve under first-best conditions and then examine the effects of second-best distortions.

Consider the demand (or marginal valuation) curve for a commodity and its MC (marginal cost) curve. If both are linear, the relation curve is concave as well as symmetric over the neighbourhood of the first-best rule. If we reasonably rule out negative quantities and prices, then the extreme values of the relation curve will not be equal unless MC cuts the demand curve at mid-point. For example, with MC^1 in Figure 9.5a, if we have a positive divergence from the first-best rule (i.e price $> MC$), the loss cannot be larger than the triangle ABC. But the maximum loss from a negative divergence is much larger. On the other hand, if we have MC^3, then the reverse is true. If we have MC^2 which cuts the demand curve at its mid-point, or if we do not know the likely position of the MC with respect to the demand curve, the relation curve may be taken to to be symmetrical.

The demand curve is, however, more likely to be isoelastic than linear over the relevant range, as shown in Figure 9.5b. If the MC is either MC^1 or MC^3 and intersects the demand curve in the middle of the range, say, AB, regarded as relevant, then the relation curve is again symmetrical. If instead we have MC^2, then the relation curve will be somewhat skewed, but not by a significant degree.

The main sources of second-best distortion seem to be
(1) differential degrees of monopolistic power;
(2) uncorrected externalities;
(3) taxation; and
(4) governmental intervention.

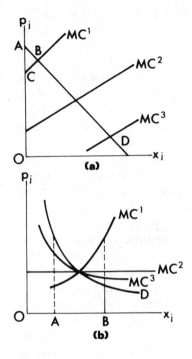

Figure 9.5

In a first-best world, optimality requires the equality of prices and
*MC*s. In the presence of uncorrected monopolistic distortion, formulation of the second-best pricing rule requires detailed knowledge of cost
and demand relationships (including cross relationships). However, on
third-best grounds, it can be argued that, unless a particular commodity
is known to be highly complementary to or competitive with some
commodities produced under highly monopolised conditions, it is not
far from optimal to make its price/MC ratio equal to the estimated
average in the economy. (Cf. Green, 1961, Mishan, 1962b, Ng, 1975d.)
Since this ratio is likely to be larger than one, this third-best rule requires pricing above *MC*. This could then be a way out of the optimal
pricing dilemma for public utilities with decreasing average costs.
(Another way out is the adoption of a multi-part tariff, on which see

Mayston, 1974*, Ng & Weisser, 1974*.) With MC smaller than AC, pricing at MC involves losses, the financing of which by non-lump-sum taxes again involves inefficiency. (For some of the difficulties involved in MC pricing, see Ruggles, 1949-50, Farrell, 1958.) However, if optimality requires not MC pricing but above MC pricing, then one may not be too far out by setting price at average cost, unless MC is very much smaller than AC.

Some qualifications to the above argument for average cost pricing may be necessary. First, monopolistic distortions need not be left uncorrected. If idealised subsidies plus lump-sum tax can be costlessly administered, the presence of monopolies need not cause any distortion. While in practice, such a perfect 'cure' for monopoly is quite impossible, some rough 'treatment' may be feasible. Let us divide the economy into three sectors: the very competitive, the very monopolised, and the intermediate. Tax the competitive sector according to its output, the monopolised sector according to its profit, and the intermediate sector by a combination of the two. Then the restrictive effect of monopoly may be partially remedied. Second, there may exist sectors with prices below MCs – e.g. public provision of goods not on efficiency but on political grounds, expenditure subject to tax deductions-making the effective prices below MCs. The deductions might initially been provided on grounds of efficiency or equity but then became outdated or subject to abuses, but yet difficult to withdraw for political reasons. If these sectors with prices below MC are so important as to roughly overbalance the above MC pricing practice of monopolistic firms, it may be optimal for public utilities to adopt the first-best rule of MC pricing. However, other considerations such as the need to prevent empire-building by public enterprises may also have to be taken into account.

Apart from monopolistic distortion, we have taxation distortion. (This distortion may be far less significant than is commonly believed; see the argument below.) Consider commodity taxation which further increases the divergence of (consumer) prices from MC. Hence, even for public utilities with MCs well below average costs, average cost pricing may still not be far from optimality. Exemption from taxation may be all that is needed.

Now consider externality. An external effect can either be an external economy or an external diseconomy. If both these beneficial and detrimental externalities are equally prevalent in the economy, it can again be argued on third-best grounds that unless a good is known to have significant externality itself or is highly complementary to or competitive with some other goods with important externalities, then the first-best rules are applicable (Ng, 1975d). However, it seems reasonable to say that, on the whole, detrimental external effects are likely to overbalance the beneficial ones. Think of a few important external effects, e.g. pollution, congestion, keeping up with the Joneses, and they are detrimental ones. If we include public goods as externalities, it is true that beneficial externalities may be just as important. But this is not of much relevance to our purpose here. For example, in determining the amount of expenditure on defence, presumably account is already being taken of the beneficial effect on all citizens. For another example, education may have important favourable external effects. But education is already provided free or heavily subsidised. For the problem of second v. third best, it is the 'unaccounted for' externalities that matter. If we confine our consideration to the unaccounted for externalities in the production and consumption of goods and services, it seems quite certain that detrimental externalities predominate. Most production processes, directly or indirectly (through input usage), involve some detrimental external effects on the environment. Moreover, the consumption of many goods also has detrimental external effects due to people's desire to keep up with or surpass their neighbours and countrymen. Thus the appearance of new fashions and new models makes their predecessors 'older', the building of bigger houses makes existing ones 'smaller'.

If we agree that detrimental externalities predominate, then this gives rise to an interesting consideration. The necessity to raise government revenue through non-lump-sum taxes has always been regarded as a form of distortion we have to live with.† But with the predominance of detrimental externalities, most goods and services have to be taxed to achieve the first-best optimum to start with. This first-best system of taxes involves, of course, complicated rate-structures to account for the

---

†The problem of minimising the cost of this distortion has given rise to a considerable amount of very sophisticated literature; see e.g. Atkinson & Stiglitz (1972)*, Baumol & Bradford (1970), Boiteux (1971)*, Bradford & Rosen (1976), Diamond & Mirrlees (1971)*, Dixit (1970), Lerner (1970), Mirrlees (1976)*, Sandmo (1976), Stiglitz & Dasgupta (1971)*.

different degrees of externalities. However, taking account of the informational and administrative costs of devising such a complicated system, it might not be far from optimal to impose a general tax (either in the form of an income tax, value-added tax, or some other tax) on all goods and services with special adjustments only to account for particularly severe forms of externality. If this average rate of taxes is not much different from that required to finance government expenditure, there need not be any real distortion at all as a result of government taxation. Considering the degrees of such externalities as environmental pollution and keeping up with the Joneses, and the fact that government sector accounts for around 30 per cent of GNP, it does not seem unlikely that such may well be the case. It is true that, due to the progressive structure of income taxation, the marginal tax rates are well above the average rates and the tax rates on the rich are well above those on the poor. This may then involve some distortion. But I think at least part of the differentiation in tax rates can be regarded as an unintended corrective to the differential externalities. The detrimental externalities of consumption due to utility interdependence (keeping up with the Joneses, etc.) are likely to be more pronounced for the rich than for the poor. Hence, even on efficiency grounds alone, the rich may have to be taxed more anyway.†

The validity of the above subjective judgements of facts (on which see Ng, 1972b, and Appendix 1A) is of course an empirical question. Before such information is available, all we have is just a rough estimate. However, we must act on the best information we have got. Decisions based on rough estimates are better than random choice or indecision (if that is an option). It is true that there are many difficulties associated with the collection of relevant information here. But further study would seem to be justified in view of the importance of the issue.

For our purpose here, government intervention may be divided into two groups, corrective and distortive intervention. Corrective intervention is undertaken to offset distortions due to externalities etc. Distor-

---

†In two interesting articles, Thompson (1974, 1979) argues that, due to the defence burden of capital accumulation and the effect of wartime price controls, the US tax/subsidy structure is roughly efficient. In the text, I have not taken account of this defence burden argument for taxation/subsidisation.

tive intervention leads to inefficiency but is undertaken for purposes of income distribution, political handouts, etc. Corrective intervention need not concern us here. For distortive intervention, it seems that some forms (e.g. farm-price maintenance, quotas, etc.) result in a positive distortion with price $> MC$ and others (such as free national health service) result in a negative distortion. Without empirical studies, it is difficult to judge the relative importance of the two opposite effects.

With respect to government intervention and the problem of second-best, there is an interesting argument that should be considered:

> Suppose that, in accordance with a second-best solution, we subsidise those sectors which we ought to, and encourage those which must become more monopolistic in their behaviour to do so. As time goes by, other constraints will appear and some of those which were effective in the past may cease to be so. All this will involve us in a process of extending subsidies and monopolisation on the one hand and trying to dismantle them on the other. While, however, it is easy thing to start subsidising or encouraging restrictive practices, it is not so easy to take the reverse of these steps. In general, one can justifiably expect that some of the imperfections which we might have encouraged in the past according to a second-best solution may harden out after some time and become constraints in their own right, at least according to the logic of the theory [of second best]. In this way we run the danger of a proliferation of constraints and the efficiency of the system will become very poor. (Athanasiou, 1966, p. 86)

In reply to the above argument, a theorist of second best may say that what we need to do is just to pose a long-run maximisation problem which takes account of possible changes in the constraints over time. Despite the possible effects on the set of constraints, it can be seen that a second-best policy is in general different from a first-best one. In fact, due to interaction between policy and constraints, the second-best solution will be even more complicated. For example, it may be optimal (on second-best grounds) to give 'tariff-compensating' subsidies to agricultural products at lower rates than static second-best solution suggests. (Given that the tariffs on industrial imports cannot be eliminiated due to political reasons, a subsidy on agricultural production has been advanced as a second-best argument to 'compensate' for the adverse effect of tariffs on agriculture. For an argument against this proposal, see Warr, 1979.) It may even be optimal to vary the rates of subsidy over time (perhaps increasing slowly) according to some complicated formulae.

The above 'second-best' reply to the argument of Athanasiou is formally correct if we ignore the problems of information and administrative costs. Taking account of these, it is obvious that a dynamic second-best solution is even more utopian than its static counterpart. Thus, if we combine our argument for a third-best policy that recognises informational and administrative costs and Athanasiou's argument on the danger of the proliferation of constraints, a powerful case can be made out for ignoring second-best considerations and adopting simple first-best rules for most cases. It is true that Athanasiou's argument involves an asymmetry between taxes and subsidies, i.e. it is easy to withdraw taxes but difficult to withdraw subsidies. However, due to the necessity of raising government revenue, most sectors are subject to various forms of taxes. It may thus not be far from optimality to impose taxes according to first-best rules in order to correct for significant distortions (such as the $M tax on an external diseconomy discussed above), refrain from introducing subsidies that can be justified only on temporary grounds, waive taxes instead of giving subsidies that can be justified on more permanent grounds, and give subsidies only if amply justified.

Summary

The theory of second best shows that the presence of irremovable distortions renders the second-best conditions exceedingly complicated; by satisfying some optimality conditions, an improvement is not ensured. However, the complicated second-best rules are neither optimal nor feasible if informational and administrative costs are taken into account. The simple first-best rules are the optimal feasible in an important class of situations (Informational Poverty), implying that analyses based on first-best assumptions are still relevant for practical policy-making. This is so since, with a reasonable concavity assumption, staying with the first-best rules maximises expected benefit. With more (but not perfect) information, third-best policies are appropriate. Some informal illustrative applications of this third-best theory are provided. In particular, average-cost pricing for public utilities may not be far from the third-best optimum and the necessity to raise government revenue through non-lump-sum taxes need not impose any real distortion. (Appendix 9A has its own summary.)

A Dollar is a Dollar: Efficiency, Equity, and Third-Best Policy

The original conjecture of 'a dollar is a dollar' is due to Ross Parish. Despite my assurance that the conjecture is worth 50% of this appendix, Parish has modestly declined my invitation to a joint authorship. (He has outlined his argument elsewhere; see Parish, 1976. It does not include the third-best equity-efficiency argument of this appendix.) I was converted to Parish's conjecture during my attempt to convince him that it is wrong. This shows that this appendix is free from ideological motivation. In fact, this is an instance of the very widespread phenomenon that many economists are very sympathetic at the intuitive and/or ideological level to many ideas of the left which unfortunately turn out to be unacceptable upon closer analysis.

In economic policy in general and in cost-benefit analysis in particular, there are two different approaches. One takes distributional issues explicitly into account by using, e.g. distributional weights such that a dollar to the rich is worth less than a dollar to the poor. (On the potential enormous efficiency costs of the application of distributional weights, see Harberger, 1978.) The other approach concentrates on the efficiency aspect of the problem only, with an explicit or implicit understanding that the result is subject to distributional qualifications. (Harberger, 1971, seems to believe that no such qualification is required but does not provide a convincing justifying argument.) In this appendix, I wish to argue that, generally, no distributional weights need to be used, i.e. analysis based on efficiency alone is worth its face value with no need for a distributional proviso. In short, a dollar is a dollar. This argument, if accepted, provides a powerful simplification in the formulation of economic policy in general and in cost-benefit analysis in particular.

The pursuit of equality by progressive income taxation is usually limited by the consideration of incentives. (Thus the progressivity of the Australian system of income taxation was reduced in February 1978, partly on the ground of incentives.) But for the disincentive effect, it is likely that most people would prefer a more equal distribution of post-tax incomes. Hence it is believed that a dollar to the rich should count less than a dollar to the poor; rationing is regarded as more equitable than the price mechanism, etc. What most people fail to see is that such distributional weighting, preferential treatment, rationing, etc. will also produce disincentive effects. So these measures are inferior to income taxation as they have efficiency costs in addition to the disincentive effect. This may not be true if these measures are used as a second-best policy to counteract the disincentive effect of taxation. However, they are not in fact used for this second-best efficiency purpose but for equity purposes. Moreover, the scope for pursuing the complicated second-best policy, if at all possible, is severely limited by informational and administrative costs. Hence the optimal feasible or the third-best policy is to treat a dollar as a dollar, leaving the objective of equity or equality to be achieved by income taxation. (This does not of course rule out measures that reduce inequality without creating any disincentive effect such as the removal of man-made barriers to equality of opportunity.) Instead of using income weighting, rationing, etc. to achieve the objective of equality, it is better to get rid of such efficiency-reducing measures and substitute for them a more progressive income tax system. The removal of income weighting, rationing, etc. will make the rich better off. Hence the compensating increase in taxes will not reduce their incentives. In fact, everyone could be made better off by the introduction of such a system.

9A.1   The Third-best Equity-incentive Argument

In an ideal first-best world where costless and neutral lump-sum transfers (fixed according to potential rather than actual incomes) are feasible, it can easily be seen that a dollar is a dollar. A dollar must be treated as a dollar to achieve efficiency, and any desired level of equality can be achieved by lumpsum transfers. If we introduce some second-best constraints ruling out lump-sum taxes and taxes on leisure, the resulting second-best system of taxation/pricing rules is very complicated, even if only the efficiency consideration is taken into account. (If taxes on all goods including leisure are possible, no inefficiency need be involved in taxation since a system of proportional taxes can be devised which is effectively equivalent to lump-sum taxes.) To illustrate the point that in a second-best world a dollar need not be a dollar, consider a simplified economy of three sectors, goods X and Y, and leisure L. Suppose that the degree of substitutability between X and Y is not strong and X is highly complementary with L. It may then be better to impose a higher tax on the consumption of X by the rich instead of just relying on income tax which is equivalent to taxing X and Y at the same rate.[†] In the real economy of thousands of goods, the second-best optimal rates of taxation require information far in excess of what is available. Taking account of informational and administrative costs, I argue in Section 9.3 above that second-best policies are not optimal. In fact, first-best rules (such as price = marginal cost) may be optimal if the available information is very inadequate and third-best rules (something less complicated than second-best rules but not as simple as first-best rules) may be desirable with more information. For our purpose here, we cannot of course rule out the possibility that the amount of information may be sufficient to justify some third-best rules instead of the first-best rule of 'a dollar is a dollar'. However, such departures from the first-best rule are justified, as will be argued below, not on equity grounds but on efficiency grounds depending on the degrees of complementarity with leisure and other interrelationships. (For simplicity, I shall refer only to the degrees of complementarities with leisure in the following; this does not affect the essence of the argument. On

---

[†]Cf. Sosnow (1974) where it is argued that it is optimal to employ more than two policy parameters to achieve equitable distribution of income and that for distributional aiding and distributional impeding programs, the usual cost-benefit rule should be modified, i.e. a dollar is not a dollar. However, Sosnow's analysis does not cover factors considered in the present paper. Similarly, Deaton (1977) analyses the equity-efficiency issues of commodity taxation, assuming a fixed labour supply.

the importance of complementarity with leisure, see Corlett & Hague, 1953, Atkinson & Stiglitz, 1972*.)

As lump-sum transfers are impracticable, the actual redistributive mechanisms take such forms as progressive income taxation, rationing, preferential treatment in government expenditure, etc. That redistribution is not pursued to achieve complete equality may be explained by the disincentive effects involved. Ideally then, the pursuit of equality should stop at a level that involves an optimal balance between equality and efficiency (or incentive). I wish to argue that: (1) Assuming that we have already achieved such an optimal balance, a dollar should be a dollar; (2) If not, it is better to achieve such balance by manipulating the income tax schedule (i.e. by making it more progressive or less) instead of using rationing, preferential treatment of the rich and the poor, etc.; a dollar should still be a dollar; (3) For any balance (optimal or not) between equality and incentive using preferential treatment, there exist a superior alternative system (that provides the same balance between equality and incentive) without using preferential treatment. This last proposition is a more interesting one and in fact subsumes the first two. Our argument differs from the well-known negative income tax proposal in that the latter is based on the first-best partial equilibrium framework which ignores the second-best complication. The analysis here takes this complication into account but justifies the principle of 'a dollar is a dollar' on third-best grounds. Nevertheless, our argument does lend support to the negative income-tax proposal and also to the attempt to separate the equity and efficiency issues by Musgrave (1969b) and others.

Consider a rational individual without money illusion. In his choice between work and leisure, he will not only take into account the amount of income he can earn by working extra hours (or extra hard) but also what he will get by this extra income. If having a higher income does not enable one to buy more parking space but rather means that one has to pay more for the same thing, and/or that projects in his favour are less likely to be undertaken, then the extra income will be worth less than it otherwise would be. It is as though the tax rate has increased. The same degree of disincentive will apply unless income is valued not so much for its purchasing power but mainly as a status symbol. However, among those people for whom status considerations are important, it is more likely that the pre-tax rather than the post-tax income will be used as an indication. Hence the same degree of incentives still applies. But the use of rationing, preferential treatment, income weighting in cost-benefit analysis, etc., will, in general, result in additional inefficiency unless they are designed as second-best measures which require detailed information. For example, using the unequal income weighting system, we may, by chance, choose a project with the greatest unweighted aggregate net benefit. But in general we will choose one with a lower aggregate net benefit.

To dramatise the point, suppose that a society is so decidedly against the inequality involved in the market mechanism (with unequal earning abilities) that it replaces the market altogether by a system of complete, equal, and permanent rationing. Then, even if labour is not rationed so that people still have the freedom of work, the remaining incentive (if any) to work can no longer be explained by differential earnings, since extra incomes do not enable one to buy anything extra at all. Even if the resulting incentive is sufficient to keep the system going, it is better to introduce a system of taxation that completely equalises post-tax incomes or a system of completely equal wage payments and let the market perform its allocative function. The objective of equality is achieved all the same but the undesirable effect of rationing need not be incurred.

In the real world, complete equality in post-tax incomes will result in an intolerably low level of incentive. Some level of inequality has to be accepted. But whatever the combination of equality and incentive aimed at, it is better to achieve it by means of income taxation than by using preferential treatment and/or dispensing with the market mechanism. With the appropriate income taxation, a dollar is a dollar. More precisely, I wish to establish the following proposition:

PROPOSITION: *For any alternative (designated A) using a system (a) of purely equality-type preferential treatment between the rich and the poor, there exists another alternative, B, which does not use preferential treatment, that makes no one worse off and achieves the same degree of equality (of real income, or utility) and raises more government revenue which could be used to make everyone better off.*

Note that this proposition is true even in the case where the pure equality-type preferential treatment just happens to be consistent with second-best efficiency considerations. This is so since alternative B, which does not incorporate pure equality-type preferential treatment, but instead uses a system b which is designed for efficiency purposes only, would already, within that system b, incorporate the second-best efficiency considerations with which system a just happens to be consistent.

However, the *existence* of alternative B does not necessarily mean that it can be identified and implemented. If system a is *designed* to take account of second-best considerations, then system b can also be so designed. But system a may only be consistent with second-best considerations by *chance* rather than by design. In addition, the informational costs of designing a system consistent with the second-best considerations may be prohibitive. Then we may not be able to identify system b. Thus, while alternative B may exist, it may not be feasible to implement. Thus, if we wish to strengthen the above proposition to be one about the existence of a *feasible* superior alternative B, it would apply only in a probabilistic sense. That it (the strengthened proposition) still applies in a probabilistic sense is due to the theory of third best. Just as it may be consistent with second-best considerations, system a may also be opposite to the requirement of second best. The argument in Section 9.3 can then be used to show that the expected gain is negative. Hence, as far as the second-best consideration is concerned, the use of system a involves negative expected gains. For simplicity, we may thus assume that system a is neutral with respect to second-best considerations. (This, in fact, gives it an advantage.)

To establish our proposition let us adopt the following simplifying assumptions: (1) there is no political constraint on redistribution through taxation; (2) the administrative cost of the pure taxation system is no higher than its alternative, for any same degree of equity attained; (3) all individuals know the relevant taxation scale, details of government expenditure, etc.; (4) there is no money illusion or similar 'irrational' preference. In Section 9A.2, we shall see that the relaxation of these assumptions does not affect our argument significantly.

Consider Figure 9A.1, where curve α represents a given income-tax

250 Welfare Economics

schedule relating post-tax to pre-tax income levels. For example, a person earning OC (= CE) will be taxed DE and left with CD as his post-tax income. With the operation of preferential treatment, etc., the rich are made worse-off and the poor *may* be made better-off. Let this be equivalent to a more egalitarian tax system β but without the preferential treatment.† Now, instead of adopting alrenative A = tax-schedule α with the given system of preferential treatment, let us adopt alternative B = tax schedule β without preferential treatment. Assuming no money illusion, alternative B offers the same degree of incentives as well as the same degree of equality in real income (using 'real income' to include the effects of preferential treatment) or utilities. To see this, consider *any* individual. Under alternative A, suppose he chooses to work to

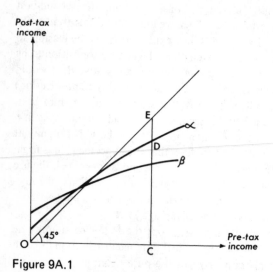

Figure 9A.1

---

†In Section 9A.3, it is shown that a *common* tax schedule (with no preferential treatment) can be devised which all individuals will regard as equivalent to alternative A, assuming a common utility function as in Mirrlees (1971)*. If this assumption is relaxed, we have to work with representative individuals. The main thrust of our argument will not be affected.

the extent such that his pre-tax income is, say, OC. His post-tax income is CD. He could have chosen any other point along the α curve within the range of his earning capacity. Hence D is his utility maximising point subject to his earning ability. Next, consider alternative B. The individual is now faced with the curve β. For any level of pre-tax income, the post-tax income is, in general, different from that under A. However, in terms of utility, they are the same by construction. Hence, the individual will still find it most advantageous to work to earn a pre-tax income of OC. This applies to any individual. Hence alternatives A and B offer the same incentive as well as the same level of equality of real income.

The argument of the preceding paragraph is based on the assumption of *perfect* preferential treatment. In other words, the degree of preferential treatment is taken to be a monotonically decreasing function of incomes across all individuals. In practice, preferential treatment in government expenditure cannot be perfect. For one thing, some expenditures benefit all people in the same geographical area. The government may choose to spend more on poor areas but a rich person living in a predominantly poor area will benefit as well. A person is not likely to change his place of residence each time as his income is increased. Hence, for any person living in a particular area, he will not be appreciably adversely affected if he earns more, for those government expenditures that are geographically specific. The increase in his income does not increase the average income of the whole area appreciably. But for the purpose of income taxation, it is his income alone that counts and not the average income of the whole area. It follows that the disincentive effect of pure income taxation (alternative B) is greater than that of income taxation with lower progressivity but with *imperfect* preferential treatment (alternative A'). Does it follow that alternative B is inferior to alternative A'? No, as the following paragraph shows.

The reason we have to make do with imperfect preferential treatment is the infeasibility or very high costs of effecting perfect preferential treatment, not that we prefer imperfect preferential treatment (alternative A') to perfect preferential treatment (alternative A) as such. Abstracting from the problems of feasibility and transaction costs, alternative A is preferable to A'. But it has been argued above that alternative B is preferable to alternative A. It follows that alternative B must be preferable to A'. This is so despite the fact that the disincentive effect is higher under B. The imperfection of alternative A' involves welfare loss in terms of inequity which must be larger than the costs of higher disincentive effects of B or A (which have the same incentives), otherwise A' would be preferable to A. Since the problem of imperfection in preferential treatment does not affect our conclusion, let us henceforth concentrate mainly on perfect preferential treatment.

It remains to be seen whether the tax schedule β will collect no less an amount of net government revenue than schedule α. If the preferential treatment under alternative A is designed as second-best measures by taking account of the different degrees of complementarities with leisure, etc., then ignoring problems of information and administrative costs, alternative B, without using such an efficiency-improving method of transfer, will yield a smaller net revenue. However, this second-best measure of preferential treatment is justified on grounds of efficiency. This is similar to, say, the argument that a commodity producing an important negative externality should be taxed more. The usual case for preferential treatment, rationing, etc., is based on equity grounds. The low-income groups are given tax concessions on their interest payments on houses not because of the consideration of the degree of complementarity of housing with leisure but because they are poor. If it can be shown that adequate housing has significant external economies or is a merit good, then perhaps the tax concession can be justified on these grounds. But purely on equity grounds, if some people are still too poor to buy a house after the operation of the optimal income-tax/subsidy, then it is optimal for them not to own a house. If we think we have not done enough in achieving equity, it is better to make the income-tax system more progressive instead of meddling with all sorts of interventions, unless these are justified on grounds of externality, second best, merit-want, etc. If measures of preferential treatment, rationing, etc., are not selected on efficiency grounds (externality, second best, etc.), then by chance they may be justified on efficiency grounds after all. But more likely they won't be justified. Moreover, on the principle of increasing marginal damages (Section 9.3) the expected gain from such policies are negative. Hence, at least in a probabilistic sense, tax schedule β without preferential treatment will collect more net revenue than tax schedule α with preferential treatment. The increased revenue collected is a measure of the superiority of alternative

B over *A*. (For a more precise demonstration of this result, see Section 9A.3 below.)

Before concluding this section let us illustrate our argument with a utility possibility map. In Figure 9A.2 U^J and U^K represent the levels of utility of two (groups of) individuals in the society. Starting from the initial position *D* on the utility possibility curve *I*, consider a project (or any change) that involves a negative aggregate net benefit (the possibility curve moves inward to II),† and a more equal distribu-

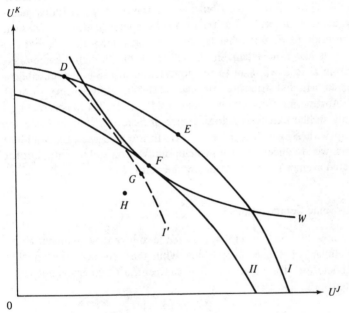

Figure 9A.2

†We are confined to the unambiguous cases where the net benefit measure shows a negative (or positive) result whether compensating variation or equivalent variation is used (the utility possibility curves do not cross in the relevant region). Cases where they do cross give rise to well-known theoretical problems in using compensation tests. However, it is clear that the differences between compensating and equivalent variations are likely to be overwhelmed by inaccuracies in the process of information collection and aggregation. Thus for cases where we can be sure that the aggregate net benefit is positive, it is likely to be positive irrespective of which measure we use. This is especially true if the redistribution effects are not very large. For cases where this is not true, see Appendix 4A.

tion at the point F. If the welfare contour W through F passes above D it appears that the change is desirable. Income weighting in cost-benefit analysis that sanctions such changes seems justified. However, to achieve the degree of equality represented by the point F, it would be better to do so by income taxation travelling along curve I from D to E. It is true that income taxation has disincentive effects and thus the point E is not sustainable. The disincentive effect will lead to a contraction of the utility possibility curve I inwards (not drawn) to pass through, say, the point G. In other words, we cannot in fact travel along the utility possibility curve I but have to travel along the utility feasibility curve I' in redistribution through income taxation. As drawn, G is inferior to F. But what is not commonly recognised is that the point F is also not sustainable. If redistribution through income taxation from D to E will lead to the contraction of the utility possibility curve, so will redistribution through cost–benefit weighting from D to F. Abstracting from second-best considerations, II will contract by a roughly similar extent as I does. Hence, instead of the point F, we will end up with H, which is inferior to G. In the presence of second-best factors, we are uncertain as to which point we will end up with, but the expected average is somewhat below the point H.

9A.2 Some Complications

Let us now discuss factors that may render our general argument above for 'a dollar is a dollar' inapplicable. While these considerations qualify our conclusion, the main thrust of the central argument is not much affected.

(1) Political Constraints on Redistribution through Taxation

It is argued above that, if we have already achieved an optimal balance between equity and incentive in our taxation system, a dollar should be treated as a dollar. If not, it is better to change the taxation schedule instead of using preferential treatment, quota, weighting, etc. What if the taxation schedule cannot be changed to the desired structure due to political constraints? (A somewhat different constraint, the institutional constraint, has been discussed by Goldfarb & Woglom, 1974. The political constraint is noted in Little & Mirrlees, 1974.) If it is true that we can't change the taxation schedule but we can effect redistribution by other means, our conclusion may have to be qualified accordingly, though there is still the ethical question of the desirability of doing good by stealth. However, why should the political constraint act only to prevent redistribution through taxation and not by other means? This may be because the voters are rather irrational. But in this respect, I suspect that they are rather rational and practical. The upper and middle classes will vote a government out of office not only for carrying out drastic changes in taxation but also for carrying out other drastic redistributive measures. Especially in the long run, the forces that operate to prevent redistribution through taxation will also operate to prevent redistribution by other means. If we are thinking in terms of a distributional equilibrium, the distribution should be in terms not so much of money income but of real income. Naturally, if the rich are penalised in other ways, they will have less tolerance of the progressivity of taxation.

(2) Transaction Costs

Our analysis has been based on the assumption that transaction costs are negligible or at least that the additional transation costs associated with redistribution through more progressive income taxation are not higher than the transaction costs of its alternatives. Apart from the disincentive effect (which has been taken into account and is not subsumed under transaction costs), the costs associated with income taxation seem to fall mainly under (a) the costs of administration on the part of both the taxpayers and the collectors, (b) the costs involved in tax evasion and enforcement, and (c) the costs of tax lobby activities and the like. We recognise that all these forms of costs are very substantial. But the relevant amounts are not the total but only the marginal costs. For good or for bad, income taxation will be with us in the foreseeable future. The incremental costs of administration of a more progressive tax schedule seem trivial. The costs of a change from one schedule to another may not be trivial but are probably not substantial However, at least in the long run, the relevant comparison is between the costs of administering two alternative schedules, the difference between which is probably quite negligible. A more progressive tax schedule may however involve higher costs in encouraging more evasion and more lobby activities. But the increase in progressivity is in lieu of some system of preferential treatment which itself is a subject of evasion and lobbying. While this is a subject where precise conclusion can hardly be expected, it does not seem probable that the costs involved in the latter (i.e. preferential treatment) will be much lower. On the other hand, the cost of administering a pure taxation system is almost certainly significantly lower than that of administering a system of taxation combined with preferential treatment in government expenditure. Hence, for the heading of transaction costs as a whole, it seems likely that our central conclusion is strengthened, not weakened.

(3) Ignorance of Benefit Distribution

My argument is based on the assumption that individuals know the distribution of costs and benefits in government expenditure across income groups or the details of preferential treatment so that the incentives are the same as an equivalent pure income taxation system. In practice, this knowledge is unlikely. On the other hand, most individuals do know the scale of income taxation. Does this asymmetrical knowledge mean that the disincentive effect of income taxation is more severe than an equivalent preferential expenditure system, as in effect argued by Feldstein (1974, p. 152)?

In the absence of perfect knowledge, an individual has to base his choice on his estimates. From the fraction of knowledge he possesses, it seems that he is as likely to overestimate as to underestimate the degree of progressivity implied in a given preferential expenditure system, depending on the psychology of the individual in question. Hence, on the whole, the degree of incentives is likely to be similar between the preferential expenditure system and the pure income taxation system.

(4) Illusion and Dogmatism

I have mentioned money illusion (which may qualify our result in the short run but is unlikely to be significant in the long run) but there could be other forms of illusion and/or dogmatism. For example, some individuals may insist on rationing the limited parking space (or any other scarce good) by quota and are quite ignorant of or unable to see the inefficiency involved and its futility in achieving more equality. If these individuals genuinely feel hurt or frustrated if we abolish the quota system even with compensating increase in the progressivity of income taxation, then it may not be true that such a move would increase social welfare.

This complication is not peculiar to our specific problem here but is quite general to many economic and social policies. The long-term solution to this may (at the risk of being too optimistic, no, idealistic) be the education of the public which frees them from their naive and dogmatic beliefs. In the meantime, the policy-makers may have to take such complications into account in some way but it is very difficult for the theorist to incorporate them formally into the analysis.

(5) Redistributive Effects of the Project Itself

My argument shows that a dollar is a dollar irrespective of whether it accrues to the poor or the rich. But my argument does not show that a billion dollars is a billion dollars. This point can be clearly seen by considering a simple example. Consider two alternative projects: project M will increase the incomes (after allowing for cost share) of all the one million individuals by $1000 each, and project N will increase the income of one single random individual by $1,000,000,000. Ruling out costless lump-sum transfers (which would make us indifferent between the two projects), it is clear that project M will be preferred to project N by all egalitarian SWFs. This preference is not based on valuing a marginal dollar to the rich lower than a marginal dollar to the poor. Rather, it is based on treating the first dollar as more valuable than the 1,000,000,000th dollar, to whoever they go. Hence the equity-incentive argument we use above does not apply here. However, the equity-incentive argument can be used to dispel the possible belief that, since a project that itself creates inequality is inferior to one with the same aggregate net benefits, a project that creates equality must be preferable to one that has the same aggregate net benefit but is distributionally neutral. Consider another project O that will yield the same aggregate net benefits of $1,000,000,000 but distributed across the economy in such a way that the poor have much higher benefits and the rich have negative benefits. While this may seem to be a good thing in itself, the incentive argument will show that project O is in fact inferior to project M.

From the above, it may be said that, for projects whose redistributive effects are marginal, one can simply choose in terms of the aggregate net benefits; for projects whose redistributive effects are significant, we should prefer the one with less redistributive effects, given the same aggregate net benefits. This seems to lend support to the concept of a conservative SWF discussed by Corden (1974, p. 107).

(6) Preference for Working, etc.

If an individual prefers to have his income by earning it instead of receiving it as a transfer welfare payment, then a cost-benefit analysis that does not take this preference into account may be misleading. This has been emphasised by Skolnik (1970). The main thrust of this kind of complication can be taken care of by appropriate shadow-pricing. For example, in the particular case considered here, the main difference is the possible preference some individuals may have for earning income instead of receiving some kind of dole money. This can largely be taken care of by putting an appropriate shadow price on employment. For a single person without dependants, his income from a low-paid job is likely to be sufficient to preclude him from receiving a subsidy (negative income-tax). All that is needed is a low or zero income-tax. So he will not have to suffer the feeling of being on the dole. For families with dependants, the negative income-tax can be effected in the form of, say, substantial child-endowment payments differentiated according to income levels. A fixed child-endowment is used in Australia with no one feeling ashamed of receiving it and the introduction of differentiation is unlikely to change this substantially.

(7) Preferential Treatment Based on Some Index of Earning Abilities

It may be thought that our argument against preferential treatment between the rich and the poor as such does not extend to preferential treatment according to some characteristics which may account for people being poor or rich. For example, preferential treatment according to some index of earning ability such as I.Q. (by, say, spending on education until the marginal returns on the less/more capable are less/more than that justified by pure efficiency considerations) or skin colour (by subsidising Afro haircuts, as suggested to me in a seminar) may be regarded as desirable as it is very difficult or impossible for people to acquire (or not to acquire) such characteristics as I.Q. However, this only means that, instead of basing our equity-purpose tax/subsidy on income levels which are liable to be affected by disincentive effects, it might be better to base it on some index of earning abilities such as I.Q. Instead of subsidising Afro haircuts, it would be better to subsidise the people concerned directly. Instead of stopping to educate the capable when the discounted net marginal returns are still positive, it would be better to educate them but impose higher taxes on them (according to I.Q.). However, if it is true that the practical difficulties of taxing intelligence (on which see Section 6.4) are too prohibitive, while preferential treatment in educational spending is more feasible, an exception to our general principle on this practical ground may be justifiable. (This is in fact a question of asymmetrical transaction costs, not a failure of our principle as such.)

(8) Unexpected Emergencies

In times of unexpected emergencies such as earthquakes, wars, etc., certain necessities may be in very short supply. In principle, we could impose appropriately higher taxes on the rich and those who happen to own the goods in short supply and pay subsidies to the poor and the victims of the disaster. Then the policy of 'a dollar is a dollar' could still be best even in these emergencies. However, due to time lags, imperfect information, etc., it may be practically infeasible to effect the required changes in taxes/subsidies in time. Rationing of basic necessities such as medical supplies (which also involves external economies) may then be the best practical solution. However, the possible desirability of violating the principle of 'a dollar is a dollar' in such emergencies does not mean that the same is true for normal times.

From the discussion above, it may be concluded that none of the complications seem to change the central argument of this appendix significantly.

9A.3 Is β the Tax Schedule We Want?

With reference to the argument of Section 9A.2, we wish to show that a common tax schedule β can be constructed that, with the elimination of the preferential system a, makes no individual worse off and also increases government revenue. We have to assume a common utility function (with respect to leisure, consumption and the preferential system) and shall comment on the relaxation of this assumption later.

Each person has a given income-earning ability. Subject to this earning ability, each person may choose different levels of pre-tax income by varying his hours and intensity of work. His choice depends, of course, on his subjective preference, the tax schedule and the system of preferential treatment. Even with the assumption of the same preference or utility function, persons of different earning abilities may have different indifference maps as defined in Figure 9A.3. (This is similar to the Mirrlees model of optimal income taxation. See Seade, 1977, for a diagrammatical illustration.) Given some mild assumptions, income varies positively and continuously with earning ability (Mirrlees, 1971). Geometrically, a person with higher earning ability has a flatter indifference curve at a given point. The equilibrium points (E^1, E^2, E^3) of three individuals under alternative A (tax schedule α and preferential system a) are depicted in Figure 9A.3.

Now let us dismantle the system of preferential treatment a. This will make the rich better off and *may* make the poor worse off. If system a is so inefficient such that its dismantling makes everyone better off, we have a stronger case for its removal. Thus, let us take the case where the poor will be made worse off by its removal. A system of perfect preferential treatment involves a degree of preferential treatment that is monotonically decreasing in incomes. (Non-perfection in preferential treatment does not affect our conclusion, see pp. 251–2.) Thus, if the rich are made better off and the poor worse off by the removal of system a (assumed perfect), there exists an intermediate income level (say C^2) at which the individual would stay indifferent by the removal of system a. This individual must exist in a model of a continuous distribution of individuals, but may not exist in the discrete case. But the actual existence of this individual is of no consequence to our argument. After the removal of system a, the new indifference curve of this individual that corresponds to the same level of utility as

Post-tax
income

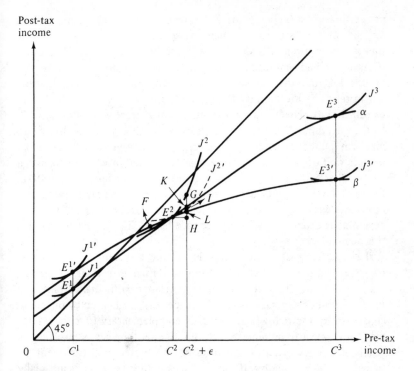

Figure 9A.3

J^2 must still pass through the point E^2. On the other hand, individual 3, who is made better off by the removal of system a, must have a new indifference curve $(J^{3'})$, that corresponds to the same level of utility J^3, passing through a lower point $E^{3'}$. With no preferential treatment against him, he now only needs a lower level of post-tax income to attain the original utility level at the same level $(0C^3)$ of pre-tax income.† Conversely, the new indifference curve $(J^{1'})$ for individual 1

---

†This is obviously true with the assumption of given earning abilities. With the relaxation of this assumption, it may be thought that $J^{3'}$ may pass above E^3 (and $J^{1'}$ below E^1) if the wage rate of individual 3 (individual 1) is sufficiently increased (reduced) by the operation of preferential system a. If this is so, it means that preferential system a in fact favours the rich rather than the poor when its full effects (including the indirect effect on earning abilities) are taken into account. This possibility may thus be disregarded. It is also clear that the indirect effect is unlikely to overbalance the direct effect.

passes through a higher point $E^{1'}$. Tracing through all points such as $E^{1'}$, E^2, $E^{3'}$, we arrive at the new tax schedule β. With the usual continuity assumptions this schedule will also be continuous and smooth. (Continuity and smoothness are not really necessary for our central proposition, but they make the illustration easier and enable it to be put in terms of the familiar tangency condition for maximisation.) Let us call the tax schedule β with no preferential treatment alternative B. If the government can collect at least as much revenue as before to maintain public expenditure it is clear that everyone will remain at least as well off as under alternative A. This is so since each person can always choose to earn the same amount of pre-tax income and attain the same level of utility as before. However, if alternative B has greater disincentive effects, many individuals may choose to earn less and government revenue may be smaller than before. Let us turn to examine this possibility.

The 'preferential' system may in fact be a system of second-best measures designed to counteract the disincentive effects of the income tax schedule α. Since the rich are confronted with higher tax-rates, these second-best measures may include, say, higher taxes on goods consumed by the rich which are highly complementary to leisure. They may thus appear to be preferential. But, in fact, they can be justified on purely efficiency grounds and need not be preferential treatment designed to achieve equality. If such is the case, then system a is not really preferential and hence it can be incorporated into alternative B, making alternatives A and B equivalent. Our purpose is not to argue against 'preferential treatment' that is in fact justified on second-best grounds (or some other efficiency grounds such as externality, merit goods). Rather we are arguing against preferential treatment to achieve equality as such. A system of truly equality-type preferential treatment may happen to go in the same general direction as required by second-best considerations. But it may also go in the reverse direction. Hence, we will assume that it is neutral in this respect. (In Section 9.3 it is argued that the expected gain of a movement towards and away from the second-best direction is probably negative. Hence, by assuming that preferential treatment is neutral in this respect, we in fact give it an advantage.)

If the new indifference curve of individual 2 does not only pass through E^2 but also stays unchanged at J^2 (at least in the neighbourhood of E^2) the new tax schedule β being flatter than α, must cut this indifference curve J^2). Individual 2 would then choose to earn a lower level of pre-tax income, say at the point F. However, the actual new indifference curve $(J^{2'})$ must be flatter than the old one J^2 at the point E^2. With no preferential treatment he would need less/more post-tax income if he were to earn a higher/lower level of pre-tax income. (Otherwise β would not be flatter than α to begin with.) Moreover, it can be shown that $J^{2'}$ must be tangential to β at E^2. The tax schedule α touches the (highest) indifference curve J^2. Both J^2 and α are reduced in slope to become $J^{2'}$ and β respectively. Moreover, the reduction in slope must be the same at the point E^2. Hence β touches $J^{2'}$ at E^2. To see this more clearly, consider a slightly higher level of pre-tax income $C^2 + \epsilon$. The slope of J^2 at E^2 (denoted by S^2) may be approximated by GH/E^2H. This approximation will become exact equality as we make ϵ approach zero, given smoothness in the curve. Similarly, the slope of $J^{2'}$ at E^2 (denoted $S^{2'}$) $\simeq IH/E^2H$, and the slope of α at E^2, $S^\alpha \simeq KH/E^2H$, $S^\beta \simeq LH/E^2H$. Since the denominators of all these slopes are the same, we may concentrate on the numerators. S^2 is larger than $S^{2'}$ by (approximately) GI, ignoring denominator. GI measures the extent to which individual 2 would be made better off by the removal of preferential system a had he chosen to earn $C^2 + \epsilon$ instead. (This is so owing to the argument of the preceding paragraph abstracting away the possible second-best effect of preferential system a. Otherwise GI may partly reflect this second-best effect which may, however, go either way.) S^α is larger than S^β by KL. KL measures the extent to which the individual who actually earned $C^2 + \epsilon$ under alternative A would be made better off by the removal of preferential system a if he were to keep earning $C^2 + \epsilon$. It must be recognised that GI need not equal KL. Although the pre-tax $(C^2 + \epsilon)$ incomes of both individuals are the same if the above hypothetical conditions prevail, they have different earning abilities. The same pre-tax income must then imply different hours or intensities of work. This difference in hours of work may then make them willing to forgo a different sum of post-tax income to remove the same system (and the same degree) of preferential treatment. However, as we make ϵ approach zero, not only do the above approximate measures of slopes become exact, the difference in the earning abilities of the two individuals also approaches zero. Given continuity, the amount by which S^2 is larger than $S^{2'}$ will then be equal to the amount by which S^α is larger than S^β at the point E^2 as the measures of these slopes are made exact. Since $S^2 = S^\alpha$ at E^2, so $S^{2'} = S^\beta$ at E^2. It is then not difficult to see that, under alternative B, not only can individual 2 attain the same level of utility as before by earning the same income as before, he has no incentive to earn a different income. Given some convexity assumption he would be positively worse off to operate at a different point.

Let us now consider the position of individual 3. Now $S^{3'}$ (slope of $J^{3'}$ at $E^{3'}$) may differ from S^3 for two reasons. One is the same as what makes $S^{2'}$ differ from S^2, i.e. the removal of preferential treatment tends to make the slope flatter. But since E^3 and $E^{3'}$ are now on two different points, there is an additional reason that may make $S^{3'}$ differ from S^3. The difference in post-tax income may make the individual have a different trade-off between consumption (or post-tax income) and leisure (related to pre-tax income). However, S^β (at $E^{3'}$) also differ from S^α (at E^3) for these two reasons. It is thus not difficult to see that S^β must equal $S^{3'}$ at $E^{3'}$. Individual 3 will choose to earn the same amount of pre-tax income as before. Similar reasoning shows that under alternative B all individuals will choose to earn the same amounts of pre-tax income as under alternative A. Alternative B thus provides the same degree of incentives and the same degree of equality in the distribution of real income (utility) as alternative A.

Even if all individuals earn the same amount of pre-tax income, can we be sure that government revenue is no smaller under alternative B? In Figure 9A.3, let C^1 (it could be zero) be the lowest pre-tax income earned and C^3 be the highest. The change in government revenue in moving from alternative A to B equals the area $E^2 E^3 E^{3'}$ weighted by population density function along the horizontal axis minus the area $E^{1'} E^1 E^2$, similarly weighted. It is clear that the weighted area $E^2 E^3 E^{3'}$ must be larger than the weighted area $E^{1'} E^1 E^2$. The former measures the aggregate amount by which all individuals earning more than C^2 are made worse off by preferential system a. The latter area measures the aggregate amount all individuals earning less than C^2 are made better off by system a. If the former area were smaller than the latter, system a would be justified on pure efficiency grounds to start with. Thus, if system a is truly preferential, the former area must be larger than the latter. For example, the use of unequal income weighting in cost-benefit analysis may sanction projects with positive unweighted aggregate net benefits. But such projects will be sanctioned without the use of unequal income weighting and would be undertaken under alternative B too. Hence, the difference in tax schedules α and β is caused by the effects of preferential measures such as unequal income weighting when they are effective in sanctioning projects with *negative* unweighted aggregate net benefits.

From the above discussion it can be seen that alternative B does not provide only the same degree of incentives and the same degree of equality, it also generates more government revenue than alternative A. This extra amount of revenue is a measure of the superiority of B (no preferential treatment but more progressive income taxation) and can be used to make everyone better off by increasing public expenditure and/or lowering taxes all around.

Our argument above is based on the assumption of the same preference for all individuals. If individual preferences with respect to leisure, consumption and preferential treatment differ, the removal of system *a* may make individuals who earned the same income better off or worse off by different amounts. Their new indifference curves will then pass through different points. We cannot then construct a new tax schedule (such as β) that will keep every individual as well off as before and earn the same income as before. We would then have to work with average individuals and construct a tax schedule that make these average individuals (one at each income level) indifferent. Some non-average individuals would be made better off and some worse off, some would earn more and some less. In principle, compensation may be effected to make no one worse off. But this is not practicable. However, this complication applies to all practical changes in the complicated real world with differentiated individuals. It does not affect the main thrust of our argument.

(A mathematical example demonstrating that each individual will choose the same amount of work under alternatives A and B is available from the author.)

Summary

The pursuit of equality by progressive income taxation is usually limited by the consideration of incentives. Despite this, it is not desirable to use distributional weights in cost-benefit analysis and other forms of preferential treatment for the poor and handicaps or limitations (e.g. rationing) for the rich. A dollar should be treated as a dollar, to whomsoever it goes. This is so because the disincentive effect will also apply to these measures, not just to progressive taxation. In addition, these measures have additional efficiency costs unless they are (but they are not) used as a second-best policy to counteract the disincentive effect of taxation. Moreover, the information and administrative costs of such a (second-best) policy are likely to be prohibitive. Hence the third-best policy of a dollar is a dollar. This central argument is presented in some detail and shown to be valid even after considering some complications.

10 Conclusion: Towards a Complete Study of Welfare?

10.1 Summary

We started off by defining welfare economics as the branch of study which endeavours to formulate propositions by which we can say that the social welfare in one economic situation is higher or lower than another. Is the welfare economics presented in this book useful in meeting its defined task?

As noted in Chapter 1, whether welfare economics is a positive or normative study depends on our definition of 'social welfare'. Defined in a positive way such as a vector or a sum or some other function of individual welfares or preferences (on the differences between welfare and preference, see Section 1.3*), welfare economics is a positive study. On the other hand, if we define social welfare normatively such as whatever we ought to pursue or maximise, then welfare economics must involve some normative aspect. Nevertheless, even with this later normative interpretation, we could leave the normative aspect (the determination of the objective function) aside and concentrate on the positive aspect. As long as it is agreed that social welfare (either in its positive or normative sense) depends somehow (positively) on individual welfares, the discussion on the conditions for and the attainment of Pareto optimality (Chapter 2) can provide a useful guide in the pursuit of social welfare.

If some persons are made worse off and some better off, can we still say something about the change in social welfare? The answer is positive if the change satisfies certain welfare criterion regarded as acceptable. In Chapter 3, Little's criterion is defended against arguments that it is inconsistent and/or redundant. But Little's criterion requires the

satisfaction of both the efficiency condition (the Kaldor criterion and/
or Scitovsky's reversal test) and the distributional condition. When the
two conflict presumably one has to be weighed against another. The
numerical measurement of surpluses (Chapter 4) may then be of some
assistance. Despite some ambiguities (such as path-dependency) at the
theoretical level, the surplus measurement can be accepted as an approximate measure of welfare change in most cases. (For some special case
where this is not so, I proposed the use of 'marginal dollar' equivalent;
see Appendix 4A.) A more tricky problem is how do we determine a
distributional improvement and how do we weigh distributional against
efficiency considerations. Different persons may have different opinions. Can we resolve our differences by some reasonable democratic
procedure? Can we base our social preferences on individual preferences? The impossibility theorems of Arrow, Kemp–Ng, and Parks, etc.,
show that social choice cannot be very satisfactorily based on individual
ordinal preferences. Subject to practical difficulties, it is possible to
reveal the intensities of individual preferences. With the concept of
finite sensibility, a marginal indifference can be used as a unit in cardinal utility measurement. Using a reasonable criterion of weak majority
preference, I then show that our SWF must be the unweighted sum of
individual utilities (Section 5.4.1*).

With a specific SWF, the optimal distribution of income can be determined if the utility feasibility frontier is also known (Section 6.1). Income distribution considerations are relevant in such issues as the degree
of progressiveness in income taxation. An important factor here is the
degree of disincentive effect. While the gross disincentive effect is relevant for the issues of tax revenue, it is the net (of income effect) disincentive effect that is relevant in determining the welfare cost (Appendix
6A*). The rigorous analysis of optimal income taxation by Mirrlees
(Section 6.3) produces a somewhat surprising result of a regressive
marginal tax-rate (though progressive in average rates). This conclusion
must be qualified by the fact that the analysis ignores external effects
(utility interdependency).

External effects are analysed in Chapter 7. In particular, the existence of conscience effect means that the welfare significance of the
problem of externalities may be much larger than suggested by traditional analysis. In Chapter 8, the discussion of public goods gives
some emphasis to the recently proposed incentive-compatible mechanism for preference revelation which opens up exciting possibilities of

tackling the free-rider problem.

It seems reasonable to say that we have learned something useful. Even if we cannot jump right to the summit of social welfare, at least we have gained some insights which may help us make some improvements. However, according to the theory of second best (Section 9.1), if we cannot jump to the summit, it seems quite impossible to make a definite improvement at all. If some of the first-best optimality conditions cannot be satisfied, the satisfaction of other first-best conditions may make matters worse. The second-best conditions are so complicated that it is practically impossible to define specifically, let alone to satisfy. This sounds to be a deadly blow to the practical usefulness of welfare economics. Fortunately, we have provided a theory of third best (Section 9.3) which shows that, in the absence of the relevant information, it is best to stick to the first-best rules even in the presence of second-best constraints. This provides a powerful case for the usefulness of welfare economics in general and analyses based on first-best assumptions in particular.

In Appendix 9A, the third-best argument is extended to cover the question of equity-efficiency trade-off. It is concluded that a (marginal) dollar should be treated as a dollar whoever it goes to, the rich or the poor. Instead of using such measures as income weighting, rationing, etc., to achieve the objective of equality, it is better to use income taxation. It is true that taxation has disincentive effects. But income weighting, rationing, etc., have efficiency costs in addition to their disincentive effects (which are not usually recognised). Thus, unless used as a second-best policy or based on some other efficiency considerations, these measures are inferior to taxation. This conclusion of 'a dollar is a dollar' provides a powerful simplification in the formulation of economic policies.†

---

†It may appear that our argument of a dollar is a dollar is inconsistent with Little's criterion (defended in Chapter 3) which takes distributional considerations into account. There is in fact no conflict. 'A dollar is a dollar' is evaluated prior to disincentive effects while Little's criterion should be applied to the final outcome including disincentive effects. See the analysis of Figure 9A.2 where the UPC moves inward due to disincentive effects. (See also p. 257 above.) If a change satisfies Little's criterion even taking account of disincentive effects, etc., then it should be adopted. But then it will also be sanctioned by 'a dollar is a dollar' unless perhaps when the distributional effects are not marginal. Little's criterion and the concept of marginal dollar equivalent may then be useful. I anticipate that it may take some reflection to assimilate the argument of this footnote.

10.2 Further Considerations

While we have covered much ground in welfare economics, we have also omitted many relevant issues which are not necessarily less important. They are left out mainly because of space limitation and also because some would have required more complicated treatment. One has first to master the basic elements of welfare economics before taking account of the complications. For those who wish to pursue further, Appendix 10A provides a very brief and incomplete guide to the literature on the following topics: changes in tastes, price-dependent preferences, merit goods, X-efficiency, rent-seeking activities, the process of public choice, etc. Even if we have successfully extended our analysis to take account of these complications (some of which are very tricky), some people may still be sceptical of the relevance (or at least the adequacy) of welfare economics to problems of social welfare. This may be due to the belief that a market economy concentrates too narrowly on purely economic objectives to the disregard of broader social objectives, that decision-making by separate economic units may not conform to over-all interests, that economic abundance may not improve happiness, etc. We shall consider these issues presently.

It has been shown (Section 2.3 and Appendix 2B) that a perfectly competitive equilibrium is Pareto-optimal under the assumptions of rational choice, absence of externalities and some minor assumptions. Thus the main factors that may account for the undesirability of a market economy are: (1) externalities, (2) irrational choice and imperfect knowledge of individuals, (3) undesirable distribution of income, (4) that the economy is not in perfectly competitive equilibrium. We have discussed problems of externalities in Chapter 7. Irrational choice and knowledge imperfection are also briefly discussed in Chapter 1. (See also the discussion of the concept of merit and demerit goods in Appendix 10A.) But we shall come back to these later. We have also devoted Chapter 6 to problems relating to distribution. It may be emphasised that what many people regard as a desirable distribution of income is usually based on ignoring the costs of arriving at that distribution (such as the disincentive effects of all practicable forms of redistribution and the loss in efficiency, freedom of choice, and liberty in general if more bureaucratic methods are used to achieve equality). Let us turn to examine briefly the possible undesirability of a market economy due to the fact that it is not in perfectly competitive equilibrium.

An actual economy is unlikely to be in a position of equilibrium since changes occur all the time. But if it is moving towards an equilibrium (even a changing one), equilibrium analyses may not be far off the mark. A more important difficulty arises if we do not have stable equilibria. But these difficulties shrink into insignificance by comparison with the fact that the economy is not perfectly competitive. The presence of the monopolistic (including oligopolistic) elements may be due to knowledge imperfection, institutional factors such as various cartel-like associations including trade unions, or to the presence of product differentiation/decreasing costs/indivisibilities (these are related factors). The presence of monopolistic elements makes the attainment of Pareto optimality impossible in practice. In principle, *if* the government knows the cost and demand conditions, it can design a system of taxes/subsidies to achieve optimality if desired. But this possibility exists only in Utopia. However, it may be argued that, if we take account of such complications as imperfect knowledge, administrative costs, political and institutional constraints, the very concept of Pareto optimality that ignores such complications (admitting only the technological constraint on production) is itself utopian. On the other hand, if the concept of Pareto optimality is defined to take account of all relevant constraints, costs, knowledge imperfection, etc., it can be argued that any given situation must be Pareto optimal or at least is in the process of moving towards a Pareto optimum. If it is possible to make everyone better off net of all relevant costs and satisfying all relevant constraints, etc., the improvement must have been made or is being made unless it is hampered by such factors as failure to recognise the possible improvement or failure to agree on the division of the gain, e.g. stalemate due to strategic bargaining. This last factor is very difficult to analyse objectively. (See, however, Nash, 1950.) But the degree of knowledge imperfection may be reduced by economic analysis, including the study of various types of costs. If the costs of a certain institutional constraint can be shown to be very high, there may be grounds for its removal. In other words, in a wider perspective, the constraint may not be taken as absolute. Analyses that ignore certain constraints or complications may also be useful by allowing deeper studies of the relevant central relationships. But in applying conclusions thus arrived at to the real world, it is important to bring back the complications and assess (we may have to be content with very rough estimates) their effects on the theoretical conclusions. With the progress of the study, more and more factors may be brought into the formal analysis itself.

After the above digression into some methodological issues, let us come back to the problem of the absence of perfect competition. In the proofs of the Pareto optimality of perfect competition, profit maximisation of firms may be built into the definition of perfect competition. Alternatively, it may be used as an independent assumption. In any case, the absence of profit maxmimisation may cause some difficulty. However, by defining profit as net of the cost of management, etc., it can be argued that utility maximisation implies profit maximisation for an owner-managed firm (Koplin, 1963, Ng, 1969, 1974b). Thus the assumption of utility maximisation or rational choice on the part of owner-managers is sufficient (together with other assumptions) for proving the Pareto optimality of a competitive equilibrium. With the separation of ownership from control, the utility maximising choice of managers need not conform completely to the interests of owners. However, if there is a competitive market for managers, they will be induced by the forces of competition to maximise profits for owners.†
Hence one may say that nonoptimality is due again to the presence of monopolistic power (of the manager).

Even abstracting away the problems of market imperfection (due to monopoly, etc.) and market failure (due to externality, etc.; see Bator, 1958 for an 'anatomy'), many people still believe that the functioning of a market economy and economic progress do not necessarily contribute to social welfare or happiness. Factors affecting welfare are not confined to economic factors and hence, it is believed, purely economic

---

†In the presence of uncertainty, the maximisation of expected profits need not be the best policy. With different attitudes towards risk by owners, there does not exist a general objective function (Diamond, 1967*, Ekern & Wilson, 1974). However, with a large number of firms, prospective owners could presumably segregate themselves by their degrees of risk aversion, i.e. risk-averse individuals buying shares of 'safe' firms. In any case, the problem of the existence of an objective function is not an important one in comparison to the problem of the conflict between managers and owners.

calculation is insufficient. Recent studies by economists on this and related issues include Easterlin (1974), Hirsch (1976), Layard (1980), MacDougall (1977), Mishan (1977) and Scitovsky (1976).

Out of a number of factors alleged to make the functioning of a market economy and/or economic growth undesirable, many are actually the familiar factors (market imperfection, externality, etc.), though usually discussed under different names. For example, in discussing the 'tyranny of small decisions', Kahn (1966) explicitly noted that the undesirable results of 'small decisions' are associated with the presence of externalities, decreasing costs, etc. Similarly, market failure due to the problem of 'option demand' discussed by Weisbrod (1964) can actually be attributed to decreasing costs. The so-called option demand refers to the fact that (present) nonconsumers of a product may also lose from the disappearance of the product as he may want to consume it in the future. But the revenue of a private producer comes only from consumers. 'It follows that the inability of the operator to make a profit does not necessarily imply the economic inefficiency of the firm' (Weisbrod, 1964, p. 476). This can be true (assuming that no externality, decreasing costs, etc., are involved) only if the firm can expect to earn more than normal profit in the future. It can then sustain a temporary loss in anticipation of eventual profit (abstracting from capital market imperfection, uncertainty, etc.). This cannot therefore be a valid ground for government subsidy. The closure of the enterprise may however be a social loss if there is decreasing costs. It can then be analysed by traditional analysis. Similarly, many of the alleged costs of economic growth can be seen to be no more than external diseconomies and can be treated as such. (For a 'spirited defence' of economic growth along this line, see Beckerman, 1975.) In the following (based on Ng, 1978a), let us concentrate on factors less amenable to traditional analysis.

As an example, consider the Harrod–Hirsch concept of positional goods. Harrod (1958) uses the concept of oligarchic wealth in connection with the problem of satiety; Hirsch (1976) developed it into the concept of positional goods and used it to question the desirability of economic growth. Positional goods are those goods or aspects of goods, services, work positions and other social relationships that are (1) scarce in some absolute or socially imposed sense and (2) subject to congestion or crowding through more extensive use.† Included as positional goods are: (1) goods of more-or-less fixed physical supply such as natural landscapes, old masterpieces, and personal services on a per capita basis; (2) those valued mainly for relative scarcity or status. For example, if we create a higher level of awards, it makes the existing awards less venerable. As more people get the bachelor degree one may need a Ph.D. to feel distinguished.

To concentrate on the contrast between positional goods and nonpositional goods, let us assume that the relative prices of different positional goods do not change with respect to each other so that we may lump them into a single composite good X. Similarly, all nonpositional goods are lumped as Y. This permits us to work with the two-dimensional Figure 10.1.

Abstracting for the moment from the problems of possible differences and changes in tastes, we operate with the same set of indifference curves. Consider a person with average income facing the budget line AA'. He may consume an average amount of both positional goods (X^0) and nonpositional goods (Y^0). (Persons of average income, even on average, may have above average consumption of Y and under average consumption of X or vice versa depending on the consumption pattern of the whole society. This divergence does not affect the main contention below.) Since positional goods are likely to be income elastic, his rich contemporary is likely to consume a disproportionately larger amount of X, e.g. at the point E^3. In other words, the income consumption curve OC is likely to be concave. However, this is not an essential assumption for the central argument here. With economic growth, our Mr Average can expect his income to increase, eventually catching up with or even surpassing the original rich man's income. Does this mean that he can eventually consume at E^3 on the indifference curve K_3? The answer is negative. Since positional goods cannot be increased with economic growth, their prices will increase relative to nonpositional goods as the latter become abundant. Thus, the average

---

†Both conditions were mentioned by Hirsch (1976, p. 27), who regarded either condition as sufficient to make a good positional. But it fits his argument better to make both conditions necessary. If a good is subject to congestion (as most goods are) but can be expanded in supply to relieve the congestion, then obviously it cannot be classified as a positional good.

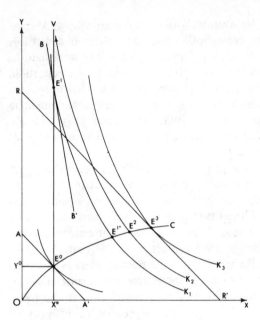

Figure 10.1

man's budget line will not move from AA' towards RR'. Rather, it will not only move out but will also rotate in a clockwise direction to a position such as BB'. Hence Mr Average can never reach the point E^3, though he may reach the point E^1 or even some point vertically above E^1 with further growth. While E^1 is beyond the reach of even the rich man before economic growth, it may lie below the indifference curve K_3. It is even likely that, no matter how high one travels along the vertical line X^0V, one can never reach, say, the indifference curve K_2 which may approach X^0V assymptotically or eventually become vertical and/or even turn rightward. Nevertheless, as we travel along X^0V upward, we hit successively higher indifference curves before they become, if at all, vertical and turn rightward. This seems to suggest that economic growth improves the welfare of Mr Average even though it cannot make him as well off as the rich. However, this may not be true if we take account of the likely effects of economic growth in raising the aspiration levels of Mr Average. With economic growth, Mr Average may aspire to attain the consumption point E^3 only to find that this aspiration is repeatedly frustrated. For example, he may work hard to earn an income sufficient to provide his children with a good education, hoping that they will then get good jobs. But since other people are doing the same thing, his children may have a better education than he had but not better than the average of their generation. They are likely to end up with no better than average jobs. The aspiration for 'good' jobs is likely to be frustrated.

To digress a little on the problem of education, it seem likely that education has an important purely competitive aspect in addition to the commonly recognised productive and consumption aspects (internal effects) and external benefits (a better educated person may make a better citizen and neighbour). The purely competitive aspect consists both in competition for (relative) distinction and for better jobs. If competition for better jobs consists in better training, this has a productive aspect as well. But to the extent that *relative* performance in educational achievement is important in getting better jobs, it also has a purely competitive aspect. It is true that, in view of the difficulty of employers in knowing the ability of applicants, educational performance is useful as an indicator (Arrow, 1973, Spence, 1973, Stiglitz, 1975, Wolpin, 1977). However, if all individuals agree not to work too hard in scoring high marks in examination, persons of highest intelligence will still come out best. Hence, to the extent that the *relative* performance counts, there is an element of external costs involved. Though the amount of the external costs is a matter scarcely anyone can be sure of, it seems not impossible that it may offset to a large extent the external benefits of education.

Returning to Figure 10.1, it can be seen that travelling along X^0V upward, the successively higher indifference curves become closer and closer to each other as measured along the income-consumption curve OC. An increase in Y from E^0 to E^1 is equivalent to the movement from E^0 to $E^{1'}$. But no matter how many times Y is increased above E^1, the indifference curve does not lie above E^2. Thus, even if we do not assume that the marginal utility of income is diminishing but rather constant as we travel along OC, the marginal utility of Y as we travel along X^0V must still be diminishing fast. The small gain in utility can therefore easily be overbalanced by the loss in frustrated aspirations.

Economic growth, to the extent that it increases socially unrealisable aspirations, may actually reduce social welfare.

It may, however, be argued that the cause of the reduction in welfare is the unrealistic aspiration rather than growth as such. What is needed is not to stop growth but to realise that growth can make an average person better off along X^0V but not along OC, i.e. more non-positional goods but not more positional goods. If aspiration can stick to this realistic path, no frustration need arise. Whether this is possible cannot be answered here as it involves the psychological and sociological problems of the formation of aspirations. In any case, it seems clear that the problem of aspiration is as important, if not more important than economic abundance, as least in the economically advanced countries.

An important consideration neglected in Hirsch's argument illustrated above is that, apart from changes in aspirations, there may also be other possible changes in tastes, abilities to enjoy, etc. For example, as Mr Average travels along X^0V, he may gradually learn how to enjoy non-positional goods more effectively. Thus, there may be changes in the shape of the indifference curves such that he may be consuming at a point along X^0V which, according to the new indifference map, lies above E^3. Let us put this in terms of Figure 10.2. With X being held

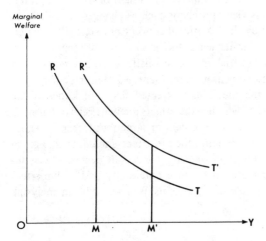

Figure 10.2

constant at X^0, we may concentrate on changes in (nonpositional) income Y. The curve RT measures the original marginal welfare of Y. With learning in consuming, it may move upward to $R'T'$. However, as the whole curve moves upward, the minimum level of income (denoted as M) sufficient to provide a non-negative level of (total) welfare may also increase to M'. (On the reasonableness of the concept of zero welfare, see Section 1.4.) This increase in M may be due to the following inter-related factors: a change in aspiration, an increase in one's customary standard of living, and increases in the prevailing social standards of living. Whether total welfare increases or not as income per capita increases depends much on the relative magnitudes of the above two movements. Welfare may thus be more a function of the *rates* of increase in income, in aspiration, etc. than in the absolute level of income. Economic growth may be important more in providing a positive rate of increase in income than in providing a high level of income.

It may also be argued that if a certain change in aspiration or something else leads to a reduction in happiness, then whatever the external factor that causes this change should be deemed to produce an external diseconomy. On the other hand, if the factor is internal (i.e. under the control of the individual concerned), then its effect will be taken into account by the individual unless imperfect foresight or irrational preference is involved. On this view, problems such as changes in aspiration, etc. can all be handled by the traditional concept of externality, imperfect foresight, etc. In a formal sense, this is so. But this seems to overstretch the concept of external economy a little. Certainly no court in the world would grant compensation for 'damages' through a change in aspiration. Moreover, the individuals affected may not know of the existence of the effects, or whether the effects are beneficial or harmful. One may then say that this is a problem of imperfect foresight. Quite so. But when we take into account long-run effects including changes in aspiration, etc., the assumption of perfect foresight becomes very dubious. Just by lumping everything into externality and/or imperfect foresight is not going to solve the problems. We have to begin analysing them.

10.3 Towards a Complete Study of Welfare

Whether a certain measure (in promoting economic growth or any other objective) will increase or decrease social welfare depends both on its effects on the objective world (a change in distribution, more production and/or more pollution, or a change in output-mix) and its effects on the subjective world (changes in knowledge, beliefs, aspirations, etc., of individuals). The subjective–objective classification is exhaustive. However, it is useful to think in terms of a third group of factors which have both subjective and objective elements and are products of the interaction of these elements. These are the institutional factors, including governments, laws, religions, families, customs, various organisations, etc. Institutions are formed by the interactions of individuals between themselves and with the objective environment. Once formed, they serve to regulate and constrain these interactions and hence affect the future course of the subjective and objective worlds. (See arrows in the right half of Figure 10.3.) All measures are originated from the subjective world (all initiatives are taken by some individuals), working through the institutional setting to affect the objective world, the institutional setting, and/or the subjective world itself. (See arrows in the left half of Figure 10.3.) In the process, it is almost certain that not only the objective world will be affected, but

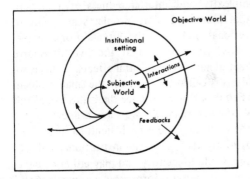

Figure 10.3

the institutional setting and the subjective world will change as well. Therefore a complete analysis of any significant policy or event has to take account of all its effects on the objective world, the institutional setting, and the subjective world.

Economic analysis (including cost-benefit analysis, an application of welfare economics) is mostly confined to the study of the objective effects. Though this may include how these objective effects are evaluated by individuals, the effects of the institutional setting and on the psychology of individuals themselves are usually excluded. This is partly due to the fact that these effects are very difficult to identify (not to mention quantify) and partly due to the division of the various fields of study largely isolated from one another. The confinement to the objective effects means that the analysis is useful mainly for relatively small changes whose institutional and subjective effects are negligible. For example, if the problem is to choose between two alternative routes for a freeway which will have similar social and environmental effects, a study of the direct costs and benefits is sufficient for the purpose. However, if the problem is whether the freeway should be built at all, the effects on the environment, etc. have also to be taken into account. For even larger problems like the desirability of economic growth, one needs a more complete analysis taking account of all significant objective, institutional, and subjective effects.

Due to increasing complexity and interrelatedness of a modern society, it seems likely that more and more problems are going to involve all objective, institutional, and subjective effects. For example, in the freeway example above, it is likely that the two alternative routes may have different social and environmental effects. If this is so, then a more complete analysis is called for even for the small problem of the choice of alternative routes. However, since the institutional and subjective effects are very tricky to analyse, we have a dilemma. We know that the effects are there but they are very difficult to study. One way out of this dilemma is to say that, since the institutional and subjective effects are almost impossible to identify and may either be beneficial or harmful, in the absence of better information, we may disregard them and concentrate on the objective effects. This is a generalisation of the theory of third best discussed in Section 9.3. This may be a valid approach for some problems at the moment but it does not mean that we should not pay more attention and resources to the study of the institutional and subjective effects, hoping to achieve a more complete analysis in the future. ('Indirect externality' may serve as a useful analytical concept in this more complete analysis; see Ng, 1975d.)

To achieve a more complete analysis, it seems that an interdisciplinary study is required. One of the relevant disciplines is psychology. Easterlin (1974) has recently brought together the results of various psychological studies of human happiness. The conclusion of this survey is that while there is a clear and positive correlation between income and (self-reported) happiness within a country at a particular time, it is uncertain whether such a positive association exists across countries and over time. Easterlin also discusses some conceptual and measurement problems of using self-reports of happiness and concluded with a qualified approval. One basic difficulty is the problem of comparability. The same amount of happiness may be described as 'very happy' in a poor country or fifty years ago but described only as 'fairly happy' in a rich country now. There is a simple method to reduce this difficulty which does not seem to have been used. This is discussed below.

The most popular method used in happiness questionnaires is to ask a respondent to tick one of the following: very happy, fairly (or pretty) happy, not very (or not too) happy. This has the advantage of being very simple but it raises problems of comparability. Cantril (1965) devises a so-called 'self-anchoring striving scale'. A respondent is to register a number from 0 to 10 with 0 representing the worst possible life and 10 representing the best, as defined by the respondent himself. This method may be useful for certain comparative studies but it does not overcome the difficulty of comparability since the same number may represent different amounts of happiness for different people. While this difficulty is very difficult to overcome completely (see, however, Section 5.4.1) it can be reduced by the following simple method. Though different persons may select different adjectives or numbers to describe the same amount of happiness, there is one level of happiness that is more objectively identifiable, the level of zero (net) happiness. No matter how large or small gross happiness an individual may have, if it is roughly equal to, in the opinion of the individual, the amount of pain or suffering, the net amount of happiness is zero and has an interpersonal significance in comparability. Hence an inter-temporal and inter-regional comparable piece of information is the proportion of people having zero, positive, and negative net happiness. Such wordings as 'not too happy' may subsume both negative, zero, *and* relatively small amounts of positive happiness. Moreover, this relatively small amount is determined by the subjective judgement of the respondent and hence not interpersonally comparable. Thus a simple way to reduce the difficulty of comparability is to pin down the dividing-line of zero happiness.

Different persons get happiness in different ways. Some feel happy serving God, some feel happy having a good family life, some feel happy being adventurous, etc. But virtually everyone likes to have happiness for himself, for his family and perhaps also for others. According to a major school of moral philosophy, happiness is the only acceptable ultimate objective in life. Yet the study of happiness is in such a primitive stage. At the risk of repetition, it may be said that more attention and more resources should be devoted to the study of happiness (eudaimonology?) taking account of the objective, subjective, and institutional factors.

It may however happen that, as studies on the desirable and undesirable institutional and subjective effects have been done, these studies, instead of being used to guide policies aiming at increasing welfare, may be used by unscrupulous politicians and bureaucrats to further their ambitions and power to the detriment of freedom and welfare. But this is true of almost everything, including electricity, explosives, nuclear power, etc. Nevertheless, are institutional and subjective factors so delicate that a dividing line ought to be drawn here? Is happiness something that is less likely to be obtained the more you try to get it? Should we have a meta-study of the desirability of pursuing different studies? But isn't this going to be even more dangerous to freedom? As I ponder more and more over these questions, I become less and less certain of their answers. It seems that the only thing I become more certain of is that I now understand Socrates more.

Summary

Analyses of the previous chapters are brought together in a summary (Section 10.1). Wider problems related to social welfare are briefly considered, such as the question 'Does economic growth increase social welfare?' Answers to such questions can only be provided by a complete analysis (eudaimonology?) of all the objective, subjective, and institutional effects. All measures originate from the subjective world, working through the institutional setting to affect the objective world, the institutional setting and/or the subjective world. Due to the increasing complexity of modern society, it is likely that more problems are going to involve significant institutional and subjective effects, making a complete multidisciplinary study more necessary (Section 10.3). As an introduction to this argument, the Harrod–Hirsch concept of positional goods and its implications on the desirability of economic growth are analysed geometrically and extended (Section 10.2). A simple method to reduce the difficulty of comparability in happiness surveys by pinning down the dividing-line of zero net happiness is also suggested (Section 10.3).

Notes and References on Some Advanced and Applied Topics

This book covers only the basic topics in welfare economics. Readers who wish to pursue the subject further may find this appendix useful as a guide to some more advanced and applied topics. These topics may also be assigned to students for writing essays or seminar papers. Topics in Sections 10A.2, 10A.3 and 10A.6 are easier to handle. Several considerations affect the selection of topics and references below. First, practical relevance and conceptual interest rank higher than technical complication. Thus such problems as the question of Pareto optimality where infinity is involved, complicated extensions of the proofs of existence, optimality of competitive equilibrium, etc., are not included. Second, such obviously relevant topics as cost-benefit analysis are excluded on the ground that they are likely to be covered by separate courses in a university curriculum. Third, my personal interests and limitations of my knowledge also exert some influence.

10A.1 Some Institutional Factors

As in most studies in welfare economics, this book concentrates on analysing what is socially optimal in some sense, as though presuming that governments will pursue social optimality. Over eighty years ago, Wicksell (1896) admonished economists for their failure to recognise the fact that governments don't behave like a benevolent despot. Collective decisions are undertaken by ordinary people like voters, politicians, and bureaucrats who usually base their decisions more on their own interests. This point has been repeatedly emphasised by Buchanan (e.g. 1975, 1978, Buchanan *et al.*, 1978). Despite substantial works in this area (e.g. Downs, 1957, Olson, 1965, Tullock, 1965, 1967b, 1976, Niskanen, 1971, Breton, 1974, Brennan & Buchanan, 1977, 1980,

Buchanan, Tollison & Tullock, 1980, Fiorina & Noll, 1978; see also surveys by Ferejohn & Fiorina, 1975, Mueller, 1976, 1979, Peacock & Wiseman, 1979), the impact on orthodox economic writings has been small. This is partly due to the complicated nature of actual public choice processes and partly due to the fact that the simple social-optimality approach can still usefully serve as an ideal to aim at, a standard to compare with, and a foundation to base further analysis on.

A very important aspect of actual democratic public choice processes is that of minority pressure groups. Governments typically succumb to the pressure of particular interest groups even at a greater cost imposed on society. Since the cost (of say higher tariffs, subsidies, etc.) is usually thinly spread across the whole society, it does not usually arouse strong protest. No satisfactory solution (within the democratic framework) to this widely recognised problem has been found. (Cf. Weingast, Shepsle & Johnsen, 1981).

Parallel to the study of the public choice processes, institutional factors in the private sector have been analysed by the literature on property rights, including the emergence and functions of private property rights, its relation with externalities, the theory and regulation of modern corporations, etc. This literature has been surveyed by Furubotn & Pejovich (1972), Schmid (1976), and Randall (1978).

Related to the problems of property rights, pressure groups, and public choice processes is the issue of rent-seeking. Individuals and groups spend resources (including time) attempting to secure rights that yield surpluses (or rents). A privileged position such as tariff protection may then only generate transitory gains at a permanent cost (Tullock, 1967c, 1975, Krueger, 1974, Posner, 1975, Buchanan, Tollison & Tullock, 1980). On the implication of rent-seeking on cost–benefit analysis, see Ng (1983).

10A.2 X-Efficiency

Welfare economics has been basically concerned with allocative efficiency. The concept of X-efficiency was advanced by Leibenstein (1966). An X-inefficient producer allows his cost of production to be higher than is necessary. For example, a monopolist, not being subject to strong competition, may opt to pursue a quiet life instead of taking trouble to achieve the lowest cost curve. Welfare losses due to X-inefficiency are said to be much more important than those due to allocative inefficiency (Comanor & Leibenstein, 1969). However, this argument ignores the gain (ease and leisure, etc.) to the producer by being X-inefficient. Taking account of this, Parish & Ng (1972) show that X-inefficiency as such gives rise to no welfare loss. However, coupled with some form of allocative inefficiency such as monopoly, the amount of welfare loss involved differs from both the Comanor–Leibenstein measure and the traditional measure that ignores X-inefficiency. For a review of this debate, see Crew (1975, pp. 154–64). (Personally, I have some slight reservations about Crew's assessment.) Perhaps partly as a response to Parish & Ng, Leibenstein (1976, 1978) has extended his critique of traditional theory by questioning the assumption of rational maximising individuals and by providing his analysis of group interactions, 'selectively rational man', 'inert area', etc. On X-efficiency in the production of public goods, see Olson (1974). For estimates of monopolistic losses, see Harberger (1954), Cowling & Mueller (1978, 1981), Sawyer (1980), Littlechild (1981).

10A.3 Merit Goods

If the consumption of a good by the voluntary decisions of individuals, given their incomes, is deemed deficient/excessive not due to the existence of externalities or pricing inefficiency, it is a merit/demerit good. A most widely accepted example of a demerit good is addictive drugs with severe harmful effects. Examples of merit goods (exercise, health-care, arts, education) are more debatable. Given that the social objective should be a function of individual welfare, the only acceptable ground for recognising merit (hereafter taken to subsume demerit) goods is the divergence of individual preference from individual welfare. In Chapter 1 we have identified three factors accounting for this divergence: concern for others, ignorance and imperfect foresight, irrationality. Since the first factor generally serves to increase social welfare at least when the other two factors are not involved, the main justifications for merit goods are ignorance and irrationality. Liberals may even hesitate in accepting this and may argue that if ignorance is the problem, what should be done is to provide more information or education. Moreover, even if some individuals are too slow to learn or are irrational, it may still be undesirable to tinker with their consumer sovereignty. If one believes that this tinkering is undesirable in itself, one is a fundamental liberal. If one believes that it is undesirable due to the undesirable effects on social welfare of say more government control, one is an instrumental liberal (Ng, 1973U).

Many writers lump under the concept of merit goods such factors as externality, distributional consideration, etc. Since these factors can be and have been analysed independently of the concept of merit goods, it is best not to include them. For some discussions on merit goods, see Head (1966, 1969), McLure (1968), Pulsipher (1971), Pazner (1972). Pazner's formal analysis (similarly that of Roskamp, 1975) consists in the inclusion of the quantities of consumption of merit goods *directly* into a social welfare function *independent* of individual welfares. But why should the society (does it have an independent mind?) care if *no* individual welfare is involved? A more satisfactory formalisation of the merit good problem is outlined below.

The social objective is to maximise social welfare as a function of individual welfares, $W = W(W^1, \ldots, W^I)$ where, abstracting from externality, $W^i = W^i(x_1^i, \ldots, x_G^i)$. Each individual maximises $U^i = U^i(x_1^i, \ldots, x_G^i)$. Define a merit good as one where $W_g^i > U_g^i (W_g^i \equiv \partial W^i/\partial x_g^i$, etc.), and conversely for a demerit good. If $W_g^i \neq U_g^i$ over the relevant range, one can then clearly see that taxes/subsidies may be desirable. As formulated these taxes/subsidies may differ over individuals. However, for administrative simplicity, a uniform measure may be more practicable. But the basic problem is how do we know that $W_g^i > U_g^i$ or the reverse? (Cf. Baigent, 1981.)

10A.4 Price-dependent Preferences and Changes in Tastes

Simple analyses take individual preferences to be given and independent of the prices of goods. Much complication is introduced when these assumptions are relaxed. Prices may affect preferences because of the intention to demonstrate one's wealth (Veblen, 1899) or because of the habit of judging quality by price (Scitovsky, 1944/5). Kalman (1968*) provides an analysis of consumer demand (deriving the Slutsky equation) where prices enter utility functions and Pollak (1977) remarks on the sparse literature on the topic, the welfare significance, and the distinction between the 'conditional' (where prices affect preference ordering itself) and the 'unconditional' interpretations (where the objects of choice are quantity–price situations).

Welfare evaluation with changes in tastes is a tricky subject to analyse. For example, Rothenberg (1953) takes welfare to be a function of the ratio of satisfaction over desire such that if both changes by the same proportion, welfare stays constant. But this clearly conflicts with the common-sense observation that a person with strong desires (e.g. appetite for food, sexual libido) and well satisfied may be much happier than a person with little desire even if fully satisfied. Gintis' (1974) analysis (see also Gorman, 1967) is to postulate a long-run utility or welfare function which determines, with the consumption history, changes in the short-run function. For some other discussions, see Harsanyi (1953/4), Weizsäcker (1971)*, and Pollak (1976)*. Stigler & Becker (1977) use the household production function approach (exposited in Michael & Becker, 1973) to analyse problems usually associated with changing tastes (e.g. addiction, advertising, fashion) while assuming *constant* tastes. This approach seems to be more suitable for analysing the 'positive' instead of the welfare aspects of the problem. For a survey of both the positive and welfare aspects of changing tastes, see Pollak (1978). For a comparison of the radical and the traditional approaches, see Burns (1980).

10A.5 Optimal Taxation and Public Pricing

Essentially the problem of optimal taxation is to discover what structure of taxes on commodities minimises the total cost imposed on the economy for any given amount of revenue raised. The problem of public pricing is to ask what are the best prices to charge for the products of public enterprises (usually public utilities). These two problems may seem to be two separate issues. Actually, both relate to government revenue on the one hand and prices of commodities on the other, though one is mainly concerned with the private sector and the other with the public sector. After the theory of second best, it is clear that the problem has to be considered in the setting of the whole economy. Commodity taxation and public utility pricing then become two sub-issues of this general problem. This is true for the essential welfare economics consideration. On a more practical level, the two sub-issues may have different relevant considerations. For example, the problem of the motivation and accountability of the manager is an important consideration in the problem of public utility pricing but not in the problem of taxation. Partly because of this, the two issues have usually been discussed separately. (Another reason is the difference in assumptions used; see Green, 1975.)

Though the rigorous analysis of optimal taxation dates from Ramsey (1927), further developments along this mathematical approach, with a few exceptions (e.g. Boiteux, 1956*, translated in 1971), had not taken place until around 1970. Since then, the literature has mushroomed. For an introduction to this literature, see Sandmo (1976), and Atkinson and Stiglitz (1980, pp. 366—93); for a synthesis of optimal commodity and income tax theories, see Mirrlees (1976*, forthcoming). The Ramsey rule states that taxes should induce equal percentage reductions in compensated demand for all commodities. This and similar rules are usually based on a one-consumer economy or some distributional neutrality assumption (Wildasin, 1977). In view of our argument in Appendix 9A, distributional neutrality is not unduly restrictive an assumption. In the 1940s and 50s, discussion on the welfare economics of taxation centered mainly on the issue of the relative 'excess burden' of direct versus indirect taxes, using mainly geometrical analysis. A survey of this literature is provided by Walker (1955). (Atkinson, 1977, compares this older literature with the new optimal tax literature.) Further contributions were made by Harberger (1964). With the development of the expenditure function technique, the excess burden of taxation and other types of welfare cost may also be analysed using this technique (Diamond & McFadden, 1974).

Early discussion of public utility pricing centered on the desirability of marginal cost pricing, as surveyed by Ruggles (1949/50). A recent discussion of pricing policies for public enterprises at undergraduate level is given in Webb (1976). The problem has been developed in many directions, including the issues of peak load (surveyed by Greene, 1970), two-part tariff (theoretical analyses by Mayston, 1974*, Ng & Weisser, 1974*, Schmalensee, 1981* and applications by Cicchetti, Gillen & Smolensky, 1977, Mitchell, 1978). See also Trebing (1971, 1976).

10A.6 Optimal Saving/Growth and Resource Exhaustion

As in the case of optimal taxation, the theory of optimal saving was pioneered by Ramsey (1928). (If he had not died young, one wonders whether there would be any interesting major topics left for us.) The

Ramsey rule here says that the amount of saving multiplied by the marginal utility of consumption equals the amount by which total utility falls short of bliss. Assuming constant elasticity of marginal utility, this gives the simple rule that the rate of saving equals the inverse of this (absolute) elasticity. The rule is derived by maximising a utility function over time without a time discount rate. Since the integral does not converge, the shortfall from bliss is minimised. Alternatively, the overtaking criterion (Weizsäcker, 1965)* may be used. While many writers are against the discount of future utility (not consumption), it seems to me quite justifiable due to the fact that we cannot be absolutely sure of our perpetual existence. (Mendel Weisser regards this as an understatement due to the second law of thermodynamics. Fortunately, this law applies only to a closed system. But is the universe an open system?) Ramsey's analysis has been extended in many directions, see Shell (1967)*, and Mirrlees & Stern (1973, Part 5)*. The less mathematically inclined may start with Sen (1961) who expressed doubts about the practical usefulness of the intertemporal utility maximisation approach. For a more practical solution, see Ng (1973c).

With the sharp increases in oil prices in the early 1970s and as a reply to the concern of the environmentalists and conservationists, economists have become more interested in the specific problem of optimal resource exhaustion instead of optimal growth in general; see, for example, the 1974 Symposium Issue of the *Review of Economic Studies** and an introduction by Solow (1974). The pioneering analysis can however be traced back to Hotelling (1931). The basic message is that the scarcity rent (the market price of the resource less extraction costs) should increase at the rate of interest and that this will tend to be achieved by the market mechanism, given the available information. Where the market rate of interest cannot be accepted as the social rate of time preference, some complications will arise (Hanson, 1977). For complications due to uncertainty about the amount of the deposit, see Gilbert (1979)*, Kemp & Long (1978, 1980); on resource utilisation with technical progress, see Kamien & Schwartz (1978) and references therein. On the effect of industrial structure, see Aivazian & Callen (1979). On the counter-productiveness of subsidising energy production, see Baumol & Wolff (1981). For a survey, see Devarajan & Fisher (1981).

10A.7 Some Specific Topics

The following are some topics of more specific scope good for writing essays or seminar papers on.

(1) Price Stability

Do consumers and/or producers benefit from price stability (of specific products)? Consult: Massell (1969), Samuelson (1972), Hueth & Schmitz (1972). The tool of analysis is mainly geometrical measurement of changes in consumer/producer surplus. For more advanced analyses, see Turnovsky *et al.* (1980)*, Newberry & Stiglitz (1982).

(2) Brain Drain

What should be done about the international emigration of highly skilled and educated people (especially from the less developed countries to the developed countries)? Consult: Bhagwati (1976), especially Chapter 5 in Vol. II; Kwok & Leland (1982). When I was conducting a seminar on this topic for students, I had to declare that I was not an instance of brain *drain* since I was in some sense 'pushed away'.

(3) Road Congestion

An application of the thoery of externality is that of road congestion. On charging for road usage to account for congestion costs, see Walters (1961). On the wider problem of transport economics, see Sharp (1973). For a geometrical survey of the general congestion problem, see Porter (1978).

(4) Market Structure and Innovation

The static efficiency of competition may be relatively trivial if the Schumpeterian thesis on the dynamic efficiency of monopoly with respect to innovation is correct. Arrow (1962) argues that the incentive to innovate is greater under competition than under monopoly. Demsetz (1969) argues that the reverse is true. Using a different argument that meets Demsetz's objection, Ng (1971d, 1977b) re-establishes Arrow's conclusion. For a review, see Needham (1975). See also Kamien & Schwartz (1975) for a survey on more general issues related to market structure and innovation. However, most writers have only considered the *amount* or degree of incentive instead of optimal incentive. This seems to be a fruitful avenue for further research as it is not true that the larger the incentive to invent the better since obviously we do not want to spend the whole national product on invention. Arrow has briefly considered the social benefit of innovation within his framework. But no one, to my knowledge, has considered this cost-benefit problem in Demsetz's or Ng's framework. It should not be difficult to undertake this analysis. (See, however, a recent study by Dasgupta & Stiglitz, 1980.)

(5) Uncertainty

I am uncertain whether I should have added a topic on uncertainty but am certain that I have to stop now as the publisher is certain to refuse to publish an over-length book with uncertain demand.

References and Author Index

Index page references are at end of each reference, in italic type.

Abbreviations

AER	: *American Economic Review*
AER/S	: *American Economic Review, Papers and Proceedings*
E.	: *Economic*
EJ	: *Economic Journal*
J.	: *Journal*
JEL	: *Journal of Economic Literature*
JET	: *Journal of Economic Theory*
JPE	: *Journal of Political Economy*
P.	: *Papers*
QJE	: *Quarterly Journal of Economics*
R.	: *Review*
RES	: *Review of Economic Studies*

AARON, Henry, *see* McGuire & Aaron

AIVAZIAN, Varoiy A., & CALLEN, Jeffrey L. (1979), 'A note on the economics of exhaustible resources', *Canadian J. E.,* **12**, 83–9 (Feb). *290*

ALCHIAN, Armen A., & DEMSETZ, Harold (1972), 'Production, information costs and economic organisation', *AER*, **62**, 777–95 (Dec). *175*

ALDRICH, John (1977), 'The dilemma of a Paretian liberal', *Public Choice*, **30**, 1–22 (Summer). *138*

ALEXANDER, S. S. (1967), 'Human values and economists' values', in S. HOOK (ed.), *Human Values and E. Policy*, A Symposium (New York: New York University Press). *32*

ALLINGHAM, Michael (1975), *General Equilibrium* (New York: Wiley). *58*

– & ARCHIBALD, G. C. (1975)*, 'Second best and decentralisation', *JET*, **10**, 157–73 (Apr). *219* n, *223, 226* n

ARCHIBALD, G. C., *see* Allingham & Archibald

ARMSTRONG, W. E. (1951), 'Utility and the theory of welfare', *Oxford E.P.,* **3**, 257–71. *14, 128*

ARROW, Kenneth J. (1950), 'A difficulty in the concept of social welfare', *JPE*, 58, 328–46. *121*

– (1951a)*, 'An extension of the basic theorems of classical welfare economics', in J. NEYMAN (ed.), *Proceedings of the Second Berkeley Symposium on Mathematical Statistics and Probability* (Berkeley: University of California Press). *56, 58*

– (1951b, 1963), *Social Choice and Individual Values* (New York: Wiley). *111-18*

– (1962), 'Economic welfare and the allocation of resources for invention', in National Bureau of Economic Research, *The Rate and Direction of Inventive Activity* (Princeton: Princeton University Press). Reprinted in ROWLEY (1972). *291*

– (1970), 'Political and economic evaluation of social effects and externalities', in J. MARGOLIS (ed.), *The Analysis of Public Output* (London: Cambridge University Press). *127*

– (1971a)*, 'The firm in general equilibrium theory', in MARRIS, R., & WOOD, A. (eds), *The Corporate Economy* (Cambridge, Mass.: Harvard University Press). *58*

– (1971b), 'The utilitarian approach to the concept of equality in public expenditure', *QJE*, 85, 409–15 (Aug). *158*

– (1973), 'Higher education as a filter'. *J. of Public E.*, 2, 193–216 (July). *159, 276*

– (1977U), 'The property rights doctrine and demand revelation under incomplete information', Harvard Institute of Economic Research, *Discussion Paper*, No. 580. *133*

– & DEBREU, Gerard (1954)*, 'Existence of an equilibrium for a competitive economy', *Econometrica*, 22, 256–90 (July). *58*

– & HAHN, F. H. (1971)*, *General Competitive Equilibrium* (San Francisco: Holden-Day). *29, 58*

– & INTRILIGATOR, Michael D. (eds) (forthcoming)*, *Handbook of Mathematical Economics, Vol. III: Mathematical Approaches to Welfare Economics* (Amsterdam: North-Holland).

– & SCITOVSKY, Tibor (eds) (1969), *Readings in Welfare Economics* (London: Allen & Unwin).

ASIMAKOPOLUS, A., *see* Kemp & Asimakopolus

ATHANASIOU, L. (1966), 'Some notes on the theory of second best', *Oxford E.P.*, 18, 83–7 (Mar). *241-2*

ATKINSON, Anthony B. (1973), 'How progressive should income tax be?' in M. PARKIN (ed.), *Essays on Modern Economics* (London: Longman). Reprinted in PHELPS (1973). *155, 157*

– (1975), *The Economics of Inequality* (Oxford: Clarendon Press). *156*

– (ed.) (1976), *The Personal Distribution of Income* (London: Allen & Unwin). *156*

— (1977), 'Optimal taxation and the direct versus indirect tax controversy', *Canadian J. of E.*, **10**, 590–605 (Nov) *289*
— & HARRISON, A. J. (1978), *Distribution of Personal Wealth in Britain* (London: Cambridge University Press). *156*
— & STIGLITZ, Joseph E. (1972)*, 'The structure of indirect taxation and economic efficiency'. *J. of Public E.*, **1**, 97–119 (Apr). *239* n, *247*
— & STIGLITZ, Joseph E. (1980), *Lectures on Public Economics* (New York: McGraw-Hill). *289*
AUMANN, Robert J. (1964)*, 'Market with a continuum of traders', *Econometrica*, **32**, 39–50 (Jan–Apr). *35* n
AUSTER, Richard D. (1977), 'Private markets in public goods (or qualities)', *QJE*, **91**, 417–30 (Aug). *212*
BAIGENT, Nick (1981), 'Social choice and merit goods', *E. Letters*, **7**, 301–5. *287*
BAILEY, Martin J. (1979), 'The possibility of rational social choice in an economy', *JPE*, **87**, 37–56 (Feb). *118*
BARBERÁ, Salvador (1977)*, 'Manipulation of social decision functions', *JET*, **15**, 266–78 (Aug). *135* n
BARONE, Enrico (1908), 'Il ministerio della produzione nello stato collectivista', *Giornale degli Economisti*, **37**, 267–93, 391–414 (Aug, Oct). English translation: 'The ministry of production in the collectivist state', in F. A. Hayek (ed.), *Collectivist Economic Planning* (London: Routledge & Kegan Paul, 1935). *60* n
BATOR, Francis M. (1957), 'The simple analytics of welfare maximisation', *AER*, **47**, 22–59 (Mar). *32, 38*
— (1958), 'The anatomy of market failure', *QJE*, **72**, 351–79 (Aug). *272*
BATTALIO, Raymond C., KAGEL, John H., & REYNOLDS, Morgan O. (1977), 'Income distributions in two experimental economies', *JPE*, **85**, 1259–71 (Dec). *159*
BAUER, P. T. (1976), 'Equal shares, unequal earnings', *Times Literary Supplement*, 23 (July). *160*
BAUMOL, William J. (1965), *Welfare Economics and the Theory of the State*, 2nd ed. (London: Bell).
— (1977), 'The public-good attribute as independent justification for subsidy', *Intermountain E. R.*, **8**, 1-10 (Fall). *190* n
— (1982), 'Contestable markets: an uprising in the theory of industry structure', *AER*, **72**, 1–15 (March). *49*
— & BRADFORD, David F. (1970), 'Optimal departures from marginal cost pricing', *AER*, **60**, 265–83 (June). *239* n
— — (1972), 'Detrimental externalities and nonconvexity of the production set', *Economica*, **39**, 160–76 (May). *170* n

—, PANZAR, John C., & WILLIG, Robert D. (1982), *Contestable Markets and the Theory of Industry Structure* (San Diego: Harcourt Brace Jovanovich). *49*

— & OATES, W. E. (1975), *The Theory of Environmental Policy: Externalities, Public Outlays, and the Quality of Life* (Englewood Cliffs: Prentice-Hall). *176*

— & ORDOVER, Janusz A. (1977), 'On the optimality of public-goods pricing with exclusion devices', *Kyklos*, **30**, Fasc. 1, 5–21. *193*

— & WOLFF, Edward N. (1981), 'Subsidies to new energy sources: Do they add to energy stocks?', *JPE*, **89**, 891–913 (Oct). *290*

BECKER, Gary S., *see* Michael & Becker, Stigler & Becker

BECKERMAN, Wilfred (1975), *Two Cheers for the Affluent Society: A Spirited Defense of Economic Growth* (New York: St. Martin's Press). *273*

BENASSY, Jean-Pascal (1976)*, 'The disequilibrium approach to monopolistic price setting and general monopolistic equilibrium', *RES*, **43**, 69–81. *58*

BENNETT, John (1981), 'A variable-production generalization of Lerner's theorem', *J. of Public E.*, **16**, 371–6 (Dec). *152*

BERGLAS, Eitan (1976), 'On the theory of clubs', *AER/S*, **66**, 116-21 (May). *212*

BERGSON (Burk), Abram (1938), 'A reformulation of certain aspects of welfare economics', *QJE*, **52**, 310-34. Reprinted in ARROW & SCITOVSKY (1969). *3, 59*

BERGSTROM, Theodore C. & CORNES, Richard C. (1981)*, 'Gorman and Musgrave are dual: an antipodean theorem on public goods', *E. Letters*, **7**, 371–8. *192*

BERRY, R. Albert (1969), 'A note on welfare comparisons between monopoly and pure competition', *Manchester School*, **1**, 39-59 (Mar). *93*

— (1972), 'A review of problems in the interpretation of producers' surplus', *Southern E. J.*, **36**, 79-92 (July). *100*

BHAGWATI, Jagdish N. (ed.) (1976), *The Brain Drain and Taxation* (Amsterdam: North-Holland). *291*

BIRKHOFF, G. (1948)*, *Lattice Theory* (New York: American Mathematical Society). *29*

BLACK, Duncan (1948), 'On the rationale of group decision making', *JPE*, **56**, 23-34 (Feb). *121*

BLAU, Julian H. (1957), 'The existence of social welfare functions', *Econometrica*, **25**, 302-13 (Apr) *117*

BLIN, Jean–Marie, & SATTERTHWAITE, Mark A. (1978), 'Individual decisions and group decisions: the fundamental differences', *J. of Public E.*, **10**, 247-68 (Oct). *135* n

BOADWAY, Robin W. (1974), 'The welfare foundations of cost-benefit analysis', *EJ*, **84**, 926-39 (Dec). *96-8*

– (1981), 'Review of Ng, *Welfare Economics*', *Canadian J. of E.*, **14**, 540–2 (Aug). *xv, 293*

– & HARRIS, Richard (1977)*, 'A characterisation of piecemeal second best policy', *J. of Public E.*, **8**, 169–90 (Oct). *228*

BOHM, Peter (1979), 'Estimating willingness to pay: Why and how?', *Scandinavian J. of E.*, **81**, 142–53. *205*

BOITEUX, M. (1971)*, 'On the management of public monopolies subject to budgetary constraints', *JET*, **3**, 219–40 (Sep). *239 n, 289*

BORDA, J. C. de (1781), 'Mémoire sur les élections au scrutin', *Mémoires de l'Académie Royale des Sciences*. English translation by A. DE GRAZIA, *Isis* (1953). *128*

BOSKIN, Michael J., & SHESHINSKI, Eytan (1978)*, 'Optimal redistribution taxation when individual welfare depends upon relative income', *QJE*, **92**, 589–601 (Nov). *156*

BRADFORD, David F., & HILDEBRANDT, Gregory G. (1977)*, 'Observable preferences for public goods', *J. of Public E.*, **8**, 111-31 (Oct). *200*

– & ROSEN, Harvey S. (1976), 'The optimal taxation of commodities and income', *AER/S*, **66**, 94–101 (May). *239 n*

– *see also* Baumol & Bradford

BRANDT, R. B. (1966), 'The concept of welfare', in S. R. KRUPP (ed.), *The Structure of Economic Science* (Englewood Cliffs: Prentice-Hall). *10*

BRENNAN, Geoffrey, & BUCHANAN, James M. (1977), 'Towards a tax constitution for Leviathan', *J. of Public E.*, **8**, 255–73. *284*

– (1980), *The Power to Tax: The Analytical Foundations of a Fiscal Constitution* (Cambridge: Cambridge University Press). *284*

– & FLOWERS, Marilyn (1980), 'All "Ng" up on clubs? Some notes on the current status of club theory', *Public Finance Quarterly*, **8**, 153–69 (Apr). *212*

– HEAD, John G., & WALSH, Cliff (1979), 'Market provision of public goods: a monopoly version of the Oakland model', *Finanzarchiv*, **37**, no. 3, 385–95. *198*

– & MCGUIRE, Thomas (1975), 'Optimal policy choice under uncertainty', *J. of Public E.*, **4**, 205–9 (Feb). *235*

BRETON, Albert (1974), *The Economic Theory of Representative Government* (Chicago: Aldine). *284*

BRITO, Dagobert, L., & OAKLAND, William H. (1980), 'On the monopolistic provision of excludable public goods', *AER*, **70**, 691–704 (Sep). *198*

BROOKSHIRE, David S., THAYER, Mark A., SCHULZE, William D. & D'ARGE, Ralph C. (1982), 'Valuing public goods: a comparison of survey and hedonic approaches', *AER*, **72**, 165–77 (March). *205*

BROWNING, Jacquelene M., & BROWNING, Edgar K. (1976), 'Welfare analytics in general equilibrium: an improved geometry', *Canadian J.E.*, **9**, 341–50 (May). *40–3*

BRUNO, Michael (1972)*, 'Market distortions and gradual reform', *RES*, **39**, 373–83 (July). *228*

BUCHANAN, James M. (1965), 'An economic theory of clubs', *Economica*, **32**, 1–14 (Feb). *211–12*

— (1975), 'Public finance and public choice', *National Tax J.*, **28**, 383–94 (Dec). *284*

— (1978), 'Markets, states, and the extent of morals', *AER/S*, **68**, 364–8 (May). *284*

— & KAFOGLIS, M. Z. (1963), 'A note on public good supply', *AER*, **53**, 403–14 (June). *285*

— & STUBBLEBINE, W. C. (1962), 'Externality', *Economica*, **29**, 371–84 (Nov). *171*

— TOLLISON, Robert, & TULLOCK, Gordon (1980), *Towards a Theory of the Rent-Seeking Society* (College Station: Texas A & M University Press). *285*

— & TULLOCK, Gordon (1962), *The Calculus of Consent* (Ann Arbor: University of Michigan Press). *284*

— *et al.* (1978), *The Economics of Politics* (London: Institute of Economic Affairs). *284*

— *see also* Brennan & Buchanan

BURNS, Michael E. (1973), 'A note on the concept and measure of consumer's surplus', *AER*, **63**, 335–44 (June). *100*

— (1977), 'On the uniqueness of consumer's surplus and the invariance of economic index numbers', *Manchester School*, 41–61 (Mar). *94*

— (1980), 'Consumer theory and individual welfare: a radical approach re-examined', *Australian E. P.*, **19**, 233–47 (Dec). *288*

— & WALSH, Cliff (1981), 'Market provision of price-excludable public goods: a general analysis', *JPE*, **89**, 166–91 (Feb). *198*

CALABRESI, Guido (1968), 'Transaction costs, resource allocation and liability rules – a comment', *J. of Law and E.*, **11**, 67–73. *183*

CALLEN, Jeffrey L., *see* Aivazian & Callen

CAMPBELL, C. B., *see* Tullock & Campbell

CANTOR, G. (1895)*, 'Beiträge zur begründung der transfiniten mengenlehre', *Math. Ann.*, **46**, 481–512. *28–9*

CANTRIL, H. (1965), *The Pattern of Human Concerns* (New Brunswick, New Jersey: Rutgers University Press). *281*

CHIPMAN, John S. (1960)*, 'The foundation of utility', *Econometrica*, **28**, 193–224 (Apr). *28*

— (1976), 'The Paretian heritage', *Revue Européenne des sciences sociales et Cahiers Vilfredo Pareto*, **14**, 65–171. *60* n

— & MOORE, James C. (1976), 'The scope of consumer's surplus arguments', in M. TANG *et al.* (eds), *Evolution, Welfare, and Time in*

Economics, Essays in Honor of Nicholas Georgescu-Roegan (Toronto: Lexington). *92*

CHIPMAN, John, S., & MOORE, James C. (1978). 'The new welfare economics 1939–1974', *International E.R.,* **19**, 547–84 (Oct) *60, 68*

CICCHETTI, Charles J., GILLEN, William J., & SMOLENSKY, Paul (1977), *The Marginal Cost and Pricing of Electricity* (Cambridge: Ballinger). *289*

CLARK, Colin (1973), 'The marginal utility of income', *Oxford E.P.,* **25**, 145–59 (July). *161*

CLARKE, Edward H. (1971), 'Multipart pricing of public goods', *Public Choice,* **11**, 17–33 (Fall). *134-7, 199-207*

– (1972), 'Multipart pricing of public goods: an example', in MUSHKIN (1972). *199-207*

– (1980), *Demand Revelation and the Provision of Public Goods* (Cambridge, Mass.: Harper & Row, Ballinger). *199*

COASE, R. H. (1960), 'The problem of social cost', *J. of Law and E.,* **3**, 1–44 (Oct). *182-5*

COFFMAN, Richard B., *see* McManus, Walton & Coffman

COLEMAN, James S. (1966), 'The possibility of a social welfare function', *AER,* **56**, 1105–22 (Dec). *124*

COLLARD, David, LECOMBER, Richard, & SLATER, Martin (eds) (1980), *Income Distribution: The Limits to Redistribution* (Bristol: John Wright). *156*

COMANOR, W. S., & LEIBENSTEIN, Harvey (1969), 'Allocative efficiency, X-efficiency, and the measurement of welfare losses', *Economica,* **36**, 304–9 (Aug). *286*

CORDEN, W. M. (1974), *Trade Policy and Economic Welfare* (Oxford: Oxford University Press). *258*

CORLETT, W. J., & HAGUE, D. C. (1953), 'Complementarity and the excess burden of taxation', *RES,* **21**, 21–30. *218, 247*

CORNES, Richard C., *see* Bergstrom & Cornes

COWLING, Keith, & MUELLER, Dennis C. (1978), 'The Social Costs of Monopoly Power', *EJ,* **88**, 727–48 (Dec). *286*

– (1981), 'The social costs of monopoly power revisited', *EJ,* **91**, 721–5 (Sep). *286*

CREW, M. A. (1975), *Theory of the Firm* (London: Longman). *286*

CURRIE, John M., MURPHY, John A., & SCHMITZ, Andrew (1971), 'The concept of economic surplus and its use in economic analysis', *EJ,* **81**, 741-99 (Dec). *92, 100-1*

CURRIE, David A., & PETERS, William (eds) (1980), *Contemporary Economic Analysis, Vol. II: Proceedings of the 1978 AUTE Conference* (London: Croom Helm).

DAHL, R. A., & LINDBLOM, C. E. (1963), *Politics, Economics and*

Welfare (New York: Harper & Row). *10*

DANZIGER, Sheldon, HAVEMAN, Robert, & PLOTNICK, Robert (1981), 'How income transfer programs affect work, savings, and the income distribution: a critical review', *JEL*, **19**, 957–1028 (Sep). *156*

DASGUPTA, Partha, & STIGLITZ, Joseph (1980), 'Industrial structure and the nature of innovative activity', *EJ*, **90**, 266–93 (June). *292*
— *see also* Stiglitz & Dasgupta

D'ARGE, Ralph C., *see* Brookshire *et al.*

D'ASPREMONT, C., & GEVERS, L. (1977), 'Equity and the informational basis of collective choice', *RES*, **44**, 199–209. *113* n

DAVID, Paul, & REDER, Melvin W. (eds) (1974). *Nations and Households in Economic Growth*, Essays in Honor of Moses Abramovitz (New York: Academic Press).

DAVIS, Otto A., & HINICH, M. (1966), 'A mathematical model of policy formation in a democratic society', in J. L. BERAD (ed.), *Mathematical Applications in Political Science*, vol. II (Dallas, Texas: Southern Methodist University Press). *127*
— & WHINSTON, Andrew B. (1965), 'Welfare economics and the theory of second best', *RES*, **32**, 1–14 (Jan). *226-7*

DEATON, Angus (1977), 'Equity, efficiency, and the structure of indirect taxation', *JPE*, **8**, 299–312. *246* n

DEBREU, Gerard (1954a)*, 'Representation of a preference ordering by a numerical function', in R. M. THRALL, C. H., COOMBS, and R. L. DAVIS (eds), *Decision Processes* (New York: Wiley). *29*
— (1954b)*, 'Valuation equilibrium and Pareto optimum', *Proceedings of the National Academy of Sciences*, **40**, 588–92.
— (1959)*, *Theory of Value* (New Haven: Yale University Press). *27, 29, 58*
— (1964)*, 'Continuity properties of Paretian utility', *International E.R.*, **5**, 285–93 *29*
— & SCARF, H. (1963)*, 'A limit theorem on the core of an economy', *International E.R.*, **4**, 235–46 (Sep). *35* n
— *see also* Arrow & Debreu

DEMEYER, Frank & PLOTT, Charles R. (1971), 'A welfare function using "relative intensity" of preference', *QJE*, **85**, 179–86. *121*

DEMSETZ, Harold (1969), 'Information and efficiency: another viewpoint', *J. of Law and E.*, **12**, 1–22 (Apr), reprinted in ROWLEY (1972). *291*
— (1970), 'The private production of public goods', *J. of Law and E.*, **13**, 292–306 (Oct). *194*
— *see also* Alchian & Demsetz

DE SERPA, Alan C. (1977), 'A theory of discriminatory clubs', *Scottish J. of Political Economy*, **21**, 33–41 (Feb). *212*
— (1978), 'Congestion, pollution, and impure public goods', *Public Finance/Finances Publiques*, **33**, 68–83. *211*

DEVARAJAN, Shantayanan, & FISHER, Anthony C. (1981), 'Hotelling's "economics of exhaustible resources": fifty years later', *JEL*, **19**, 65–73 (Mar). *290*

DIAMOND, Peter A. (1967)*, 'The role of the stock market in a general equilibrium model with technological uncertainty', *AER*, **57**, 759–76 (Sep). *272 n*

− & MCFADDEN, D. L. (1974), 'Some uses of the expenditure function in public finance', *J. of Public E.*, **3**, 3–21 (Feb). *289*

− & MIRRLEES, James A. (1971)*, 'Optimal taxation and public production', *AER*, **61**, 8–27, 261–78 (Mar). *239 n*

DIXIT, Avinash K. (1970), 'On the optimum structure of commodity taxes', *AER*, **60**, 295–301 (June). *239 n*

DODSWORTH, J. R. (1975), 'Reserve pooling: an application of the theory of clubs', *Economia Internazionale*, **28**, 103–18 (Feb–May). *212*

DOWNS, Anthony (1957), *An Economic Theory of Democracy* (New York: Harper). *284*

DREZE, J., & POUSSIN, D. de la Vallée (1971)*, 'A tatonnement process for public goods', *RES*, **38**, 133–50. *199*

DUMMETT, Michall, & FARQUHARSON, Robin (1961), 'Stability in voting', *Econometrica*, **29**, 33–43 (Jan). *135 n*

DUPUIT, Jules (1944), 'De la mesure de l'utilité des travaus publics', *Annales des Ponts et Chaussées*, translated by R. H. BARBACK in *International E.P.*, **2**, (1952). *83–110*. Reprinted in ARROW & SCITOVSKY (1969). *84-5*

DUSANSKY, Richard, & WALSH, John (1976), 'Separability, welfare economics, and the theory of second best', *RES*, **43**, 49–51. *227-8*

EASTERLIN, Richard A. (1974), 'Does economic growth improve the human lot? Some empirical evidence', in DAVID & REDER (1974). *273, 281*

EDWARDS, W., *see* Luce & Edwards

EDGEWORTH, F. Y. (1881), *Mathematical Psychics* (London: Kegan Paul). *35, 128*

EKERN, Steiner, & WILSON, Robert (1974), 'On the theory of the firm in an economy with incomplete markets', *Bell J. of E. and Management Science*, **5**, 171–80 (Spring). *272 n*

FAIR, Ray C. (1971), 'The optimal distribution of income', *QJE*, **85**, 551–79 (Nov). *149 n*

FAITH, Roger L., & THOMPSON, Earl A. (1981), 'A paradox in the theory of second best', *E. Inquiry*, **19**, 235–44 (Apr). *232*

FARQUHARSON, Robin (1969), *Theory of Voting*, (New Haven: Yale University Press). *135 n*

− *see also* Dummett & Farquharson

FARRELL, M. J. (1958), 'In defence of public-utility price theory' *Oxford E.P.*, **10**, 109–23 (Mar). *238*

— (1976), 'Liberalism in the theory of social choice', *RES,* **43,** 3–10. *138*

FELDSTEIN, Martin S. (1974), 'Distributional preferences in public expenditure analysis', in H. M. HOCHMAN & PETERSON (eds), *Redistribution Through Public Choice* (New York: Columbia University Press). *256*

FEREJOHN, John A., & FIORINA, Morris P. (1975), 'Purposive models of legislative behavior', *AER/S,* **65,** 407–14 (May). *285*

— & GRETHER, David M. (1977a)*, 'Weak path independence', *JET,* **14,** 19–31 (Feb). *126, 133*

— — (1977b)*, 'Some new impossibility theorems', *Public Choice,* **30,** 34–43 (Summer). *126*

FIORINA, Morris P., & NOLL, Roger G. (1978), 'Voters, bureaucrats and legislators: a rational choice perspective on the growth of bureaucracy', *J. of Public E.,* **9,** 239–54 (Apr). *285*

— *see also* Ferejohn & Fiorina

FISHBURN, Peter C. (1970a)*, 'Arrow's impossibility theorem: concise proof and infinite voters', *JET,* **2,** 103–6 (Mar). *117*

— (1970b), 'Intransitive indifference in preference theory: a survey', *Operations Research,* **18,** 207–28. *128*

— (1970c), *Utility Theory for Decision Making* (New York: Wiley). *29*

— (1972)*, *Mathematics of Decision Theory* (The Hague: Mouton). *27*

— (1973)*, 'Interval representations for interval orders and semiorders'. *J. of Mathematical Psychology,* **10,** 91–105. *128*

— (1974)*, 'On collective rationality and a generalised impossibility theorem', *RES,* **41,** 445–57 (Oct). *126*

FISCHER, Dietrich, & SCHOTTER, Andrew (1978), 'The inevitability of the "paradox of redistribution", in the allocation of voting weights', *Public Choice,* **33,** No. 2, 49–67. *211* n

FISHER, Anthony C., & PETERSON, Frederick M. (1976), 'The environment in economics: a survey'. *J. of E. Literature,* **14,** 1–33 (Mar). *166*

— *see also* Devarajan & Fisher

FISHER, Irving (1927), 'A statistical measure for measuring "marginal utility" and testing the justice of a progressive income tax', in HOLLANDER (ed.), *Economic Essays Contributed in Honour of J. B. Clark* (London: Macmillan). *161*

FITZROY, Felix R. (1974)*, 'Monopolistic equilibrium, non-convexity and inverse demand', *JET,* **7,** 1–16 (Jan). *58*

FLEMING, Marcus (1952), 'A cardinal concept of welfare', *QJE,* **66,** 366–84. *129*

FLOWERS, Marilyn, *see* Brennan & Flowers

FOSTER, C. D., & NEUBURGER, H. L. I. (1974), 'The ambiguity of the consumer's surplus measure of welfare change', *Oxford E.P.*, **26**, 66–77 (Mar). *100*

FOSTER, E., & SONNENSCHEIN, H. (1970)*, 'Price distortion and economic welfare', *Econometrica*, **38**, 281–97 (Mar). *228*

FRIEDMAN, David (1980), 'Many, few, one: social harmony and the shrunken choice set', *AER*, **70**, 225–32 (Mar). *39*

FRIEDMAN, Milton (1947), 'Lerner on the economics of control', *JPE*, **55**, 405–16 (Oct). *152*

– (1953), 'Choice, chance, and the personal distribution of income', *JPE*, **61**, 277–90 (Aug). *158*

FRISCH, Ragnar A. K. (1932), *New Methods of Measuring Marginal Utility* (Tübingen: Mohr). *161*

FURUBOTN, Eirik B., & PEJOVICH, Svetozar (1972), 'Property rights and economic theory: a survey of recent literature', *J. of E. Literature*, **10**, 1137–62 (Dec). *285*

GAERTNER, Wulf, & KRÜGER, Lorenz (1981), 'Self-supporting preferences and individual rights: the possibility of Paretian libertarianism', *Economica*, **48**, 17–28 (Feb). *138*

GEVERS, L., *see* D'Aspremont & Gevers

GIBBARD, A. (1973)*, 'Manipulation of voting schemes: a general result', *Econometrica*, **41**, 587–601 (July). *135* n

– (1974), 'A Pareto-consistent libertarian claim', *JET*, **7**, 388–410. *138*

GIFFORD, Adam, Jr, & STONE, Courtenay C. (1975), 'Externalities, liability, separability, and resource allocation: comment', *AER*, **65**, 724–7 (Dec). *169*

GILBERT, Richard J. (1979)*, 'Optimal depletion of an uncertain stock', *RES*, **46**, 47–57 (Jan). *290*

GILLEN, William J., *see* Cicchetti, Gillen & Smolensky

GINTIS, Herbert (1974), 'Welfare criteria with endogenous preferences: the economics of education', *International E.R.*, **15**, 415–30 (June). *288*

GLAISTER, S. (1974), 'Generalised consumer surplus and public transport pricing', *EJ*, **84**, 849–67 (Dec). *95*

GOLDFARB, Robert S., & WOGLOM, Geoffrey (1974), 'Government investment decisions and institutional constraints on income redistribution', *J. of Public E.*, **3**, 171–80 (May). *255*

GOOD, I. J. (1977), 'Justice in voting by demand revelation', *Public Choice*, **29**, 65–70 (Spring Supplement). *136*

GOODMAN, Leo A., & MARKOWITZ, Harry (1952), 'Social welfare functions based on individual rankings', *American J. of Sociology*, **58**, 257–62. *144*

GORMAN, W. M. (1953)*, 'Community preference fields', *Econometrica*, **21**, 63–80 (Jan). *64* n, *83*

– (1967), 'Tastes, habits, and choices', *International E. R.*, **8**, 218–22

(June). *288*

GOULD, J. R. (1977), 'Total conditions in the analysis of external effects', *EJ,* **87,** 558–64 (Sep). *170* n

GRAAFF, J. de V. (1957), *Theoretical Welfare Economics* (London: Cambridge University Press). *46, 61*

GRANDMONT, Jean-Michel (1977)*, 'Temporary general equilibrium theory', *Econometrica,* **45,** 535–72 (Apr). *58*

— (1978)*, 'Intermediate preferences and the majority rule', *Econometrica,* **46,** 317–30 (Mar). *123*

GREEN, H. A. John (1961), 'The social optimum in the presence of monopoly and taxation', *RES,* **29,** 66–77 (Oct). *228, 237*

— (1975), 'Two models of optimal pricing and taxation', *Oxford E.P.,* **27,** 352–82 (Nov). *289*

— (1976), *Consumer Theory,* revised ed. (London: Macmillan). *93* n, *95*

GREEN, Jerry, KOHLBERG, Elon, & LAFFONT, Jean-Jacques (1976)*, 'Partial equilibrium approach to the free-rider problem', *J. of Public E.,* **6,** 373–94 (Nov). *202*

GREEN, Jerry, & LAFFONT, Jean-Jacques (1977a)*, 'Characterisation of satisfactory mechanisms for revelation of preferences for public goods', *Econometrica,* **45,** 427–38 (Mar). *199* n

— — (1977b), 'Imperfect personal information and the demand-revealing process: a sampling approach', *Public Choice,* **29,** 79–94 (Spring). *206*

— — (1978a)*, 'An incentive compatible planning procedure for public good production', *Swedish J.E.,* **80,** 20–33. *199*

— — (1978b), *Incentives in Public Decision Making* (Amsterdam: North-Holland). *199* n

GREENE, Robert L. (1970), *Welfare Economics and Peak-Load Pricing* (Gainesville, Fla: University of Florida Press). *289*

GRETHER, David M., *see* Ferejohn & Grether

GRILICHES, Zvi, *et al.* (eds) (1978), *Income Distribution and Economic Inequality* (Somerset, N. J.: Halsted). *156*

GROVES, Theodore (1970U), 'The allocation of resources under uncertainty: the informational and incentive roles of prices and demands in a team'. Ph.D. dissertation, University of California, Berkeley. *134, 199–207*

— (1973), 'Incentives in teams', *Econometrica,* **41,** 617–33 (July). *199–207*

— (1976), 'Information, incentives and the internalisation of production externalities', in LIN (1976). *199–207*

— (1979)*, 'Efficient collective choice when compensation is possible', *RES,* **46,** 227–41 (April). *137*

– & LEDYARD, John (1977a)*, 'Optimal allocation of public goods: a solution to the "free rider problem"', *Econometrica*, **45**, 783–809 (May). *135, 199*

– – (1977b), 'Some limitations of demand-revealing processes', *Public Choice*, **29**, 107–24 (Spring Supplement). *205* n

– – (1980)*, 'The existence of efficient and incentive compatible equilibria with public goods', *Econometrica*, **48**, 1487–506 (Sep). *199*

– & LOEB, Martin (1975), 'Incentives and Public Input', *J. of Public E.*, **4**, 211–26 (Aug). *199*

GUESNERIE, Roger (1977), 'On the direction of tax reform', *J. of Public E.*, **7**, 179–202.

GUITTON, H., *see* Margolis & Guitton

GWILLIAM, K. M., & NASH, C. A. (1972), 'Evaluation of urban road investment: a comment', *Applied Economics*, **4**, 307–15. *93*

HAGUE, D. C., *see* Corlett & Hague

HAHN, F. H., *see* Arrow & Hahn

HAMMOND, Peter J. (1977), 'Dynamic restrictions on metastatic choice', *Economica*, **44**, 337–50 (Nov). *123*

HANSON, Donald A. (1977), 'Second best pricing policies for an exhaustible resource', *AER/S*, **67**, 351–4 (Feb). *290*

HANSSON, B. (1969), 'Group preferences', *Econometrica*, 50–4 (Jan). *123* n

– (1976)*, 'The existence of group preference functions', *Public Choice*, **28**, 89–98 (Winter). *117*

HARBERGER, A. C. (1954), 'Monopoly and resource allocation', *AER*, **45**, 77–87 (May). *286*

– (1964), 'Taxation, resource allocation, and welfare', in *The Role of Direct and Indirect Taxes in the Federal Revenue System*, National Bureau of Economic Research and Brookings Institution (Princeton: Princeton University Press). *289*

– (1971), 'The three basic postulates for applied welfare economics: an interpretive essay', *J. of E. Literature*, **9**, 785–97 (Sept). *100, 244*

– (1978), 'On the use of distributional weights in social cost-benefit analysis', *JPE*, **86**, S87–S120 (Apr). *244*

HARDY, J. D., *et al.* (1952, 1967), *Pain Sensations and Reactions* (Baltimore; New York: Hafner (reprinted 1967)). *131–2*

HARRIS, Richard, *see* Boadway & Harris

HARRISON, A. J., *see* Atkinson & Harrison

HARROD, Roy F. (1958), 'The possibility of economic satiety', in *Problems of United States Economic Development*, vol. I (New York: Committee for Economic Development). *273*

HARSANYI, John C. (1953), 'Cardinal utility in welfare economics and in the theory of risk-taking', *JPE*, **61**, 434–5 (Oct). *125*

− (1953–4), 'Welfare economics of variable tastes', *RES*, **21**, 204−13. *288*

− (1955), 'Cardinal welfare, individualistic ethics, and interpersonal comparisons of utility', *JPE*, **63**, 309-21 (Aug). *125-6, 129*

HATTA, Tatsuo (1977)*, 'A theory of piecemeal policy recommendations', *RES*, **44**, 1-21 (Oct). *228*

HAUSE, John C. (1975), 'The theory of welfare cost measurement', *JPE*, **83**, 1145-82 (Dec). *89 n, 90, 99-100*

HAUSMAN, Jerry A. (1981)*, 'Exact consumer's surplus and deadweight loss', *AER*, **71**, 662−76 (Sep). *90*

HAVEMAN, Robert, *see* Danziger, Haveman & Plotnick

HAYEK, F. A. von (1945), 'The use of knowledge in society', *AER*, **35**, 519-30 (Sep). *48*

HEAD, John (1966), 'On merit goods', *Finanzarchiv*, **25**, 1-29 (Mar). Reprinted in HEAD (1974). *287*

− (1969), 'Merit goods revisited', *Finanzarchiv*, **28**, 214-25 (Mar). Reprinted in HEAD (1974). *287*

− (1974), *Public Goods and Public Welfare* (Durham, North Carolina: Duke University Press).

− (1977), 'Misleading analogies in public goods analysis', *Finanzarchiv*, **36**, No. 1, 1-18. *194*

− *see also* Brennan, Head & Walsh

HELLER, Walter P., & STARRETT, David A. (1976) 'On the nature of externalities', in LIN (1976). *167*

HELPMAN, R. C. Elhanan (1974), 'Optimal income taxation for transfer payments under different social welfare criteria', *QJE*, **88**, 656−70 (Nov). *155*

HELPMAN, Robert C. E. (1974), 'Optimal income taxation for transfer payments under different social welfare criteria', *QJE*, **88**, 656−70 (Nov). *155*

− & HILLMAN, A. L. (1977), 'Two remarks on optimal club size', *Economica*, **44**, 293−6 (Aug). *212*

HENDERSON, A. (1941), 'Consumer's surplus and the compensating variation', *RES*, **8**, 117-21. *86*

HICKS, John R. (1939), 'Foundations of welfare economics', *EJ*, **49**, 696-712 (Dec). *46, 60*

− (1940), 'The valuation of social income', *Economica*, **7**, 105-24. *60, 85 n*

− (1941), 'The rehabilitation of consumer's surplus', *RES*, **8**, 108-16. *60, 85*

− (1943), 'The four consumers' surplus', *RES*, **11**, 31-41. *86*

HILDEBRANDT, Gregory G., *see* Bradford & Hildebrandt

HILDENBRAND, Werner (1977)*, 'Limit theorems on the case of an economy', in INTRILIGATOR (1977). *35*

− & KIRMAN, A. P. (1976), *Introduction to Equilibrium Analysis* (Amsterdam: North-Holland). *58*

HILDOCK, C. (1953), 'Alternative conditions for social orderings', *Econometrica*, **21**, 81. *124*

HILLMAN, A. L., *see* Helpmann & Hillman

HINICH, M., *see* Davis & Hinich

HIRSCH, Fred (1976), *Social Limits to Growth* (Cambridge, Mass: Harvard University Press). *273–4*

HOCHMAN, Harold M., & PETERSON, George E. (eds) (1974), *Redistribution Through Public Choice* (New York: Columbia University Press). *157*

– & RODGERS, J. D. (1969), 'Pareto-optimal redistribution', *AER*, **59**, 542–57 (Sep). *207*

HOOK, S. (ed.) (1967), *Human Values and Economic Policy: A Symposium* (New York: New York University Press).

HORVAT, Branko (1972), 'A model of maximal economic growth', *Kyklos*, **25**, fasc. 2, 215–28.

HOTELLING, Harold (1931), 'The economics of exhaustible resources', *JPE*, **39**, 137–75 (Apr). *290*

– (1938), 'The general welfare in relation to problems of taxation and of railway and utility rates', *Econometrica*, **6**, 242–69 (July). Reprinted in ARROW & SCITOVSKY (1969). *94–5*

HUETH, Darrall, & SCHMITZ, Andrew (1972), 'International trade in intermediate and final goods: some welfare implications of destabilising prices', *QJE*, **86**, 351–65 (Aug). *291*

HURWICZ, Leonid (1960)*, 'Optimality and informational efficiency in resource allocation processes', in K. J. ARROW *et al.* (eds), *Mathematical Methods in the Social Sciences* (Stanford: Stanford University Press). Reprinted in ARROW & SCITOVSKY (1969). *48*

– (1972)*, 'On informationally decentralised systems', in R. RADNER & B. McGUIRE (eds), *Decision and Organisation* (Amsterdam: North-Holland). *48, 202*

– (1972U)*, 'On the dimensional requirements of informationally decentralised Pareto-satisfactory processes', paper presented at the conference seminar on decentralisation, Northwestern University.

– (forthcoming)*, 'Incentive aspects of decentralization', in Arrow & Intriligator. *48*

INADA, Ken-Ichi (1970), 'Majority rule and rationality', *JET*, **2**, 27–40 (Mar). *123*

INTRILIGATOR, Michael D. (ed.) (1977)*, *Frontiers of Quantitative Economics*, vol. III (Amsterdam: North-Holland).

– *see also* Arrow & Intriligator

JENCKS, C., *et al.* (1972), *Inequality: A Reassessment of the Effect of Family and Schooling in America* (new York: Basic Books). *159*

JEWITT, Ian (1981)*, 'Preference structure and piecemeal second best policy', *J. of Pub. E.*, **16**, 215–31 (Oct). *228*

JOHANSEN, Leif (1963), 'Some notes on the Lindahl theory of determination of public expenditures', *International E.R.*, **4**, 346–58 (Sep). *193* n

JOHNSEN, Christopher, *see* Weingast, Shepsle & Johnsen

JUSTER, F. T. (1978), *The Distribution of Economic Well-Being* (New York: Wiley). *157*

KAFOGLIS, M. Z., *see* Buchanan & Kafoglis

KAGEL, John H., *see* Battalio, Kagel & Reynolds

KAHN, Alfred E. (1966), 'The tyranny of small decisions: market failures, imperfections, and the limits of economics', *Kyklos*, **19**, fasc. 1, 23–47. *273*

KAHN, R. F. (1935), 'Some notes on ideal output', *EJ*, **45**, 1–35 (Mar). *225* n

KALAI, Ehud, & SCHMEIDLER, David (1977), 'Aggregation procedure for cardinal preferences: a formulation and proof of Samuelson's impossibility conjecture', *Econometrica*, **45**, 1431–8 (Sep). *121*

KALDOR, N. (1939), 'Welfare propositions of economics and interpersonal comparisons of utility', *EJ*, **49**, 549–52 (Sep). *60*

– (1947), 'A comment', *RES*, **14**, 49. *60*

KALMAN, Peter J. (1968)*, 'Theory of consumer behavior when prices enter the utility function', *Econometrica*, **36**, 497–510 (July/Oct). *287*

KAMIEN, Morton I., & SCHWARTZ, Nancy L. (1975), 'Market structure and innovation: a survey', *J. of E. Literature*, **13**, 1–37 (Mar). *291*

– – (1978), 'Optimal exhaustible resource depletion with endogenous technical change', *RES*, **45**, 179–96 (Feb). *290*

KANEKO, Mamoru, & NAKAMURA, Kenjiro (1979), 'The Nash social welfare function', *Econometrica*, **47**, 423–35 (Mar). *149*

KAPTEYN, Arie, & VAN HERWAARDEN, Floor G. (1980), 'Interdependent welfare functions and optimal income distribution', *J. of Pub. E.*, **14**, 375–97 (Dec). *156*

– *see also* Van Herwaarden, Kapteyn & Van Praag

KAWAMATA, Kunio (1977)*, 'Price distortion and the second best optimum', *RES*, **44**, 23–9 (Oct). *228*

KEARL, J. R., POPE, Clayne L., WHITING, Gordon C., & WIMMER, Larry T. (1979), 'A confusion of economists?', *AER/S*, **69**, 28–37 (May). *23*

KELLY, Jerry S. (1977), *Arrow Impossibility Theorems* (New York: Academic Press). *138*

KEMP, Murray C. (1968), 'Some issues in the analysis of trade gains', *Oxford E.P.*, **20**, 129–61 (July). *228*

– & ASIMAKOPOLUS, A. (1952), 'A note on "social welfare functions" and cardinal utility', *Canadian J.E.*, **18**, 195–200. *124*

– & LONG, Ngo Van (1978), 'The optimal consumption of depletable resources: comment', *QJE*, **92**, 345–53 (May). *290*

– – (1980), 'Eating a cake of unknown size: pure competition versus social planning', Essay 5 of *Exhaustible Resources, Optimality, and Trade* (Amsterdam: North-Holland). *290*

— & NG, Yew-Kwang (1976), 'On the existence of social welfare functions, social orderings and social decision functions', *Economica,* **43**, 59–66 (Feb). *118–21, 140–6, 254* n

— — (1977), 'More on social welfare functions: the incompatibility of individualism and ordinalism', *Economica,* **44**, 89–90 (Feb). *120, 254* n

KENNEDY, C. (1953), 'The economic welfare function and Dr. Little's criterion', *RES,* **20**, 137–42. *68–9*

— (1963a), 'Welfare criteria – a further note', *EJ,* **73**, 338–41 (June). *68–9*

— (1963b), 'Two comments (II)', *EJ,* **73**, 780–81 (Dec). *68–9*

KIRMAN, Alan, & SONDERMANN, Dieter (1972)*, 'Arrow's theorem, many agents and invisible dictators', *JET,* **5**, 267–77 (Oct). *117*

— *see also* Hildenbrand & Kirman

KLAPPHOLZ, K. (1964), 'Value judgments and economies', *British J. for the Philosophy of Science,* (Aug). *15, 23*

KOHLBERG, Elon, *see* Green, Kohlberg & Laffont

KOPLIN, H. T. (1963), 'The profit maximisation assumption', *Oxford E.P.,* **15**, 130–39 (July). *50, 272*

KRAMER, G. (1973)*, 'On a class of equilibrium conditions for majority rule', *Econometrica,* **41**, 285–97. *119*

KRELLE, Wilhelm, & SHORROCKS, Anthony F. (eds) (1978), *Personal Income Distribution* (Amsterdam: North-Holland). *157*

KRUEGER, Anne O. (1974), 'The political economy of the rent-seeking society', *AER,* **64**, 291–303 (June). *285*

KRÜGER, Lorenz, *see* Gaertner & Krüger

KWOK, Viem and LELAND, Hayne (1982), 'An economic model of the brain drain', *AER,* **72**, 91–100 (March). *291*

LAFFONT, Jean-Jacques (ed.) (1979), *Aggregation and Revelation of Preferences* (Amsterdam: North-Holland). *135* n

— *see also* Green, Kohlberg & Laffont, Green & Laffont

LANCASTER, Kelvin (1968), *Mathematical Economics* (London: Collier-Macmillan). *46*

— *see also* Lipsey & Lancaster

LAYARD, R. (1980), 'Human satisfactions and public policy', *EJ,* **90**, 737–50 (Dec). *273*

LAU, Lawrence J., SHESHINSKI, Eytan, & STIGLITZ, Joseph E. (1978)*, 'Efficiency in the optimum supply of public goods', *Econometrica,* **46**, 269–84 (Mar). *192*

LECOMBER, Richard, *see* Collard, Lecomber & Slater

LEDYARD, John, & ROBERTS, D. J. (1974U)*, 'On the incentive problem with public goods', Northwestern University, Centre for Mathematical Studies in Economics and Management Science, *Discussion Paper* No. 116. *202*

— *see also* Groves & Ledyard

LEIBENSTEIN, Harvey (1966), 'Allocative efficiency vs. X-efficiency', *AER*, **56**, 392–415. *285*

— (1976), *Beyond Economic Man: A New Foundation for Microeconomics* (Cambridge, Mass.: Harvard University Press). *286*

— (1978), 'On the basic proposition of X-efficiency theory', *AER/S*, **68**, 328–32 (May). *286*

— *see also* Comanor & Leibenstein

LEIMAN, Ephraim (1978), 'Inequality as a public good: unambiguous redistribution and optimality', in SANDMO, A. (ed.), *Essays in Public Economics* (Lexington, Mass.: Lexington-Heath). *211*

LELAND, Hayne, *see* Kwok & Leland

LERNER, Abba P. (1944), *The Economics of Control* (New York: Macmillan). *152-3*

— (1970), 'On optimal taxes with an untaxable sector', *AER*, **60**, 284–94 (June). *239* n

LIN, Steven A. (ed.) (1976). *Theory and Measurement of Economic Externalities* (New York: Academic Press).

LINDBLOM, C. E., *see* Dahl & Lindblom

LIPSEY, Richard G., & LANCASTER, Kelvin (1956), 'The general theory of second best', *RES*, **24**, 11–32 (Oct). *218-20*

— — (1959), 'McManus on second best', *RES*, **26**, 225–6 (June). *226* n

LITTLE, Ian M. D. (1949), 'The foundations of welfare economics', *Oxford E.P.*, **1**, (N.S.), 227–46 (June). *66*

— (1951), 'Direct versus indirect taxes', *EJ*, **61** 577–84 (Sep). *218*

— (1952), 'Social choice and individual values', *JPE*, **60**, 422–32 (Oct). Reprinted in PHELPS (1973). *118*

— (1957), *A Critique of Welfare Economics*, 2nd ed. (London: Oxford University Press). *32, 61, 66-72*

— & MIRRLEES, James A. (1974), *Project Appraisal and Planning for Developing Countries* (London: Heinemann). *255*

LITTLECHILD, S. C. (1981), 'Misleading calculations of the social costs of monopoly power', *EJ*, **91**, 348–63 (June). *286*

LIU, Pak-Wai & WONG, Yue-chin (1982), 'Educational screening by certificates: an empirical test', *E. Inquiry*, **20**, 72–83 (Jan). *159*

LLOYD, Peter J. (1974), 'A more general theory of price distortions in open economies', *J. of International E.*, **4**, 365–86 (Nov). *228*

LOEB, Martin (1977), 'Alternative versions of the demand-revealing process', *Public Choice*, **29**, 15–26 (Spring Supplement). *199* n

— *see also* Groves & Loeb

LONG, Ngo Van, *see* Kemp & Long

LUCE, R. D. (1956), 'Semiorders and a theory of utility discrimination', *Econometrica*, **24**, 178–91. *128*

— & EDWARDS, W. (1958)*, 'The derivations of subjective scales from just noticeable differences', *Psychological R.*, **65**, 222–37. *109* n, *161* n

– & SUPPES, P. (1965)*, 'Preference, utility, and subjective probability', in R. D. LUCE, R. R. BUSH, & E. GALANTER (eds), *Handbook of Mathematical Psychology*, vol. III (New York: Wiley). *29*

MACDOUGALL, Donald (1977), 'Economic growth and social welfare', *Scottish J. of Political Economy*, **24**, 193–206 (Nov). *273*

McFADDEN, Daniel (1969), 'A simple remark on the second best Pareto optimality of market equilibria', *JET*, **1**, 26–38 (June). *227*
– *see also* Diamond & McFadden

McGUIRE, Martin (1974), 'Group segregation and optimal jurisdiction', *JPE*, **82**, 112–32 (Jan–Feb). *211*
– Martin C., & AARON, Henry (1969), 'Efficiency and equity in the optimal supply of a public good', *R. of E. and Statistics*, **51**, 31–9 (Feb). *192 n*

McGUIRE, Thomas, *see* Brennan & McGuire

MACHLUP, Fritz (1940), 'Professor Hicks' statics', *QJE*, **54**, 280–2. *89*
– (1957), 'Professor Hicks' revision of demand theory', *AER*, **47**, 119–35. *89*

McKENZIE, Lionel W. (1951), 'Ideal output and the interdependence of firms', *EJ*, **61**, 785–803. *225 n*

MACKENZIE, W. J. M. (1967), *Politics and Social Science* (Harmondsworth: Penguin Books). *127*

McLURE, Charles E. (1968), 'Merit wants: a normatively empty box', *Finanzarchiv*, **27**, 474–83 (June). *287*

McMANUS, Maurice (1959)*, 'Comments on "the general theory of second best"', *RES*, **26**, 209–24 (June). *220, 225 n*
– (1975)*, 'Inter-tastes consistency in social welfare functions', in PARKIN & NOBAY (1975). *119 n*
– (1978)*, 'Social welfare optimisation with tastes as variables', *Weltwirtschaftliches*, **114**, 101–23. *119 n*
– WALTON, Gary M., & COFFMAN, Richard B. (1972), 'Distributional equality and aggregate utility: further comment', *AER*, **62**, 489–96 (June). *152 n*

MALINVAUD, E. (1971)*, 'A planning approach to the public goods problems', *Swedish J.E.*, **73**, 96–112. *199*
– (1972), *Lectures on Microeconomic Theory* (Amsterdam: North-Holland). *94 n, 95*

MARGOLIS, J., & GUITTON, H. (eds) (1969), *Public Economics* (London: Macmillan).

MARKOWITZ, Harry, *see* Goodman & Markowitz

MARSCHAK, Thomas A. (forthcoming)*, 'Organization design', in Arrow & Intriligator. *48*

MARSHALL, Alfred (1920), *Principles of Economics*, 8th ed. (London: Macmillan). *84–5*

MAS-COLELL, Andreu, & SONNENSCHEIN, Hugo (1972)*, 'General

impossibility theorems for group decisions', *RES,* **39,** 185-92 (Apr). *126*

MASKIN, Eric (1978), 'A theorem on utilitarianism', *RES,* **45,** 93-6 (Feb). *129*

MASSELL, Benton F. (1969), 'Price stabilisation and welfare', *QJE,* **83,** 284-98 (May). *291*

MAYSTON, David J. (1974)*, 'Optimal licensing in public sector tariff structures', in M. PARKIN & A. R. NOBAY (eds), *Contemporary Issues in Economics* (Manchester: Manchester University Press). *237-8, 289*

— (1975U)*, 'Alternatives to irrelevant alternatives', *University of Essex Discussion Paper* No. 61. *144*

— (1980), 'Ordinalism and quasi-ordinalism in the theory of social choice', paper presented at the 1978 AUTE Conference; in Currie & Peters. *140, 145–6*

MEADE, James E. (1955a), *The Theory of Customs Unions* (Amsterdam: North-Holland). *218*

— (1955b), *Trade and Welfare* (London: Oxford University Press). *218*

— (1964), *Efficiency, Equality, and the Ownership of Property* (London: Allen & Unwin). *160*

— (1976), *The Just Economy* (London: Allen & Unwin). *157*

MICHAEL, Robert T., & BECKER, Gary S. (1973), 'On the new theory of consumer behavior', *Swedish J.E.,* **75,** 378-96 (Dec). *288*

MILL, J. S. (1844), *Essays on Some Unsettled Questions of Positive Economics.* *6*

MILLER, Nicholas R. (1977), 'Logrolling, vote trading, and the paradox of voting', *Public Choice,* **30,** 51-76 (Summer). *125*

MILLERON, J.-C. (1972)*, 'Theory of value with public goods: A survey article', *JET,* **5,** 419-77 (Dec). *193* n

MIRRLEES, James A. (1971)*, 'An exploration in the theory of optimum income taxation', *RES,* **38,** 175-208 (Apr). *14, 153-6, 160, 250, 290*

— (1976)*, 'Optimal tax theory: a synthesis', *J. of Public E.,* **6,** 327-58. *239* n, *289*

— (forthcoming)*, 'The theory of optimal taxation', in ARROW & INTRILIGATOR. *289*

— & STERN, N. H. (eds) (1973)*, *Models of Economic Growth* (London: Macmillan). *290*

— *see also* Diamond & Mirrlees, Little & Mirrlees

MISHAN, Ezra J. (1952), 'The principle of compensation reconsidered', *JPE,* **60,** 312-22 (Aug). *64* n

— (1962a), 'Welfare criteria: an exchange of notes', *EJ,* **72,** 234-44 (Mar). *61*

— (1962b), 'Second thoughts on second best', *Oxford E.P.,* **14,** 205-17 (Oct). Reprinted in MISHAN (1969b). *224, 237*

– (1963), 'Welfare criteria: are compensation tests necessary?', *EJ*, **73**, 342–50 (June). *77*
– (1969a), *Welfare Economics: An Assessment* (Amsterdam: North-Holland). *61*
– (1969b), *Welfare Economics: Ten Introductory Essays* (New York, Random House). *2*
– (1971), 'The postwar literature on externalities: an interpretative essay', *J. of E. Literature*, **9**, 1–28 (Mar). *105, 167*
– (1973), 'Welfare criteria: resolution of a paradox', *EJ*, **83**, 747–67 (Sep). *73-5*
– (1977), *The Economic Growth Debate: An Assessment* (London: Allen & Unwin). *273*
– (1980), 'The new welfare economics: an alternative view', *International E.R.*, **21**, 691–705 (Oct). *73*
MITCHELL, Bridger M. (1978), 'Optimal pricing of local telephone service', *AER*, **68**, 517–37 (Sep). *289*
MOHRING, Herbert (1971), 'Alternative welfare gain and loss measurement', *Western E.J.*, **9**, 349–68 (Dec). *100*
MOORE, James C., *see* Chipman & Moore
MORAWETZ, David (1977), 'Income distribution and self-rated happiness: some empirical evidence', *EJ*, **87**, 511–22 (Sep). *207*
MORRISON, Clarence C. (1968), 'Generalisation on the methodology of second best', *Western Economic Journal*, **6**, 112–20 (Mar). *219*
MUELLER, Dennis C. (1967), 'The possibility of a social welfare function: comment', *AER*, **57**, 1304–11 (Dec). *125*
– (1976), 'Public choice: a survey', *J. of E. Literature*, **14**, 395–433 (June). *285*
– (1979), *Public Choice* (Cambridge: Cambridge University Press). *14, 120, 285*
– *see also* Cowling & Mueller
MURAKAMI, Y. (1961), 'A note on the general possibility theorem of the social welfare function', *Econometrica*, **29**, 244–6 (Apr). *117-18*
MURPHY, John A., *see* Currie, Murphy & Schmitz
MUSGRAVE, Richard A. (1959), *The Theory of Public Finance* (New York: McGraw-Hill). *190* n
– (1969a), 'Provision for social goods', in MARGOLIS & GUITTON (1969). *190* n
– (1969b), 'Cost-benefit analysis and the theory of public finance', *J. of E. Literature*, **7**, 797–806 (Sep). *247*
MUSHKIN, S., (ed.) (1972), *Public Prices for Public Products* (Washington: Urban Institute.
NASH, C. A., *see* Gwilliam & Nash
NASH, John F., Jr (1950), 'The bargaining problem', *Econometrica*, **18**, 155–62. *149, 271*
NATH, S. K. (1969), *A Reappraisal of Welfare Economics* (London:

Routledge & Kegan Paul). *31-2, 52*

NEEDHAM, D. (1975), 'Market structure and firms' R & D behavior', *J. of Industrial E.*, **23**, 241–55 (June). *291*

NEGISHI, T. (1960–1)*, 'Monopolistic competition and general equilibrium', *RES*, **28**, 196–201. *58*

NEUBURGER, H. L. I., *see* Foster & Neuburger

NEWBERRY, David M. G. and STIGLITZ, Joseph E. (1982), 'Risk aversion, supply response, and the optimality of random prices: a diagrammatic analysis', *QJE*, **97**, 1–26 (Feb). *291*

NG, Yew-Kwang (1969), 'A note on profit maximisation', *AEP*, **8**, 106–10 (June). *50, 272*

– (1969U), 'A study of the interrelationships between efficient resource allocation, economic growth, and welfare and the solution of these problems in market socialism', Ph.D. thesis, University of Sydney. *8*

– (1971a), 'Recent developments in the theory of externality and the Pigovian solution', *E. Record*, **47**, 169–85 (June). *170–2, 179, 183–4*

– (1971b), 'The possibility of a Paretian liberal: impossibility theorems and cardinal utility', *JPE*, **79**, 1397–402 (Nov–Dec). *138*

– (1971c), 'Little's welfare criterion under the equality assumptions', *E. Record*, **47**, 579–83 (Dec). *71, 77* n

– (1971d), 'Competition, monopoly, and the incentive to invent', *Australian E.P.*, **10**, 45–9 (June). *291*

– (1972a), 'Pareto conditions, behavioural rules, and the theory of second best', *Australian E.P.*, **11**, 124–5 (June). *226*

– (1972b), 'Value judgments and economists' role in policy recommendation', *EJ*, **82**, 1014–18 (Sep). *15, 23, 240*

– (1973a), 'Income distribution as a peculiar public good: the paradox of redistribution and the paradox of universal externality', *Public Finance/Finances Publiques*, **28**, No. 1, 1–10. *270–11*

– (1973b), 'The economic theory of clubs: Pareto optimality conditions', *Economica*, **40**, 291–8 (Aug). *211–12*

– (1973c), 'Optimum saving: a practicable solution', *Indian J. of E.*, **53**, 285–94 (Jan). *138, 290*

– (1973U), 'Interpretations of the Pareto principle and its compatability with Liberalism', paper presented to the Third Australasian Conference of Economists, Adelaide. *287*

– (1974a), 'The economic theory of clubs: optimal tax/subsidy, *Economica*, **41**, 308–21 (Aug.) *211–12*

– (1974b), 'Utility and profit maximisation by an owner-manager: towards a general analysis', *J. of Industrial E.*, **23**, 97–108 (Dec). *274*

– (1975a), 'Bentham or Bergson? Finite sensibility, utility functions, and social welfare functions', *RES*, **42**, 545–70 (Oct). *14, 128* n, *129–33, 150–1, 254* n

– (1975b), 'Coase's theorem and first party priority rule: reply', *E. Record*, **51**, 272–74 (June). *183*
– (1975c), 'The paradox of universal externality, *JET*, **10**, 258–64 (Apr). *216*
– (1975d), 'Non-economic activities, indirect externalities, and third-best policies', *Kyklos*, **29**, No. 3, 507–25. *176, 217, 237, 239, 281*
–(1975U), 'The Benthamite social welfare function: its justification and implications', paper presented to the Fifth Australasian Conference of Economists, Brisbane (Aug). *133*
– (1977a), 'Towards a theory of third best', *Public Finance/Finances Publiques*, **32**, 1–15. *228–42*
– (1977b), 'Competition, monopoly, and the incentive to invent: a reply', *Australian E.P.*, **16**, 154–6 (June). *291*
– (1978a), 'Economic growth and social welfare: the need for a complete study of happiness', *Kyklos*, **31**, No. 4, 575–87. *273–82*
– (1978b), 'Optimal club size: a reply', *Economica*, **45**, 407–10 (Nov). *212*
– (1980), 'Optimal corrective taxes/subsidies when revenue-raising imposes excess burden', *AER*, **70**, 744–51 (Sep). *169*
– (1981a) 'All "Ng" up on clubs? A "Bran-new Flawer" of Brennan–Flowers', *Public Finance Quarterly*, **9**, 75–8 (Jan). *212*
– (1981b), 'Welfarism: a defence against Sen's attack', *EJ*, **91**, 527–30 (June). *22*
– (1981c), 'Bentham or Nash? On the acceptable form of social welfare functions', *E. Record*, **57**, 238–50 (Sep). *129, 149*
– (1982aU), 'Does Pareto optimality require the reallocation of the numeraire? A response to Sandler–Tschirhart's survey of clubs-theory', typescript. *212* n
– (1982b), *Theory and Decision*, **17**,141–7. 'Beyond Pareto optimality. The necessity of interpersonal cardinal utilities in distributional judgments and social choice', *Zeitschrift für Nationalökonomie (J. of E.)*. **42**, 207–33. *121*
– (1983), 'Rents and pecuniary externalities in cost–benefit analysis', *AER.*, **73**, 63–70. *285*

– & WEISSER, Mendel (1974)*, 'Optimal pricing with a budget constraint – the case of the two-part tariff', *RES*, **41**, 337–45 (July). *237–8, 289*
– (1984), 'Interpersonal level comparability implies comparability of utility differences', typescript. *15*
– *see also* Kemp & Ng, Parish & Ng.
NISKANEN, William (1971), *Bureaucracy and Representative Government* (Chicago: Aldine). *284*
NOBAY, A. R., *see* Parkin & Nobay
NOLL, Roger G., *see* Fiorina & Noll
OAKLAND, William H. (1972), 'Congestion, public goods and welfare', *J. of Public E.*, **1**, 339–57 (Nov). *211*

– (1974), 'Public goods, perfect competition, and underproduction', *JPE*, **82**, 927–39 (Sep–Oct). *194–8*

– *see also* Brito & Oakland

OATES, W. E., *see* Baumol & Oates

OKUN, Arthur M. (1975), *Equality and Efficiency: The Big Tradeoff* (Washington: Brookings Institution). *157*

OKUNO, Masahiro (1976)*, 'General equilibrium with money: indeterminancy of price level and efficiency', *JET*, **12**, 402–15 (June). *58*

OLSON, Mancur (1965), *The Logic of Collective Action: Public Goods and the Theory of Groups* (Cambridge, Mass.: Harvard University Press). *284*

– (1974), 'On the priority of public problems', in R. MARRIS, *The Corporate Society* (New York: Wiley). *192 n, 286*

ORDOVER, Janusz A., *see* Baumol & Ordover

ORR, Larry L. (1976), 'Income transfers as a public good: an application to AFDC', *AER*, **66**, 359–71 (June). *207*

OSANA, Hiroaki (1977)*, 'Optimal tax-subsidy system for an economy with Marshallian externalities', *Econometrica*, **45**, 329–40 (Mar). *58*

– (1978)*, 'On the informational size of message spaces for resource allocation processes', *JET*, **17**, 66–78 (Feb). *48*

OSBORNE, D. K. (1976)*, 'Irrelevant alternatives and social welfare', *Econometrica*, **44**, 1001–15 (Sep). *115 n, 121*

OTANI, Yoshihiko, & SICILIAN, Joseph (1977)*, 'Externalities and problems of nonconvexity and overhead costs in welfare economics', *JET*, **14**, 239–51 (Apr). *170 n*

OZGA, S. A. (1955), 'An essay in the theory of tariffs', *JPE*, **63**, 489–99 (Dec). *218*

PANZAR, John C., *see* Baumol, Panzar, & Willig

PARETO, V. (1909), *Manuel d'Économie politique* (Paris: Girard & Brière). *59*

– (1935), *The Mind and Society*, vol. 4, edited by Arthur Livingston, and translated by the editor and Andrew Borgiorno (London: Cape). *31 n*

PARISH, Ross M. (1972), 'Economic aspects of pollution control', *Australian E.P.*, **11**, 32–43. *176*

– (1976). 'The scope of benefit-cost analysis', *E. Record*, **52**, 302–14 (Sep). *244*

– & NG, Yew-Kwang (1972), 'Monopoly, X-efficiency, and the measurement of welfare loss', *Economica*, **39**, 301–8 (Aug). *286*

PARK, Robert E. (1967), 'The possibility of a social welfare function: comment', *AER*, **57**, 1300–4 (Dec). *125*

PARKIN, Michael, & NOBAY, A. R. (eds) (1975), *Current Economic Problems* (Cambridge: Cambridge University Press).

PARKS, Robert P. (1976), 'An impossibility theorem for fixed preferences: a dictatorial Bergson–Samuelson welfare function', *RES*, **43**, 447–50 (Oct). *119*

PATTANAIK, Prasanta K. (1971), *Voting and Collective Choice* (Cambridge: Cambridge University Press). *123*

— (1978), *Strategy and Group Choice* (Amsterdam: North-Holland). *135* n

— *see also* Sen & Pattanaik

PATINKIN, Don (1963), 'Demand curves and consumer's surplus', in C. CHRIST *et al.*, *Measurement in Economics: Studies in Mathematical Economics and Econometrics in Memory of Yehula Grundfeld* (Stanford: Stanford University Press). *92*

PAULY, M. (1970), 'Cores and clubs', *Public Choice*, **9**, 53–65 (Fall). *211*

PAZNER, Elisha A. (1972), 'Merit wants and the theory of taxation', *Public Finance/Finances Publiques*, **27**, No. 4, 460–72. *287*

PEACOCK, Alan T., & WISEMAN, Jack (1979), 'Approaches to the analysis of government expenditure growth', *Public Finance Quarterly*, **7**, 3–23 (Jan). *285*

PECHMAN, Joseph, A., & TIMPANE, Michael (eds) (1975), *Work Incentives and Income Guarantees: The New Jersey Negative Income Tax Experiment* (Washington, D.C.: Brookings Institution).

PEJOVICH, Svetozar, *see* Furuboton & Pejovich

PEN, Jan (1971), *Income Distribution*, translated by T. S. PRESTON, (London: Allen Lane, The Penguin Press). *157*

PETERSON, Frederick M., *see* Fisher & Peterson

PETERSON, George E., *see* Hochman & Peterson

PETHIG, Rudiger (1979), 'Environmental management in general equilibrium: a new incentive compatible approach', *International E.R.*, **20**, 1–27 (Feb). *199*

PFOUTS, R. W. (1953), 'A critique of some recent contributions to the theory of consumers' surplus', *Southern E.J.*, **19**, 315–33 (Jan). *85*

PHELPS, Edmund S., *et al.* (1970), *The Microeconomic Foundations of Employment and Inflation Theory* (New York: Norton). *1*

— (1972), *Inflation Policy and Unemployment Theory: The Cost-Benefit Approach to Monetary Planning* (New York: Norton). *1*

— (ed.) (1973), *Economic Justice: Selected Readings* (Harmondsworth: Penguin Books). *157*

— (ed.) (1975), *Altruism, Morality, and Economic Theory* (New York: Russell Sage Foundation). *8*

PIGOU, Arthur C. (1912), *Wealth and Welfare*. Later editions (1920, 1924, 1929, 1932) assume the title *The Economics of Welfare* (London: Macmillan). *59*

— (1922), 'Empty economic boxes: a reply', *EJ*, **32**, 458–65. *1*

— (1932), *The Economics of Welfare*, 4th ed. (London: Macmillan). *48, 59, 151*

PLOTNICK, Robert, *see* Danziger, Haveman & Plotnick

PLOTT, Charles R. (1972), 'Ethics, social choice, and the theory of economic policy', *J. of Mathematical Sociology*, **2**, 181-208. *115, 143*

- (1973)*, 'Path dependence, rationality and social choice', *Econometrica*, **41**, 1075-91. *133*
- *see also* Demeyer & Plott

POLINSKY, A. M. (1972), 'Probabilistic compensation criteria', *QJE*, **86**, 407-25 (Aug). *72* n

POLLAK, Robert A. (1976)*, 'Habit formation and long-run utility functions', *JET*, **13**, 272-97 (Oct). *288*
- (1977), 'Price dependent preferences', *AER*, **67**, 64-75 (Mar). *287*
- (1978), 'Endogenous tastes in demand and welfare analysis', *AER/S*, **68**, 374-9 (May). *288*
-- (1979), 'Bergson–Samuelson social welfare functions and the theory of social choice', *QJE*, **93**, 73-90 (Feb). *119*

POPE, Clayne L., *see* Kearl *et al.*

PORTER, Richard C. (1978), 'The economics of congestion: a geometric review', *Public Finance Quarterly*, **6**, 23-52 (Jan). *211, 291*

POSNER, Richard (1975), 'The social cost of monopoly and regulation', *JPE*, **83**, 807-27 (Aug). *285*

POUSSIN, D. de la Vallée, *see* Dreze & Poussin

PULSIPHER, Allan G. (1971), 'The properties and relevancy of merit goods', *Finanzarchiv*, **30**, 266-86 (Mar). *287*

QUIRK, James, & SAPOSNIK, Rubin (1968), *Introduction to General Equilibrium Theory and Welfare Economics* (New York: McGraw-Hill). *58, 63, 115* n

RAMSEY, F. P. (1927), 'A contribution to the theory of taxation', *EJ*, **37**, 47-61 (Mar). *255, 289*
- (1928), 'A mathematical theory of saving', *EJ*, **38**, 543-59 (Dec). Reprinted in ARROW & SCITOVSKY (1969). *289*

RANDALL, Alan (1978), 'Property institutions and economic behavior', *J. of E. Issues*, **12**, 1-21 (Mar). *285*

RAPANOS, Vassilis T. (1980), 'A comment on the theory of second best', *RES*, **47**, 817–19. *228*

REDER, M. W. (1947), *Studies in the Theory of Welfare Economics* (New York: Columbia University Press). *32*
- *see also* David & Reder

REITER, Stanley (1977), 'Information and performance in the (new)[2] welfare economics', *AER/S*, **67**, 226–34 (Feb). *48*

REYNOLDS, Morgan O., *see* Battalio, Kagel & Reynolds

RILEY, John G. (1979), 'Testing the educational screening hypothesis', *JPE*, **87**, S225–52 (Oct). *159*

RIVLIN, Alice M. (1975), 'Income distribution – can economists help?', *AER/S*, **65**, 1-15 (May). *157*

ROBERTS, Donald J. (1974), 'The Lindahl solution for economies with public goods', *J. of Public E.*, **3**, 23-42 (Feb). *193* n

ROBERTS, Kevin W. S. (1980a)*, 'Possibility theorems with interpersonally comparable welfare levels', *RES*, **47**, 409–20. *121, 138*
– (1980b)*, 'Interpersonal comparability and social choice theory', *RES*, **47**, 421–39. *113 n, 138*
– (1980c)*, 'Social choice theory: the single-profile and multi-profile approaches', *RES*, **47**, 441–50. *119, 138*
– see also Ledyards & Roberts
ROBERTSON, D. (1962), 'Welfare criteria: an exchange of notes', *EJ*, **72**, 226–29 (Mar). *61*
ROBBINS, Lionel (1932), *An Essay on the Nature and Significance of Economic Science* (London: Macmillan). *15, 59*
– (1938), 'Interpersonal comparison of utility: a comment', *EJ*, **48**, 635–41 (Dec). *284*
RODGERS, J. D., see Hochman & Rodgers
ROSEFIELDE, Steven (1981), *Economic Welfare and the Economics of Soviet Socialism: Essays in Honour of Abram Bergson* (Cambridge: Cambridge University Press).
ROSEN, Harvey S., see Bradford & Rosen
ROSKAMP, Karl W. (1975), 'Public Goods, Merit Goods, Private Goods', *Public Finance/Finances Publiques*, **30**, No. 1, 61–9. *287*
ROTHENBERG, Jerome (1953), 'Welfare comparisons and changes in tastes', *AER*, **43**, 885–90 (Dec). *288*
– (1961), *The Measurement of Social Welfare* (Englewood Cliffs: Prentice-Hall). *128*
ROWLEY, Charles K. (ed.) (1972), *Readings in Industrial Economics*, vol. II (London: Macmillan).
– (1978), 'Liberalism and collective choice: A return to reality?', *Manchester School*, **46**, 224–51 (Sep). *138*
RUGGLES, Nancy (1949/50), 'Recent developments in the theory of marginal cost pricing', *RES*, **17**, 107–26. Reprinted in TURVEY (1968). *238, 289*
SADKA, Efrain (1976), 'On income distribution, incentive effects, and optimal income taxation', *RES*, **43**, 261–7. *155*
SAMUELSON, Paul A. (1942), 'Constancy of the marginal utility of income', in O. LANGE et al., *Studies in Mathematical Economics and Econometrics in Memory of Henry Schultz* (Chicago: Chicago University Press). *92*
– (1947), *Foundations of Economic Analysis* (Cambridge, Mass.: Harvard University Press). *52, 100, 121, 218*
– (1950), 'Evaluation of real national income', *Oxford E.P.*, **2**, 1–29 (Jan). *65, 76 n*
– (1954), 'The pure theory of public expenditure', *R. of E. and Statistics*, **36**, 387–9 (Nov). *191, 214*
– (1955), 'Diagrammatic exposition of a theory of public expenditure', *R. of E. and Statistics*, **37**, 350–6 (Nov). *191*
– (1956), 'Social indifference curves', *QJE*, **70**, 1–22 (Feb). *79–83*

— (1967), 'Arrow's mathematical politics', in HOOK (1967). *118, 121*
— (1969), 'Pure theory of public expenditure and taxation', in MARGOLIS & GUITTON (1969). *192 n*
— (1972), 'The consumer does benefit from feasible price stability', *QJE*, **86**, 476–98 (Aug). *291*
— (1977), 'Reaffirming the existence of reasonable Bergson–Samuelson social welfare functions', *Economica*, **44**, 81–8 (Feb). *120, 140*
— (1981), 'Bergsonian welfare economics', in Rosefielde. *121*
SANDLER, Todd (1977), 'Impurity of defence: an application to the economics of alliances', *Kyklos*, **30**, fasc. 3, 443–60. *212*
— (1978), 'Public good and the theory of second best', *Public Finance/Finance Publiques*, **33**, No. 3, 331–44. *223*
— & TSCHIRHART, John T. (1980), 'The economic theory of clubs: an evaluative survey', *JEL*, **18**, 1481–521 (Dec). *212 n*
SANDMO, Agnar (1976), 'Optimal taxation: an introduction to the literature', *J. of Public E.*, **6**, 37–54 (June). *239 n, 289*
SAPOSNIK, Rubin, *see* Quirk & Saposnik
SATTERTHWAITE, M. A. (1975)*, 'Strategy-proofness and Arrow's conditions', *JET*, **10**, 187–217 (Apr). *135 n*
— *see also* Blin & Satterthwaite
SAWYER, Malcolm (1980), 'Monopoly welfare loss in the United Kingdom', *Manchester School*, **48**, 331–54 (Dec). *286*
SCHMALENSEE, Richard (1976), 'Another look at the social valuation of input price changes', *AER*, **66**, 239–43 (Mar). *100*
— (1981)*, 'Monopolistic two-part pricing arrangements', *Bell J. of E.*, **12**, 445–66 (Autumn). *289*
SCHMEIDLER, David, *see* Kalai & Schmeidler
SCHMID, A. Allan (1976), 'The economics of property rights: a review article', *J. of E. Issues*, **10**, 159–68 (Mar). *282*
SCHMITZ, Andrew, *see* Currie, Murphy & Schmitz, Hueth & Schmitz, and Turnovsky *et al.*
SCHOTTER Andrew, *see* Fischer & Schotter
SCHULZE, William D., *see* Brookshire *et al.*
— *see also* Newberry & Stiglitz
SCHWARTZ, Nancy L., *see* Kamien & Schwartz
SCITOVSKY, Tibor (1941), 'A note on welfare propositions in economics', *RES*, 77–88 (Nov). Reprinted in ARROW & SCITOVSKY (1969). *60, 63, 66*
— (1942), 'A reconsideration of the theory of tariffs', *RES*, **9**, 89–110. *79–83*
— (1944/5), 'Some consequences of the habit of judging quality of price', *RES*, **11**, 100–5. Reprinted in *P. on Welfare and Growth* (Stanford: Stanford University Press, 1964). *287*
— (1976), *The Joyless Economy* (Oxford: Oxford University Press). *273*

— *see also* Arrow & Scitovsky

SEADE, Jesus K. (1977). 'On the shape of optimal tax schedules', *J. of Public E.*, **7**, 203–35 (Apr). *260*

— (1978), 'Consumer's surplus and Linearity of Engel curves', *EJ*, **88**, 511–23 (Sep). *90 n*

SEN, Amartya K. (1961), 'On optimising the rate of saving', *EJ*, **71**, 479–96 (Sep). *290*

— (1963), 'Distribution, transitivity, and Little's welfare criteria', *EJ*, **73**, 771–78 (Dec). *67*

— (1967), 'The nature and classes of prescriptive judgments', *Philosophical Quarterly*, **17**, 46–62 (Jan). *19-20*

— (1969a), 'Planners' preferences: optimality, distribution, and social welfare', in MARGOLIS & GUITTON (1969). *152 n*

— (1969b), 'Quasi-transitivity, rational choice, and collective decisions', *RES*, **36**, 381–93 (July). *126*

— (1970a), *Collective Choice and Social Welfare* (Amsterdam: North-Holland). *15, 19-22, 26, 114, 127, 143*

— (1970b), 'Interpersonal aggregation and partial comparability', *Econometrica*, **38**, 393–409 (May). *15*

— (1970c), 'The impossibility of a Paretian liberal', *JPE*, **78**, 152-7 (Jan-Feb). *137-8*

— (1973a), *On Economic Inequality* (Oxford: Clarendon Press). *157*

— (1973b), 'On ignorance and equal distribution', *AER*, **63**, 1022-4 (Dec). *152 n*

— (1973c), 'Behaviour and the concept of preference', *Economica*, **40**, 241–59 (Aug). *8*

— (1974), 'Informational bases of alternative welfare approaches: aggregation and income distribution', *J. of Public E.*, **3**, 387–404 (Nov). *15*

— (1976), 'Liberty, unanimity, and rights', *Economica*, **43**, 217–45 (Aug). *138*

— (1977a), 'Social choice theory: a re-examination', *Econometrica*, **45**, 53–89 (Jan). *138*

— (1977b), 'On weights and measures', *Econometrica*, **44**, 1539–72 (Oct). *15, 113 n*

— (1978U), 'Strategy and revelation: informational constraints in public decisions', typescript. *135 n*

— (1979a), 'The welfare basis of real income comparison: a survey', *JEL*, **17**, 1–45 (Mar). *83*

— (1979b), 'Personal utilities and public judgments; or what's wrong with welfare economics?', *EJ*, **89** (Sep). *22*

— (forthcoming), 'Social choice theory', in Arrow & Intriligator. *138*

— & PATTANAIK, P. K. (1969), 'Necessary and sufficient conditions for rational choice under majority decision', *JET*, **I**, 128–202 (Aug).

SENGUPTA, Manimay (1978)*, 'On a difficulty in the analysis on strategic voting', *Econometrica*, **46**, 331–43 (Mar). *135* n

SHAFER, Wayne, & SONNENSCHEIN, Hugo (1976)*, 'Equilibrium with externalities, commodity taxation, and lump sum transfers', *International E.R.*, **17**, 601–11 (Oct). *58*

SHALIT, Haim, *see* Turnovsky, Shalit & Schmitz

SHARP, C. H. (1973), *Transport Economics* (London: Macmillan). *291*

SHELL, Karl (ed.) (1967)*, 'Essays on the theory of optimal economic growth', (Cambridge, Mass.: MIT Press). *290*

SHEPSLE, Kenneth A., *see* Weingast, Shepsle & Johnsen

SHESHINSKI, Eytan (1971U)*, 'On the theory of optimal income taxation', HIER *Discussion Paper* No. 172. *154*
— *see also* Boskin & Sheshinski, Lau, Sheshinski & Stiglitz

SHIBATA, Hirofumi (1971), 'A bargaining model of the pure theory of public expenditure', *JPE*, **79**, 1–29 (Jan). *175*

SHONE, R. (1976), *Microeconomics: A Modern Treatment* (London: Macmillan). *58*

SICILIAN, Joseph, *see* Otani & Sicilian

SILBERBERG, Eugene (1972), 'Duality and the many consumer's surplus', *AER*, **55**, 942–52 (Dec). *94*

SKOLNIK, M. L. (1970), 'A comment on Professor Musgrave's separation of distribution from allocation', *J. of E. Literature*, **8**, 440–42. *258*

SLATER, Martin, *see* Collard, Lecomber & Slater

SLUTSKY, Steven (1977), 'A characterisation of societies with consistent majority decision', *RES*, **44**, 211–25 (June). *123*

SMITH, Vernon L. (1977), 'The principle of unanimity and voluntary consent in social choice', *JPE*, **85**, 1125–40 (Dec). *203* n
— (ed.) (1979), *Research in Experimental Economics* (New York: Greenwich). *203*
— (1980), 'Experiments with a decentralized mechanism for public good decisions', *AER*, **70**, 584–99 (Sep). *203*

SMOLENSKY, Paul *see* Cicchetti, Gillen & Smolensky

SOLOW, Robert M. (1974), 'The economics of resources or the resources of economics', *AER/S*, **64**, 1–14 (May). *290*

SONDERMANN, Dieter, *see* Kirman & Sondermann

SONNENSCHEIN, Hugo (1977)*, 'Some recent results on the existence of equilibrium in finite purely competitive economies', in INTRILIGATOR (1977). *58*
— *see also* Foster & Sonnenschein, Shafer & Sonnenschein, Mas-Colall & Sonnenschein

SOSNOW, Neil D. (1974), 'Optimal policies for income redistribution', *J. of Public E.*, **3**, 159–69 (May). *246* n

SPENCE, Michael (1973), 'Job market signalling', *QJE,* **87,** 355–74 (Aug). *159, 276*

STARRETT, D. A. (1972)*, 'Fundamental nonconvexities in the theory of externalities', *JET,* **4,** 180–99 (Apr). *170* n
– *see also* Heller & Starrett

STERN, N. H., *see* Mirrlees & Stern

STERNBACH, Richard A., & TVERSKY, Bernard (1964), 'On the psychophysical power function in electric shock', *Psychonomic Science,* **1,** 217–18. *109* n

STIGLER, George J., & BECKER, Gary S. (1977), 'De gustibus non est disputandum', *AER,* **67,** 76–90 (Mar). *288*

STIGLITZ, Joseph E. (1975), 'The theory of "screening", education, and the distribution of income', *AER,* **65,** 283–300 (June). *159, 276*
– (1976U), 'Utilitarianism and horizontal equity: the case for random taxation', *Technical Report* No. 214, Economics Series, Institute for Mathematical Studies in the Social Sciences, Stanford University. *159*
– & DASGUPTA, P. (1971)*, 'Differential taxation, public goods, and economic efficiency', *RES,* **38,** 151–74 (Apr). *192, 239* n
– *see also* Atkinson & Stiglitz, Dasgupta & Stiglitz, Lau, Sheshinski & Stiglitz, and Newberry and Stiglitz

STIGUM, Bernt P. (1969)*, 'Competitive equilibrium under uncertainty', *QJE,* **83,** 533–61 (Nov). *58*

STROTZ, R. (1958), 'Two propositions related to public goods', *R. of E. and Statistics,* **40,** 329–31 (Nov). *192* n

STONE, Courtenay C., *see* Gifford & Stone

STUBBLEBINE, W. C., *see* Buchanan & Stubblebine

SUGDEN, Robert, & WEALE, Albert (1979), 'A contractual reformulation of certain aspects of welfare economics', *Economica,* **46,** 111–23 (May). *129*

SUPPES, P., *see* Luce & Suppes

SWAN, Peter L. (1975), 'The Coase theorem and "sequential" Pareto optimality', *E. Record,* **51,** 269–71 (June). *183*

TARASCIO, V. J. (1968). *Pareto's Methodological Approach to Economics* (Chapel Hill, N.C.: University of North Carolina Press). *59*

TAUBMAN, Paul (1975), *Sources of Inequality in Earnings* (Amsterdam: North-Holland). *157-8*
– (1976), 'Earnings, education, genetics, and environment', *J. of Human Resources,* **11,** 447–61 (Fall). *159*

TAYLOR, M. J. (1968), 'Graph theoretical approaches to the theory of social choice', *Public Choice,* 35–48 (Spring). *127*

THAYER, Mark A., *see* Brookshire *et al.*

THOMPSON, Earl A. (1968), 'The perfectly competitive production of collective goods', *R. of E. and Statistics,* **50,** 1–12 (Feb). *193*

— (1974), 'Taxation and national defence', *JPE*, **82**, 755-82 (July/Aug). *240 n*

— (1979), 'An economic basis for the "national defence argument" for protecting certain industries', *JPE*, **87**, 1-36 (Feb). *240 n*

— *see also* Faith & Thompson

THUROW, Lester C. (1971), 'The income distribution as a pure public good', *QJE*, **85**, 327-36 (May). *207*

— (1981), *The Zero-sum Society: Distribution and the Possibilities for Economic Change* (London: Penguin). *157*

TIDEMAN, T. Nicolaus, & TULLOCK, Gordon (1976), 'A new and superior process for making social choices', *JPE*, **84**, 1145-59 (Dec). *134, 199-205*

— — (1977), 'Some limitations of demand revealing process: comment', *Public Choice*, **29**, 125-8 (Spring Supplement). *205 n*

— — (1981), 'Coalitions under demand revealing', *Public Choice*, **36**, 323–8. *135*

TIEBOUT, C. M. (1956), 'A pure theory of public expenditures., *JPE*, **64**, 416-24 (Oct). *211*

TIMPANE, Michael, *see* Pechman & Timpane

TINBERGEN, Jan (1972), 'Some features of the optimum regime', in TINBERGEN *et al., Optimum Social Welfare and Productivity* (New York: New York University Press). *160*

— (1975), *Income Distribution: Analysis and Policies* (Amsterdam: North-Holland). *157*

TREBING, Harry M. (ed.) (1971), *Essays on Public Utility Pricing and Regulation* (East Lansing: Institute of Public Utilities, Michigan State University). *289*

— (ed.) (1976), *New Dimensions in Public Utility Pricing* (East Lansing: Institute of Public Utilities, Michigan State University). *289*

TSCHIRHART, John T., *see* Sandler & Tschirhart

TULLOCK, Gordon (1965), *The Politics of Bureaucracy* (Washington: Public Affairs Press). *284*

— (1967a), 'The general irrelevance of the general impossibility theorem', *QJE*, **81**, 256-70 (May). *127*

— (1967b), *Toward a Mathematics of Politics* (Ann Arbor: University of Michigan Press). *284*

— (1967c), 'The welfare costs of tariffs, monopolies and theft', *Western E.J.*, **5**, 224-32 (June). *285*

— (1975), 'The transitional gains trap', *Bell J. of E.*, **6**, 671-8 (Autumn). *285*

— (1976), *The Vote Motive* (London: Institute of Economic Affairs). *284*

— (1977), 'Demand-revealing process, coalitions, and public goods', *Public Choice*, **29**, 103-5 (Spring Supplement). *206*

– & CAMPBELL, C. B. (1970), 'Computer simulation of a small voting system', *EJ*, **80**, 97–104 (Mar). *127*
– *see also* Buchanan & Tullock, Tideman & Tullock
TURNOVSKY, Stephen J., SHALIT, Haim, & SCHMITZ, Andrew (1980)*, 'Consumer's surplus, price instability, and consumer welfare', *Econometrica*, **48**, 135–52 (Jan). *291*
TURVEY, Ralph (ed.) (1968), *Public Enterprise, Selected Readings* (Harmondsworth: Penguin Books).
TVERSKY, Bernard, *see* Sternbach & Tversky
ULPH, David (1977), 'On the optimal distribution of income and educational expenditure', *J. of Public E.*, **8**, 341–56. *158*
VAN HERWAARDEN, Floor, KAPTEYN, Arie, & VAN PRAAG, Bernard (1977), 'Twelve thousand individual welfare functions', *European E.R.*, **9**, 283–300 (Aug). *161*
– *see also* Kapteyn & Van Herwaarden
VAN PRAAG, Bernard M. S. (1968)*, *Individual Welfare Functions and Consumer Behavior* (Amsterdam: North-Holland). *161*
– *see also* Van Herwaarden, Kapteyn & Van Praag
VEBLEN, Theodor (1899), *The Theory of the Leisure Class* (New York: Macmillan). *287*
VICKREY, William (1945), 'Measuring marginal utilities by reactions to risk', *Econometrica*, **13**, 319–33 (Oct). *125*
– (1961), 'Counterspeculation, auctions and competitive sealed tenders', *J. of Finance*, **16**, 8–37 (May). *199 n*
VINER, Jacob (1950), *The Customs Unions Issue* (New York: Carnegie Endowment for International Peace). *218*
WALKER, David (1955), 'The direct–indirect tax problem: fifteen years of controversy', *Public Finance*, **10**, 153–77. Reprinted in HOUGHTON, R. W. (ed.), *Public Finance* (Harmondsworth: Penguin Books, 1973). *289*
WALKER, Ian (1980), 'Review of Ng, *Welfare Economics*', *Manchester School*, **48**, 220–1 (June). *xv*
WALSH, Cliff (1975), 'First-party-priority revisited', *E. Record*, **51**, 275–7. *183*
– *see also* Brennan, Head & Walsh and Burns & Walsh
WALSH, John, *see* Dusansky & Walsh
WALSH, Vivian C. (1970), *Introduction to Contemporary Microeconomics* (New York: McGraw-Hill). *58*
WALTERS, A. A. (1961), 'The theory measurement of private and social cost of highway congestion', *Econometrica*, **29**, 676–97 (Oct). *291*
WALTON, Gary M., *see* McManus, Walton & Coffman
WARR, Peter (1979), 'Tariff compensation without omniscience', *E. Record*, **55**, 20–32 (Mar). *242*

WEALE, Albert, *see* Sugden & Weale

WEBB, Michael G. (1976), *Pricing Policies for Public Enterprise* (London: Macmillan). *289*

WEINGAST, Barry R., SHEPSLE, Kenneth A., & JOHNSEN, Christopher (1981), 'The political economy of benefits and costs: a neoclassical approach to distributive politics', *JPE,* **89**, 642–64 (Aug). *285*

WEISBROD, Burton A. (1964), 'Collective-consumption services of individual-consumption goods', *QJE,* **78**, 471–7 (Aug). *273*

WEISSER, Mendel, *see* Ng & Weisser

WEIZSÄCKER, Carl C. von (1965)*, 'Existence of optimal programs of accumulation for an infinite time horizon', *RES,* **32**, 85–104. *290*

– (1971)*, 'Notes on endogenous change of tastes', *JET,* **3**, 345–72 (Dec). *288*

WELDON, J. C. (1952), 'On the problem of social welfare functions', *Canadian J.E.,* **18**, 452–63 (Nov). *124*

WHINSTON, Andrew B., *see* Davis & Whinston

WHITING, Gordon C., *see* Kearl *et al.*

WICKSELL, Knut (1896), *Finanztheoretische Untersuchungen* (Jena: Gustav Fischer). *284*

WILDASIN, David E. (1977), 'Distributional neutrality and optimal commodity taxation', *AER,* **67**, 889–98 (Dec). *289*

WILES, P. J. D. (1964), *The Political Economy of Communism* (Cambridge, Mass.: Harvard University Press). *48*

WILLIG, Robert D. (1976), 'Consumer's surplus without apology', *AER,* **66**, 589–97 (Sep). *100*

– *see also* Baumol, Panzar, & Willig

WILSON, Robert B. (1969), 'An axiomatic model of logrolling', *AER,* **59**, 331–41 (June). *125*

– *see also* Ekern & Wilson

WIMMER, Larry T., *see* Kearl *et al.*

WINCH, David M. (1965), 'Consumer's surplus and the compensation principle', *AER,* **55**, 395–423 (June). *90-2*

– (1971), *Analytical Welfare Economics* (Harmondsworth: Penguin Books). *220*

– (1980), 'Review of Ng, *Welfare Economics*', *EJ,* **90**, 684–5 (Sep). *xv*

WISEMAN, Jack, *see* Peacock & Wiseman

WOGLOM, Geoffrey, *see* Goldfarb & Woglom

WOLFF, Edward N., *see* Baumol & Wolff

WOLPIN, Kenneth I. (1977), 'Education and screening', *AER,* **67**, 949–58 (Dec). *276*

WONG, Yue-chin, *see* Liu & Wong

YAARI, Manahem E. (1981), 'Rawls, Edgeworth, Shapley, Nash: theories of distributive justice re-examined', *JET*, 24, 1−39 (Feb). *148*

YEH, Y. (1972), 'On the situation utility possibility curve', *Kyklos*, **38**, 413-20. *39*

Subject Index